Aigun

HEILUNGKIANG

Sungari

Harbin

Changchun

KIRIN

Tumen

ssuri

NINGHSIA-HUI
Autonomous Region

Mongolian

Autonomous

Region

Mukden
(Shenyang)

LIAONING

Yalu

Huhehot

Great Wall

Peking

Tientsin

Port Arthur-Dairen

HOPEI

Paoting

Yinchwan

Taiyuan

Tsinan

Tsingtao

Lanchow

Yenan

SHANSI

(Yellow)

SHANTUNG

Hui-ning

Hwang Ho

Chengchow

Grand Canal

KIANGSU

Sian

SHENSI

HONAN

Hwai

Hofei

Nanking

Shanghai

HUPEI

Yangtze

Wuhan

ANHWEI

Hangchow

SZECHWAN

Chengtu

CHEKIANG

Chungking

Tung-t'ing

P'o-yang

Nanchang

Changsha

KIANGSI

Foochow

HUNAN

Juichin

FUKIEN

Kweiyang

KWEICHOW

Amoy

TAIWAN

KWANGSI-CHUANG
Aut Region

KWANGTUNG

Swatow

Canton

Nanning

Macao

HONG KONG

The American Foreign Policy Library
Edwin O. Reischauer, Editor

The United States and China

Third Edition

John King Fairbank

Harvard University Press
Cambridge, Massachusetts
1971

For
Lorena King Fairbank
1874–

Introduction to the Third Edition
by Edwin O. Reischauer

"The Harvard University Press can offer the readers of its Foreign Policy Library no more timely or important book than John King Fairbank's *The United States and China.*" This was the first sentence in the "Introduction" by Sumner Welles to this now classic work when it first appeared in 1948. It is equally true of the present Third Edition, twenty-three years later.

The Chinese people constitute between a quarter and a fifth of all mankind; the much less numerous American people control about a third of the world's wealth. The relationship or lack of relations between these two great nations, their understanding or misconceptions of each other, their cooperation or friction, will play a large part in determining the fate of humanity. No one has written more clearly or more perceptively about China during the past quarter century than Professor Fairbank, and no one has contributed more to American understanding of that country, its great traditions, and its tumultuous present conditions.

The portions of this book carried over from earlier editions still sparkle with insights that anyone interested in China should read — or reread, as I have just done with great pleasure and refreshed enlightenment. The extensive new sections on more recent events constitute the clearest, most balanced, and most judicious brief presentation of an extraordinarily complex and obscure subject that I have yet seen. In both parts, Professor Fairbank has neatly folded in the latest conclusions of a host of able young scholars working in the Chinese field. He is in a good position to do this, for he, more than anyone else, is responsible for the vigorous development of this field of scholarship in the United States, and the authorities he quotes are largely his own disciples.

As Professor Fairbank points out, the first edition of this work came out on the eve of the Communist victory in China and the second edition just before China entered on a decade of disastrous and quite unpredictable internal difficulties — the Great Leap Forward and the Cultural Revolution. No one can foresee what will happen within China or in its relations with the United States and other countries even in the immediate future. But *The United States and China* is no narrow intelligence analysis of the latest scraps of evidence from China, nor is it an exercise in the murky art of futurology. It views the Chinese people, the great flow of their traditions, and their current hopes and anguish as a whole, clarifying what has happened in the past and making more understandable whatever may transpire in the future. This is why this work has been a classic for more than two decades and will continue to be one for many years to come.

Preface to the Third Edition

This volume tries to outline what we know about China. To do this in a few words, however well chosen, is as a matter of fact impossible; but hundreds have tried it, ever since the time of Marco Polo, simply because China fascinates the foreigner.

The first edition of this book in 1948 was written just before the Chinese Communist Party came to power, on the eve of disaster to the longstanding American interest in China. The second edition of 1958 was written after the first eight years of the Communist achievement in transforming Chinese life, on the eve of Mao Tse-tung's effort at instant industrialization, the Great Leap Forward, and its disastrous shortfall. The third edition has been written after the moral disaster created in American life by our bombing in Vietnam.

China's modern history, and American relations with East Asia, the Chinese culture area, seem extraordinarily disaster-prone and inconclusive. The Korean War of 1950–53 is still not concluded except by a truce. Chairman Mao's Great Proletarian Cultural Revolution of 1966–69 subsided only in a stalemate. Neither the Chinese nor the American people can feel in the 1970's that their future is certain and secure. After almost 200 years of often extensive contact, we are almost as far apart as when our contact began in 1784.

Our new approach to China in the 1970's has to be made in the context of our Vietnam stalemate in the 1960's. We have to begin by accepting our bitter Vietnam experience as a non-victory, a frustration of our original good intentions, a proof that they were not sufficiently valid or realistic. All the aspects of our reliance on our advanced technology of destruction — and the general disruption of the local society with so much suffering for so many victims — have made Vietnam a shame and humiliation to us.

In the long view Vietnam has marked the final end of the era of gunboat diplomacy, of the century of unequal treaties, in our relations with East Asia. Within the old Chinese culture area, the Chinese, Japanese, Vietnamese, and Koreans all suffered an invasion of Western power exemplified in the mid-nineteenth century by Western gunboats; all were righteously coerced into giving the Westerners, who then represented the forefront of civilization, charters of special privileges spelled out in unequal treaties. Yet in the end all these peoples developed a modern nationalism that got rid of foreign privilege. The Japanese did so by the end of the nineteenth century, whereas Vietnam and Korea became for a time the outright colonies of France and Japan, and achieved independence only after 1945.

The rise of modern mass nationalism in China has thus occurred in an East Asian context of comparable experience among neighboring peoples. In particular China's national revolution has run parallel to that of Vietnam in several respects: In each case Western gunboat diplomacy coerced the ruling dynasty to take the foreign invader into the old power structure. But foreign contact gradually inspired a new nationalism in these peasant-and-ruling-class societies and eventually a revolution to supplant the old ruling class with a form of national communism. The revolution wiped out the basis for foreign privilege or foreign rule along with the old ruling class. China and Vietnam are thus not unrelated.

When I first put this book together, I could profit by two experiences — first of all, an experience of living in China, four years as a graduate student in Peking, 1932–35, with a good deal of traveling about, and two years as an official under the American Embassy, first in Chungking, 1942–43, and then in Nanking, 1945–46, during the onset of the Chinese Communist rise to power. My second experience had come from inaugurating the Regional Studies program on China at Harvard in 1946: this area-study approach brought each of the social science disciplines to bear and gave a more analytic structure to the Chinese history that I had taught there after 1936. I learned a great deal from faculty colleagues.

By the late 1950's, the victorious Communists were building up the Chinese state and remaking the society, while the China specialists in America, having been generally denounced and investigated in the Joe McCarthy era, were still "controversial." But new talent and important books had begun to emerge from our universities, and the second edition of this book benefited more than ever from the work of others.

Today in late 1970, the People's Republic has experienced the ups and downs of the Great Leap of 1958–60 and the Cultural Revolution of 1966–69, two periods of intense trauma, hope, effort, and disillusionment, while the American people, disillusioned on their part by Vietnam, are trying to disengage there in order to deal with multiform evils at home. While scholarship on China has been largely stultified or at least not published in the People's Republic, it has flourished in America, and the rewriting of this edition has been indebted to the flood of publications indicated in the bibliography. (An author cited in the text will be found in the index together with references to pages where his work is listed in the Suggested Reading.)

The bibliography is indeed an indication of my indebtedness to others and might equally well be listed in a section called Acknowledgments.

J.K.F.

October 1970

Contents

Contents

Contents

Contents

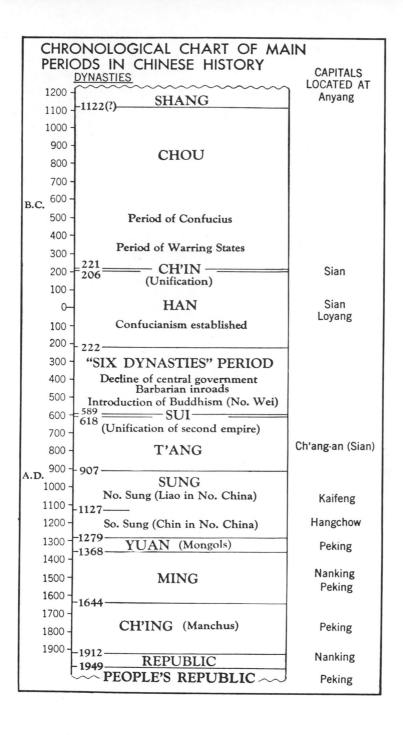

CHRONOLOGICAL CHART OF MAIN
PERIODS IN CHINESE HISTORY

DYNASTIES

CAPITALS
LOCATED AT

B.C.		
1200	SHANG	Anyang
1100	1122(?)	
1000		
900	CHOU	
800		
700		
600		
500	Period of Confucius	
400	Period of Warring States	
300		
200	221 CH'IN	Sian
	206 (Unification)	
100		
0	HAN	Sian
100	Confucianism established	Loyang
200	222	
300	"SIX DYNASTIES" PERIOD	
400	Decline of central government	
	Barbarian inroads	
500	Introduction of Buddhism (No. Wei)	
600	589 SUI	
	618	
700	(Unification of second empire)	
800	T'ANG	Ch'ang-an (Sian)
A.D. 900	907	
1000	SUNG	
	No. Sung (Liao in No. China)	Kaifeng
1100	1127	
1200	So. Sung (Chin in No. China)	Hangchow
1300	1279 YUAN (Mongols)	Peking
	1368	
1400		
1500	MING	Nanking
		Peking
1600	1644	
1700		
1800	CH'ING (Manchus)	Peking
1900	1912	
	REPUBLIC	Nanking
	1949	
	PEOPLE'S REPUBLIC	Peking

ADMINISTRATIVE AREAS
UNDER THE
CH'ING DYNASTY

Province boundaries
■ Seats of Governors-general (and some Governors)
○ Seats of Governors alone
• Other cities

TAIWAN

Tainan

CHEKIANG

Min R.
Foochow
Ch'üan-chou
FUKIEN
Amoy
NAMOA IS.
Swatow

KIANGSI
Kiukiang
Poyang Lake
Nanchang
Kan R.

HONG KONG

Yochow
Tungting Lake

KWANGTUNG
Canton
Macao
Chao-ch'ing

HUNAN
Changsha
Hsiang R.

Kweilin

KWANGSI
Hsi (West) R.

HAINAN

KWEICHOW
Kweiyang

Nanning

GULF OF TONGKING

Chungking

Yangtze R.

Yunnan-fu
YUNNAN

Red River

VIETNAM

LAOS

SIAM

1 The Chinese Scene

The Contrast of North and South

The Chinese people's basic problem of livelihood is readily visible from the air: the brown eroded hills, the flood plains of muddy rivers, the crowded green fields and hives of simple huts that form the villages, the intricate silver network of terraces and waterways that testify to the back-breaking labor of countless generations — all the overcrowding of too many people upon too little land, and the attendant exhaustion of the land resources and of human ingenuity and fortitude in the effort to maintain life.

To any traveler who has flown through the vast gray cloud banks and mists and sunshine of continental China, two pictures will stand out as typical, one of North China and one of the South. On the dry North China plain to the south of Peking where Chinese civilization had its first flowering and established its institutional forms, one sees in summer an endless expanse of dusty green fields over which are scattered clusters of darker green, the trees of tiny earth-walled villages. It is very like the view of our Middle West, where farmsteads and

1

their clumps of trees are dispersed at rough half-mile intervals all over the verdant plain. But where our corn belt has a farm, on the North China plain there is an entire village. Where one American farmer's family is established with its barn and sheds among its fields in Iowa or Illinois at a half-mile interval from its neighbors roundabout, in China an entire community of several hundred persons lives in its tree-studded village, at a half-mile interval from neighbor villages. About seven tenths of the earth's surface in this region is under human cultivation, mainly by hand, and for each square mile of cultivated land there are at least a thousand human mouths to feed. This is why the American people in spite of their farming background have no appreciation of the population density which subtly conditions every act and thought of a Chinese farmer.

In South China the typical picture is quite different, and like nothing to which we are accustomed. There during much of the year the rice fields are flooded and present a water surface to the airborne observer. The green terrain is hilly and the crescent-shaped rice terraces march up each hill almost to the top and on the other side descend again from near the crest, terrace upon terrace in endless succession, each embankment conforming to the lay of the land like the contour lines of a geographer's chart. In fact the curving pattern of the rice terraces seen from above is a visual index to the slope of the valleys in which they are built — narrow concave strips of paddy field touch the hilltops, and lower terraces grow broader and longer and bulge out as they descend to the valley floor. Gray stone footpaths are built on many of the embankments and the latter form intricate patterns like the product of some giant's doodling. When the sun is out one sees it from the air reflected brilliantly in the water of the rice fields. The sun seems in fact to be shining up through the fields from below, so that the whole ornate network of the embankments and paths and hilltops appears to rush beneath one as though on a great rolling screen, a black lacework moving across the bright silver of shining water.

No one can fly over the rugged green hills of the South without wondering where the 750 millions of China live and what they eat — such vast reaches of mountain and valley seem largely uncultivable and sparsely settled. One's picture of a big empty landscape is mirrored statistically in the estimate that six sevenths of the population have to concentrate on one third of the land. The really inhabited part of China, at a rough estimate, is only about half as large as the really inhabited part of the United States, yet it supports almost four times as many people. This is made possible only by crowding almost 1500 human beings onto each square mile of cultivated earth in the valleys and flood plains. The United States has some 570,000 square miles under cultivation and could greatly increase this area; China has perhaps 450,000 square miles of cultivated land (less than one-half acre of food-producing soil per person) with little prospect of increasing this area by more than a small fraction, even if it is used more intensively.

Little is known in statistical terms about the life of the Chinese people upon their crowded land, but sampling studies, in which American investigators once took a leading part, give us some general indications. The great contrast is between the dry wheat-millet area of North China and the moist rice land of the South. These economic regions divide along a line roughly halfway between the Yellow River and the Yangtze on the thirty-fourth parallel. Let us look at the factors of rainfall, soil, temperature, and human usage which create this striking contrast.

First of all, the rainfall depends upon the continental character of the Chinese climate and the seasonal air flow to which it gives rise. To put it very simply, the Asiatic land mass

▓▓ Approximate limit of cultivation	▨ Loess area
•••• Approximate limit of rice cultivation	— Navigable rivers

0   100   200   300   400   500   1000
Miles

changes temperature more readily than the Western Pacific and its currents, and the cold dry air which is chilled over the continent in the wintertime tends to flow southeastward to the sea, with minimum precipitation. Conversely, the summer monsoon of moisture-laden sea air is drawn inward and northward over the land mass by the rising of the heated air above it, and precipitation occurs mainly during the summer. This southerly wind of summer crosses the hills of South China first, and they receive a heavy rainfall, which remains relatively dependable with a variation of only about 15 percent in the amount of precipitation from one year to the next. North China being farther from the South China Sea receives less rainfall and, moreover, the amount of precipitation over the decades has varied as much as 30 percent from one year to the next. Since the average rainfall of the North China plain is about 20 to 25 inches, like the rainfall of the great American dustbowl, it is hardly more than sufficient to maintain cultivation at the best of times. This high degree of variability from year to year is a most serious problem. North China is normally on the subsistence margin as regards its water supply, and the periodic failure of rainfall means drought and famine. From the point of view of water supply, South China has the better of it.

As regards soil, however, South China suffers by comparison, for the constant seepage of water through its warm earth has dissolved and leached away mineral foods of great importance for plant life. The leached soil resulting is relatively unproductive, and the situation is saved partly by the fact that the constant run-off from the hills brings down new deposits for the cultivated lowlands. Even so, the heavy population centers of the South are to be found mainly on the alluvial flood plains of the Yangtze or on the river deltas, like those inland from Shanghai or around Canton. The soil of North China, on the other hand, thanks to the relative lack of water,

5

remains unleached and richer in minerals. Sometimes, indeed, as in Mongolia, mineral salts are brought to the surface by evaporating water and, in the absence of rainfall to wash them away, form a saline crust which makes cultivation impossible.

Temperature plays its part in preserving the soil of North China, since the severe continental winters, not unlike those of the Middle West, limit the growing season to about half the year. In southernmost China crops are grown the year around and rice is double-cropped. Too easily we forget that Shanghai is in the latitude of New Orleans and Suez, while Canton is in that of Havana and Calcutta, well into the tropics. This helps to explain why the greater part of the Chinese people live in the more fecund rice economy of the South.

Thus the factors of rainfall, soil, and temperature are in a rough balance both North and South, the North having soil which is highly fertile when water is sufficient, but having too often an insufficiency of water and much cold weather; and the South having no lack of water and favorable temperatures but generally infertile soil. In both cases the resources of nature are supplemented by unremitting human endeavor, of which the night soil (human excrement) industry is but one of the more spectacular forms. Without the redolent returning to the land of human waste or equivalent fertilizers no region of China could sustain its present population. It is no accident that Chinese cities from the air can be seen surrounded by a belt of dense green crops which fade out at the periphery. Each urban center maintains its surrounding truck gardens.

A population map (see p. 7) will show that the Chinese people are packed into four main regions, which include but a small part of the total area of the country. The first region is the North China plain, the second is the mountain-locked plain of Szechwan in the west, the third is the lower Yangtze valley from Hankow to Shanghai, including the Hunan rice bowl south of Hankow, and the fourth is the Canton delta in

the south. Early travelers compared China to Europe in the variety of dialects and the size of different provinces. For example, three regions along the course of the Yangtze in Central China — Szechwan province in the west, the twin provinces of Hupeh and Hunan north and south of Wuhan, and the lower Yangtze delta — are each of them comparable to Germany in area and bigger in population.

Trade and transport routes in South China have followed the waterways, and the great modern cities — Canton, Shanghai, Wuhan — have grown up where sea trade can meet the waterborne commerce of the interior. Yet China's foreign trade has never lived up to the foreign merchant's great expectations. Stretching so far from north to south, from the latitude of Canada to that of Cuba, China remains a subcontinent largely sufficient unto herself. As George Washington's contemporary, the great Ch'ien-lung Emperor, put it in his famous edict to King George III, "Our celestial empire possesses all things in prolific abundance and lacks no product within its own borders. There is therefore no need to import the manufactures of outside barbarians."

In spite of the immensity and variety of the Chinese scene, we need not be surprised that this subcontinent has remained a single political unit where Europe has not; for it is held together by a way of life even more deeply rooted than our own, and stretching even farther back uninterruptedly into the past.

Cultural Origins

The exciting discovery in 1929 of a skull of Peking man (at Chou-k'ou-tien near Peking) was of tremendous archaeological significance because the excavators subsequently found not one but many skeletal remnants of paleolithic man, not isolated but together with the bones of contemporary animals, human tools, and evidence of the use of fire. Finding these cul-

8

tural evidences together in one place was most unusual. This is still the chief paleolithic find in China, but excavations during construction since 1949 have added to the number of paleolithic sites. Evidently the culture of Peking man was indigenous and isolated.

In the subsequent ice age, geologists believe that the chill gales blowing from the European ice cap picked up the dust and silt which had been produced by the drying up of the Central Asian plateau and moved it in vast dust storms to the region of Northwest China. Today a blanket of fine, yellow, windborne soil lies to a depth of 150 feet or more over an area of some 100,000 square miles in this region. This is the famous loess soil so typical of the area south of the Ordos desert near the great bend of the Yellow River. The period of the deposition of the loess must have seen constant cyclonic gales more fierce than anything North China ever sees today. It can hardly have been a pleasant time to live there and it has been suggested that Peking man, whose paleolithic sites are found below the level of the loess, was forced to withdraw from North China in this period.

After the last glacial period a neolithic culture of Homo sapiens developed, especially in the region near modern Sian, which the archaeologist Chang Kwang-chih calls the "nuclear area" of Chinese civilization, below the southern bend of the Yellow River. Here on the border between wooded highlands to the west and swampy lowlands to the east, the early hunting and fishing ancestors of the Chinese began to domesticate plants and animals and made the transition to village-farming. Two distinct layers of pottery have been found: red painted pottery, mainly in the nuclear area, and overlying it a thinner, lustrous black pottery, which is widely distributed throughout North China, the Yangtze Valley, and even the southeast coast, indicating a great expansion. By the time this expansion occurred, China's neolithic culture already had very distinct characteristics: cultivation of millet and rice; silk culture; building with stamped-earth to make walls (in courses pounded within a wooden frame); pottery tripods; divination by the use of "oracle bones" (scapulimancy), and other features. Thus the evidence has accumulated to show that Peking man was eventually succeeded by a distinctive neolithic culture, traits of which have persisted down to the present day.

Archaeologists are still debating the degree to which cultural diffusion from the Near East across Central Asia contributed to the formation of Chinese civilization. Excavations in the Kansu corridor on the caravan route to the northwest have thus far been insufficient to settle this question. Some have called ancient China "a civilization by osmosis" on the grounds that the neolithic culture of the Near East appears to have antedated that of China by many hundred years, if not millennia. It is therefore inferred to have contributed to ancient China such cultural elements as the use of wheat, bronze, iron, the chariot, and other techniques or concepts. Whatever the proportion of indigenous and imported contributions in the Chinese cultural amalgam, it is significant that any cultural elements that were diffused into China from the Near East came across the Central Asian land barrier as ideas or methods stripped of all but the essentials and so could more easily be given Chinese garb and assimilated.

In a similar fashion peoples from North and Central Asia have continually entered the Chinese scene and have sometimes ruled over it but they have never been numerous enough to overwhelm Chinese civilization. The arid steppe land north of the Great Wall has been a breeding ground of nomad invaders but never in such numbers that they could displace the dense population of agrarian China.

In racial stock the Chinese have a deceptive homogeneity which does not stand up under anthropological inspection. It appears that the so-called Mongoloid type is made up of very diverse strains in which flat noses and hawk noses, black hair and some red hair, beards and the lack of beards, are thoroughly intermixed, and supposedly common denominators such as the Mongolian eye fold are by no means universal.

The Harmony of Man and Nature

No matter what elements of civilization — peoples or cultural traits — came to China, they all became integrated in a distinctly Chinese way of life, nourished, conditioned, and limited by the good earth and the use of it. To cite but one example, from neolithic times the people of North China have taken full advantage of the quality of vertical cleavage which is characteristic of the loess and made pit dwellings or cave homes in it. Many hundreds of thousands in the Northwest still live in caves cut into the sides of loess cliffs. They are cool in summer, warm in winter, and secure against everything but earthquakes.

The loess of Northwest China seems never to have supported forests. Where forest land occurred, the Chinese, like other early peoples and recent American pioneers, achieved its deforestation. The consequent erosion through the centuries has changed the face of their country. Erosion today is a major problem. Through its waterborne loess deposits the Yellow River has built up the broad flood plain of North China between Shansi province and the sea, and the process still goes on. Nothing can so vividly convey a feeling of man's impotence in the face of nature as to watch the swirling coffee-colored flood of the Yellow River flowing majestically within its dikes across, and twenty feet above, the crowded plain two hundred miles from the sea; and to realize that this vast yellow torrent is steadily depositing its silt and building its bed higher above the surrounding countryside until the time when human negligence or act of God will allow it again to burst from the dikes and inundate the plain.

Deforestation, erosion, and floods have constantly been met by human efforts at water control. The planting of trees and damming of tributaries in the limitless western watershed of "China's Sorrow" is a recent achievement of the People's Republic. In all previous periods the rulers of China have been periodically confronted with a fait accompli in the debouching of the Yellow River upon the North China plain in full flood, and have lacked the scientific knowledge and the means to get behind this pressing fact. In the earliest period, however, flooding of the plain was no more of a problem than the reclamation of it from its primitive swamp and fen condition; techniques of water control were developed for drainage purposes as well as for irrigation and the prevention of floods. Thus many generations of labor have been spent upon the land to make it what it is today, protected by dikes, crossed by canals and roads worn into the earth, irrigated by streams and wells, divided by paths and parcels of grave land in their groves of trees, and all of it handed down from generation to generation.

This land which modern China has inherited is used almost entirely for human food production. China cannot afford to raise cattle for food. Of the land which can be used at all, nine tenths is cultivated for crops and only about 2 percent is pasture for animals. By comparison, in the United States only four tenths of the land which is used is put into crops, and almost half of it is put into pasture. Some amelioration of this situation might be possible if the Chinese in their great Northwest should become herdsmen, but this is not their tradition. Their society and all its mores and institutions have been based from the beginning upon intensive agriculture which takes the fullest advantage of human labor.

The human implications of intensive agriculture can be

seen most strikingly in the rice economy which is the backbone of Chinese life everywhere in the Yangtze valley and the South. Rice plants are ordinarily grown for their first month in seedbeds, while subsidiary crops are raised and harvested in the dry fields. The fields are then irrigated, fertilized, and plowed (here the water buffalo may supplement man's efforts) in preparation for the transplanting of the rice seedlings. This transplanting is done by human hands, the rows of planters bending from the waist as they move backward step by step through the ankle-high muddy water of each terrace. This goes on in the paddy fields of a whole subcontinent — certainly the greatest expenditure of muscular energy in the world. When the rice is mature, the field is drained and it is harvested, again by hand. Given an unlimited supply of water and of human hands, there is probably no way by which a greater yield could be gained from a given plot of land. In this situation land is economically more valuable than labor, or to put it the other way, good muscles are more plentiful than good earth. The Chinese farmer cannot afford to put his labor into extensive agriculture which would yield less per acre. He has lacked both the land and the capital for mechanized or large-scale methods. Obliged to rely on his own family's labor power, he has been obliged to rely on intensive hand gardening in order to feed them.

The heavy application of man power to small plots of land has its social repercussions, for it sets up a vicious interdependence between dense population and intensive use of the soil whereby each makes the other possible. Population density provides both the incentive for intensive land use and the means. Once established, this economy developed its inertia and set its own human standards, whereby the back-breaking labor of many hands became the accepted norm and inventive efforts at labor saving remained the exception. Early modernizers of China in their attempts to introduce the machine constantly ran up against the vested interest of Chinese man power, since in the short run the machine appeared to be in competition with human hands and backs. Thus railways were attacked as depriving carters and coolies of their jobs, and there was no premium upon invention.

This is only one of many ways in which the ecology of the Chinese, their adaptation to physical environment, influenced their culture. Life on the great river flood plains has always been a hard life, in which man is dependent upon nature more than upon his own initiative. "Heaven nourishes and destroys" is an ancient saying. On the broad stretches of the plain the patient Chinese farmer was at the mercy of the weather, dependent upon Heaven's gift of sun and rain. He was forced to accept natural calamity in the traditional forms of drought, flood, pestilence, and famine. This is in striking contrast to the lot of the European who lived in a land of variegated topography. Western man, either on the Mediterranean or on the European continent, was never far from a water supply, and could always supplement agriculture by hunting or fishing, provided he exercised initiative. From ancient times seaborne commerce has played an immediate part in Western man's economy. Exploration and invention in the service of commerce have exemplified Western man's struggle against nature, rather than a passive acceptance of it.

A different relation of man to nature in the West and in the East has been one of the salient contrasts between the two civilizations. Man has been in the center of the Western stage. The rest of nature has served as neutral background or as his adversary. Thus Western religion is anthropomorphic and Western painting anthropocentric. To see how great this gulf is we have only to compare Christianity with the relative impersonality of Buddhism, or a Sung landscape and its tiny human figures dwarfed by crags and rivers with an Italian primitive in which nature is an afterthought.

14

And yet, paradoxically, Chinese man has been so crowded upon the soil among his fellows that he is also a most socially minded human being, ever conscious of the interplay of personalities and social conventions around him; for he is seldom in all his life beyond earshot of other people.

2 The Nature of Chinese Society

Mao Tse-tung's real claim to immortality lies in his effort to smash the ancient ruling class tradition. His bucolic distaste for the evils of city life and bureaucracy is deeply felt. It rings a bell in the Chinese mind and touches feelings that go far back; for the old China was the world's great example of upper class government from the city over the countryside, by the few over the many.

Social Structure

Since ancient times there have been two Chinas: the myriad agricultural communities of the peasantry in the countryside, where each tree-clad village and farm household persists statically upon the soil; and the overlay of walled towns and cities peopled by the landlords, scholars, merchants, and officials — the families of property and position. There has been no caste system, and the chance to rise from peasant status has not been lacking. Yet China has always remained a country of farmers, four fifths of the people living on the soil they till. The chief social division has therefore been that between town and countryside, between the 80 percent or more of the population who have stayed put upon the land and the 10 or 20 percent of the population who have formed a mobile upper class. This bifurcation still underlies the Chinese political scene and makes it difficult to spread the control of the state from the few to the many.

If we look more closely at this inherited social structure, we note that the upper levels have included really several classes — the landowning gentry, the scholar-literati, and the officials, as well as the merchants, the militarists, and their hangers-on. This composite upper stratum has been the active carrier of China's literate culture in its many aspects. Within this minority segment of the Chinese people have been developed most of the literature and the fine arts, the higher philosophy, ethics, the political ideology of the state, the sanctions of power, and much of the wealth that accompanied them. Culture has filtered down to the masses.

The Peasant: Family and Village. Even today the Chinese people are still mostly peasants tilling the soil, living mainly in villages, in houses of brown sun-dried brick, bamboo, or whitewashed wattle, or sometimes stone, with earth or stone floors, and paper, not glass, in the windows. At least half and sometimes two thirds to three quarters of their meager material income is used for food. The other necessaries of life, including rent, heat, lighting, clothing, and any possible luxuries, come from the tiny remainder. They lack even the luxury of space. Peasant dwellings have usually about four small room sections for every three persons. Sometimes family members of both sexes and two or three generations must all sleep on the same brick bed. There is little meat in the diet, and so simple a thing as iron is scarce for tools or for building. The per capita consumption of steel in the United States is several hundred times that in China. Man power still takes the place of the machine for most purposes. In this toilsome, earthbound existence the hazards of life from malnutrition and disease until recently have given the average baby in China, as in India, little more than twenty-six years of life expectancy. Human life compared with the other factors of production is abundant and therefore cheap.

To an American with his higher material standard of living the amazing thing about the Chinese peasantry is their ability to maintain life in these poor conditions. The answer lies in their social institutions which have carried the individuals of each family through the phases and vicissitudes of human existence according to deeply ingrained patterns of behavior. These institutions and behavior patterns have been the oldest and most persistent social phenomena in the world. China has been the stronghold of the family system and has derived both strength and inertia from it.

The Chinese family has been a microcosm, the state in miniature. The family, not the individual, has been the social unit and the responsible element in the political life of its locality. The filial piety and obedience inculcated in family life have been the training ground for loyalty to the ruler and obedience to constituted authority in the state.

This function of the family to raise filial sons who would become loyal subjects can be seen by a glance at the pattern of authority within the traditional family group. The father was a supreme autocrat, with control over the use of all family property and income and a decisive voice in arranging the marriages of the children. The mixed love, fear, and awe of children for their father was strengthened by the great respect paid to age. An old man's loss of vigor was more than offset by his growth in wisdom. As long as he lived in possession of his faculties the patriarch possessed every sanction to enable him to dominate the family scene. According to the law he could sell his children into slavery or even execute them for improper conduct. In fact, of course, Chinese parents were by custom as well as by nature particularly loving toward small children, and they were also bound by a reciprocal code of responsibility for their children as family members. But law and custom provided little check on parental tyranny if they chose to exercise it.

The domination of age over youth within the old-style family was matched by the domination of male over female. Chinese baby girls in the old days were more likely than baby boys to suffer infanticide. A girl's marriage was, of course, arranged and not for love. The trembling bride became at once a daughter-in-law under the tyranny of her husband's mother. In a well-to-do family she might see secondary wives or concubines brought into the household, particularly if she did not bear a male heir. She could be repudiated by her husband for various reasons. If he died she could not easily remarry. All this reflected the fact that a woman had no economic independence. Her labor was absorbed in household tasks and brought her no income. Peasant women were universally illiterate. They had few or no property rights. Until the present century their subjection was demonstrated and reinforced by the custom of foot-binding. This crippling practice by which a young girl's feet were tightly wrapped from about age five to prevent normal development seems to have begun about the tenth century. The "lily feet" so produced, with the arch broken and lesser toes curled under, meant the suffering of hundreds of millions of young girls but had great aesthetic and erotic value for men. During a girl's childhood and adolescence she endured the pain in her feet in order to attract a good husband. Daily care of her feet, washing them, cutting the nails, maintaining circulation, was a very private matter since she kept them constantly bound and covered. Eventually a husband's interest in these small sensitive objects made them genuinely erogenous — still another Chinese invention! In daily life bound feet, stumping about on one's heels, also kept womankind from venturing far abroad.

The inferiority of women imposed upon them by social custom was merely one manifestation of the hierarchic nature of a society of status. It exemplified an entire social code and cosmology. Philosophically, ancient China had seen the world as the product of two interacting complementary elements, *yin* and *yang*. Yin was the attribute of all things female, dark, weak, and passive. *Yang* was the attribute of things male, bright, strong, and active. While male and female were both necessary and complementary, one was by nature passive toward the other. Building on such ideological foundations, an endless succession of Chinese male moralists worked out the behavior pattern of obedience and passivity which was to be expected of women. These patterns subordinated girls to boys from their infancy and kept the wife subordinate to her husband and the mother to her son. Forceful women, whom China has never lacked, usually controlled their families by indirection, not by fiat.

Status within the family was codified in the famous "three bonds" emphasized by the Confucian philosophers; namely, the bonds between ruler and subject (prince and minister), father and son, and husband and wife. To an egalitarian Westerner the most striking thing about this doctrine is that two of the three relationships were within the family, and all were between superior and subordinate. The relationship of mother and son, which in Western life often allows matriarchal domination, was not stressed in theory, though naturally important in fact.

Within the extended family every child from birth was involved in a highly ordered system of kinship relations with elder brothers, sisters, maternal elder brother's wives, and other kinds of aunts, uncles, and cousins, grandparents, and in-laws too numerous for a Westerner to keep in mind. These relationships were not only more clearly named and differentiated than in the West but also carried with them more compelling rights and duties dependent upon status. A first son, for example, could not long remain unaware of the Confucian teaching as to his duties toward the family line and his precedence over his younger brothers and his sisters.

Chinese well habituated to the family system have been prepared to accept similar patterns of status in other institutions, including the official hierarchy of the government. The German sociologist Max Weber characterized China as a "familistic state." One advantage of a system of status (as opposed to our individualist system of contractual relations) is that a man knows automatically where he stands in his family or society. He can have security in the knowledge that if he does his prescribed part he may expect reciprocal action from others in the system. It has been observed that a Chinese community overseas gains strength by organizing its activities to meet new situations in a hierarchic fashion.

The life cycle of the individual in a peasant family is inextricably interwoven with the seasonal cycle of intensive agriculture upon the land. The life and death of the people follow a rhythm which interpenetrates the growing and harvesting of the crops. The peasant village which still forms the bedrock of Chinese society is built out of family units; village, family, and individual follow the rhythm of seasons and crops, of birth, marriage, and death.

Socially, the Chinese in the village have been organized primarily in their kinship system and only secondarily as a neighborhood community. The village has ordinarily consisted of a group of family and kinship units (clans) which are permanently settled from one generation to the next and continuously dependent upon the use of certain landholdings. Each family household has been both a social and an economic unit. Its members derived their sustenance from working its fields and their social status from membership in it.

The Chinese kinship system is patrilineal, the family headship passing in the male line from father to eldest son. Thus the men stay in the family while the girls marry into other family households, in neither case following the life pattern which Western individuals take as a matter of course. Until recently a Chinese boy and girl did not choose each other as life mates, nor did they set up an independent household together after marriage. Instead, they entered the husband's father's household and assumed responsibilities for its maintenance, subordinating married life to family life in a way that modern Americans would consider insupportable.

From the time of the first imperial unification, before Christ, the Chinese abandoned the institution of primogeniture by which the eldest son would have retained all the father's property while the younger sons sought their fortunes elsewhere. The enormous significance of this institutional change can be seen by comparison with a country like England or Japan where younger sons who have not shared their father's estate have provided the personnel for government, business, and empire. By the abolition of primogeniture, the Chinese created a system of equal division of the land among the sons of the family. They left the eldest son only certain ceremonial duties, to acknowledge his position, and sometimes an extra share of property; otherwise the land was divided. This constant parcelization of the land tended to destroy the continuity of family landholding, forestall the growth of landed particularism among great officials, and keep peasant families on the margin of subsistence. Under this system the prime duty of each married couple was to produce a son who could maintain the family line, and yet the birth of more than one son might mean impoverishment.

Contrary to a common myth, a large family with several children has not been the peasant norm. The scarcity of land, as well as disease and famine, set a limit to the number of people likely to survive in each family unit. The large joint family of several married sons with many children all within one compound, which has usually been regarded as typical of China, appears to have been the ideal exception, a luxury which only the well-to-do could afford. The average peasant family was limited to four, five, or six persons. Division of the land among the sons constantly checked the accumulation of property and savings and the typical family had little opportunity to rise in the social scale. The peasantry were bound to the soil not by law and custom so much as by their own numbers.

Yet Chinese peasant life was richly sophisticated in folklore and the civilities and happenings of an ancient folk culture. Life was not normally confined to a single village but rather to a whole group of villages that formed a market area.

The Market Community. Even today this pattern can be seen from the air — the cellular structure of market communities, each centered on a market town surrounded by its ring of satellite villages. The old Chinese countryside was a honeycomb of these relatively self-sufficient areas. Each one, if we visualize it in an ideal model such as that of G. William Skinner, centered on a market town from which footpaths (or sometimes waterways) radiated out to a first ring of about six villages and continued on to a second ring of say twelve villages. Each of these eighteen or so villages had perhaps 75 households and each family household averaged five persons — parents, perhaps two children, and a grandparent. No village was more than about two and a half miles from the market town, within an easy day's round trip with a carrying pole, barrow, or donkey (or a sampan on a waterway). Together, the village farmers and the market town shopkeepers, artisans, landowners, temple priests, and others formed a community of roughly 1500 households or 7500 people. The town market functioned periodically — say every first, fourth, and seventh day in a ten-day cycle — so that itinerant merchants could visit it regularly while visiting the adjoining markets five miles away in similar cycles — say every second, fifth, and eighth day or every third, sixth, and ninth day. In this pulsation of the market cycle, one person from every household might go to the market town on every third day, perhaps to sell a bit of local produce or buy a product from elsewhere, but in any case meeting friends in the tea shop, at the temple, or on the way. In ten years he would have gone to market a thousand times.

Thus while the villages were not self-sufficient, the larger market community was both an economic unit and a social universe. Marriages were commonly arranged through matchmakers at the market town. There festivals were celebrated, a secret society might have its lodge meetings, and the peasant community met representatives of the ruling class — tax gatherers and rent collectors.

The Gentry Class

The gentry dominated Chinese life, so much so that sociologists have called China a gentry state and even ordinary people may speak of the "scholar gentry" as a class. But do not let yourself be reminded of the landed gentry with their roast beef and fox hunts in merry England, for "gentry" in the case of China is a technical term with two principal meanings and an inner ambiguity. It requires special handling.

Non-Marxists generally agree, first of all, that the gentry were not a mere feudal landlord class, because Chinese society was not organized in any system that can be called feudalism, except possibly before 221 B.C. While "feudal" may still be a useful swear word, it has little value as a Western term applied to China. For instance, an essential characteristic of feudalism, as the word has been used with reference to medieval Europe and Japan, has been the inalienability of the land. The medieval serf was bound to the land and could not himself either leave it or dispose of it, whereas the Chinese peasant both in law and in fact has been free to sell and, if he had the means, to purchase land. His bondage has resulted from a press of many circumstances but not from a legal institution similar to European feudalism. Nor has it been maintained by the domination of a professional warrior caste. Avoidance of the term feudal to describe the Chinese peasant's situation in life by no means signifies that it has been less miserable. But if the word feudal is to retain a valid meaning for European and other institutions to which it was originally applied, it cannot be very meaningful in a general Chinese context.

The Chinese gentry can be understood only in a dual, economic and political sense, as connected both with landholding and with officeholding. The narrow definition, following the traditional Chinese terminology, confines gentry status to those *individuals* who held official degrees gained normally by passing examinations, or sometimes by recommendation or purchase. This has the merit of being concrete and even quantifiable — the gentry in this narrow sense were degree-holders, as officially listed, and not dependent for their status on economic resources, particularly landowning, which is so hard to quantify from the historical record.

Yet in an agrarian society one can hardly ignore the importance of landholding as one source of upper-class strength. The main point about the gentry as individuals was that they were public functionaries, playing political and administrative roles, in addition to any connection with the landlord class. Yet, being Chinese, they were also enmeshed in family relations, on which they could rely for material sustenance. This political-economic dualism has led many writers to define the term gentry more broadly, as a group of *families* rather than of individual degree-holders only. Both the narrow and the broad definitions must be kept in mind.

Looked at descriptively, the gentry families lived chiefly in the walled towns rather than in the villages. They constituted a stratum of families based on landed property which intervened between the earth-bound masses of the peasantry, on the one hand, and the officials and merchants who formed a fluid matrix of overall administrative and commercial activity, on the other. They were the local elite, who carried on certain functions connected with the peasantry below and certain others connected with the officials above.

For the peasant community the gentry included the big landowners, the economic base of the great ruling class. Their big high-walled compounds enclosing many courtyards, replete with servants and hoarded supplies and proof against bandits, dominated the old market towns. This was the type of "big house" celebrated in both Chinese and Western novels of China. As a local ruling class the gentry managed the system of customary and legal rights to the use of land. These ordinarily were so incredibly diverse and complicated that decided managerial ability was required to keep them straight. The varied tenant relationships, loans, mortgages, customary payments, and obligations on both sides formed such a complex within the community that many peasants could hardly say whether they were themselves mainly small landowners or mainly tenants. In general, the peasant's loss of title to his land was more likely to make him a tenant and decrease his share of its product than to make him a displaced and homeless wanderer. Peasant poverty was reflected sometimes in the increase of landless laborers in the villages, but it was marked chiefly by the increased payment of land rent.

There have been two schools of thought about China's rural

poverty. One school has stressed the exploitation of the peasant by the ruling class through rents, usury, and other exactions, resulting in a maldistribution of income. This idea of landlord class exploitation has of course fitted Marxist theory and is now an article of faith concerning the old China. The other school, as Ramon Myers points out, has been more "eclectic"; it has stressed the many reasons for the low productivity of the old farm economy: farms of two acres per family were too small; even these tiny plots were improperly used; "peasants had insufficient capital and limited access to new technology; there was little control over nature; primitive transport increased marketing costs." Supporters of this interpretation point to the fact that most Chinese farmers owned their land, some were partly owners and partly tenants, and only about one quarter or one fifth were outright tenants, so that landlord exploitation of tenants was far from the general rule and less of a problem than the general lack of capital and technology compared with labor.

Without attempting final judgment, we may suggest one rule: that social status and class prerogatives must have figured in the rural scene along with all the agronomic factors, and any explanation must be social and historical as well as economic. For example, as in all farming, the seasonal need of capital permitted usurious interest on loans, which ran as high as 12 percent a month, depending on what the traffic would bear. Since capital was accumulated from the surplus product of the land, landowners were usually money-lenders. The gentry families thus rested in part upon property rights and money power, as well as social prestige. In the early twentieth century, they still dominated the back country in most provinces. Modern developments like absentee landlordism strengthened rather than weakened their position, by stressing economic claims untempered by personal relations.

For the officials of the old China the gentry families were

one medium through whom tax collections were effected. By this same token they were for the peasantry intermediaries who could palliate official oppression while in the process of carrying it out. The local officials dealt with conditions of flood or famine or incipient rebellion and the multitude of minor criminal cases and projects for public works, all through the help of the gentry community. It was the buffer between populace and officialdom.

The economic role of the gentry families was no more than half the story, for they had very important political-administrative functions in the Chinese state which made them unlike any group in Western history. Here we meet a problem of historical interpretation, created by the ambivalence of the term gentry, which in the present literature on China may refer either to landowning families or to degree-holding individuals. Unfortunately for the clarity of the term, the latter group was not entirely included within the former. Peasants without landlord-family backing occasionally rose through the examination system to become degree-holders and officials. Thus a poor man, by his educational qualifications alone, could become a member of the gentry in the narrow sense used above, even though he was not connected with a gentry family. This fact makes the term "gentry" ambiguous and therefore subject to dispute.

The view taken here is that the degree-holding individuals were in most cases connected with landowning families, and the latter in most cases had degree-holding members. Until the subject is clarified by further research we can only proceed on the assumption that, in general and for the most part, the gentry families were the out-of-office reservoir of the degree-holders and the bureaucracy. The big families were the seedbed in which officeholders were nurtured and the haven to which dismissed or worn-out bureaucrats could return.

In each community the gentry had many important public functions. They raised funds for and supervised public works — the building and upkeep of irrigation and communication facilities such as canals, dikes, dams, roads, bridges, ferries. They supported Confucian institutions and morals — establishing and maintaining schools, shrines, and local temples of Confucius, publishing books, especially local histories or gazetteers, and issuing moral homilies and exhortations to the populace. In time of peace they set the tone of public life. In time of disorder they organized and commanded militia defense forces. From day to day they arbitrated disputes informally, in place of the continual litigation which goes on in any American town. The gentry also set up charities and handled trust funds to help the community, and made contributions at official request to help the state, especially in time of war, flood, or famine. So useful were these contributions that most dynasties got revenue by selling the lowest literary degrees, thus admitting many persons to degree-holding status without examination. While this abused the system, it also let men of wealth rise for a price into the upper class and share the gentry privileges, such as contact with the officials and immunity from corporal punishment.

The local leadership and management functions of the gentry families explain why officialdom did not penetrate lower down into Chinese society. The imperial government remained a superstructure which did not directly enter the villages because it rested upon the gentry as its foundation. The many public functions of the local degree-holders made a platform under the imperial bureaucracy and let the officials move about with remarkable fluidity and seeming independence of local roots. Actually, the Emperor's appointee to any magistracy could administer it only with the cooperation of the gentry in that area. All in all, in a country of over 400 million people, a century ago, there were less than 20,000 regular imperial officials but roughly one and a quarter million scholarly degree-holders.

Continued domination of the gentry families over the peasantry was assured not only by landowning but also by the fact that the gentry mainly produced the scholar class from which officials were chosen. This near-monopoly of scholarship was made possible in turn by the nature of the Chinese language.

The Chinese Written Language — The Scholar

Chinese writing is not only different to look at, it is based on utterly different principles from the phonetically written tongues of western Asia and Europe, many of which look to us just as baffling as Chinese but are in fact closely similar to our own language. Thai children, for example, when they study Thai in school go through much the same process as American children, learning the sounds to associate with a number of otherwise meaningless symbols, or alphabet. As far as their mode of thought and study is concerned, they could just as well learn the English alphabet (with various adjustments to convey Thai sounds) and then proceed to write down words heard in everyday life and develop their vocabularies and powers of self-expression. With a Chinese child it is different. He learns symbols which have meaning because of their appearance, and which exist like pictures or like the figure 5, apart from any sounds.

The Chinese writing system has been the most distinctive ingredient of Chinese culture throughout its history. The earliest Chinese characters have been found at the archaeological site of the ancient Shang dynasty capital of Anyang, which is in Honan province north of the Yellow River. Excavations there in the decade 1928–1937, and at scores of other Shang sites discovered since 1949, in this region where the Yellow

River enters the North China plain, have revealed a vigorous state and society that flourished there ca. 1400–1100 B.C. Its warriors fought in horse-drawn chariots. Its priests used ceremonial bronze vessels of pre-eminent craftsmanship and also practiced bone divination. The ancient kings' diviners took the auspices by applying a hot point to flat slips of bone, producing cracks which could be interpreted as the advice of the ancestors. Characters were scratched on these "oracle bones" and the results were recorded there. This written language was both pictographic and symbolic, in either case ideographic rather than phonetic.

The Chinese language today consists of well over forty thousand characters in the biggest dictionary. But these boil down to about seven thousand necessary for a newspaper font, including about three thousand that one needs to know in order to be really literate. The form of these characters has hardly changed since the early Christian era. Until a generation ago the Chinese were still getting along with a written language comparable in age to ancient Greek and Latin, so terse that it usually had to be seen to be understood — the sound alone being inadequate. This was one factor helping to keep China, down to the twentieth century, in its archaic Confucian mold. The language inhibited easy contact with alien societies, whose students of Chinese found it even harder then than now.

Chinese Writing. Chinese characters began as pictures or symbols. The ancient character ⊙ (later written 日) was the sun, and ☽ (later 月) the moon. Sun and moon together 明 meant bright, illustrious, clear. 木 meant a tree, two trees 林 meant a forest, and three 森, a dense growth. The symbols 一 二 三 are certainly easier than "one, two, three." 囗 indicates an enclosure or "to surround," while a smaller square 口 is the sign for the mouth and by extension means a hole, a pass, a harbor, and the like.

In its early growth the Chinese written language could not

expand on a purely pictographic basis (like the joining of "sun" and "moon" to make "bright," noted above). A phonetic element crept into it. As a result most Chinese characters are combinations of other simple characters. One part of the combination usually indicates the root meaning, while the other part indicates something about the sound.

For example, take the character for east, 東 , which in the Peking dialect has had the sound "tung" (pronounced like "doong," as in Mao Tse-tung's name). Since a Chinese character is read aloud as a single syllable and since spoken Chinese is also rather short of sounds (there are only about four hundred different syllables in the whole language), it has been plagued with homophones, words that sound like other words, like "soul" and "sole" or "all" and "awl" in English. It happened that the spoken word meaning freeze had the sound "tung." So did a spoken word meaning a roof beam. When the Chinese went to write down the character for freeze, they took the character for east and put beside it the symbol for ice 冫, which makes the character 凍 ("tung," to freeze). To write down the word sounding "tung" which meant roof beam, they wrote the character east and put before it the symbol for wood 木 making 棟 ("tung," a roof beam).

These are simple examples. Indeed any part of the Chinese language is simple in itself. It becomes difficult because there is so much of it to be remembered, so many meanings and allusions. When the lexicographers wanted to arrange thousands of Chinese characters in a dictionary, for instance, the best they could do in the absence of an alphabet was to work out a list of 214 classifiers, one of which was sure to be in each character in the language. These 214 classifiers, for dictionary purposes, correspond to the 26 letters of our alphabet, but are more ambiguous and less efficient.

In spite of its cumbersomeness the Chinese written language was used to produce a greater volume of recorded literature than any other language before modern times. One sober estimate is that until 1750 there had been more books published in Chinese than in all the other languages in the world put together.

Perhaps enough has been said to indicate why written Chinese became a monopoly of the scribes. The Chinese language had the character of an institution, rather than a tool, of society. Men worshiped it, and devoted long lives to mastering even parts of its literature, which was a world of its own, into which one might gain admittance only by strenuous effort. The Chinese writing system was not a convenient device lying ready at hand for every schoolboy to pick up and use as he prepared to meet life's problems. It was itself one of life's problems. If little Lao-san could not find the time for long-continued study of it, he was forever barred from social advancement. Thus the Chinese written language, rather than an open door through which China's peasantry could find truth and light, was a heavy barrier pressing against any upward advance and requiring real effort to overcome — a hindrance, not a help to learning.

Consequently, much of Chinese learning stopped with the language and the classical literature. Students were exhausted merely by the mastery of them. In the old days a boy needed ten years of leisure in which to master the myriad literary allusions to be found in the classics. Only a gentry family could normally afford it.

The Scholar. The scholar class produced by mastery of the characters was closely integrated with both the gentry families beneath it and the official system above. When successful as a degree-holder and perhaps an official, the scholar found his channel of expression and achievement through the established structure of government. He could become an official, however, only by mastering the official ideology of the state as set down in the canonical works of the Chinese classics. These

33

texts were part of a system of ideas and ritual practices in which the scholar-official learned and applied the Confucian rules and attitudes on the plane of verbal conduct while participating in the personal relationships, political cliques, organized perquisites, and systematic squeeze which distinguished the official class on the plane of practical action.

For the scholar who did not rise into official life there was always the alternative of the family system from which he had sprung. His status as a degree-holder gave him contact with the lower fringes of official power and through this personal contact he could serve his family by representing its interests. This function again called for the use of Confucian ideas in verbal and literary expression. In this way the scholar, whether in official life or out of it, was wedded to the established order of family and state. His living depended upon them and in practice he served them both. As a cultivated gentleman incapable of manual labor or trade and trained to be the bearer of the family-state ideology, he had no alternative.

It was the security of the individual boy in the gentry family which made it possible for him to take the risk involved in the investment of his time in scholarship. His preparation for the examinations and for official life required many years of study. Yet the examinations were a gamble and talented youths could be fed into the system only from sources that had means. The risk and mobility of official life contrasted with the security and stability of the landed gentry. The point of balance between them was the examination system. In a society which seems to us remarkable for its emphasis upon personal relations, the Chinese examinations appear to have been amazingly impersonal and universalistic. When the system was functioning effectively at the height of a dynasty, every effort was made to eliminate personal favoritism. Candidates were locked in their cubicles, several thousand of which in long rows covered a broad area at each provincial capital. Papers were marked with the writer's number only. Such precautions were, of course, necessary for the maintenance of any rational and objective standards in the selection of candidates for office. They expressed the Chinese ruler's genuine need of talented personnel to maintain an efficient administration. Once the best talent of the land had been chosen by this impersonal institution, however, it was then perfectly consistent that the officials should conduct a highly personal administration of the government, following a "virtue ethic" which attached importance to the qualities of individual personality rather than a "command ethic" which laid emphasis upon an impersonal and higher law.

The fact and the myth of social mobility in the Chinese state are still matters of debate. Most dynasties which supported the examination system as a mechanism for the selection of talent gave extensive lip service to the myth that all might enter high position, depending only upon ability. Western writers for long assumed that the Chinese examinations were a really democratic institution, providing opportunity for the intelligent peasant to rise in the world. In fact, however, this seems to have happened rather seldom. The many years of assiduous study required for the examinations were a barrier which no ordinary peasant could surmount. The legend of the villagers who clubbed together to support the studies of the local peasant genius has been an inspiring tradition. But it was not an every day occurrence.

Of the various avenues open to the common peasant, advancement could not usually be sought through the opening up of new land or founding of new enterprises, nor, for most people, through the investment of profits and savings. This fact has given Chinese life a character far different from our own and makes the American doctrine of individualism and free enterprise, when transplanted to China, an almost incomprehensible and rather dubious jumble of slogans. In Chinese circumstances, advancement for the common man has lain in the direction of connections with the bureaucracy. Entrance into the official class or into the penumbra of money handlers and fixers which surrounded it was a goal to be achieved through personal contacts and personal services. This route on the whole led through the gentry and not around them.

Thus landlords, scholars, and officials were all parts of a composite ruling class. Landowning families having some agricultural surplus could give their sons leisure for study to become scholars. Scholars, with a mastery of classical learning, could pass examinations and become officials. Officials, with the perquisites and profits of bureaucratic government, could protect and increase their family landholdings. The structure was flexible, automatically self-perpetuating, and very stable.

Nondevelopment of Capitalism — The Merchant

In all of Chinese history one of the most urgent questions which a Westerner will ask is the reason why the Chinese merchant class failed to break away from its dependence upon officialdom and create an independent industrial and entrepreneurial power. The answer is not simple but it can be attempted.

First of all, the Chinese merchant had an attitude of mind quite different from that of the Western entrepreneur extolled by our classical economists of the last century. According to the doctrine of the latter, the economic man can prosper most by producing, and securing from his increased production the profit which the market will give him. In the Chinese tradition, however, the economic man will do best not by increasing production but by increasing his own share of what has already been produced. He will rise by competing against his fellows directly rather than by creating new wealth through the conquest of nature, or the increased exploitation of her resources, or applications of improved technologies. This bespeaks the fact that the Chinese economy has had from early times a maximum of people competing for a minimum of natural resources, instead of great continents and new industries to develop. The incentive for innovative enterprise, to win a market for new products, has been less than the incentive for monopoly, to control a market by paying for an official license to do so. The tradition in China has been not to build a better mousetrap but to get the official mouse monopoly.

The ideal gentleman in China was, therefore, the man who had risen above the necessity to produce and was able to devote himself to leisure and the scholarly pursuits which symbolized it. The person most esteemed was he who had achieved leisure, not he who (like the modern big-time operator with his telecommunications and office staffs working day and night) outdid his fellows in setting the pace of frenzied business activity. This leisurely ideal could be seen only recently in the Chinese village where a leisure class appeared at the top level of the peasantry although at an amazingly low level of income. The relatively well-to-do peasant, though still bone poor by our standards, would seize the first opportunity to change his status from that of a laborer who uses his back and hands in the fields to that of a gentleman who wears a long gown and affects some literate interest. The long fingernails of old China were certainly the cheapest badge of leisure ever invented.

From the earliest period official position was the key to wealth and leisure, for the official had the greatest opportunity to increase his share of the things already produced. With his official status went the power to settle human affairs and profit thereby. More specifically, the official represented the Emperor's power to conscript corvée labor, to levy taxes, to dispense justice, and to regulate the economic and social activities of the people.

Coming from the local gentry, Chinese officials usually brought to their careers the attitude of a rentier class. They sought perquisites rather than opportunities for enterprise. It is this aspect of the "bureaucratic spirit" which most irks modern exponents of the "entrepreneurial spirit."

Now the merchant was a competitor of the official, since he also was occupied not in agricultural production but in manipulations and exchanges which would secure a greater share of the goods already available. In theory the merchant from ancient times had been regarded by the scholar-official as nonproductive and parasitic. His activities in transporting produce from place to place were given no credit in the classical literature. He was placed at the bottom of the social scale. In actual fact, however, the merchant was kept in check by the official as a minor ally whose activities could be used and milked in the interest of the official class or of the state. As Etienne Balazs has pointed out, commercial transactions were always subject to the superintendence and taxation of the officials. Government monopolies of staple articles, like salt and iron in ancient times, or like tea, silk, tobacco, salt, and matches more recently, have been an expression of the overriding economic prerogatives of the state. No merchant class was allowed to rise independently and encroach upon these prerogatives.

On the other hand, it was always possible to work out a close community of interest between the merchant and the official, for official patronage and support were necessary for any big commercial undertaking. Both could profit where neither could succeed alone. Merchants, bankers, brokers, and traders of all sorts were therefore a class attached as subordinates to the bureaucracy. As handlers and manipulators of goods and capital, they assisted the officials not only in extracting the surplus from commerce but also in extracting the surplus from agriculture.

Merchants indeed could move with some ease into the gentry class through purchase of land and literary degrees and intermarriage. The fact that farmers were free to sell their land gave the merchant class an opportunity to buy it and gain both steady income and social prestige. Unlike Europe, China had little foreign trade in which a merchant could invest. Land remained the great object of his investment, and so the merchant class produced landlords more readily than independent commercial capitalists.

Chinese guild organization, though capable of great feats of passive resistance in the form of strikes or noncooperation, bears out the subservience of merchants to officials. The strength of the guild institution has lain in the craft guild which the artisans of a certain handicraft have used to preserve their monopoly of technical processes and productive rights. Merchant guilds such as led the way in early European trade have been notably weak in China. The Canton Cohong, one of the main examples, was notoriously a tool of court officials.

China's premodern financial system has offered another body of evidence. Savings which represented accumulated capital were ordinarily invested in moneylending because of the high interest rates obtainable. The usurious rates were an index of the farmer's high seasonal demand for money, both to pay his taxes and for subsistence until the next harvest. Short-term credits to farmers paid higher interest than long-term industrial loans. As a result there was less incentive in China than in America for investment of savings in industrial production.

One sign of the predominance of agriculture in the Chinese economy was the restricted use of money. Creation of credit among the villages was retarded by the relative self-sufficiency of the peasant household and its dependence upon short-term purchases from sources close at hand. Similarly the government used to rely heavily upon taxation in kind and the payments of stipends in grain. The capital at Peking, for example, was fed by grain shipments from the provinces via the Grand Canal. In addition the government had at its command resources of corvée labor which received no money wages.

The old currency system itself was extremely complex, a bimetallic system using both silver and copper. The unit of account for silver (the ounce or tael) varied from place to place and also as between trades and agencies of government. Twenty different silver tael units of account might be in common use in one city at one time, requiring a different "currency" for each major commodity, like salt or cotton cloth, and for payments going to certain other places. It was not possible to maintain a minted currency of fixed value. Reliance had to be placed upon the clumsy circulation of pure silver, each ingot of which had to be weighed and also assayed for its purity. Meanwhile few governments could refrain from debasing the copper coinage. The resulting multiplicity of currency units, and exchange arrangements among them, represented the domination of the money manipulator, who profited by this complexity, over the investor who wanted to put his money into planned productive enterprises. One may surmise that this inefficiency of the money system was tolerated because it helped the ruling class's money operations more than it hindered them, just as the scholars tolerated an ideographic language the difficulty of which preserved their semi-monopoly over it. In any case this inefficient money system bespoke a loose, decentralized economy in which commercial activity was mainly limited to local trade. It was much like medieval Europe.

In this context it is possible to find an explanation of the nondevelopment of capitalism in China in the fact that the merchant was never able to become established outside the control of the gentry and their representatives in the bureaucracy. In feudal Europe the merchant class was able to develop in the towns. Since the landed ruling class in Europe were settled in their manors upon the land, the European towns could grow up outside the feudal system instead of being integrated in it. Medieval burghers gained their independence by having a separate habitat in these new towns, and a new political authority to protect them, in the persons of the kings of national states.

In China these conditions were lacking. The early abolition of feudalism and the dependence of the Emperor and his officials upon the local gentry left no political power outside the established order to which the merchant could turn for special protection. In addition the gentry families of China early became the dominant class in the towns, which grew up primarily as administrative centers. The essential connection of the gentry with officialdom drew them into these centers. The gentry family's best security, in short, lay not in a sole reliance upon landowning but in a union of landowning with official prerogatives. Family property in itself was no security but officials who were family members could give it protection.

Thus the gentry class, as an elite stratum over the peasant economy, inevitably congregated in the towns. The villages depended upon the towns economically as centers of handicraft production and of exchange. They depended upon the larger towns also politically as centers of administration and of the authority necessary to maintain peace and order. Finally, the towns were cultural centers as well as walled havens of protection against bandits or irate peasants, and for all these reasons they were the seat of the gentry. But the latter found their security in land and office, not in trade and industry. Between them, the gentry and officials saw to it that the merchant remained under control and contributed to their coffers instead of setting up a separate economy. Behind these institutional factors lay still another: the different status of the individual, to be noted in the next chapter.

China as an "Oriental" Society

If we put together all the foregoing elements — peasant villages, landlord gentry families, merchants, scholars, and officials — we have a structure of social classes different from anything in Europe or America, with a different type of economic organization and political control. A pioneer Marxist historian in this field, K. A. Wittfogel, classifies traditional China as a representative of an ancient "oriental" type of society, fundamentally distinct from the more recent modern society of Europe and America. He compares China with other ancient empires of Egypt, Mesopotamia, and India and also with the empires of the Incas, the Aztecs, or the Maya in pre-Columbian America. All these ancient societies were organized under centralized monolithic governments in which the bureaucracy was dominant in almost all aspects of large-scale activity — administrative, military, religious, and economic — so that no sanction for private enterprise ever became established. An imperial monopoly of administrative activities in the collection of taxes, maintenance of local order, dispensing of justice, or management of the civil service may not seem unusual to us. Centralized control over the military also may not seem unexpected, nor even efforts to control religious life and thought. But these governments' customary monopoly of large-scale economic activity will seem to Americans most different and "unnatural."

To understand this difference we must recall that ancient China was a younger contemporary of ancient Egypt and Mesopotamia. These empires had common features such as universal kingship, land-based economy, ideographic writing. China's evolution remained comparatively uninterrupted whereas in the Eastern Mediterranean the Phoenicians and Greeks developed city-states, seafaring, and alphabetic writing. Subsequently, the Greco-Roman world and the European Middle Ages both saw the growth of dominant social classes which were originally outside the framework of government and were based on private property. The Greek city-state, for instance, was dominated by a propertied class which manipulated the government and made every effort to prevent the growth of an independent bureaucracy. In this Greek society of private property, taxes were collected by tax farmers, the mines and customs were farmed out to private individuals, slaves were used as scribes, and the citizens who took office were rotated so rapidly that no one official could accumulate personal power based on official position. Under the Roman Republic the taxes and customs were collected by tax farmers, and public works were made the responsibility of private persons. In feudal Europe the enlargement of the sphere of private activity was of course even more striking, in the military and administrative sectors as well as in the economic. It is no accident that the modern West found the roots of individualism in Greek philosophy and Roman law as well as in the medieval town.

Without attempting hard and fast generalizations, we may note certain characteristics of the economic life of China and other politically centralized "oriental" countries which distinguish them from our own. In the first place these societies have been based upon agricultural production. Their governments have performed the function of controlling the economic ingredients of this production. This has involved control in varying degrees over the land, the man power, and the water supply. In ancient times the ruler's claim to the disposal of the land and of the people on it was seldom questioned, although it was usually found through experience that private land-owning was a useful incentive to peasant production and did not impede the collection of taxes. The institution of compulsory corvée labor by the people at the behest of the government usually became well established. This made possible the construction of enormous public works which still amaze us, like the pyramids of Egypt or the Great Wall of China.

Control of the water supply for agricultural production was a strategic factor in the growth of the government's economic function. It was typical of these societies that, unlike Western Europe, they were in regions of semi-aridity where the water supply of great rivers, if properly used, would supplement the insufficiency of rainfall. But irrigation and flood prevention to be effective must be centrally controlled. Both irrigation ditches and river dikes must be maintained throughout their length according to an overall program.

Once established, a government of this type found itself dependent upon the extension of the same principle of economic control. The building and maintenance of canals for transportation purposes and of highways for transport and communication were paralleled by the growth of the civil service. Scribes and administrators were essential to collect the agricultural surplus and superintend the public works. The concentration of population in enormous capital cities at the imperial administrative center went hand in hand with an increased density of man power upon the land. When urban handicraft industry stimulated exchange between town and countryside, there was no opportunity for the new industrial and merchant class to escape the overshadowing domination of government. The idea never occurred to them.

In effect this meant that heavy industry, which in these early societies was represented by such things as the Great Wall or the Grand Canal and other heavy waterworks, was from the first in the hands of the government. Private enterprise might develop freely in small-scale agricultural production within the grip of government taxation, but this was not a capitalist type of private enterprise. From the peasants' more assiduous cultivation of their privately owned land, the bureaucracy would garner a greater surplus by taxation. By the same principle they also stood ready to collect from the merchant or industrial producer any surplus he might accumulate. Many merchants appear in the records of ancient China but never as a class having political power. Early Emperors specifically barred them from taking the examinations for entrance into official life. The growth of commerce was less important to the rulers of a politically centralized "oriental" state than continued supervision of the agricultural economy. The state depended upon land taxes more than trade taxes.

Behind this disesteem of commerce lay the fact that the agrarian economy of China has always been decentralized, fragmented, and unintegrated. Given the relative self-sufficiency of each farming locality, trade and a money economy have remained at a minimum in spite of the centralization of political power for tax collections and public works.

More fundamentally, the establishment of these institutions of agriculture, public works, and bureaucracy was accompanied by a persistent pattern of assumptions and expectations in the minds of the people, expressed in the evaluations of the classical literature, which placed the official high and the merchant low in public esteem, and perpetuated by the educational system based on the classics. Instead of a philosophy of individual initiative and enterprise, or the limitless possibilities of invention and personal acquisitiveness, these "oriental" societies subscribed to a philosophy of hierarchic status with an emphasis upon individual conformity.

Chinese Militarism. The pattern of an "oriental" society is also visible in China's treatment of the soldier. The standard dogma perpetuated by civilian chroniclers has been that

45

"good iron is not used to make a nail nor a good man to make a soldier." This expressed the idea of the literatus who governs by moral sanctions and uses every opportunity to disparage the warrior who takes power by force. Disparagement of the soldier is deeply ingrained in the old Chinese system of values. Yet few empires in history have had a more impressive military record. Every dynasty has been founded by the sword. In periods of strong government, as under the Han, the T'ang, the early Ming, or the early Ch'ing (see chart, page xvii), powerful military expeditions have gone beyond China's borders into Annam or Korea, or across the wastes of Mongolia and Central Asia. Decades at a time have seen an endless succession of rebel hordes, imperial armies, and alien invaders marching across the face of the land. The nomad dynasties of conquest were actually supported by a professional military caste.

Nevertheless the Chinese military tradition is of a different type from the European or the Japanese. Once an imperial regime was set up, civilian government was esteemed over military. It took a soldier to found a dynasty but he and his descendants invariably found it easier to rule as sages, through civilian officials. This is undoubtedly because power over the Chinese economy invariably settled in the hands of administrators, bureaucrats who got wealth in the form of revenues, not warriors who got it in the form of loot. Chinese history has had no counterpart to the Elizabethan or medieval Japanese institutions of maritime adventure and piracy whereby the country waxed strong on its overseas takings. No doubt one factor was the early disappearance of feudalism. In China the fighting man gave place to the administrator some thousand years before he did so in Japan. Just as the commercial society of the United States prefers civilian to military government, so the bureaucratic polity of China sought constantly to avoid domination by any independent military power.

The Nature of Chinese Society

In practice this meant that the problem of force in China was essentially a police problem, how to maintain surveillance over an unarmed and settled population and muster enough strength to suppress those who might turn bandit. Once a dynasty had become well established, armies for the attack and destruction of enemies were not needed within the Wall. This created the constant problem of reconciling the police institutions of China proper with the type of warfare required on the Chinese frontier against the professional fighting men of the steppe. Unlike the Mongols or the Manchus, Chinese farmers could never become a nation in arms in which each individual had a stake in the tribal or national cause. Like Chairman Mao, rulers continually dreamed of making every farmer a soldier too, but this created at best a defensive rather than a striking force. Chinese armies until recent times were much more a form of public works, created at times of crisis by the same conscription of cheap man power that provided the corvée labor gangs for building a Great Wall, a Grand Canal, or a Burma Road.

The Chinese military thus remained a part of the state's bureaucracy, fed by its revenues and a tempting source of corruption. But unlike the technology-based military of industrial states today, the Chinese military machine was not a major component of the economy. It served the dynastic cause of order and unity, which meant peace and even prosperity within the state; but the primary means for preserving the social order was indoctrination in the orthodox principles of social conduct (*li*), and the secondary means was suasive coercion through rewards and punishments. The use of physical violence to maintain order was seen as a last resort, a confession that indoctrination and suasion had been ineffective and the regime perhaps lacked that popular acquiescence which constituted the Mandate of Heaven. Consequently China's military tradition included many nonviolent methods — mediation by third parties, negotiation, espionage, bribery and subversion, splitting followers from leaders, intimidation and cajolery, and all forms of deception. In short, as the ancient military classic of the fourth century B.C., the *Sun-tzu,* stated, "the acme of skill in warfare is to subdue the enemy without fighting." The objective was the enemy's submission, not necessarily his destruction, a psychological rather than a physical result. Plainly, this Chinese tradition has a new relevance for the nuclear age of deterrence and mass mobilization.

3 The Confucian Pattern

Confucius and Karl Marx had even less in common than the ideologies which bear their names, and the differences between Confucianism and Marx-Lenin-Maoism are as great as the similarities. Yet both traditional China and Communist China have stressed the role of ideology, and no one can understand Chiang Kai-shek or even Mao Tse-tung without knowing something of the Confucian tradition.

Superficial Western observers, looking only at the texts of the Confucian classics, have been impressed with their agnostic this-worldliness and their ethical emphasis upon proper conduct in personal relations. In its larger sense as a philosophy of life, we have generally associated with Confucianism those quiet virtues so artfully described in Lin Yutang's *My Country and My People:* patience, pacifism, and compromise; the golden mean; conservatism and contentment; reverence for the ancestors, the aged, and the learned; and, above all, a mellow humanism — taking man, not God, as the center of the universe.

All this need not be denied. But if we take this Confucian view of life in its social and political context, we will see that its esteem for age over youth, for the past over the present, for established authority over innovation, has in fact provided one of the great historic answers to the problem of social stability. It has been the most successful of all systems of conservatism. For most of two thousand years the Confucian ideology was made the chief subject of study in the world's largest state. Nowhere else have the sanctions of government power been based for so many centuries upon a single consistent pattern of ideas attributed to one ancient sage.

Naturally, in the course of two thousand years many changes have occurred within the broad limits of what we call Confucianism — periods of decline and revival, repeated movements for reform, new emphases and even innovations within the inherited tradition. The range of variety may be less broad than among the multiple facets of Christianity but it is certainly comparable. Consequently the term Confucianism means many things and must be used with care.

As a code of personal conduct Confucianism tried to make each individual a moral being, ready to act on ideal grounds, to uphold virtue against human error, especially against evil rulers. There were many Confucian scholars of moral grandeur, uncompromising foes of tyranny. But their reforming zeal, the dynamics of their creed, aimed to reaffirm and conserve the traditional polity, not to change its fundamental premises.

That Confucian ideas persist in the minds of Chinese politicians today should not surprise us. Confucianism began as a means of bringing social order out of the chaos of a period of warring states. It has been a philosophy of status and consequently a ready tool for autocracy and bureaucracy whenever they have flourished. Unifiers of China have been irresistibly attracted to it, for reasons that are not hard to see.

When Chiang Kai-shek on Christmas Day 1936 was released by the mutinous subordinates who had forcibly held him at Sian, he returned to Nanking amid unprecedented national rejoicing. Yet four days later he submitted his resignation. "Since I am leading the military forces of the country, I should set a good example for my fellow servicemen. It is apparent that my work failed to command the obedience of my followers; for otherwise the mutiny . . . would not have occurred . . . I sincerely hope that the central executive committee will censure me for my negligence of duties. After the Sian incident, it is no longer fit for me to continue in office."

Nine years later in his famous wartime book, *China's Destiny*, Chiang Kai-shek said: "To cultivate the moral qualities necessary to our national salvation . . . we must revive and extend our traditional ethical principles. The most important task is to develop our people's sense of propriety, righteousness, integrity, and honor. These qualities are based upon the Four Cardinal Principles and the Eight Virtues, which in turn are based on Loyalty and Filial Piety."

These two examples could be multiplied. They demonstrate the degree to which China down to recent decades remained a Confucian state. In the first case no one wanted Chiang to resign, nor did he intend to do so, and his resignation was elaborately declined. In the second case no one expected that China's national salvation in the midst of Japanese aggression, blockade, and inflation could be achieved through moral qualities alone, nor did Chiang think so. But in both cases his words delineated the traditional Confucian way.

Countless Chinese leaders before Chiang Kai-shek have quoted Confucius while fighting off rivals or alien invaders, who, like the Japanese, have invoked the Sage on their part while trying to take over China. Peking today sings a different tune, but there are Confucian overtones in the Marxist-Maoist orchestration. The crucial role of ideology under communism lends particular interest to China's ideological past.

The United States and China

Confucian Principles

The principles of Confucian government, which still lie somewhere below the surface of Chinese politics, were worked out before the time of Christ. Modifications made in later centuries, though extensive, have not been fundamental.

First of all, from the beginning of Chinese history in the Shang and Chou periods (from prehistoric times before 1400 B.C. to the third century B.C.) there was a marked stratification into the classes of the officials and nobility on the one hand, and the common people on the other. Thus the term "hundred names" (*pai-hsing*) referred originally to the clans of the officials who were in a category quite different from the common people (*min*). It was not until much later that the modern term "old hundred names" (*lao-pai-hsing*) became transferred to the populace. This difference between the ancient ruling class and the common people gave rise to a particular type of aristocratic tradition which has been preserved and transmitted through Confucianism down to the present. The Confucian aristocrat has been the scholar-official, and Confucianism his ideology.

In the result, this Confucian aristocracy of merit or talent came closer to the original Greek idea of aristocracy, "government by the best," than did the subsequent European hereditary aristocracies of birth. In the era of warring states, when the empire was not yet unified and philosophers flourished, Chinese thinkers of all major schools turned against the principle of hereditary privilege, invoked by the rulers of the many family-states, and stressed the natural equality of men at birth: men are by nature good and have an innate moral sense — in Donald Munro's phrase, an "evaluating mind." This means that man is perfectible. He can be led in the right path through education, especially through his own effort at self-cultivation, within himself, but also through the emulation of

52

models outside himself. In his own effort to do the right thing, he can be influenced by the example of the sages and superior men who have succeeded in putting right conduct ahead of all other considerations. This ancient Chinese stress on the moral educability of man has persisted down to the present. It still inspires the government to do the educating.

Government by Moral Prestige. The Confucian ideology did not, of course, begin with Confucius (551–479? B.C.). The interesting concept of the Mandate of Heaven, for example, went back to the early Chou period (ca. 1027–770 B.C.). According to the classic *Book of History,* the wickedness of the last ruler of the preceding dynasty of Shang, who was a tyrant, caused Heaven to give a mandate to the Chou to destroy him and supplant his dynasty, inasmuch as the Shang people themselves had failed to overthrow the tyrant. As later amplified this ancient idea became the famous "right of rebellion," the last resort of the populace against tyrannical government. It emphasized the good conduct or virtue of the ruler as the ethical sanction for preserving his rule. Bad conduct on his part destroyed the sanction, Heaven withdrew its Mandate, and the people were justified in deposing the dynasty, if they could. Consequently any successful rebellion was justified, and a new rule sanctioned, by the very fact of its success. "Heaven decides as the people decide." The Chinese literati have censored bad government and rebels have risen against it in terms of this theory. It has also reinforced the belief that the ruler should be advised by learned men in order to ensure his right conduct.

Confucius and his fellow philosophers achieved their position by being teachers who advised rulers as to their conduct, in an age when feudal princes were competing for hegemony. Confucius was an aristocrat and maintained at his home a school for the elucidation and transmission of the moral principles of conduct and princely rule. Here he taught the upper class how to behave. He emphasized court etiquette, state ceremonies, and proper conduct* toward one's ancestors and in the famous five degrees of relationship. One of the central principles of this code was expressed in the idea of "proper behavior according to status" (*li*). The Confucian gentleman or *chün-tzu* ("the superior man," "the princely man") was guided by *li*, the precepts of which were written in the classics.

It is important to note that this code which came to guide the conduct of the scholar-official did not originally apply to the common people, whose conduct was to be regulated by rewards and punishments rather than moral principles.

This complex system of abstruse rules which the Confucians became experts at applying stemmed from the relationship of Chinese man to nature, which has already been mentioned. This relation had early been expressed in a primitive animism in which the spirits of land, wind, and water were thought to play an active part in human affairs. The idea is still prevalent in the practice of Chinese geomancy or *feng-shui* (lit., "wind and water"), which sees to it that buildings in China are properly placed in their natural surroundings. Temples, for example, commonly face south with protecting hills behind them and a water course nearby. In its more rationalized form this idea of the close relation between human and natural phenomena led to the conception that human conduct is reflected in acts of nature. To put it another way, man is so much a part

* "When he [Confucius] was in his native village, he bore himself with simplicity, as if he had no gifts of speech. But when in the ancestral temple or at court, he expressed himself readily and clearly, yet with a measure of reserve . . . At court, when conversing with the higher great officials, he spoke respectfully. When conversing with the lower great officials, he spoke out boldly . . . When he entered the palace gate, he appeared to stoop . . . When he hastened forward, it was with a respectful appearance . . . When the prince summoned him to receive a visitor, his expression seemed to change . . . When his prince commanded his presence, he did not wait for the carriage to be yoked, but went off on foot . . . He would not sit on his mat unless it was straight." Translated by D. Bodde from *Shih Chi.*

of the natural order that improper conduct on his part will throw the whole of nature out of joint. Therefore man's conduct must be made to harmonize with the unseen forces of nature, lest calamity ensue.

This was the rationale of the Confucian emphasis on right conduct on the part of the ruler, for the ruler was thought to intervene between mankind and the forces of nature. As the Son of Heaven he stood between Heaven above and the people below. He maintained the universal harmony of man and nature by doing the right thing at the right time. It was, therefore, logical to assume that when natural calamity came, it was the ruler's fault. He might acknowledge this by issuing a penitential edict, like that of Chiang Kai-shek quoted above. It was also for this reason that the Confucian scholar became so important. Only he, by his knowledge of the rules of right conduct, could properly advise the ruler in his cosmic role.

The main point of this theory of "government by goodness," by which Confucianism achieved an emphasis so different from anything in the West, was the idea of the virtue which was attached to right conduct. To conduct oneself according to the rules of propriety or *li* in itself gave one a moral status or prestige. This moral prestige in turn gave one influence over the people. "The people are like grass, the ruler like the wind"; as the wind blew, so the grass was inclined. Right conduct gave the ruler power.*

---

* In the *Analects* Confucius said: "When a prince's personal conduct is correct, his government is effective without the issuing of orders. If his personal conduct is not correct, he may issue orders but they will not be followed." (See Chiang Kai-shek's statement at the beginning of this chapter.) In the *Great Learning* it was said: "the ruler will first take pains about his own virtue. Possessing virtue will give him the people. Possessing the people will give him the territory. Possessing the territory will give him its wealth. Possessing the wealth, he will have resources for expenditure. Virtue is the root, wealth is the result." Compare Chiang Kai-shek in *China's Destiny:* "So long as we have a few men who will set an example, the people in a village, in a district, or in the whole country will unconsciously act likewise. As the grass is bent by the wind, so the social tone is influenced by the example of such men."

On this basis the Confucian scholars established themselves as an essential part of the government, specially competent to maintain its moral nature and so retain the Mandate of Heaven. Where the Legalist philosophers of the Ch'in unification had had ruthlessly efficient methods of government but little moral justification for them, the Confucianists offered an ideological basis. They finally eclipsed the many other ancient schools of philosophy. As interpreters of the *li*, they became technical experts, whose explanations of natural portents and calamities and of the implications of the rulers' actions could be denied or rejected only on the basis of the classical doctrines of which they were themselves the masters. This gave them a strategic position from which to influence government policy. In return they provided the regime with a rational and ethical sanction for the exercise of its authority, at a time when most rulers of empires relied mainly upon religious sanctions. This was a great political invention.

Early Achievements in Bureaucratic Administration. Theory, moreover, was matched by practice in the techniques of government. The bureaucratic ruling class came into its own after the decentralized and family-based feudalism of ancient China gave way to an imperial government. The unification of 221 B.C., in which one of the warring states (Ch'in) swallowed the others, required violent dictatorial methods and a philosophy of absolutism (that of the so-called Legalist philosophers). But after the short-lived Ch'in dynasty was succeeded by the Han in 206 B.C., a less tyrannical system of administration evolved. The Emperors came to rely upon a new class of administrators who superintended the great public works — dikes and ditches, walls, palaces, and granaries — and who drafted peasant labor and collected the land tax to support them. These administrators supplanted the hereditary nobility of feudal times and became the backbone of the imperial regime. They incorporated many of the Legalist methods in a new amalgam, imperial Confucianism.

In the two centuries before Christ the early Han rulers firmly established certain principles. First, that political authority in the state was centralized in the one man at the top who ruled as Emperor. Second, the Emperor's authority in the conduct of the administration was exercised on his behalf by his chief ministers, who stood at the top of a graded bureaucracy and who were responsible to him for the success or failure of their administration. Third, this bureaucracy was centralized in the vast palace at the capital where the Emperor exercised the power of appointment to office. His chief task became the selection of civil servants, with an eye to the maintenance of his power and his dynasty. For this reason the appointment of relatives, particularly from the maternal side, became an early practice. (Maternal relatives were the one group of persons completely dependent upon the ruler's favor as well as tied to him by family bonds, in contrast to paternal relatives who might compete for the succession.) Fourth, the early Han rulers developed the institution of inspection which later became the censorate, whereby an official in the provinces was checked upon by another official of lower rank, who was sent independently and was not responsible for the acts of his superior.

In this and in many other ways the central problem of the imperial administration became that of selecting and controlling bureaucrats. It was here that Confucianism gained strength from certain Legalist methods, and ancient China, as H. G. Creel has shown, led the world in developing the basic principles of bureaucratic government: namely, the impersonal use of specifically delegated powers in fixed areas of jurisdiction by appointed and salaried officials who regularly reported their acts during limited terms of office. For more than two thousand years this system of territorial bureaucracy has been epitomized in the walled administrative city of the district or *hsien* (in recent years also called "county").

To find the talent for officialdom the Han Emperors subsidized schools and began to set written examinations. This practice continued, and when the imperial structure was reinvigorated under the T'ang dynasty (A.D. 618–907), the examination system became firmly established as the main avenue to office. For more than a thousand years, down to 1905, this imperial institution produced administrators who had established their qualifications for official life by thoroughly indoctrinating themselves in the official orthodoxy — surely another of the great political inventions.

The Classical Orthodoxy

The Confucian doctrines were transmitted through the Chinese classics. As might be expected, these ancient books have formed a canon, the texts of which have been interpreted and reinterpreted through the centuries. In this process later texts, sometimes written for the purpose, have become canonized as more ancient, and books of early importance have fallen into obscurity. In the early Han period the classics usually mentioned were the *Book of Changes* (for divination), the *Book of History*, the *Odes* (ancient folk poems), the *Book of Ceremonies and Proper Conduct*, and the *Spring and Autumn Annals* (chronicles of Confucius' own state of Lu, in Shantung province) with their commentaries. It was not until the T'ang that the ancient book of the philosopher Mencius (fl. 324–314 B.C.) was elevated to the position of a classic. By degrees there was accumulated a canon of thirteen classics, which with their commentaries today fill some 120 volumes. In order to simplify this unwieldly corpus of ancient texts, scholars of the Sung (A.D. 907–1279) selected the famous Four Books (the *Analects of Con-*

fucius, the *Book of Mencius,* the *Doctrine of the Mean,* and the *Great Learning*), which were so brief that any gentlemen could master them.

The apothegms and aphorisms of the Four Books depict paternal government as the key to social order and the defense of the state. "If your Majesty," says Mencius to King Hui, "will indeed dispense a benevolent government to the people, being sparing in the use of punishments and fines, and making the taxes and levies light, so causing that the fields shall be plowed deep, and the weeding of them be carefully attended to, and that the strong-bodied during their days of leisure shall cultivate their filial piety, fraternal respectfulness, sincerity, and truthfulness, serving thereby at home their fathers and elder brothers and, abroad, their elders and superiors — you will then have a people who can be employed, with sticks which they have prepared, to oppose the strong mail and sharp weapons of the troops of Ch'in and Ch'u."*

Though eminently rational in form, this official doctrine had its religious side, expressed in the official rites at the Confucian temples, the pantheon of sages and their tablets, and the ritual veneration of them — all forming a state cult closely allied to the veneration of ancestors in the people's homes below and the Emperor's ritual acts above. While not anthropomorphic, this was a religious cult. One might call it a cult of state humanism, based on faith in the power of virtuous conduct to capture men's hearts and so lead them in the path of order under wise and benevolent authority.

* As Chiang Kai-shek put it 2250 years later in his book *Chinese Economic Theory,* "the government's duties are to support the people on the one hand and to protect them on the other. National plans for the support of the people are plans for the people's livelihood. But since this livelihood must also be protected, plans for livelihood become plans for the national defense . . . From the Chinese standpoint, therefore, Western economics is merely the study of private enterprise or of market transactions, whereas Chinese economic theory is a combination of the people's livelihood and national defense."

The vicissitudes of the Confucian creed, like those of Catholicism, are a most instructive study and show how deeply it has penetrated Chinese life. In the third to sixth centuries after Christ, during the decline of central authority which followed the Han Empire, Confucianism was all but eclipsed by Buddhism. But in the second great imperial period of China's long history, under the T'ang and Sung dynasties of the seventh to thirteenth centuries, the Confucian system was re-established and remolded into a form more stable and enduring than ever.

The revival of Confucian government under the T'ang was part of a general revival of Chinese society in politics, administration, literature and art as well as thought. The T'ang rulers in the seventh century and until the middle of the eighth century extended their control in all directions, into Korea and Annam and over the nomad tribes and the settled oases of Central Asia. Meanwhile the T'ang capital at Ch'ang-an (modern Sian) became a metropolitan center of almost two million persons and a focus of travel and trade from Byzantium and all the Middle East.

It is interesting to note that in the early period of T'ang strength, when the state and the economy were expanding and both the legal system and the examinations were functioning vigorously, the revived Confucian bureaucracy was remarkably tolerant of foreign creeds. Foreign visitors brought with them all the variety of medieval religions: Judaism, the fifth century Christian heresy known as Nestorian Christianity, and Manichaeism and Zoroastrianism from Persia. But when the first great rebellion threatened the dynasty in the middle of the eighth century, and its problems of revenue and military control continued to grow more pressing, the self-confidence of Chinese power was evidently shaken, and the cosmopolitan spirit declined with it.

After the collapse of the T'ang and the successive incursions of barbarian rulers on the northern frontier, the Sung dynasty failed to recapture the international position which the early T'ang had achieved. Chinese rulers throughout the Sung were on the defensive against the peoples of the steppe. Handicraft production and domestic and overseas trade brought financial well-being to the government, but they were offset by military weakness. The later Sung became a great commercial empire whose exports of copper cash, silk, and porcelain reached all of Eastern Asia and spread into Indonesia, India, the Middle East, and Africa. The Sung period saw the development of a highly sophisticated urban life, the perfection of landscape painting, and the use and abuse of paper money long before its introduction in Europe. But through all this period China's reaction to the invaders from Inner Asia remained rather unwarlike. Chinese influence abroad was based on commerce and culture rather than on military power.

This experience of foreign aggression in the Sung period of the eleventh and twelfth centuries (and the Mongol conquest which followed it in the thirteenth century) strengthened in Chinese society an ethnocentricity which has remained one of its chief characteristics. Of course many other factors also influenced the thought of this period, but during it the Confucian orthodoxy was reinforced and never lost its grip thereafter.

Neo-Confucianism. This new orthodoxy was an all-embracing system of thought which has been known to the West as Neo-Confucianism. It was more systematic and more complete than the ancient classics and by a reinterpretation of them gave Confucianism more metaphysical content than it had had before. In its new form Confucianism was rounded out to provide more of the answers which man asks of life. The absorption of definitely idealistic elements, mainly from Buddhism, undoubtedly made Confucianism more satisfactory to Chinese intellectuals and so offered Christianity, when it came to China by sea in the sixteenth century, a good deal less of a

61

spiritual vacuum to fill. By that time there was more to Confucianism than met the missionary's eye when he perused the religiously arid Chinese classics.

The greatest of the Neo-Confucian synthesizers was the twelfth-century philosopher Chu Hsi (1130–1200), whose historic role in China has sometimes been compared with that of St. Thomas Aquinas (d. 1274) in the West. As would be expected, his work was the culmination of the efforts of several generations of Confucian writers reaching back to the T'ang dynasty, who had had large numbers of disciples and whose writings had established a number of philosophical elements which Chu Hsi was able to combine.

The Neo-Confucian system of the Sung, which became orthodox for seven hundred years thereafter, had its basis in an absolute first principle called the Supreme Ultimate, subsisting beyond time and space. The Supreme Ultimate in turn was manifest in an infinitude of *li* (not the old Confucian term) which may be translated here as laws or principles of form. Each separate type or category of thing has its *li* and each *li* is a manifestation of the Supreme Ultimate. Physical matter, on the other hand, consists of the primordial ether or first substance (*ch'i*), the stuff of the physical universe. In each thing, therefore, the *li* and *ch'i*, or law and matter, are mutually essential and complementary. A house, for example, must be made of bricks (*ch'i*), but they must be put together according to a plan (*li*). The comparability of this system to the Platonic ideas is plain.

In dealing with the ethical problem of evil, Chu Hsi asserted that the nature of any living creature is the *li* of that creature as found combined with the *ch'i*. The *li* in itself is perfectly good but in the physical world it is always found in combination with *ch'i*. Evil consists in the obscuring of the *li* by the *ch'i*. Thus there is no active principle of evil. It results from situations which arise. (In our modern parlance, "Dirt is not dirt but only something in the wrong place.") Man's instincts are fundamentally good. The highest Confucian virtue therefore became an unswerving determination and honesty expressed in the term *ch'eng,* "complete sincerity." By means of complete sincerity of heart the *li* or principles can be cleansed of the *ch'i* or physical obstructions which obscure them. This remains today one of the fundamental Chinese ideals, and explains why Japanese and Chinese diplomats, or Nationalist and Communist negotiators, can hurl no verbal thunderbolt more devastating than the charge of "insincerity."*

The doctrine of original goodness was expressed in the opening lines of the famous *Three Character Classic* which echoed Confucius' *Analects* and was studied first by every schoolboy for generation after generation: "At men's beginning their nature is fundamentally good, by nature they are similar but in practice they grow apart." It is not surprising that the Western missionary's somber conception of original sin has always had difficulty in overcoming this happier Confucian view.

In politics the Neo-Confucianists believed that the ruler must gain understanding in the true principles of government and become a sage by moral self-discipline. In practice the new Confucian orthodoxy put its primary stress upon the moral development of man. It became an ever more effective mechanism for the inculcation, through the study of the classics and the examination system, of the Confucian doctrines of loyalty and social responsibility and conformity. For the indi-

---

* Compare *The Doctrine of the Mean:* "Sincerity is the way of Heaven . . . He who possesses sincerity is he who, without an effort, hits what is right, and apprehends, without the exercise of thought — he is the sage who naturally and easily embodies the right way . . . It is only he who is possessed of the most complete sincerity . . . who can transform others."

Compare Chiang Kai-shek (*China's Destiny*): "Sincerity is the moving spirit of real action. With sincerity, a man works for a just cause in perfect self-possession, pushing steadfastly and calmly onwards, unheedful of difficulties and dangers, until he finally succeeds."

vidual this philosophy was essentially monistic rather than dualistic, the *li* and *ch'i* being complementary and harmonious. Hell, heaven, and personal immortality were not conceived of, nor was a personal deity.

After the expulsion of the Mongols and the re-establishment of Chinese control over China under the Ming dynasty (1368–1644), the Sung Neo-Confucianism, because of its very inclusiveness, became a straightjacket on the Chinese mind. The Ming rulers used it as a tool of government. Chu Hsi's system became a dogma. Mencius became the greatest sage after Confucius. The Four Books and Five Classics (see p. 58) became the intellectual fare of all ambitious men, as though Chinese society could find refuge by turning back into its own cultural heritage and could protect itself by staying within an established framework of ideas. This age saw the introduction of the famous "eight-legged essay," a style which put a premium upon balanced and antithetic forms of writing. Its influence can be seen in the habit of alternating sentences of six and four characters and of presenting no idea without balancing it against an opposite, which characterizes the traditional essay style.

Individualism, Chinese Style. To Western observers, China has presented a puzzling contrast: a great richness of human personality but little tradition of civil liberties. As in all countries, the creative Chinese writer, artist, or craftsman expressed his individuality, while the hermit or recluse could become a private individualist outside his community. But what was the degree of individualism in the sense of individual rights within the old society?

Instead of simply applying a legalistic Western yardstick, we may well follow W. T. deBary in appraising the actual concerns and solutions of Chinese philosophers. The individual, first of all, had to claim his status or rights within the social scene, among his fellow men. Confucius had said, "If I am not to be a man among men, then what am I to be?" Second, the Confucian emphasis on the individual's conduct supporting the social order was only the outward half of the story. The other, inward half stressed the individual's self-cultivation. But this had meant from early times the fulfillment of his personality by living as "a man among men," in proper relations with those around him and so according to moral principles. Selfishness was to be curbed by duty, and duty defined in social terms. Mencius said, "Between father and son there should be affection; between sovereign and minister, righteousness; between husband and wife, attention to their separate functions; between old and young, a proper order; and between friends, fidelity." Thus Chinese man defined his "self" by his relations to others and to the Tao or Way which united them all, through the "web of reciprocal obligations." This by no means diminished the importance of conscience and morality. On the contrary, trying to stay within the bounds of orthodoxy might intensify the individual's moral problems, but these problems were perceived as "situation-centered," in Francis L. K. Hsu's phrase, not "individual-centered" as in America.

In the sixteenth century a new school of Confucian philosophy arose that gave the individual more scope. Wang Yang-ming (1472–1529), a high official whose thinking was to have great influence in both China and Japan, led a revolt against the Neo-Confucian orthodoxy by asserting that men have a common moral nature and therefore each individual has intuitive moral knowledge within his own mind. The possibilities of sagehood lie within him. Thus his task is to achieve a moral self-reformation. This is to be done mainly through study, but study must include thought, reflection, and the unending search for truth, not as mere verbal formulas but through personal experience. While it did not attack the traditional social order, Wang Yang-ming's subjective approach urged the individual to achieve a disciplined unity between learning and conduct, thought and action, or in today's terms, between theory and practice. This was a quite restricted form of individualism; in the end, as deBary remarks, it may be "more adaptable to a socialist society than modern Western types of individualism." (This is pursued further below, page 118.)

At the end of the seventeenth century under the Manchu dynasty (1644–1911) certain Confucian scholars began to develop a more pragmatic and critical view of the classics and their doctrines. This was called the "Han learning," as opposed to the "Sung learning." It was part of a general movement of critical scholarship manifest in historical, geographical, and textual studies. But for all their obvious intellectual vigor, these later scholars clearly remained within the Confucian straightjacket. Their enormous and exhaustive compendia (the largest was in 36,300 chapters) stand today as a monument to the vitality of Chinese scholarship in carrying on and developing a great tradition, but not to its creative originality in meeting the new and unprecedented problems which have confronted the Chinese people.

The Nondevelopment of Science

The history of technology in China confronts us with still another paradox. Until late medieval times China was at least on a par with and in many ways ahead of Western Europe in technological inventiveness and systematic observations of nature (such as the recording of sunspots). China had led the way in the development of paper and printing, chemical explosives, the mechanical clock, cartography, seismography, the beginnings of pharmacology, discoveries in magnetism (the compass) and in aspects of mathematics, and the perfection of numerous handicraft processes such as bronze-casting, porcelain manufacture, and the making of silk.

During the first thirteen centuries of the Christian era, according to the historian of Chinese science Joseph Needham, successive clusters of technological inventions came to Europe from China. In addition to the more famous items mentioned above, the wheelbarrow and barrow with a sail or sailing carriage, the crossbow, the kite, deep drilling techniques, cast iron, iron-chain suspension bridges, canal locks, the fore-and-aft rig, watertight compartments, the sternpost rudder, the assembly of eccentric, connecting rod and piston-rod for the interconversion of rotary and longitudinal motion, among other things, all seem to have been known in China much earlier than elsewhere.

Yet these brilliant early achievements did not lead to the establishment of an organized technology and the formulation of a body of scientific principles — in other words, the creation of science as a persisting institution, a system of theory and practice socially transmitted, consciously developed and used. Europe made this breakthrough by the beginning of the seventeenth century. Why did China not do so? The reader will at once be reminded of other early Chinese inventions, such as the methods of bureaucratic administration, including the examination system (and even the perverse erotic invention of bound feet). In many ways China was ahead of Europe but subsequently fell behind.

In approaching this question, our Europocentric self-esteem may be chastened if we recognize how recent is the Western pre-eminence in many lines of technology and science that we today take for granted. Needham concludes that the knowledge of mathematics, astronomy, and physics in Europe and China had coalesced by the mid-seventeenth century, although China did not catch up in knowledge of botany until the end of the nineteenth century. He argues that in medicine the two traditions have still not coalesced, and that Western medicine for all its tremendous advances in the nineteenth century hardly surpassed the practical therapeutic results of the old Chinese medical system before 1900. (After all, leeches were being used to bleed patient-victims in London down to the 1880's.) Granted the superiority of the West in modern chemistry, surgery, and a multitude of other lines, the question is still a relative one. Why did China lag behind? But even more, why did Europe so dynamically forge ahead? The latter question, perhaps the real mystery, is beyond our scope. Here let us look at factors in Chinese life which seem to have inhibited the independent development of modern science.

In the realm of thought, during the era of Neo-Confucianism from the thirteenth to the nineteenth centuries, the teaching of Chu Hsi urged that sincerity of heart was to be approached by a study of external objects, "the investigation of things," after which one might proceed to the understanding of one's self. This phrase, "the investigation of things," however, was interpreted to mean not scientific observation but rather the study of human affairs. Human society and personal relationships continued to be the focus of Chinese learning, not the conquest of man over nature.

The growth of science was also inhibited by the Chinese failure to work out a fuller system of logic whereby ideas could be tested by ideas, by confronting one statement systematically with another. Philosophers assumed that their principles were self-evident when stated. They made less distinction than the Greeks between grammar and rhetoric, and therefore between abstract and concrete or general and particular. Chinese writers relied more heavily on general ideas of proportion, the balance of opposites, and the harmony of the natural order. Their famous method of chain reasoning, which was a clincher for Chinese scholars of twenty centuries, was from the Greek point of view a fancy series of non sequiturs.*

* Take the following key passage from the *Great Learning:*
"The ancients who wished to be illustriously virtuous throughout the kingdom, first ordered well their own states. Wishing to order well their states, they first regulated their families. Wishing to regulate their families, they first cultivated their persons. Wishing to cultivate their persons, they first rectified their hearts. Wishing to rectify their hearts, they first sought to be sincere in their thoughts. Wishing to be sincere in

Underlying this weakness in logic was the physical nature of the Chinese written language. The use of an ideographic script for the transmission of the cultural inheritance from one generation to the next gave the characters themselves an independent status. They seemed to be enduring entities, not mere tools for the expression of ideas. For example, the virtues of which Confucius and Chu Hsi and their millions of disciples have thought and written have been represented in writing by specific symbols to which extensive philosophical connotations have become attached. It is not in the nature of the Chinese language to express these ideas in other terms which are interchangeable or synonymous. The five Confucian virtues of *jen, i, li, chih,* and *hsin* 仁 義 禮 智 信 (roughly equivalent to benevolent love, righteousness, propriety, wisdom, and faithfulness) are not easily expressed by other characters or by circumlocutions. The tyranny of terms is greater in Chinese than in an alphabetic language. The Chinese have been less able to escape from it than Western thinkers. To question the Confucian virtues would have been to deny the existence of the written characters which expressed them.

This tyranny of language was reinforced by an educational method in which the Chinese student traditionally memorized the classics before he understood them. Only after the characters were firmly established in the eye and ear, and in the muscular coordination of the hand in writing them, was their meaning studied and discussed. The enormous weight of the classic texts which had to be mastered put a premium upon

---

their thoughts, they first extended to the utmost their knowledge. Such extention of knowledge lay in the investigation of things.

"Things being investigated, knowledge became complete. Their knowledge being complete, their thoughts were sincere. Their thoughts being sincere, their hearts were then rectified. Their hearts being rectified, their persons were cultivated. Their persons being cultivated, their families were regulated. Their families being regulated, their states were rightly governed. Their states being rightly governed, the whole kingdom was made tranquil and happy. From the Son of Heaven down to the mass of the people, all must consider the cultivation of the person the root of everything besides."

memory, which already played an inordinate part in the learning of Chinese characters. The linguistic system of China was a natural matrix for authoritarian thinking.

One concomitant of the tyranny of language and its emphasis upon memory was the nonuse of the hands in connection with intellectual work. To be sure, the scholar sought to develop his calligraphy into a fine art. But once he put on his long gown he gave up manual work, which was a sign of a different social level. Chinese life pressed so closely upon subsistence, and learning was so clearly established as a path to economic security, that the scholar set great store upon the badge of learning, his long gown, and the ritual observance of the scholarly life, in which there was no time or occasion for manual labor. People who worked with their hands were not scholars. Scholars therefore did not meet the artisan in his workshop and the craftsman who needed new techniques. This separation of hand and brain stands in marked contrast to the example of the early European pioneers of science from Leonardo on down, who often came from the tradition of craftsmanship and, although scholars, were not debarred by the mores of their society from setting up their own laboratories. In early modern Europe the heritage of learning and the manual skills of technology might be focused in one man of genius. This seldom if ever happened in China.

Behind these shortcomings in thought and action may be seen economic and social circumstances which acted as a check upon the development of science. The state monopoly over large-scale economic organization and production was inimical to private enterprise whenever it threatened to assume large-scale proportions by the use of inventions and machinery. Again, the abundance of man power militated against the introduction of laborsaving mechanical devices. The dominant position of the official class and their power to tax without check by law made it difficult for new projects to develop except under their wing. The Chinese lag was in motivation rather than ability, in social circumstances rather than innate genius. In short, the nondevelopment of science was an aspect of the nondevelopment of an industrial economy. This in turn went back to the essentially agrarian and bureaucratic nature of the Confucian state.

Traditional China was not unchanging nor static nor inert. On the contrary there were continual change and great variety, but always within the limits of a distinctive cultural and institutional pattern. This overall pattern persisted so strongly because, within their geographic confines, Chinese institutions — economic, political, social, cultural — over the centuries had developed great self-sufficiency, balance, and stability. Continuity, in short, had created inertia in the sense of momentum, persistence in established channels, not inertness.

The deep-laid inertia of the Confucian pattern in Chinese political life during two millennia explains why China's modern revolution against it has been so grievously long-drawn-out. Yet we can really appreciate the persistent vigor of this pattern only if we realize how nomadic conquest of China, far from destroying, served to reinforce it.

4 Alien Rule and Dynastic Cycles

The unfolding of Chinese-Russian relations in the next decades must have overtones of China's past relations with invaders from the north. We should look at the historical record not as a portent of the future but as a source of insight and perspective.

During the last thousand years North China has been ruled more than half the time by alien invaders. This is one of the facts of history which inspired Japanese militarists in their schemes for conquest and rule through Chinese puppets. Alas for the Tanakas and Doiharas — they studied Chinese history all too well, but did not bring it down to date! Modern Chinese nationalism is a new force in history, and the past glories of the Mongol and Manchu conquests cannot be revived today.

Yet the record must be kept in mind, not with the thought that Russia can do today what Japan could not do yesterday, but in order to understand the complex problems of the Russo-Chinese relationship. For the twentieth-century nationalism of modern China must find its boundaries and achieve expression on a geographical and cultural frontier, between China and

Russia, where the centuries have produced distinctive institutions and remarkable patterns.

Nomad Conquest

The great continuing contrast in the life of Eastern Asia has been that between the steppe and the sown, between the pastoral nomads of the plateaus of Inner Asia and the settled villages based on the intensive agriculture of China. This contrast is a striking one in nearly every respect.

On the steppe, population is thinly scattered and there are today perhaps two million Mongols and hardly more than that number of Tibetans in the arid plateau regions which more than equal the area occupied by some 750 million Chinese. The thinness of population in Central Asia in itself makes the life of the steppe nomad vastly different from the crowded life of China. "Nomadism" of course does not mean aimless wandering over the grasslands so much as the seasonal removal of camps and flocks from one known place to another, to the hills in summer and the lowlands in winter, as climate and rainfall make necessary, in search of pasture. Just as intensive agriculture has molded China, so the sheep economy of Central Asia has conditioned the nomad. From his flocks he secures food, sheepskins for clothing, shelter in the form of felt for his yurt, and fuel in the form of sheep dung. Cultivation of the soil being unreliable, he relies upon the management of his animals for a livelihood and upon his horses for a mobility that will save him from the aridity of the steppe. He must therefore be constantly resourceful and ready for new ventures. Custom does not tie him to the land, but he remains inevitably dependent upon a certain minimum of trade with settled regions. He is often more free than the Chinese farmer and at the same time more poor than the Chinese landlord, since he cannot accumulate immobile wealth from generation to generation. He is also a trained hunter and horseman, and so a potential warrior.

Early in the settled history of China the great military striking power of the mounted barbarian archers became a constant problem to the farming peoples of the plain. So powerful have been the barbarian invasions of North China that a succession of Chinese states and dynasties has been of barbarian origin: the Northern Wei dynasty (A.D. 386–534) in the interregnum after the Han, and the Liao dynasty (907–1127) of the Khitan Mongols, are almost as well known as the Yuan dynasty of the Mongols (1279–1368) and the Ch'ing dynasty of the Manchus (1644–1911).

Chinese defensive efforts in the third century B.C., when the First Emperor of Ch'in joined together existing local walls to make the original Great Wall of China, to keep out the nomads, were followed by constant later efforts to achieve security, either through defensive attack or bribery and payments or through diplomacy and negotiation. In some eras, like that of the Han, the T'ang, or the Ming, native Chinese dynasties have conducted great military campaigns into the steppe. In the process of invasion and counter-invasion during the centuries there has been a great mixing of population. There has also grown up in Chinese society a vast body of lore and tradition concerning the barbarians and how to deal with them. The steppe nomads, in fact, gave China her background in foreign and international relations before the advent of the modern West.

Thus the relations of the Chinese with the nomads of Central Asia have significance not only for China but for us, for in modern times the West has taken the place of the barbarian menace. The modern invasion of China by the Western world, from the point of view of the Confucian way of life, is only the most recent in a long series of invasions of alien cultures carried by alien peoples. There is of course no comparison between the impact of the nomads upon Chinese life and the impact of the West. But the Chinese response to the West has been conditioned by Chinese experience in meeting the nomads.

The fact that China's agrarian way of life could not expand into the steppe and that the nomad herdsmen could never permanently dominate the life of China led to a seesaw of Chinese-barbarian relations in the frontier region beyond the Great Wall. In these border areas, so aptly termed by Owen Lattimore "the Inner Asian Frontiers of China," a mixed economy of marginal agriculture and pastoralism formed the background for mixed political relations. Nomad leaders at times became settled territorial rulers. Chinese officialdom at other times exercised its sway over border tribes.

Lattimore suggests that the alternations of Chinese advance and retreat and barbarian submission and domination on the frontier was a product of interaction between two cycles: the cycle of dynastic rise and decline within China and the cycle of unification and dispersion among the tribes of the steppe. When a nomad leader, drawn by the trade at the border region, extended his power over it, he was obliged to take on settled ways. While this might lead the barbarians further toward domination of China south of the Wall, sedentary life would also in the end lead to a weakening of barbarian vigor and a decline of their new and transitory power over the sown.

Nomad invaders found that it was possible to rule China only in the Chinese way. Usually they achieved power by taking the advice of border collaborators who understood the Confucian system and could operate it in their behalf. One of its merits was that it could maintain an organized state no matter who might have inherited the Mandate of Heaven, so long as the inheritors would abide by Confucian principles.

The First Sino-Foreign Empires

The Khitan Mongols, from whom North China got the name "Cathay," maintained an empire for over two centuries (907–1127) on both sides of the Great Wall, including parts of North China, Manchuria, and Mongolia. Their original way of life, as studied by Wittfogel, had been only seminomadic, for they appear to have relied on agricultural crops, especially millet, as well as on sheep, horses, and pigs. Indeed, they rose to power by the very fact that they straddled the frontier between steppe and sown and could thus combine the military force of nomad cavalry with the economic sustenance of peasant tillage. The federation of tribes that founded the empire was led by the imperial Yeh-lü clan, who prolonged their rule by adopting the Chinese institution of hereditary monarchy and many of the forms of Confucian government. The result was a dual state, Chinese in the south, barbarian in the north, the southern half governed through institutions of civil bureaucracy inherited from the T'ang, the northern half by men on horseback. Thus while the Emperor's officials for one area were being recruited through the classical examination system, the mounted archers of the north were being mobilized and trained to serve in his elite guard, the *ordo* (from which derives our term "horde"). Eventually a dozen *ordos* were set up in separate areas, totaling perhaps 600,000 horsemen, a mobile shock force held in reserve.

Aside from this interesting dualism of government, the Liao Empire contributed little to Chinese culture. Its population was only about four million, less than one tenth, perhaps one twentieth, the size of the Sung Empire to the south, yet the Liao cavalry had such striking power that the Sung finally paid them annual subsidies to keep peace on the border.

When the Liao state was taken over by the Jurchen tribes of northern Manchuria, who called their dynasty Chin or "golden" (1127–1234), the same pattern continued: the Sino-barbarian Chin Empire could combine the horses of the grasslands and the grain of North China to mount military assaults and force the Sung southward. (The Northern Sung, 960–1127, had their capital at Kaifeng, on the Yellow River; the Southern Sung, 1127–1279, at Hangchow, south of the Yangtze.) But these Sino-barbarian achievements were in the realm of power, not of culture, and had historical significance mainly as a foretaste of the disaster to come.

The Mongol conquest and the Yuan dynasty set up by it in China (1279–1368) have been viewed by succeeding generations of Chinese scholars as an unhappy interlude during which the Chinese people were under a foreign tyranny. It is true that the Yuan dynasty lasted less than a century and the Mongol power generated by Chingis Khan (ca.1167–1227) and spread over China by the great Khubilai (1214–1292) withered and disintegrated with unusual rapidity after the Mongols became rulers of China. This egregious failure of the Mongols to maintain themselves in China stands out in such marked contrast to the later success of the Manchus that it deserves more than passing analysis.

The Mongols finally succeeded in imposing themselves over all China by the sword in 1279 after two generations of fighting and maneuvering, only to be expelled in 1368. The Manchus came to the throne with relative ease in 1644 and maintained a regime which the Chinese literati of the nineteenth century still stood ready to defend with their lives and fortunes. The key to this contrast lies in the failure of the Mongols and the success of the Manchus in strengthening the Confucian system and using it for their own ends.

Of the factors that operated to prevent the Mongols from ruling China in Chinese fashion, the most immediate was probably their inability to assimilate Chinese culture and make it their own: they were full nomads, unaccustomed to agriculture or settled life. Their background was illiterate, their language different, their daily food and costume outlandish, their moral and legal codes at variance with Chinese tradition. This difficulty was reinforced by the fact that the Mongols in China were but one part of the great Mongol Empire which was the product of the organizing genius of the Great Khan, Chingis (Genghis, lit., "Emperor within the Seas," the title he took in 1206), and his sons and grandsons.

It is startling to note that Chingis in early middle age was still a vassal of a minor Mongol chieftain, among a tribal people who did not yet recognize the common linguistic bond later expressed in the name Mongol. His achievement in unifying and inspiring these tribes of the steppe to embark upon the greatest course of territorial conquest in early history can be understood only by reference to the propitious circumstances of the time in Central Asia.

About the year 1200 there stretched across that region from east to west a belt of settled communities founded on agriculture and connected with one another by trade. China was divided between the Chinese Sung dynasty in the south at Hangchow and the alien Chin dynasty in the north at Peking. In Northwest China was a kingdom founded by a Tibetan people. Westward in Chinese Turkestan were the Uighur Turks and west of them in Russian Turkestan were Turkish Moslem sultanates such as Bokhara and Samarkand. Finally in Persia there was the Abbassid caliphate with its capital at Baghdad. Commerce among these settled states gave them wealth but none of them was warlike nor strong enough to dominate its neighbor. They were a tempting prize for invaders from the steppe.

Another east to west belt of peoples stretched across Central Asia on the north. These were the nomad tribes of the arid plateau country. They were Turkish, Mongolian, and Tungusic in various mixtures and lived by an extensive pastoral economy. They had the nomad's mobility and comparative self-sufficiency; their patriarchal clan organization made them amenable to strong leadership.

Chingis rose through adversity from the lower nobility and built his power on personal loyalty. He asserted his mission to rule the world as the delegate of the eternal blue sky. He gave his tribal name, Mongol, to all the tribes that joined him. He codified their customary law, borrowing the Uigur script for the purpose, and declared it supreme and universal. He organized his warriors on a family principle under clans, tribes, and divisions of the empire. In all these ways he created a nation in arms. His carefully selected personal bodyguard or *ordo* formed an elite corps from which he drew his generals. The war machine thus created depended upon flying columns of Mongol cavalry, disciplined, hard-riding, and ruthless, who lived always for the loot which lay ahead and which gave them a constant incentive to expansion. Their compound bows and armor-piercing arrows and their sudden and deceptive battle tactics made them an irresistible force and the scourge of Asia. The descendants of Chingis set up their khanates in southern Russia, in Persia, and Turkestan, as well as in China.

This international scope of the Mongol Empire makes it comparable to the expansion of Europe as a cause of cultural and institutional mixing. In both cases the representatives of one kind of society invaded several others. Mongol conquerors who overran settled agricultural states in South Russia, Persia, and China met a bewildering variety of languages, religions, and local customs, yet in each case faced certain general problems — how to maintain order, how to conduct a civil administration through a bureaucracy and secure tax collections, how to retain the Mongol grip on power, and therefore in the final analysis how to maintain their own identity, unity, and vigor. It is truly amazing how far these illiterate warriors succeeded in these exacting tasks. The Mongols of the Golden Horde ruled in South Russia for 200 years and those in Persia for a century. In both countries, as in China, they seem to have built up the political institution of centralized despotism. During the thirteenth century contact among these far-flung domains was kept up by the famous Mongol post routes across the grasslands and oases of Central Asia, the strategic inner core of the empire. This made possible Europe's first direct contact with Cathay.

Unfortunately for the Mongols, their grip proved less strong than their striking power. In China they faced the problem of ruling in a Chinese fashion and yet retaining political control in Mongol hands. To do this it was essential not only that they have force in reserve and that they maintain order which would bring prosperity, but that they also give opportunity for the exercise of Chinese talent in the official system.

Early in their career of conquest the Mongols had learned the necessity of employing experienced civil administrators who knew how to levy taxes, manage finance, and recruit a bureaucracy. For this work in China they relied mainly upon Chinese but they also used in their administration other seminomads of the border region and many foreigners. Marco Polo (in China 1275–1292) was such a person. There were also others from Europe and a great number of Moslems, both Persian and Turkish, as well as Uighur administrators drawn from the states of Central Asia. The Mongols revived the examination system as a means of recruiting Chinese but it never worked well enough to get the best Chinese talent into the government.

The splendors of the reign of Khubilai, his new capital built at Peking, his extension of the imperial post roads and of the Grand Canal from Hangchow to Peking, and the great commercial development of such centers as Hangchow and Canton, described by Polo, demonstrated the vigor of Mongol rule in its heyday. But Mongol leadership after Khubilai soon deteriorated. The early fourteenth century saw a succession of weak rulers and finally dissension among the Mongol clans. Lamaism, the type of Buddhism developed in Tibet, spread its superstitious practices among the Mongol tribes. Lamaist excesses in China outraged the Confucian literati and stigmatized the Mongols as a people of primitive culture. Yellow River floods, financial difficulties, and at the last an inflation of paper currency undermined the regime. Rebels arose in several southern provinces to compete for the succession, and the strong man who succeeded among them expelled the Mongols and founded the Chinese Ming dynasty in 1368.

From the moment of its establishment one of the chief preoccupations of the Ming was to defend itself against the Mongol power. The first Emperor sent big expeditions into the steppe against the Mongols. He recovered Manchuria, secured the allegiance of a new dynasty in Korea, and was finally able to engineer the Mongols' collapse and disintegration into eastern and western kingdoms. The second Ming Emperor personally led four expeditions against them. He assisted the western Mongols to crush the eastern Mongols and later helped the eastern Mongols to crush the western. Even so, the Chinese were not able to wipe out the Mongol threat, for they could not destroy nor could they Sinify the steppe society across the Gobi desert. They were therefore forced to fall back on the age-old expedient of using one barbarian tribe against another and preserving the forms of a suzerain-vassal relationship with them all. In the end this led to their undoing, for they could not keep under control the Manchu state which grew up as a vassal on their northeastern frontier.

The Manchu Achievement

The Manchus who ruled China from 1644 to 1911 were a non-Chinese people of different habitat, language, and culture. Yet they succeeded in maintaining their power by traditional Confucian means for as long a period as any Chinese dynasty. The secret of this achievement may lie in the fact that, while they governed in a Chinese fashion, their alien origin and background helped them to retain political vigor within the ruling group. Some understanding of their success may help us to account for the tardy development of Chinese nationalism in modern times.

The essential point about the Manchu conquest of 1644 is that the Manchus by the time they came to power in China had already mastered the Confucian art of government and reconciled their own political institutions with it. Their development to this stage of political sophistication had been made possible by the fact that they were a border people on the frontier of the Chinese state where tribalism and bureaucracy could be synthesized.

Modern Western students of the Chinese frontier under Lattimore's inspiration have worked out an interpretation of the way in which the Chinese and barbarian societies interacted. In China, intensive agriculture was the basis for a bureaucratic government, in a region where land was scarce in relation to man power and the state depended upon revenue derived from the land. On the steppe, nomad pastoralism was the basis for a tribal form of government, in a region where man power was more scarce than land and the power of a chieftain consisted in his ability to command the personal loyalty of the warriors. The Chinese populace had to be governed through an officialdom. The non-Chinese barbarians could be controlled only through personal vassal relations. The Manchus were fortunate in coming from a region where these two systems met and intermixed.

Manchuria in the sixteenth century had been brought under the Chinese type of intensive agriculture only in the southernmost region below Mukden on either side of the Liao

River. Northwestern Manchuria was still a nomad area. The northeast, the original home of the Manchus, was a partly forested region suitable for hunting and fishing and the use of horses as well as for some agriculture. The Ming had recognized the frontier nature of South Manchuria by organizing it in military districts rather than under a civil administration only. By establishing hereditary and registered military units at strategic points, separate from the civil administration of this agricultural area, the Ming Chinese sought to maintain both a military buffer against barbarian inroads, and a check upon any separatist tendencies of local Chinese officials; for they could not overlook the fact that South Manchuria was a hostage to fortune which could be cut off from North China at the bottleneck of Shanhaikuan, where the Great Wall escarpment comes to the sea.

In their rise to power the Manchus took full advantage of their strategic position on a frontier where they could learn Chinese ways and yet not be entirely subjected to Chinese rule. The founder of the Manchu state, Nurhachi (1559–1626), began as a minor chieftain on the eastern border of the agricultural basin of South Manchuria. Like Chingis among the Mongols, he brought adjoining tribes under his personal rule and early in the seventeenth century set up his capital at Mukden. His successor subjugated Korea on the east and made alliances with the Mongol tribes on the west in Inner Mongolia. In 1636 he gave the name Manchu to his people and proclaimed the Ch'ing ("Pure") dynasty.

The Manchus by this time had made several incursions into North China but had not yet been able to defeat the Ming. The Ming regime in China, however, had grown progressively weaker. Rebellion was already endemic. The leading figure in the disorder of the time was a Chinese rebel named Li Tzuch'eng whose banditti had raided widely in Northwest China and even into Szechwan and the Yangtze valley. This leader had finally secured literate advisers and begun to set up a framework of dynastic government. In 1644 he succeeded in capturing Peking and had the dynastic succession within his grasp. But he was unable to consolidate institutionally the position that he had won by force. Chinese officialdom and the scholar-gentry class who provided the personnel of government were not drawn to him. Meanwhile a loyal Ming official in charge at Shanhaikuan invited the Manchus inside the Wall. They came at his bidding, destroyed the rebel Li, and stayed. Within forty years they had completed the conquest of China and their government of the empire remained stable for two centuries thereafter. Their success where a Chinese rebel had failed was essentially an achievement in the creation of political institutions.

The Manchus' first problem (as studied by Franz Michael) had been to develop beyond the state of tribal politics. This they did by creating a territorial administration over their lands, paralleled by a military organization of all the Manchu fighting men in eight divisions, each with a different flag or banner. The Manchu bannermen had lands assigned to them but these lands were kept scattered and the banners did not become territorial units. Mongols and Chinese who came over to the Manchus were taken into the system and organized their own banner units. Nurhachi appointed his sons to head the banners but their power was brought under central control in a state council. In this way the originally personal relations between the head of the state and his loyal tribal chieftains were put into an impersonal institutional form.

Finally, the early Manchu rulers, like the Liao, Chin, and Yuan Emperors before them, took over the terminology, forms, and ideas of Confucianism and used them, as they were meant to be used, for the support and maintenance of political authority. They promoted study of the classics and the veneration of ancestors, set up the state cult of Confucius, talked and wrote of the "way of the ruler" (like the Japanese in Manchukuo three centuries later), extolled the Confucian virtues, and accepted the idea that the ruler rules by virtue of his moral goodness. More than a decade before their entrance into China, they had created in Mukden a miniature civil administration in imitation of Peking. The Six Ministries and other elements typical of Ming government were formally established and staffed by a bureaucracy in which Manchus, Mongols, and Chinese were represented. When they entered North China and assumed the Mandate of Heaven they were fully prepared to solve their fundamental problem, how to rule in the Chinese way but maintain their identity as Manchus.

Several circumstances aided them in this achievement. For onc thing, unlike the Mongols, they had no vast empire to the west to distract them from the all-important problem of China. Having come from the frontier of South Manchuria, rather than from the Mongolian steppe itself, they did not have to leap the great cultural gap between the steppe and the sown. The unusually long and vigorous sixty-year reigns of two early emperors also provided a strong executive leadership: the K'ang-hsi Emperor (reigned 1662–1723) and the Ch'ienlung Emperor (reigned 1736–1796) were both hard-working and conscientious sovereigns who commonly saw their ministers every day at dawn, studied the classics assiduously, traveled widely over the empire, and maintained a vigorous personal rule.

The various devices by which the Manchus sought to preserve their dynastic vitality are an interesting study. In order to preserve their identity as a racial group they closed their homeland to Chinese immigration and maintained North Manchuria as a hunting land outside the Chinese agricultural economy. To check Chinese immigration from South Manchuria northward, they built a willow palisade several hundred miles long (a big ditch with willows planted along it) to mark the boundary beyond which the Chinese should not expand. They organized Manchuria under a Manchu military government. In spite of a periodic overflow of Chinese settlers in time of famine, they succeeded on the whole in checking further Chinese settlement. North of the Chinese basin in the south, Manchuria remained a sparsely populated vacuum down to the late nineteenth century — a tempting prize for Russian and Japanese imperialists.

In addition to this geographical basis the Manchus sought to preserve themselves by maintaining their racial purity. They banned intermarriage between Chinese and Manchus and fostered differences of custom between the two groups. Manchu women, for example, were not supposed to have bound feet. Manchus were not supposed to engage in trade or labor. The Manchu clan organization was preserved by their shamanistic religious system.

Manchu military control of China was maintained by the establishment of banner garrisons at strategic points. There was a military cordon of twenty-five garrisons at strategic cities around Peking, to preserve the capital as a symbol of imperial power. There was a northern belt of garrisons to defend North China against Mongol inroads. Finally, there were garrisons of Manchu bannermen in the bigger provincial capitals, Nanking, Hangchow, Chengtu, Foochow, and Canton. These garrisons in a separate Manchu military quarter in the big cities symbolized force held in reserve. The only Chinese troops given a recognized existence were provincial forces who were used mainly as a constabulary on the post routes and against bandits but lacked any training as a striking force.

In order to preserve strong leadership, the early Manchu Emperors arranged that the imperial princes should be pensioned and given wealth but not allowed to become territorial lords. They were kept at Peking out of power. Every effort was made to avoid the historic curse of government by women and eunuchs, which had resulted so often in palace intrigue.

In the civil administration of China the Manchus used a system of dual appointments, whereby both Chinese and Manchus were placed in charge of important functions. At first they relied on Chinese allies from South Manchuria who had been enrolled usually as Chinese bannermen or bond servants, especially dependent upon and loyal to the Manchu rulers. Eventually the formula was to have capable Chinese do the work and loyal Manchus check upon them. At the capital Manchus outnumbered Chinese, but in the provinces Chinese officials far predominated. In order to draw into their service the most able and promising Chinese, the Manchus saw to it that the examination system continued to function with highest prestige and efficiency.

To absorb the energies of Chinese scholars produced by the examination system, the Manchu Emperors became great patrons of literature and sponsored enormous projects of criticism and compilation. The K'ang-hsi Emperor at the turn of the eighteenth century, like Dr. Johnson and the Encyclopedists in the contemporary West, presided over the production of a famous dictionary and of a vast encyclopedia in 5020 chapters. His great successor, the Ch'ien-lung Emperor, sponsored an edition of the twenty-four dynastic histories and a collection of all Chinese literature in "The Complete Library of the Four Treasuries." This compilation included 3462 works. It was too large to print and only seven copies were made by hand. The printed catalog alone ran to 92 chapters.

By means of this vast project the Manchu court in fact conducted a literary inquisition, one of their objects being to suppress all works that reflected on alien rulers. In searching out rare books and complete texts for inclusion in this master library, the compilers were able at the same time to search out all heterodox works which should be banned or destroyed. They paid high prices for rare works and even conducted house-to-house canvasses. The works proscribed included studies of military or frontier affairs, criticisms anti-barbarian in tone, and chiefly items which extolled the preceding Chinese dynasty of the Ming. Altogether, some 2320 works were suppressed. This was thought control on the largest scale.

By these various expedients and devices the alien rulers of China under the Ch'ing dynasty maintained their racial and social identity, preserved their military and administrative control, and yet gave prestige and opportunity to Chinese of talent. The Manchu possession of temporal power in the Chinese state turned Chinese men of genius to literary and cultural activity. It also preserved in early modern China the nonnationalistic tradition that it makes little difference who governs as long as he governs in the proper fashion.

In Chinese politics this experience of alien rule confirmed rather than weakened the Confucian tradition because it put it on a universal rather than a regional or racial plane. The fact that an alien Emperor followed Confucianism confirmed the fact that it was, as it claimed to be, an all-embracing and universal philosophy of government, to which there was no civilized alternative. The Chinese way in politics, like the rice economy of the paddy fields, appeared to be more fundamental than dynasties or races.

The Nature of Chinese Nationalism. Undoubtedly this is one reason why culture (the way of life) has been more fundamental in China than nationalism. The early Chinese Emperors began by asserting that they ruled over all mankind without distinction of race or language. Barbarian invaders who succeeded them found it expedient to continue and reinforce this tradition. To any Confucian ruler, Chinese or alien, the important thing was the loyalty of his administrators and their right conduct according to the Confucian code. Color and speech were of little account as long as a man understood the classics and could act accordingly. The successful barbarian rulers were those who acknowledged this fact by becoming assiduous classical scholars, calligraphers, and connoisseurs. They proved their legitimacy by quoting Confucius, conducting the rites, granting amnesties, maintaining the examination system, appointing officials, and issuing edicts in the manner of preceding Sons of Heaven. So long as they did so, they wrought no revolution in the Chinese political system and were accepted. This ability to persist under alien rule was also a measure of the extent to which Confucian government was a "benevolent despotism." It mattered little who was the despot as long as he fitted "benevolently" into the system.

Thus the long experience of alien rule has produced a fascinating paradox: the Chinese people in the nineteenth century entered the modern world singularly backward in one of its major qualities, the spirit of nationalism, yet in their twentieth century revolution the inherited pride of culture or "culturalism" has inspired a new cultural nationalism which may in the future outdo the merely political nationalisms that originated in Europe.

This different relationship between culture and political loyalty in China and in the West deserves more study. France and Germany, for instance, became nations only after the time of Charlemagne, who ruled both areas. Though frequently at war, these two nations have shared the common culture of Christendom; Descartes and Bach, Leibniz and Pasteur, Rousseau and Marx, are their common heritage. In China, by contrast, the state has remained ideally coterminous with the whole culture. Polity and culture have almost fused. This may be seen in the way that China since the unification of 221 B.C. has clung to two great political myths: the unity of the Chinese empire and its superiority to all outsiders.

Until the Mongol conquest of the thirteenth century the

myth of superiority was obviously justified by the facts of China's superior size, technology, wealth, and level of culture. The idea of the Chinese Emperor's supremacy over mankind through his rule-by-virtue was rudely shattered when the unvirtuous Mongols conquered China by sheer power. But the Ming Chinese rulers made a comeback and combined virtue and power to reassert the myth of imperial supremacy. In this way the very ancient idea of universal kingship, used by early rulers in Mesopotamia, Egypt, India, and even Central America, was able to persist in China down to modern times.

The ideal myth of unity, so long associated in Chinese thinking with the absence of civil war and therefore with domestic peace, order, and prosperity, gained a new lease on life from the Manchu dynasty. When its bannermen in the eighteenth century brought Western Mongolia, Sinkiang, and Tibet under Peking's rule, this meant simply that the "Chinese empire" was in fact the "empire of East Asia" (China and Inner Asia), long a strategic and now a political unit. The consolidation of this whole area under the rule of the Ch'ing dynasty has now been followed in recent decades by its absorption into the expanded Chinese nation, first under the rule of the Kuomintang and then of the Chinese Communist Party. Both parties assert tenaciously even today that only one China, no two Chinas, is conceivable, and that this one China of the Han Chinese rightly includes as cultural minorities the Mongolian, Tibetan, Uighur Turkish, and many other ethnic groups.

The Dynastic Cycle

One basic approach to China's history of the early twentieth century is to regard it as a dynastic interregnum. Viewed in the light of the famous twenty-four histories of Chinese dynastic periods, the efforts of Sun Yat-sen, Chiang Kai-shek, and Mao Tse-tung to seize and organize central power are variations on an ancient theme. China's two thousand years of recorded politics have produced apparent rhythms and pulsations. Always, even though the current struggle might ravage the Middle Kingdom, most Chinese have had utter faith that unity would come again.

Anyone who seeks historical uniformities, or who makes societies and civilizations his units of study, will find the Chinese chronicles inexhaustible. Nowhere else are there so many recorded facts of imperial administration waiting to be selected, ordered, and generalized about by philosophers of history or by Marxist and anti-Marxist system-makers or by ordinary political pundits and historians in off moments. Here if anywhere one might hope to catch History in the act of repeating herself. Only the unimaginative can resist the idea that if we can read correctly the story of China's last two millennia, we can foresee her next two decades — a vain hope but an entrancing one.

Students of several generations have been impressed by the peculiarly parallel sequences in ancient China and in the Greco-Roman world: an age of philosophers and warring states, an age of unification and empire, and an age of disintegration and collapse of central power. Thus Confucius and his disciples are noted to have been roughly contemporary with Plato and Aristotle; Alexander the Great precedes the First Emperor of the Ch'in by only a century; and the imperial systems of Rome and Han flourished contemporaneously. Similarly the barbarians on the northern frontier grew more dangerous as each of these empires declined, and the economic and political disintegration within the "universal state," in Toynbee's phrase, was marked by the spread of foreign religions to which the distressed people turned for solace. The entrance of the northern nomads into China and the spread of Buddhism in the period from the third to the sixth centuries after Christ were actually contemporary with the inroads of the Goths and Vandals and the spread of Christianity in the West. To all who seek intellectual security in the formulation of laws which govern human affairs, these parallels have been a starting point both for generalization and for further research.

Within Chinese history the most interesting uniformity which strikes the superficial observer is the sequence of phases centering about the Han and the T'ang dynasties. Preceding each of these imperial periods was a time of intellectual ferment marked, respectively, by the philosophers of the late Chou period, and the flourishing of Taoism and Buddhism after the Han. Each phase of imperial greatness was inaugurated by a short-lived powerful dynasty which unified the state, the Ch'in (221–206 B.C.) and the Sui (A.D. 589–618). Both the Han and the T'ang, once established on the basis of a new unity, achieved an expansion of Chinese political power in neighboring regions, especially Central Asia, and a corresponding development of foreign contact.

Stimulated by this parallelism between two major dynasties, students have attempted numerous formulations of cycles. Underlying all these attempts is the fundamental phenomenon observed by Chinese historians and recorded by them so assiduously, namely, the dynastic cycle. In the twenty-four dynastic histories there is naturally a certain recurrence of ideas, since the chroniclers in each case were recording the life history of a ruling family which came to power, had its heyday, and shuffled from the scene. Toward the close of each regime, for example, natural calamities, comets, eclipses, and other heavenly portents become more numerous in the record, evidence that the improper conduct of the ruler is losing him the Mandate of Heaven.

Autosuggestion, indeed, on the plane of public morale and social psychology may have played its part in the dynastic cycle. For so great was the dynasty's dependence on its moral prestige that its loss of "face" in certain instances might set in motion a process in which the ideology, as it were, turned against the regime and hastened its downfall. Once the literati who set the tone of public opinion became convinced that a dynasty had lost its moral claim to the throne, little could save it. This is a factor in Chinese politics today.

Time after time dynastic decline went hand in hand with the increasing inefficiency of the ruling house. The family in power accumulated over the generations a heavy load of dead wood and dead weight, fastened upon it by the family system. This was most flagrantly visible in the peculations and profligacy of maternal relatives who became entrenched in the imperial household. Wine, women, and song at the court led to increasing personal weakness of the rulers. This danger attended the Sinification of barbarian conquerors. The Mongol khans, for example, became effete and were undone by their own excesses.

The economic interpretation of Chinese history has been used even more extensively to explain the dynastic cycle. This approach concentrates particularly upon the land tax, which in the agrarian economy of China has been the chief source of government revenue and power. One process which seems to have appeared in each dynasty was the progressive withdrawal of land from taxation, for the benefit of the ruling official class and to the detriment of the imperial revenues. At the beginning of a dynasty the land and the population were usually estimated and recorded in a rough sort of census. New tax registers could be used as a firm basis for revenue collection. As time went on there ensued a struggle between the interests of the imperial government and of the individuals who dominated it. Gradually the ruling class were able to increase their landholdings and to remove them from taxation by various expedients such as the destruction of tax registers, official connivance, or legal falsification. This created a vicious spiral in which a greater burden was placed upon the land of the peasantry which still paid taxes, at the same time that the demands of the government for revenue were likely to increase. In this way a progressively smaller proportion of the land was expected to pay a progressively larger amount of revenue. Peasant disorders eventually resulted.

In some cases the final collapse of a dynasty came through peasant rebellion under fanatical religious leadership. Since no dynasty has tolerated an organized opposition, its opponents have had recourse to secret societies. For example, as the Mongol administration lost its efficiency and morale in the middle of the fourteenth century, revolt became endemic in many provinces. Some of these revolts were led by secret groups like the White Lotus Society which had a symbolic ritual, esoteric signs and passwords, oaths sealed in blood, and an underground organization. Other revolts were led by religious leaders, usually Buddhist, who might proclaim the imminent advent of the bodhisattva Maitreya. Some rebels claimed to be legitimate successors to the preceding Sung dynasty. Others were content to be mere bandit chiefs who became local warlords and competed in the struggle for the survival of the fittest to receive the Mandate of Heaven. A bandit chieftain in Hupeh got control of much of the central Yangtze region, another chieftain seized part of Honan, another rose at the same time in the lower Yangtze, and finally a pirate leader arose in Fukien. Each of them assumed a dynastic title. The eventual founder of the Ming dynasty got himself established in the richest area of the country, around Nanking, and knew how to combine clever politics with the forcible seizure of power. He was himself the son of a laborer and had been a Buddhist monk before seeking his fortune in rebellion. He conciliated the common people, maintained discipline among his forces, and prevented plundering. By 1368 he had conquered or absorbed his rivals and was able to seize Peking, where his last successor was not dispossessed until 1644, almost three centuries later.

It is an interesting coincidence that the Ming Emperors reigned for 276 years and their successors, the Manchus, for 267 years — spans which attest the stability of the monarchy's political institutions, no matter whether Chinese or non-Chinese were on the throne.

5 The Political Tradition

The imperial system survived until 1912, the year Woodrow Wilson was elected President of the United States. The leaders of modern China grew up under it. Even the generation who dominate the Chinese scene today need think back only sixty or seventy years to recall the imperial splendor of the old Empress Dowager, the lavish trappings of despotism, the eunuchs, concubines, and court attendants, palace guards and palanquins, formal audiences, kowtow and lesser rituals, within the high red walls and gold-tiled roofs of the palace at Peking. These things have barely passed away. To look at modern China, as we usually do, without seeing them in the background makes no more sense than to look at the United States without any recollection of Washington and Jefferson, Dan Boone and Abe Lincoln, manifest destiny, or the rise of the common man and John D. Rockefeller.

Bureaucracy

One key to the understanding of the Communist administration in China today is the fact that the old imperial government was a bureaucracy of the most thoroughly developed and sophisticated sort. To the American who has confronted the problems of bureaucracy only recently, the effort of modern Chinese to escape from the evils and capitalize upon the good points of their own bureaucratic tradition is a matter of absorbing interest.

The old government centered in the capital. Without question the vast symmetrical plan of Peking makes it the most magnificent of all capital cities. Paris and London, Washington and Moscow, are creations of yesterday and do not attest, in the balance of gate against gate and avenue against avenue, the omnipotence of oriental despots who created their capital city as an outer cover to their palace. Peking centers upon the moats and red walls of the Forbidden City. Within it the yellow-roofed throne halls rising from their marble platforms form the main axis of the whole metropolis. Behind them a great man-made hill of earth protects them from the north. Before them were broad avenues, and today a great square stretches south to the old front gate of the city. No Western capital is so plainly a symbol of centralized and absolute monarchy.

At Peking, for the greater part of thirteen centuries the civil administration of China was divided among the famous Six Ministries (or Boards) of civil office (appointment of officials), revenue, ceremonies, war, punishments, and public works (such as flood control). This structure, adumbrated in the first imperial system of the Ch'in and Han, had been formally established under the T'ang. In addition to the Six Ministries there were two other independent hierarchies of administration, the military establishment and the Censorate, as well as a number of minor offices: the imperial academy of literature, a court to review criminal cases, a historiographer's office, the imperial stud, and offices in charge of banquets and sacrificial worship. At the apex of everything the Ming had created the Grand Secretariat, in which high officials assisted the Emperor in his personal administration of affairs. One of the few Manchu innovations was to add in 1729 a less formal body, the Grand Council, which handled military and other important matters and so became the real top of the administration.

Spread out over the eighteen provinces of China under the Manchu dynasty was a network of territorial divisions. Each province was divided into several circuits (*tao*) and below them into prefectures, departments, and *hsien* (districts or counties) in descending order. The mandarins in charge of these divisions with their ubiquitous assistants and subordinates formed the main body of the territorial magistracy. Like civil servants trained in the classics at Oxford and Cambridge, they were supposedly omnicompetent, responsible for the collection of revenue, maintenance of order, dispensing of justice, conduct of literary examinations, superintendence of the postal service, and in general for all public events within their areas. Theoretically, they stood *in loco parentis* to the people and were called, or rather called themselves, the "father and mother officials."

The imperial civil service was divided into nine ranks, each of which was divided into upper and lower grades. Each rank was entitled to a particular and very fine costume, including a colored button on the cap and insignia such as "mandarin squares" embroidered on the front and back of the gown. Prerogatives, titles, and dignities were minutely set forth in the statutes. High officials might be rewarded with the right to wear a peacock feather or bear the title of "Junior Guardian of the Heir Apparent."

Intervening between the hierarchy of local officials and the government at the capital stood the higher administration in each province. This consisted of a governor-general who was in most cases responsible for two provinces and, as his junior colleague, a governor responsible for a single province. These two officials were of course so placed as to check each other, for they were expected to act and report jointly on important matters. Under the Ch'ing (Manchu) dynasty, frequently the governor-general was a Manchu and the governor Chinese. Beneath them were four provincial officers who exercised province-wide functions: a treasurer, judge, salt comptroller, and grain intendant (who supervised the collection of grain for the capital).

Official business over the far-flung Chinese empire was conducted as in all bureaucracies by a flow of documents of many kinds. In their special forms and designations these multifarious communications mirrored the elaborate proliferation of red tape. A governor addressed his imperial master in certain prescribed forms and addressed his subordinates in others. Every communication began with a clear indication of its nature as a document to a superior, an equal, or a subordinate. Similarly there were special forms for memorials submitted to the Emperor and edicts issued from him. Each document also went through a certain procedure of preparation, transmission, and reception. Hundreds of thousands of brush-wielding scriveners were kept busy year in and year out transcribing, recording, and processing official communications. In the imperial archives in the Peking palace are more than one hundred different types of documents which were in common use.

The flow of paper work was maintained by an official post which reached all corners of the empire but was limited to the transportation of official mail, official shipments (as of funds), and persons traveling on official business. This postal system was made up of some two thousand stations stretched out along five main and many subsidiary routes which ran into Manchuria, across Mongolia, westward to Turkestan and Tibet, southeastward through the coastal provinces, and southward through the interior of Central China. Couriers and travelers on these routes were provided with official tallies entitling them to the use of the transportation facilities, which in different areas might be horses, camels, donkeys, chairs (palanquins), or boats. In time of crisis couriers could cover 250 miles a day. (See map, p. 129.) Such speed was achieved by the use of horses in relays, a system which the Mongols had developed to cover the distances of Central Asia. In the early nineteenth century this pony express regularly transmitted messages from Canton to Peking in less than three weeks and from Shanghai to Peking in one week.

Central Controls. Given this network of officials, connected by a flow of documents and persons along the postal routes, it was the problem of the capital to stimulate the local bureaucrats to perform their functions and yet prevent them from getting out of hand. This control was achieved by the application of techniques common to bureaucracies everywhere, in addition to the special measures (noted above) whereby the Manchus sought to preserve their dynasty.

Among these techniques the first was the appointment of all officers down to the rank of district magistrate by the Emperor himself. This made them all aware of their dependence upon the Son of Heaven and their duty of personal loyalty to him. Circulation in office was another device. No official was left in one post for more than three years or at most six years. Ordinarily when moving from one post to another the official passed through the capital and participated in an imperial audience to renew his contact with the ruler.

Thus Chinese officialdom was a mobile body which circulated through all parts of the empire without taking root in any one place. In this it was aided by its reliance upon the Mandarin (Peking) dialect as a lingua franca of universal currency in official circles. Frequently an official would arrive at his new post to find himself quite incapable of understanding the local dialect and therefore the more closely confined to his official level.

One means to prevent officials taking local root was the "law of avoidance" according to which no mandarin could be appointed to office in his native province, where the claims of family loyalty might impair devotion to the imperial regime.

Another custom, which interrupted an official's rise to power, was the rule of three years' mourning (actually some twenty-five months) after the death of his father, during which an official retired to a life of quiet abstention from worldly activities. As Arthur Waley says, this was "a sort of 'sabbatical' occurring as a rule toward the middle of a man's official career. It gave him a period for study and reflection, for writing at last the book that he had planned . . . for repairing a life ravaged by official banqueting, a constitution exhausted by the joint claims of concubinage and matrimony."

In general the bureaucratic principle was to set one official to check upon another. This was done particularly through the system of joint responsibility. The Six Ministries each had two presidents, one Manchu and one Chinese, who watched each other. It was common to appoint one man after he had gained prominence to several offices so that he was not able to master any one of them, and at the same time to appoint many men to perform one job so that no one of them could completely control it. Indeed many offices were sometimes created to carry on the same function, checking each other through their duplication of activity. The result of this duplication of offices and mutual responsibility was to hedge each official about with a multiplicity of commitments in each of which others were concerned. It was something like the unlimited liability of a partnership in which there were dozens of partners. Over and above all these immediate checks created by the involvement of many officials in a common responsibility, there was the system of the Censorate. Under it some fifty-six censors selected for their loyalty and uprightness were stationed in fifteen circuits through the provinces with the duty of keeping the Emperor informed upon all matters concerning the welfare of the people and the dynasty. The early Ch'ing rulers even invented an eyes-alone type of memorial by which designated officials could send secret reports, to be opened only by the Emperor and returned with his comments only to the sender. The ruler thus had his informers throughout the bureaucracy.

The evils inherent in bureaucracy were all too evident. All business was in form originated at the bottom and passed upward to the Emperor for decision at the top, memorials from the provinces being addressed to the Emperor at the capital. The higher authority was thus left to choose alternatives of action proposed, and yet the proposal of novel or unprecedented action was both difficult and dangerous for the lower official. The greater safety of conformity tended to kill initiative at the bottom. On the other hand the efficiency of the one man at the top was constantly impaired by his becoming a bottleneck. All business of importance was expected to receive his approval. All legislation and precedent were established by his edict. Modern China still suffers from this tradition.

In view of the complete and arbitrary power which the imperial bureaucracy asserted over the whole of Chinese life, it is amazing how few and how scattered the officials were in number. The total of civil officials for whom posts were statutorily available, both at the capital and in the provinces, was hardly more than 9000. The military officials were supposed to number only about 7500. It is true, of course, that there was an increasing number of supernumerary or "expectant" officials who might be assigned to various functions without receiving substantive appointments. There was also the vast body of clerks and factota necessary for the copying, recording, negotiating, and going and coming in each Chinese official's establishment or yamen. Down to the gatemen, runners, and chair-bearers, these human elements in the official machine no doubt totaled millions. But if we look for the men of genuine official status who could take official action and report it in the hierarchy as representatives of his imperial majesty, we find them few and thinly spread, totaling at a rough estimate hardly more than 30 or 40 thousand "officials" at most, ruling over a country of about 200 million which grew to perhaps 400 million by the middle of the nineteenth century. Of the nine ranks, for example, the seventh rank near the bottom of the scale began with the district magistrate who was responsible for a population on the order of 250,000 persons. This relative smallness of the imperial administration no doubt reflects the fact that it depended upon the gentry class to lead and dominate the peasantry in the villages.

Government as Organized "Corruption." Another anomaly of the bureaucracy was its low salaries. According to the official red-book, a governor-general in charge of two provinces as big as European countries received from his imperial master a salary equivalent in our terms to $300 a year. To this nominal sum was added a larger payment drawn from the provincial rather than the imperial treasury. For the governor-general in question this supplementary salary (*yang-lien,* lit. "to nourish honesty") would be equivalent to some $41,000 a year. But still, when added together from all sources, such salaries could not begin to meet the needs of an officer who had to employ a great retinue of private secretaries and special assistants.

The imperial officials were held responsible for all public events within their jurisdiction but not for all public funds. Budgeting and accounting procedures were rudimentary. The bureaucracy lived by what we today would call systematized corruption which sometimes became extortion. This was a necessary concomitant of the system of intricate personal relationships that each official had to maintain with his superiors, colleagues, and subordinates.

Among the bureaucracies of history, the Chinese has been distinguished by the way in which the twin institutions of "squeeze" and nepotism reinforced each other. The former operated through forms of politeness rather than secrecy. Junior officials in the course of their duties gave their superiors customary "gifts." But like all prices in old China, the amount of such a gift resulted from the working out of a personal relationship. The squeeze system was no more cut and dried than any other part of the man-to-man bargaining which pervaded Chinese life. The extralegal sums which passed between officials were larger but no different in kind from the small commissions extracted until only recently from every money transaction by underpaid houseboys.

Nepotism supported the squeeze or leakage system by giving an added sanction for personal arrangements contrary to the public interest. Even classic texts extolled duty to family, and particularly filial piety, as superior to any duty to the state. Thus the interest of the imperial administration at the capital, which needed the sustenance of revenue from the provinces, was constantly in conflict with the multifarious private interests of all the officials, each of whom had to provide for his relatives and his further career. High office commonly meant riches. The favorite minister of the Ch'ien-lung Emperor, when tried for corruption and other crimes by that Emperor's successor in 1799, was found to have an estate worth in our terms of that period more than one billion dollars — probably an all-time record. Another high Manchu, who fell into disfavor at the time of the Opium War in 1841, was found to have an estate of some 425,000 acres of land, $30,000,000 worth of gold, silver, and precious stones, and shares in ninety banks and pawnshops. I would not suggest that Westerners have been backward or less adept in the art of graft. But in China corruption remained longer into modern times an accepted institution, unashamed and unafraid.

Communist China's vast new bureaucratism must be seen against this tradition. Today's totalitarianism, though utterly unprecedented in its total effect, has certain ancient foundations to build on. It also faces the age-old problem of how to keep the bureaucrats energetic, efficient, and honest.

Law

In the Western tradition bureaucracy has been tempered by law. Against the tyranny of officialdom the individual has had recourse to legal protection. Our civil liberties rest upon this. But the law in Chinese life has not been similarly developed to protect the individual either in his political rights or in his economic position. The early use of law by the Legalist school of the third century B.C. was as a tool of absolutism to aid in administrative unification. Later the imperial government under the Han continued to use certain Legalist practices, like that of mutual responsibility among family members. Thus the "Confucian state," for all its exaltation of the name and teachings of Confucius, came to incorporate elements of the Legalist tradition as well. This tradition has lingered on and been reasserted from time to time ever since.

Modern students of legal history have only begun to look at the enormous and ramified documentation of Chinese law. The great T'ang code of the eighth century and its successors in the Sung, Yuan, Ming, and Ch'ing periods still await analysis by Western scholars. But it is plain that by any pre-modern standard the Chinese codes were monuments of their kind. As with so many other aspects of Chinese society, the old legal system was "unmodern" yet in the context of its times we should be slow to call it "backward." Early European observers had been well impressed with Chinese justice. It was only after the eighteenth and nineteenth century reforms of law and punishments in the modern West that China was left behind.

Nevertheless the Chinese concept of law was fundamentally different from legal conceptions in the West. It began with the ancient Chinese idea of the order of nature, the necessity of human actions harmonizing with it, and the ruler's function of maintaining this harmony. Since the ruler swayed the people by his virtuous conduct and moral example, not by law, it was felt that enlightened and civilized persons would be guided by such an example and by the norms of proper conduct without the need of regulations. Punishment was necessary in this theory only for barbarous and uncivilized persons who could not appreciate the teachings of the sages and the ruler's example and so must be intimidated. Rewards and punishments were useful in order to make clear the activities proper to each person according to his status. But they were always considered in theory a secondary means of securing people's right conduct. The object was to "punish only to be able to stop punishing."

Certain generalizations can be attempted about this Chinese legal system. First of all, the law was not regarded as an external and categorical element in society; there was no "higher law" given to mankind through divine revelation. Moses received his golden tablets on a mountain top, but Confucius reasoned from daily life without the aid of any deity. For his rules of propriety, he did not claim any metaphysical sanction. Rather disingenuously, he merely said they came from the moral character of the natural universe itself, from this world, not from another world beyond man's ken. It followed that legal rules were but one expression of this morality — models or examples to be followed, or working rules of administration or ritual observance. So the breaking of such rules was a matter of practical expedience rather than of religious principle. Law was subordinate to morality. Its sanction lay in reason or the common social experience which underlay morals. This avoided the unhappy dualism which grew up in the West between the letter of the law and the dictates of common sense morality.

In practice the Chinese imperial code was chiefly penal, a corrective for the untutored. It was also administrative, and prescribed the details of the rites. In other words, the code was nearly all public law, referring to administration, marriage, inheritance, and other matters relative to and important in government administration. The law occupied a comparatively small share of the public scene. The people avoided litigation in the magistrate's court, where plaintiffs as well as defendants could be interrogated with prescribed forms of torture, and everyone would have to pay fees to the yamen underlings. The magistrates hired personal law secretaries to advise them; aside from these there was no legal profession, no private lawyer class to represent clients. Justice was official, weighted on the side of the state and social order. It operated vertically, from the state upon the individual, more than it did horizontally, to resolve conflicts between one individual and another.

Within its limited sphere, the Ch'ing legal system, as analyzed by Derk Bodde and others, was elaborately organized, and it functioned, once it got into action, with a good deal of exactitude. The five punishments (beating with the light and heavy bamboo, penal servitude, exile, and death) were imposed by a hierarchy of courts running from the hsien magistrate's yamen up through the prefecture and province to the capital and eventually, for death sentences, to the Emperor. Cases were reported to and reviewed by superiors. Appeals could be made. Magistrates were under deadlines to apprehend criminals and could be severely disciplined for wrong judgments.

The great Ch'ing code listed 436 main statutes and about 1900 supplementary or sub-statutes, which provided specific penalties for specific crimes. The magistrate's problem was to find the statute most applicable to a given case. In doing so he might follow precedent or reason by analogy, but the law was not built up by cases, and although thousands of cases were collected and published with private commentaries to help the magistrates, there was rather little development of generalized doctrine and principles. The statutes were sometimes contradictory and their applicability uncertain. In general, the law was neither primary nor pervasive within the state, and it was felt that to appeal to the letter of the law, like Shylock, was to disregard true morality or to admit the moral weakness of one's case. The law had to be tempered by circumstance in order to achieve justice. Legality was an inferior substitute for morality. As the traditional saying put it, "when a state is about to perish, the regulations increase in number."

One major aim of this legal system was to preserve the Confucian hierarchy of relationships, the social order. Thus penalties for the same act varied according to the social and especially the kinship status of the actors. Filial disobedience was the most heinous crime. A son who merely struck his parent could be decapitated whereas a parent who beat his son to death, if provoked by the son's disobedience, would deserve only 100 blows (by custom "100" was normally 40 blows) of the heavy bamboo and might be let off entirely. A wife's striking her husband deserved 100 blows, whereas a husband's striking his wife was punishable only if she was badly injured and lodged a complaint. A younger man's scolding his paternal uncle was more heavily punished than his scolding the grandson of his great grandfather's brother. Back of such provisions lay a concern for ritual to maintain social harmony and for punishment as necessary retribution when the social order had been violated. Contributing to the death of one's parent was a capital offense even when quite unintended. T. T. Ch'ü cites a case: "Teng Feng-ta fell while engaged in a fight, his opponent on top of him. The latter picked up a stone and Teng's son fearing that it would be hurled at his father grabbed a knife and made for the attacker. The latter moved and the knife entered Teng's father's belly, killing him. The authorities considered that the son had sought to rescue his father. They presented his case to the emperor and asked that his sentence be reduced from 'dismemberment' to 'immediate beheading.' This was granted."

Since formal law mainly served the interests of state and society, private law remained underdeveloped in this legal system. Resolution of conflicts among the people was therefore achieved through various nonofficial channels. Conflicts arising from business deals and contracts might be settled within craft or merchant guilds. Disputes between neighbors might be mediated by village elders, neighborhood associations, or gentry members. In particular, the heads of extended family or clan organizations, so-called "common descent groups," in addition to maintaining the religious rituals of ancestor reverence, supporting schools for clan members' children, and arranging their marriages, would make every effort to keep their members out of court by assuring their tax payments and settling disputes among them. After all, the legal system was part of the government, which remained superficial, far above the level of daily life in the villages. Most conflicts were therefore resolved extralegally by mediation and appeals to old custom and local opinion.

This nondevelopment of Chinese law along lines familiar to the West was plainly related to the nondevelopment of capitalism and an independent business class in the old China. There was no idea of the corporation as a legal individual. Big firms were family affairs. Business relations were not cold impersonal matters governed by the general principles of the law and of contract in a world apart from home and family. Business was a segment of the whole web of friendship, kinship obligations, and personal relations which supported Chinese life. In old China the law, sanctity of contract, and free private enterprise never became a sacred trinity.

In short, "the law" in China was an arm of the state and something to avoid — a very different institution from that which has nourished political leadership, guided legislation, trained statesmen, served corporations, and protected individual rights among the legal-minded and litigious American people.

Religion

Another part of China's heritage from her past, which lies behind modern authoritarianism, was the peculiarly passive attitude of the common people toward government, the apparent irresponsibility of the individual citizen toward affairs of state. Sun Yat-sen once complained that his people were like "a heap of loose sand." Many writers during the century of Western contact from the 1840's to the 1940's deplored the selfish opportunism, competitive jealousy, and disregard for others which they discerned in individual conduct outside the bonds of family, clan, and personal relations. It was a perennially fascinating paradox — this contrast, to the Western way of thinking, between loyalty to family and friends and disregard of the public interest, between the most meticulous sense of responsibility when responsibility was customarily expected and clearly undertaken, and a callous irresponsibility regarding the suffering of strangers or public evils that concerned no one in particular.

Obviously this un-Western ideal of conduct springs partly from the fact that the Chinese family has outweighed the community both as an object of loyalty and a source of benefits.

But the secret of the paradox undoubtedly lies also in the passive and individualistic aspects of China's religions. This passivity complements, and also conduces to, authoritarian government. To understand it we should look briefly at the religious alternatives to the Confucian doctrine.

Taoism. Taoism (_tao_ means "the path," "the way") has expressed the common people's naturalistic cosmology and belief in certain traditional superstitions. It has also provided an escape from Confucianism, profiting by each revulsion of scholars against the overnice ritualism and detailed prescriptions of the classics. It has been a refuge from the world of affairs. It is aptly said that the Chinese scholar has been a Confucian when in office and a Taoist when out of office.

Traditionally Taoism stems from Lao-tzu (lit., "The Old Master") who was claimed by his followers to have been an elder contemporary of Confucius. The school of thought ascribed to him became a repository for a variety of beliefs and practices which Confucianism had refused, including early popular animism, alchemy, ancient magic, the search for the elixir of immortality and the Isles of the Blest, early Chinese medicine, and mysticism generally, both native and imported from India. Finally the Taoist church as an organization in China was influenced profoundly by Buddhism.

In general the Taoist philosophical writers who followed the brilliant literary example of Chuang-tzu (fl. 339–329 B.C.) raised their doubting questions from what we would now call a relativistic point of view. It was Chuang-tzu who delighted succeeding generations by writing that he had dreamed that he was a butterfly playing in the sunshine; and after he awoke he could not be sure whether he was still Chuang-tzu who had dreamed that he was a butterfly, or actually a butterfly dreaming that it was the philosopher Chuang-tzu. The early Taoists were bright people. Applying the idea of the unity of opposites, they argued that human moral ideas are the reflection of human depravity, that the idea of filial piety springs from the fact of impiety, that the Confucian statement of the rules of propriety is really a reflection of the world's moral disorder. Following this line of thought, the typical Taoist took refuge in a philosophy of passivity expressed in the term *wu-wei*, meaning "action by inaction" or "effortlessness." This took the form of laissez-faire, of following one's unrationalized inner nature and accepting without struggle the experience of life. This was plainly the philosophy of those who condemned government meddling and moral crusading and who sought to be resigned to the burdens of life since they could not be avoided. The famous "Seven Sages of the Bamboo Grove" got a great reputation for bibulous irresponsibility in pursuit of the elixir of life and a good time. One practical Taoist contribution came from their protoscientific experiments. Their search for elixirs and herbs built up the great Chinese pharmacopoeia, on which the world is still drawing, and also contributed to the technology of porcelain, dyes, alloys, and other Chinese inventions like the compass and gunpowder.

The Taoist church, as distinct from the philosophers, reached the masses with an imposing pantheon and many sects but failed to build up a worldly organization or appeal to the literati. Monasteries and temples remained disconnected units, catering to popular superstition. By its nature Taoism could not become a vigorous organized force in Chinese politics. It expressed an alternative to Confucianism but left the field of practical action to the Confucians.

Buddhism. The Buddhist element in Chinese life is difficult for Westerners to assess because of our ignorance of Buddhism. Its influence in setting the tone of oriental life is familiar to us through Buddhist art, but its ideas are little studied.

In retrospect we can see that the Buddhist age in China, roughly from the fourth to the ninth centuries after Christ, when a foreign religion from India with a new system of values and institutions became dominant in Chinese life, is the chief prototype of the modern invasion of China by the West. What example does China's experience of this foreign religion set before us? Neither Christianity nor Marxism form exact parallels. Yet China's acceptance of foreign faiths today has overtones of the past. Religious enthusiasm among Chinese rebel movements is an ancient thing. In the case of Buddhism the new faith was taken up first by the barbarian invaders who were entering China from the north. But it was never a political tool of a foreign power.

To understand the appeal of Buddhism in China, we must note its major conceptions. One of the most ancient tenets of Buddhism is that life is painful and that it is not limited to the mortal span with which we are familiar; this is the concept of transmigration.

The Buddha, who lived probably during the sixth century B.C. in Nepal, was born of a noble family and began life as an aristocrat. After renouncing his palace and its harem and luxuries he achieved through meditation an illumination in which he realized the great principle of the wheel of the law or the wheel of the Buddha.

This may be defined as a theory of the "dependent origination" of life: that everything is conditioned by something else in a closed sequence, so that in effect the misery of life is dependent upon certain conditions, and by eliminating these conditions it is possible to eliminate the misery itself. Thus desire originates in dependence upon sensation, which in turn originates in dependence upon contact and the six senses, and so on. The Buddhist objective therefore becomes to cut the chain of conditions which bind one into this sequence of passions, desires, and attachments. From this premise that misery is conditioned and that the conditions can be destroyed, the early Buddhists developed many theories.

One central idea of peculiar interest today is that of the

dharmas. This is actually a theory of elements or atoms, according to which an entity does not exist in itself but is made up of its parts. The old Buddhist monks believed that man himself is composed merely of these many parts or dharmas; he has no personality, soul, or self. The dharmas are of several types. Some relate to form and substance, others to sensation, and others to mental activity. Taken together they make a very neat explanation of experience and form a basis for the denial of the existence of self. This is just what the Buddhist sought, as a way of escaping life's misery. Since all the elements of experience could be analyzed to be disparate, unconnected, and atomic, both in space and in time, it was held that a proper realization of this truth could lead to elimination of the self and a release from the wheel of the law. This sort of escape or enlightenment, as you prefer, has been sought by mystics the world over and was eagerly pursued in medieval China.

Early Buddhism was institutionalized in a monastic order that developed its rule on lines which may be compared and contrasted with the monasticism of Christianity at a later date. By these early Buddhist monks the sutras (traditional sermons and teachings of the Buddha) were finally written down.

Buddhism in China. By the time of its expansion from North India to the Far East the Buddhist school of the Mahayana (the "greater vehicle") had wrought profound changes in the ancient doctrines and made them more likely to appeal to the masses of the population. One of these developments was the idea of salvation, which became possible through the intercession of the bodhisattva (or "enlightened ones") who had attained to the enlightenment of the Buddha but continued their existence in this world in order to rescue others. Probably the most famous of these deities has been the so-called Chinese Goddess of Mercy or Kuan-yin, who is an abstraction of the

114

principle of compassion. Another is the Buddha of Endless Light, Amitabha (in Chinese O-mi-t'o-fo). Salvation of others through the efforts of these enlightened ones was made possible on the theory that merit could be transferred. Along with this went the concept of charity, which supplemented the original Buddhist faith and has made it in China and Japan a more positive social force.

The Mahayana school also developed a positive doctrine of nirvana, the state which it was the object of Buddhist effort to attain but which the Buddha himself had regarded as so completely indescribable that he had said nothing about it.

The Buddhist teachings were set forth in the great Buddhist canon or tripitaka. Translation of sutras from this canon became the chief work of the first Buddhist monks in China. They and their followers faced enormously complex linguistic as well as intellectual problems — how to translate from Sanskrit, which was polysyllabic, highly inflected, and alphabetic like English and other Indo-European languages, into the monosyllabic, uninflected, ideographic script of China; how to convey, in that rather terse and concrete medium, the highly imaginative and metaphysical abstractions of Indian mysticism.

In attempting to transfer or "translate" their new and alien ideas into terms meaningful for their Chinese audience, the early Buddhist missionaries ran into the problem that has faced all purveyors of foreign ideas in China ever since: how to select certain Chinese terms, written characters already invested with established meanings, and invest them with new significance without letting the foreign ideas be subtly modified, in fact sinified in the process. For example, the Chinese character *tao* ("the way"), already so much used in Taoism and Confucianism, might be used variously for the Indian dharma or for yoga or for the idea of enlightenment, while *wu-*

wei, the "nonaction" of Taoism, was used for nirvana. The result was at least ambiguity, if not some watering down of the original idea.

Abstract ideas from abroad when expressed in Chinese characters could hardly avoid a degree of sinification. In addition, exotic values were resisted. As Arthur Wright remarks, "The relatively high position which Buddhism gave to women and mothers was changed in these early translations. For example, 'Husband supports wife' became 'The husband controls his wife,' and 'The wife comforts the husband' became 'The wife reveres her husband.'"

Barbarian invaders of North China, in the fourth century and after, accepted Buddhism partly because, like themselves, it came from outside the old order which they were taking over. Buddhist priests could be allies in fostering docility among the masses. For the Chinese upper class who had fled to the south, Buddhism also offered an explanation and solace, intellectually sophisticated and aesthetically satisfying, for the collapse of their old society. Emperors and commoners alike sought religious salvation in an age of social disaster. When the rulers of the brief Sui dynasty (589–618) and of the early T'ang (618–907) revived a strong central government, they patronized Buddhism as a state religion. Great works of art, statues and rock-cut temples, have come down from this period. Fruitful comparisons and contrasts can be made between the roles of clergy and monasticism, the growth of sects and relations of church and state, during this age of faith in China and its later counterpart in medieval Europe. Buddhist monasteries, for example, served as hostels for travelers, havens of refuge, and sources of charity. They also became great landowners and assumed quasi-official positions in the administration.

The early period of borrowing and domestication had been

followed by one of acceptance and independent growth. The native Buddhism was influenced extensively by Taoism, and influenced it in return. New sects arose in China, catering to Chinese needs. Best known to us today through its influence on Oriental art was the school which sought enlightenment through practices of meditation (called in Chinese Ch'an, or in the Japanese pronunciation, Zen).

The Buddhist contribution to Chinese culture still awaits thorough appraisal but perhaps enough has been said to indicate the very complex interaction between such elements as Indian Buddhism, the barbarian invaders, native Taoism, and the eventual growth, flowering, and decay of Chinese Buddhism.

A comparison of Buddhism's role in China with that of Christianity in Europe should show one striking difference on the political plane. After the revival of strong government in the T'ang, the imperial bureaucracy eventually sought to bring the Buddhist church under firm control. Under Buddhist influence, Confucianism was gradually reinvigorated in the form of Neo-Confucianism. But so little had Buddhism disrupted the political tradition that the government had relatively little difficulty in reducing the economic power of the Buddhist monasteries. The several persecutions of Buddhism were in part a struggle to keep land out of the hands of the church and more easily amenable to taxation. No struggle between church and state developed in medieval China comparable to that in the West. The church — whether Buddhist or Taoist — was quite unable to achieve independence of the temporal power. Their priesthoods and temples in recent centuries have remained loosely decentralized, dependent on local support but without organized lay congregations or any nationwide administration, and passive in matters of politics. Meanwhile by its persistent proscription of religious organization, Confucianism more easily succeeded in dominating both the field of ethics and the major aspects of religious life, notably the family cult of ancestor reverence.

As a result of all this, in modern times China's resistance to Christianity has been not only ideological but also institutional — against any organized church independent of official control.

Chinese Humanism

The preceding pages have stressed certain political and social institutions which on the whole tended toward authoritarian government in traditional China. Since most imperial governments, East and West, have been authoritarian down to recent times, this should be neither a surprise nor a stigma. The pertinent question today is whether China's political tradition can offer inspiration for democracy as well as for totalitarianism.

The answer must be yes, but within certain limits. There was a strong and indeed inspiring tradition that the Confucian scholar had a moral responsibility to speak out against misgovernment. The famous maxim (Buddhist-tinged, to be sure) was handed down from a Sung reformer: "A scholar should be the first to become concerned with the world's troubles and the last to rejoice in its happiness." Scholar-officials in disfavor at the late Ming court were publicly beaten with the bamboo; no laws protected them. Nevertheless those of the Tung-lin ("Eastern forest") Academy in the early seventeenth century inveighed against the misrule of the eunuchs, suffering torture and death accordingly. Chinese history has not lacked heroes who attacked evil in terms of principle — only the principles have been a bit different from our own. If we speak of a Chinese tradition of humanism, we must note the difference in values which sets it apart from our Western tradition.

These different values can be perceived in the rich heritage of China's art and literature. T'ang poetry and Sung landscape painting represent a society which in its day outshone that of Europe, an aesthetic level which the West has not surpassed. But even a superficial glance at the status of the individual in Chinese art and literature will disclose that his place is less prominent than in the West. The Chinese tradition was humanistic, in short, in its concern for man-in-society, in its preoccupation with human relations in this world, especially the problem of conduct.

China's long experience of crowded community and family life produced a body of accepted norms of conduct. The individual farmer had first of all to accept the austerity of a bamboo-and-vegetable (as opposed to our iron-and-meat) standard of material wealth. This fostered in him the virtue of frugality. As in most peasant societies, he esteemed personal honesty, industry, and thrift. He also accepted the Buddhist virtue of contentment with little and limitation of wants. The old saw ran, "Acknowledgment of limits leads to happiness." Chinese life was marked, finally, by a special concern for propriety. The individual acknowledged the strength of social conventions and subordinated himself to them. He paid special respect to the old, he revered past generations, he yielded to family. In all these social forms there was a heavy discipline.

The Chinese type of humanism included a concern for the dignity of the individual, but from a social point of view. "Face" has been a social matter. Personal dignity has been derived from right conduct and the social approval it has secured. "Loss of face" came from failure to observe the rules of conduct so that others saw one at a disadvantage. Personal worth was not considered innate within each human soul, as in the West, but had to be acquired. Chinese humanism recognized that some persons had more gifts than others — human beings, though by nature good, were not equal in their capacities; there was no theory that each had an immortal soul.

On the contrary, right conduct was attuned to a hierarchic society in which some people dominated others because of their status. The center of Confucian moral life, *jen* or "benevolent love," was a distinctly un-Christian though logical doctrine which called for loving others in a graded fashion, beginning with one's own father, family, and friends. Chinese humanism, indeed, was something of an upper-class luxury. The niceties of right conduct in social relations were less to be expected from the unlettered.

All this meant that the acts of a person were to be judged mainly by their contribution to social welfare and stability. The individual as such was not exalted. He was neither unique, immortal, nor the center of the universe. The proper study of mankind was mankind. Emphasis upon individual self-expression tended too often toward license and anarchy, and so the Chinese tradition emphasized social conduct. Compromise and tolerance, perspective and sense of humor, wisdom concerning human nature, character achieved through self-discipline, were all parts of a structure of goals and sanctions which gave each individual his motivation within his community.

Certainly this code may be called humanistic, in its concern for human affairs, yet it fostered paternalism in government and permitted a high degree of authoritarianism. The Emperor and his officials had sweeping prerogatives over the goods and persons of the economy. They created at will state monopolies of salt and iron, controlled production or distribution of various goods, conscripted labor gangs and soldiery on a vast and merciless scale, forbade social gatherings and all unlicensed organizations, and generally ruled without fear of any higher law. Yet this absolutism was tempered by an all-pervading concern with human relations and social stability.

In spite of the theories and devices of autocracy, the Chinese tradition distinctly did not put the state above mankind. It was not *étatism*. But the main reason for this, less a matter of theory than of circumstance, was that the government remained superficial, merely the top layer of the whole society.

Recent generations have seen this ancient structure collapse. Nationalism, science, democracy, and other dynamic elements of a worldwide civilization have shattered the old scheme of things. Today under Communism it is being refashioned with emphasis upon the authoritarian and collectivist elements in the great tradition. But Mao Tse-tung's "mass line," his concern to involve the whole people in politics and self-betterment, is far different from the Stalinist brand of Communism. The Chinese tradition, moreover, is rich and various. Tomorrow other elements may emerge from it.

The foregoing pages should indicate the continuing vigor of the Chinese heritage. One stimulus to China's adaptation to modern life has been her tradition of superiority. This cultural pride forms a more than adequate basis for national cohesion. Another stimulus has been the poverty of the people. Between the pride bequeathed from a long past and the poverty presented in everyday life, there has been no lack of incentive for change and growth.

6 The
Western
Impact

Powerful invaders were nothing new to the Middle Kingdom in the nineteenth century. The unprecedented novelty of the Western invaders was their technological superiority, for it constituted a claim to institutional and cultural superiority also. For a people who had regarded themselves during three millennia as the originators of material culture and the center of civilization, this Western claim could not be acknowledged. Yet the invading British devoted themselves throughout the Victorian era to asserting their superiority worldwide. Progress in all its forms seemed to be on their side. As the record steadily accumulated against China, her ruling class suffered a profound demoralization. The Western impact of the 1840's and 1850's was a stunning blow. To the next generation, however, from the 1860's through the 1890's, the West became a model to imitate, the better to strengthen China to deal with the West. Finally, in the twentieth century the West has been an inspiration for China's three revolutions, Republican, Nationalist, and Communist. Clearly its "impact," whether blow, model, or inspiration, has been both varied and changing.

Indeed, "the West" includes even more variety and complexity than our pet generality "China." Since 1840 the West has gone through revolutionary changes almost if not quite as profound as those in China. Neither the West nor its impact has been a single, simple thing. Why even speak of the multiform impact of a multifaceted West? Why be so simplistic? The reader is warned.

Yet one basic fact remains: the West was the homeland and inventor of the technological and other kinds of progress that convulsed the globe in the nineteenth and twentieth centuries. The West could therefore modernize from within its own civilization, one nation learning from another — and the peripheral giants, America and Russia, learning from them all — without shame or self-doubt. China, however, given her own distinctive tradition, had to modernize from without. Steamships and railways came in foreign hands. The center of modern innovation was obviously outside China. All things Western came by sea and to Chinese recipients were indiscriminately "foreign" (*yang*, "oceanic," "from overseas"). Thus the ordinary friction match was called foreign fire; kerosene, foreign oil; cement, foreign mortar; rifles, foreign guns; galvanized iron, foreign iron. Modern man in China could never forget the West, and since his civilization had consciously developed on the basis of its own central superiority, he could never overlook the self-confident Western claims to Western superiority. China's sense of identity could hardly be impaired, but her self-confidence could be severely shaken. In this rather general, pervasive sense there certainly was a Western impact. Similarly China's "response" to the West was also an enormous fact, a mixture of many processes, complex and interacting.

Perhaps the best starting point is to note how the beginnings of Sino-Western contact have cast long shadows over later events. The American role in China has had exotic nuances which came not from American life but from the precedents established by our European predecessors in the East. Sino-American relations developed within the shadow of older Sino-European relations.

European versus Chinese Expansion

The expansion of Europe which brought Western civilization into direct contact with China can be described in general terms under the headings of capitalism, nationalism, and Christianity. These headings may serve to remind us of the characteristics of Western society. The growth of capitalism can be traced from the time when the crusades aided in the revival of trade between Western Europe and the Eastern Mediterranean through waters which had been closed off by Arab domination. This revival was accompanied by the development of commercial techniques and eventually the rise of towns with their urban classes, stimulation of industrial production, the accumulation of investment capital and its use through new techniques of banking and finance. This economic development during the later Middle Ages was paralleled by the gradual rise of the national states.

Except by hindsight it cannot be said that either of these phenomena, capitalism or nationalism, was inevitable. Neither of them followed patterns that were familiar to the ancient world. Older societies, for example, had been organized in city states or else in universal empires. The nation state was something new. It appears to have had many roots — in the self-consciousness and the kingship institution of the Germanic tribes, in the economic needs of new enterprises growing beyond the limits of the city-state type of economy, in the growth of representative institutions as a means of bringing people into larger political groupings than had been possible in the direct assemblies of the ancient world.

124

Once the national states for these and other reasons had become self-conscious units, the rivalry and warfare among them encouraged economic expansion and technological innovation. Capitalism and nationalism, which are of course no more than convenient overall abstractions for descriptive purposes, thus appear to have interacted upon each other as aspects of a single expansive process. In doing so they stimulated learning, science, and invention. None of these developments had equal counterparts in China.

The expansive energy of Christian evangelism, particularly that of the Jesuits and other orders in the time of the Counter Reformation, may no doubt be compared more easily with Chinese experience in the time of the Buddhist expansion. But the crusading zeal of the Spanish and Portuguese against the infidel Moors in Spain and later overseas represents a type of religious enthusiasm foreign to the traditional Confucian mind. Taken with the other factors mentioned above, the proselytizing energy of early modern Europe must be viewed as still another manifestation of a social growth quite different in its nature and processes from the traditional society of China.

The West approached China through the medium of China's foreign trade. The Western impact can be understood only against this commercial background. The sixteenth century Portuguese and the seventeenth century Dutch and British adventurers and merchants who opened the China trade discovered unknown regions, just as their colleagues of the same generations were opening up the New World. The all-important difference was that Eastern Asia, far from being a virgin continent, was already the center of an enormous and ramified commercial life of its own. The early Western ventures of exploration and trade were but small increments in channels of commerce already centuries old. It is a striking fact that British trade was opened at Canton in 1637, within a very few years of the founding of New England. Yet British trade with China was not able to expand outside of Canton until the nineteenth century, when New England had long since become part of a new and independent nation ready itself to aid in expanding the Canton trade.

The contrast between European expansion in America and its retardation in China must be understood from the Asian as well as the European side. It was not solely that European expansionist hopes and rivalries became more easily focused upon the wide open opportunities of the New World. The very size and richness of the Far Eastern empires, China and Japan, made them at first too strong to coerce, too sophisticated and too self-sufficient to best in trade.

The Arab Role. Except for brief intervals the trade between medieval China and the West down to the modern period was mediated through the Arabs.

It is not always remembered that the Arab expansion of the seventh and eighth centuries across North Africa and into Spain, which made the Mediterranean a "Moslem lake," was paralleled by a similar expansion to the east. The battle of Tours (732) at which the Arabs were turned back in France may be compared with the battle of Talas (751) at which Arab forces in Central Asia north of the Pamirs defeated a Chinese army of the T'ang dynasty. The spread of Islam into Chinese Turkestan, and the accession of Moslem dynasties in India in the twelfth century and later, were part of a continuing expansion toward the east which carried Arab merchants all the way to China and eventually set up Moslem sultanates on the Malay Peninsula and the islands of Indonesia. The Indian Ocean in late medieval times was equally a "Moslem lake" in which the spice trade from the East Indies to the Levant formed but one of the staples. China was a participant in this Arab trading world.

The Chinese records show early "tribute missions," by which we may understand traders, arriving from the Roman East in the Han period, but refer only vaguely to Chinese trading expeditions to the south or west. Chinese ships no doubt reached India, perhaps even Arabia, by the fifth century, and by 758 Islamic Arab traders were present at Canton in numbers sufficient to burn and loot the city. When the Sung dynasty in the twelfth century was forced by the barbarian invasions to withdraw to South China, there was an increased concern for the maritime trade, which already had a history of a thousand years and yet had not to that time become a mjaor focus of Chinese energies. Under the Sung, trade was already confined to certain ports and foreign traders to a certain quarter of the city. Sung ceramics, whether carried by Chinese or Arab ships, are found throughout the Middle East and far down the east coast of Africa. In the Mongol era, Khubilai Khan, asserting his claim to rule all mankind, sent a dozen missions to Southeast Asia to secure the vassalage of the native rulers. While these costly efforts led to no permanent results for the Mongols, they acknowledged the existence of a well-established Chinese trade. This commercial background makes sense of the otherwise startling and inexplicable Ming expeditions into and across the Indian Ocean in the early fifteenth century.

The Ming Explorations. These amazing expeditions between 1405 and 1433 took Chinese ships to India, the Persian Gulf, and the East African coast almost a century before the more famous Portuguese navigators reached those places by sea around Africa. China's precedence over Europe at that time in naval architecture, navigation (the magnetic compass had been a Chinese invention), and the nautical arts in general was clearly demonstrated. But it is quite plain that this achievement had little significance in the Chinese scheme of things. Perhaps there is no more telling point of contrast between the China and Europe of the fifteenth century than their respective attitudes toward maritime exploration.

The Ming expeditions were under the superintendency of the chief court eunuch of the time, a Moslem named Cheng Ho. There were seven separate ventures. The first in 1405 was composed of sixty-two ships carrying 28,000 men. The fourth voyage in 1413–1415 sent ships as far west as the terminus of navigation in the Persian Gulf and to Aden. Seven Chinese reached Mecca. Chinese vessels touched the coast of Africa as well as Arabia. So-called tribute missions came to China from these places — from Bengal eleven times in this period and from a score of other states. The King of Malacca came to the Chinese court four times in person.

The motive of the Ming court in supporting these vast undertakings is by no means clear. It is true that the eunuchs were able to use the tribute missions and strange gifts from faraway potentates as a means of flattery and ingratiation at court. Elephants and ostriches, strange products and stranger tales, could be used to gain imperial favor. Giraffes brought from Arabia were touted as unicorns — in Chinese mythology a symbol of imperial virtue and an occasion for flowery congratulations to the ruler.

A traditional Chinese explanation of these voyages, that they were intended to seek out a deposed Emperor who still claimed the throne, hardly seems like the full story. Perhaps their motivation was a combination of political and commercial interests: their political sanction lay in the desire of the Ming court to perfect its claim to rule all men by bringing the maritime trading nations of the world into the traditional suzerain-vassal relationship which was demanded by Confucian theory as an alternative to the direct rule of the Son of Heaven. Ming suzerainty was vigorously asserted over the tribes of Central Asia in the early fifteenth century. The Cheng Ho expeditions seem to have been equally an effort to assert Chinese suzerainty over rulers accessible by sea.

The comparison between these Ming expeditions through the Indian Ocean and the contemporary Portuguese expeditions down the coast of Africa is both spectacular and instructive. Portuguese exploration of the African coast had begun as early as 1270. From 1418 Prince Henry the Navigator sent out expeditions almost every year. But Cape Verde was not reached until 1445, by which time the Ming court had already ceased its activity. In size the Chinese fleets were much larger than the Portuguese, they sailed farther, and were undoubtedly comparable if not superior in technical abilities of seamanship. Yet the Chinese fleets, for all their competence, lacked any incentive to reach Europe around Africa or even to establish trading posts. The similar capabilities of the Chinese and Portuguese voyagers make the contrast between their motivations all the greater. The Chinese simply lacked the expansive urge which the Europeans had, and this fact made all the difference. Strategically, the Ming court was obliged to face a recrudescent Mongol threat and ward off repeated invasions of the northern frontier. Maritime expeditions were no help against the Mongols. But the main point demonstrated by the Ming voyages and their cessation fifty years before Vasco da Gama was China's self-sufficiency.

Early Maritime Contact. After the Portuguese entered the channels of China's maritime commerce, from 1514, they began a process of trade and evangelism which was to culminate three centuries later in the unequal treaty system of our own day. The chief focus of the new Sino-European relationship was trade. The Portuguese carried the silks of China to Japan as well as the spices of the Indies to Europe. Their commercial empire was built on a far-flung network of fortified trading posts, in India, at Malacca, at Nagasaki, and after 1557 at Macao near Canton. Development of bigger ships and guns and of skill in navigating by compass, astrolabe, and written sailing directions gave the Portuguese their century of supremacy in the eastern seas. They were eclipsed in the seventeenth century by the Dutch and British, whose East India Companies were better organized and financed, but the same network of trading posts continued to facilitate European penetration of the Far East. Each one was an outpost containing the seeds of empire — claims to national sovereignty, zeal for Christian evangelism, demands for Western legal practices, fluid capital funds, and superior military technology — all planted on Oriental shores and ready to sprout when conditions permitted.

The Spanish from Manila and the Dutch from Batavia soon expanded over the adjacent territories to create colonial domains. But Japan and China, under new centralized regimes in the seventeenth century, were able to keep the Europeans quarantined for the time being at designated ports like Nagasaki, Macao, and Canton, which became the predecessors of the nineteenth century treaty ports.

The striking contrast between the Japanese and Chinese responses to Western contact was one of timing as well as degree: Japan reacted more rapidly and extremely, though China eventually followed a somewhat similar pattern. Within forty years after the first Portuguese reached Japan in 1542, the Jesuits had seventy-five priests at work there and some 150,000 converts. After a century, however, by 1640, Japan was closed to Western intercourse and Christianity was proscribed. In China the process went more slowly. St. Francis Xavier, one of the founders of the Jesuit order, had entered Japan in 1549 but he died off the coast of China in 1552. During the next two centuries he was followed in the effort to Christianize China by some 463 selected and highly trained evangelists whose devotion and pertinacity have seldom been surpassed. The great Jesuit pioneer Matteo Ricci (1552–1610) took twenty years to work his way step by step from the Portuguese community at Macao to the court at Peking.

The Jesuits came to China opportunely, when late Ming society was in disarray and bright minds craved new ideas, even from abroad. Ricci quickly saw how to make his way into the scholar-official elite. He gave up his original Buddhist monk's costume for a scholar's gown. He gave up preaching in a chapel and held conversations with small, select groups. He accepted the early classics of Han Confucianism, quoting them for Christian purposes, and disputed only the more systematic tenets of Sung Neo-Confucianism. He permitted reverential kowtows to one's ancestors or the Emperor as secular rites compatible with Christian faith. All this cultural accommodation, combined with his own impressive personality, his command of Chinese, and a display of Western technology — a clock, prisms, a map of the world, Euclidean geometry — won him acceptance. Like a Chinese scholar, he found patrons among the officials, living and traveling in their entourages. He and his colleagues established friendships, based on the art of learned discourse and polite etiquette, with several high officials of the late Ming, including some in the Tung-lin Academy group of moral reformers. In the end Ricci had an imperial stipend at Peking and was buried in a plot granted by the Emperor.

His successors served as Chinese officials heading the astronomical bureau in charge of the imperial calendar under both the late Ming and the early Ch'ing. Indeed they were the first technical experts from the West, retained by the Manchu rulers as useful courtiers who could map the empire or build fountains for the Summer Palace in imitation of Versailles. Several hundred Jesuit publications in classical Chinese made available much of the scientific learning of Europe, while representing Christianity as a system of wisdom and ethics compatible with Confucius' original teaching.

After functioning at Peking for more than a hundred years, interpreting China to Europe and Europe to China, the Jesuits were undone by the Rites Controversy, a long altercation in which the rival Dominican and Franciscan friars, coming to China from their success in far different circumstances in the Philippines, accused the Jesuits of a permissiveness that flouted the positive laws of the Church. When the Pope supported this attack, the great K'ang-hsi Emperor supported his courtiers the Jesuits. Between two such potentates, each superior to the other, no compromise was possible. K'ang-hsi's successor proscribed Christianity as a heterodox subversion. Eventually the Pope suppressed the Jesuit order.

Through this early contact the elite of Chinese scholarship at Peking had been made acquainted with the best of Western learning. With what result? One of the greatest seventeenth century literati (Ku Yen-wu) could only repeat the old wives' tale recorded in the official Ming History: "Portugal is south of Java . . . She sent an envoy for the purpose of buying small children to cook and eat." The imperial encyclopedia of 1747 called Ricci a liar: "His description of the five continents is nothing more than a wild fabulous story." After all, Cheng Ho had sailed west seven times in the Ming dynasty and never come across Italy, Portugal, or Europe. The early knowledge of the West in China had little influence, and although trade continued, it was kept under control at Canton, on the southern edge of the empire.

Meanwhile the early Russian contact by land across Siberia was slower to develop, though in the end more permanent. Cossack bands penetrated North Manchuria in the middle of the seventeenth century, but the power they could muster there, across the barren continental reaches of Siberia, could not yet compare with that of European warships on the China coast. After the treaty of Nerchinsk in 1689 the Manchus obliged the Russians to remain outside the Amur watershed for a century and a half. A trade treaty in 1728 let Russia maintain a nondiplomatic ecclesiastical mission — a few priests and language students — at Peking, while her traders were kept tightly controlled at Kiakhta, an emporium far off on the Siberian border of Mongolia, a counterpart to Canton on the southern seacoast of the empire. Thus Russian commercial relations were controlled like those of all other foreigners, but from the first the Russian political contact by land was different from that of the Europeans by sea. Russia gradually became a territorial neighbor, like the Mongol tribes of Inner Asia, but more distant.

China's Impact on Europe

Europe was the aggressor in opening relations with China. The impact of the new relations was therefore felt first in Europe. This is really no paradox, for the responsiveness to stimuli which led Europeans overseas made them sensitive to what they found there. Until a century and a half ago, China played a greater part in Western life than the West did in China. American understanding of Chinese society today is still colored and a bit befuddled by this inheritance from our own past.

The Europeans' discovery of Asia by sea in the sixteenth and seventeenth centuries revolutionized their view of the world. Before the great sea voyages, and except for the brief contact with Cathay in the time of Marco Polo, the only other contemporary society known to Europe had been that of the Moslems and Turks, the infidel on the border of the known world against whom medieval Christendom had struggled. Even in the sixteenth century in Europe there were still more books published on the Turks than on the New World. But the discovery of mighty kingdoms and ancient societies in Asia which were non-Christian and had actually survived for centuries without benefit of Christianity eventually had a profound effect on Western thought.

The implication of these new facts was fully developed only in the eighteenth century Enlightenment. In it the conflict between natural morality and revealed religion came to a head. And China was taken as evidence to support the argument that the deity could be found through the natural order without revelation. The favorable picture of Cathay so brilliantly sketched by the Jesuit letters of the seventeenth century from Peking tended to show that virtuous conduct, in many ways adequate to Christian standards, could be achieved without revealed religion. This afforded a basis for the separation of morality and religion as sought by the Enlightenment. The translation of the Confucian classics into Latin at Paris in 1687 provided textual evidence. Writers like Leibniz, who had already been profoundly influenced by China, asserted that the Chinese were actually superior in the practical organization of their society and the administration of its affairs, even though Europe remained superior in theoretical studies. For a generation which sought to show how the natural law underlay human institutions even in the absence of religion, China provided a perfect answer. In the China portrayed in the classics, a philosopher-king indeed appeared to be the benevolent father of his people.

Among the writers of the Enlightenment, Voltaire gave enormous prestige to Chinese government by his discussion of it in his *Essay on Morals* published in 1756. He stated that the highest achievement of China was "morality and law." The Chinese officials were benevolent guardians of the people, the whole kingdom a family, and the public weal the first duty of government. As evidence of this he pointed to the Chinese officials' concern for public works, roads, and canals, and other activities fostering economic prosperity. He pointed out that the laws not only punished crime but also recompensed virtue, as when the Emperor honored virtuous persons on the suggestion of his ministers.

The physiocrats in seeking the reform of administration in France and other countries also got inspiration from China. As prophets of the industrial revolution and the rise of the modern middle class, the physiocrats stressed the inviolability of private property. In their reaction against mercantilism they argued that the private individual should be able to accumulate wealth without government supervision. The leader of the physiocrats, Dr. Quesnay, who was known as the "Confucius of the West," published his book *The Despotism of China* in 1767. In it he argued that the Emperor of China, although an absolute monarch, ruled within the framework of natural law. Chinese society approached Quesnay's idea of perfection. There was no hereditary nobility. The son succeeded to the goods of his father but could succeed to his father's dignity only by study and self-improvement. China seemed to him a deistic society which worshiped the Supreme Being. Property rights seemed well assured. Taxes were regulated by the Emperor and no lands except temples were exempt. Quesnay did observe that commerce was not sufficiently encouraged and that corruption among the officials and the despotism of the ruler were only partly tempered by fear of rebellion. But on the whole his estimate was favorable and had wide influence.

Eighteenth century Europe also had a vogue of chinoiserie, the use of Chinese motifs in art, architecture, landscape gardening, ceramics, and other household furnishings such as wallpaper and latticework. Blue-and-white Ming porcelain, both imported and imitated, graced the mansions of the well-to-do. Chippendale furniture and Wedgewood china used Chinese patterns. The Chinese vogue in England reached its height in the ten-story pagoda built in Kew Gardens in 1763.

China's impact on early modern Europe was thus highly selective, mediated through thinkers and craftsmen who found in the example of China certain things that they wanted to find. This set a style that still persists among travelers who take to China, prefabricated, their later impressions of the place.

In the nineteenth century this secondhand idealized view of the Enlightenment was rudely shattered by the maledictions of treaty-port merchants and consuls not interested in philosophy.

The Tribute System

During a full century, from 1842 to 1943, China labored under the handicap of the unequal treaties by which she was opened to Western commercial and religious enterprise. Although the unequal treaty system was finally abolished before the Communist victory, it still meets the need for a focus of patriotic resentment in retrospect. National disasters in the United States, like the Civil War or the Great Depression, have commonly been utilized in the appeals of domestic politics; so the leaders of modern China have found the treaty system a valuable symbol of national humiliation. Chiang Kai-shek, in his book *China's Destiny*, attributed to it all modern China's ills — economic, political, social, psychological, and moral — and the Communist denunciations are even more violent and comprehensive.

To understand the one-sidedness and inequality of the unequal treaties which the Western powers imposed upon the Chinese empire, one must look at the ancient tribute system which China first imposed upon Western visitors. This old Chinese system was just as unequal as the treaty system that supplanted it.

The tribute system was an application to foreign affairs of the Confucian doctrines by which Chinese rulers gained an ethical sanction for their exercise of political authority. Just as the virtuous ruler by his moral example had prestige and influence among the people of the Middle Kingdom, so he irresistibly attracted the barbarians who were outside the pale of Chinese culture. To a Confucian scholar it was inconceivable that the rude tribes of the frontier should not appreciate Chi-

137

na's cultural superiority and therefore seek the benefits of Chinese civilization. Since the Emperor exercised the Mandate of Heaven to rule all mankind, it was his function to be compassionate and generous to all "men from afar." The imperial benevolence should be reciprocated, it was felt, by the humble submission of the foreigner.

Once the foreigner had recognized the unique position of the Son of Heaven it was unavoidable that these reciprocal relations of compassionate benevolence and humble submission should be demonstrated in ritual form, by the ceremonial bestowal of gifts and of tribute respectively. Tribute thus became one of the rites of the Chinese court. It betokened the admission of a barbarian to the civilization of the Middle Kingdom. It was a boon and privilege, and not ignominious. As the original Chinese culture-island spread through the centuries, from the ancient nuclear area over the rest of China, to absorb barbarian tribes, the formalities of tribute relations were developed into a mechanism by which barbarous regions outside the empire might be given their place in the all-embracing Sinocentric cosmos.

When Europeans first came to China by sea these formalities were naturally expected of them. According to the collected statutes of the Manchu dynasty, a tributary ruler of a foreign state should receive an imperial patent of appointment which acknowledged his tributary status. There should also be conferred upon him a noble rank and an imperial seal for use in signing his memorials, which should be dated by the Chinese calendar. When his tribute missions came, they should be limited in size to one hundred men, of whom only twenty might proceed to the capital, by the imperial post. At the capital the mission was lodged, carefully protected, and entertained. Eventually it was received in audience by the Emperor. This was the time of all others when the tribute envoys performed the kowtow.

Early European envoys, like the unhappy Hollanders who presented tribute at the Manchu court in 1795, were inclined to feel that this calisthenic ceremony more than offset the imperial benevolence which filtered down to them through the sticky hands of the officials who had them in charge. The full kowtow was no mere prostration of the body but a prolonged series of three separate kneelings, each one leading to three successive prostrations, nose upon the floor. The "three kneelings and nine prostrations" left no doubt in anyone's mind, least of all in the performer's, as to who was inferior and who superior. Egalitarian Westerners usually failed to appreciate that this abasement of the individual who kowtowed was a normal aspect of the ceremonial life in a society of status. The Emperor kowtowed to Heaven and his parents, the highest grandees kowtowed to the Emperor. In a less formal way friends might kowtow to each other, as polite Japanese almost do today. From a tribute bearer it was therefore no more than good manners.

The secret of the tribute system was the fact that it had become a vehicle for trade. The Ming chroniclers, by including the long defunct Roman East, fictitious principalities, and border tribes, had listed more than 120 tributaries. The Manchus put the border tribes under a special office and reduced their list of genuine tributaries to less than a dozen including the still shadowy countries of the "Western Ocean" whose merchants had already appeared at Canton. Because the Manchu empire chiefly sought stability in its foreign relations, it dealt only with neighboring countries or with those who came to China. If foreign merchants came and their ruler wanted to promote their trade, he could present tribute. It was as simple as that.

The trading states of East Asia presented tribute to the Chinese court in order to maintain their trade and friendly relations and were duly enrolled as tributaries. Certain ports and markets were designated for them. Thus tribute and trade from Korea came by land through Shanhaikuan, from the Liu-ch'iu (Ryukyu) Islands through Foochow, from Siam through Canton. When the first Europeans reached Canton, they were similarly enrolled and almost without realizing it became part of China's tributary firmament. Until the nineteenth century the diplomatic missions sent from Western powers to China, although they totaled more than a score, did little or nothing to shatter the Chinese institution of tribute and the conviction of superiority which it signified. It was still possible for the Ch'ien-lung Emperor, in his famous mandate of 1793 to King George III, to compliment the barbarian ruler on his "respectful humility" while at the same time refusing to permit any exchange of diplomatic representatives or expansion of British trade outside Canton.

The Canton System and Its Collapse. The old Canton trade in its heyday (c. 1760–1840) was carried on under a working compromise between the Chinese system of tributary trade and European mercantilism. During the Napoleonic wars one of the great survivors of the mercantilist era, the British East India Company, based on India, beat out its Continental competitors and brought the growing tea exports of Canton into a profitable triangular trade between England, India, and China. Fleets of East Indiamen voyaged annually from London to Canton, where the company by its charter monopolized all British trade and dealt with a comparable monopoly on the Chinese side — a licensed guild of about a dozen firms, or "hongs." These Chinese hong merchants were responsible to the imperial officials for the foreign trade and traders. The foreigners in turn were restricted by various regulations which, for example, confined them largely to their factories and kept them outside the walls of Canton. Thus by mutual agreement during most of the eighteenth century, in spite of continual disputes, the old Canton trade proved mutually profitable

140

within the limits imposed by two, Chinese and foreign, systems of trade regulation.

Western expansion, and free trade in particular, disrupted the Canton system after the East India Company lost its monopoly of Britain's China trade in 1833. Unfortunately for the repute of private enterprise in the Orient, it reached the China coast at this time chiefly in the form of the opium trade conducted by private traders. This historical circumstance has poisoned Sino-Western relations ever since.

The opium was grown and taxed chiefly in areas under East India Company jurisdiction in India. Opium was carried to China by private British and Indian traders, as well as by Americans who competed as best they could by buying opium in Turkey. They usually found Chinese merchants and mandarins eager to flout the Emperor's prohibitions of smoking and importation. The result was an illegal trade — openly connived at by British, American, Chinese, and other merchants and officials — too valuable to the British Indian exchequer to be refrained from, too necessary to the balancing of the tea export trade to be given up by the merchants, and too profitable to them and to venal Chinese officials to be easily suppressed.

In the retrospect of Chinese patriots today it makes little difference that the opium traffic was a fully bilateral activity, or that its evils hardly exceeded those of the contemporary smuggling of Africans for sale in the United States. In China the opium trade remains a classic symbol of Western commercial imperialism — foreign greed and violence demoralizing and exploiting an inoffensive people. British humanitarians denounced it as such at the time.* A century later we can see it as part of an unavoidable conflict, Western expansion clashing head-on with China's traditional order. Conflict was

---

* One devout Scottish opium captain noted in his journal on December 2, 1832: "Employed delivering briskly. No time to read my Bible."

bound to come. Opium provided the first occasion, though not the last. Similarly, the West was bound to win. (Whether that was a good thing depends on what you think of modern life.)

In the Chinese view, the Western barbarians have always been outlandish in their physical characteristics, generally uncouth and smelling of mutton fat. In slang they have been called "foreign devils" (*fan-kuei* or *yang-kuei-tzu*), "big noses" (*ta-pi-tzu*), or "hairy ones" (*mao-tzu*). The official history of the Ming had described in some detail the Portuguese method of boiling and eating little Chinese children. Nineteenth century mission orphanages were thought to make medicine out of children's eyes and hearts. Foreign diplomats seemed to the mandarins wily and inscrutable, unpredictable "as dogs and sheep." Peasant mothers used to shield their babies from a foreigner's unlucky glance and especially the black magic of his camera. All in all, the white peril in nineteenth century China was a good deal more sinister than the yellow peril of the 1900's in America.

Moreover, since the white barbarians came by ship, the traditional Chinese defensive strategy was completely reversed. The sea now took the place of the steppe. China's frontier was no longer on the Great Wall or at the Jade Gate in Kansu, but at Canton and Shanghai. Age-old conceptions had to be reversed accordingly.

The Treaty System

The legal structure established by the unequal treaties in the period 1842–1860 resulted directly from the two wars fought by the British against the Ch'ing government. The first war in 1840–1842, which has been called, particularly in China, the Opium War, resulted directly from the doughty Commissioner Lin Tse-hsu's vain effort to suppress the drug trade at Canton. But the British expeditionary force was sent to Canton and thence up the coast to secure privileges of general commercial and diplomatic intercourse on a Western basis of equality, and not especially to aid the expansion of the opium trade. The latter was expanding rapidly of its own accord, and was only one point of friction in the general antagonism between the Chinese and British schemes of international relations.

The principles embodied in the Treaty of Nanking in 1842 were not fully accepted on the Chinese side and the treaty privileges seemed inadequate from the British side. Consequently the treaty system was not really established until the British and French had fought a second war and secured treaties at Tientsin in 1858. Even then the new order was not acknowledged by the reluctant dynasty until an Anglo-French expedition had occupied Peking itself in 1860. The transition from tribute relations to treaty relations occupied a generation of friction at Canton before 1840, and twenty years of trade, negotiation, and coercion thereafter.

Although the new treaties were signed as between equal sovereign powers, they were actually quite unequal in that China was placed against her will in a weaker position, wide open to the inroads of Western commerce and its attendant culture. By the twentieth century, after three generations of energetic Western consuls had developed its fine points, the treaty structure was a finely articulated and comprehensive mechanism. It was based first of all on treaty ports, at first five in number and eventually more than eighty. (See map, page 144.)

The major treaty ports had a striking physical and institutional resemblance to one another. Each had a crowded, noisy bund and godowns (warehouses) swarming with coolies, who substituted for machinery, under the supervision of Chinese compradors (business managers), who managed affairs beneath the overlordship of the foreign taipan (firm managers). Each treaty port centered in a foreign section newly built on

U. S. S. R.

Nerchinsk

Khabarovsk

MANCHURIA

U. S. S. R.

Harbin

Kirin

Vladivostok

Changchun

Urga (UlanBator)

OUTER

MONGOLIA

Mukden

KOREA

Kalgan

Peiping
(Peking)

Dairen
Pt. Arthur

Paotow

Tientsin

Yellow R.

Tsinan

Tsingtao

KYUSHU

Yenan

Chengchow

Kaifeng

Hsuchow

Former Course of
the Yellow River

Lanchow

Sian

Nanking

Shanghai

Ningpo

Wuhan
(Hankow)

Yangtze R.

Chengtu

Changsha

Chungking

Foochow

TAIWAN
(FORMOSA)

Kweiyang

Kweilin

Amoy

Kunming

Canton

Swatow

Hong Kong(Br.)
Macao (Pt.)

Hanoi

VIET-
NAM
(INDOCHINA)

BURMA

LUZON

HAINAN I.

★ Early treaty ports   o Other cities

——— Important railroads (in 1948)

Miles

0   100   200   300   400   500   1000

144

the edge of a teeming Chinese city and dominated by the tall white flagstaff of Her Majesty's Consulate. Its institutions included the club, the race course, and the church. It was ruled by a proper British consul and his colleagues of other nations and protected by squat gunboats moored off the bund. At Canton, Amoy, Swatow, and Foochow this foreign community got further protection by being established on an island adjacent to the shipping. At Ningpo, Shanghai, and other places the foreign area was separated from the Chinese city by a river, canal, creek, or other waterway.

Extraterritoriality. This legal system, under which foreigners and their activities in China remained amenable only to foreign and not to Chinese law, was not a foreign nor a modern invention. In a manner rather like that of the Turks at Constantinople, the Chinese government in medieval times had expected foreign communities in the seaports to govern themselves under their own headmen and by their own laws. This had been true of the early Arab traders in China. The British and Americans at Canton before the Opium War demanded extraterritoriality because they had become accustomed to the protection of their own laws in their relations with the Moslem states of North Africa and the Ottoman Empire and had suffered from Chinese attempts to apply Chinese criminal law to Westerners, without regard for Western rules of evidence or the modern Western abhorrence of torture. But most of all the foreign traders needed the help of their own law of contract.

As applied in the treaty ports, extraterritoriality became a powerful tool for the opening of China because it made foreign merchants and missionaries, their goods and property, and to some extent their Chinese employees, converts, and hangers-on, all immune to Chinese authority. France in particular undertook the protection of Roman Catholic missions and communicants. All this was, to say the least, an impairment of Chinese sovereignty and a great handicap to China's self-defense against Western exploitation. The Japanese, who were saddled with the same system after 1858, made tremendous efforts to get out from under it and did so by the end of the century.

A further essential of the treaties was the treaty tariff, which by its low rates prevented the Chinese from protecting their native industries. Since, for various reasons, the administration of the low treaty tariff was not effective in Chinese hands, a foreign staff was taken into the Chinese customhouse. This Chinese employment of foreigners followed ancient precedents and was one of the most constructive features of the treaty system. Under Sir Robert Hart as Inspector General, the Westerners who served as commissioners of Chinese Maritime Customs became leading figures in every port, guardians both of the equality of competition (by enforcement of the regulations for foreign trade) and of the modest Chinese revenue of about 5 percent derived from it. The growth of trade gave Peking important, because uncommitted, new revenues which could be used for modern needs.

Under the new dispensation of the treaties Western civilization brought to China a rich fare of good and evil. The opium trade which supplied 10 or 15 percent of the revenue of British India went hand in hand with the Protestant missionary movement which was nourished by the shillings and dimes of devout congregations in the Christian West. Beginning in the 1830's British and American Protestant missionaries found that modern medicine carried more weight in China than the scriptures. Missionary hospitals were soon attempting to repair the ravages of disease, including the effects of opium. In Chinese eyes this was no more anomalous than the general gap between Christian precept and imperialist practice.

By the most-favored-nation clause (the neatest diplomatic device of the century) all foreign powers shared whatever privileges any one of them could squeeze out of China. The treaty system kept on growing as the fortunes of the Manchu dynasty deteriorated. The dynasty became increasingly dependent upon British administrative and diplomatic support. During the century of the treaties the Chinese people were consequently subjected to a gradually accelerating, cumulative, and often violent process of change. The opium trade that had begun as a joint Sino-foreign traffic was taken into the country. After the 1880's China's native opium production began to supplant the Indian product, importation of which ceased in 1917. From the treaty ports along the coast and up the Yangtze, Western ways as well as goods spread into the interior, aided in the remote centers by zealous evangelists like those of the China Inland Mission. Christianity opened the way for the acceptance of Western values which upset the old order entirely.

Today this influx of Western goods, ways, and ideas during the treaty century is rather indiscriminately condemned by Chinese patriots in retrospect as simple "imperialism" —military, commercial, financial, or cultural as the case may be. Indeed, all Sino-foreign contact of this period almost without exception is now termed "imperialistic," so that the term covers everything and thereby ceases to mean much for analytic purposes. Missionary hospitals, for example, are classed as "cultural imperialism." But this blanket use of "imperialism" to malign even the noblest motives of Western philanthropy may well remind us of one basic fact: the West expanded into China, not China into the West. The foreigners even in their best moments were in this sense aggressive; they were agents of change, and thus destructive of the old order. Americans of today, feeling themselves catapulted forward by technological progress, have no one but their forebears to blame for it; but the Chinese can blame the outside world for having forced modern changes upon them, and for having done it in a certain way. How it was done is thus the question at issue.

The degree of China's victimization and exploitation by the treaty powers is no problem for politicians or true believers, who believe what they prefer, but it will be endlessly debated by historians. The question is so difficult to decide because it involves both objective facts and subjective feelings and neither alone can settle it. A degree of Chinese humiliation can be assumed, though it seems to be greater now in retrospect than it was at the time in fact. But what actually happened under the treaty system?

Here we confront new evidence from researchers in economic history which may alter the picture of China's victimization. This new perspective is derived from work in China, Taiwan, Japan, the United States, and Britain. It stresses the vast size and long-developed maturity of China's domestic trade and the growing power of the merchant class in the Ming and early Ch'ing periods, a power only indirectly acknowledged in the official records. As Rhoads Murphey has pointed out, even Adam Smith could perceive that China's "home market" was as big as that of "all the different countries of Europe put together." The extensive interprovincial trade meant that China was already highly commercialized and, as always, self-sufficient. Lancashire textiles, for example, failed to sweep the Chinese market simply because China's handwoven cotton cloth was a superior and on the whole cheaper product for local purposes. It still supplied most of North China's needs as late as 1930. After all the long struggle to "open" the Chinese market, the chief Western import for Chinese mass consumption turned out to be kerosene — a product more of geological conditions than of Western industrial pre-eminence. Modern economy when it did develop, mainly in the treaty port sector, was to a large extent in Chinese hands. Chinese compradors of course had long managed nearly all the foreigners' business within China. It now appears that much of the nominally foreign enterprise in the treaty ports was a convenient cover for investment by Chinese entrepreneurs. Meanwhile the honeycomb pattern of the rural market towns and their surrounding villages continued to handle the Chinese people's largely self-sufficient commercial life. The foreigner, his trade goods and investment funds, were unable to compete or have much effect at this level. The great rural sector of the economy ran into crisis conditions for many reasons after 1911 and rescue has been under way only since 1949, but the foreign impact and the treaty ports were only one element in this crisis. This new picture does not fit into the framework of Leninist imperialism, although it rather suits chairman Mao's anti-urban stress on the self-sufficiency of the Chinese countryside.

The Demographic Disaster

China's ills in the nineteenth and twentieth centuries have been intensified by the unhappy conjunction of two processes: Western invasion and dynastic change. At the same time that Western contact began to undermine the Confucian social order, an accumulation of domestic problems was weakening the government. From the end of the eighteenth century the Manchus, already 150 years upon the throne, had begun to experience all the difficulties which had undone preceding dynasties. In particular, peace and prosperity had brought an unprecedented increase of population, so tremendous as to constitute almost a new type of crisis in itself, with disastrous repercussions on livelihood, administration, and public morale. Today, as Ping-ti Ho puts it, "China's population is a world problem."

The Population Record. Records of previous dynasties portray a peculiar stability of population from the Han period at the time of Christ down to the end of the Ming dynasty in 1644. The imperial registration of A.D. 2 recorded a population of 59.9 million. Population was then concentrated mainly in the Yellow River area with relatively little habitation south of the

149

Yangtze. In the next millennium and a half these figures were hardly exceeded. At the end of the T'ang dynasty, around A.D. 900, the population was recorded as totalling about 53 million. Under the Southern Sung around A.D. 1200, when the north was under barbarian control, the figure was 45 million. In the Ming period, from 1368 to 1644, with China united and at peace, the totals vary between 50 and 60 million. The Manchu dynasty in 1651 recorded 10 million families or households, each of which was estimated at six persons.

It seems evident that the official population estimates of dynasties erred on the short side of the facts. This was because tax payments were due from an administrative area partly according to the estimated population total. This created an incentive for short reporting both by the people themselves and by the authorities responsible for tax payments to the capital. There never was a genuine census of the modern type, recording precise data as of a given date on age and sex distribution, marital status, migration, and all the other minutiae necessary for scientific analysis. The Chinese figures, on the contrary, resulted from an administrative procedure of registration and estimation, conducted for government purposes to find out the number of persons capable of cultivating land, laboring on public works, bearing arms, or paying taxes. Popular cooperation was not to be expected. Whole categories of persons were omitted. Uniform schedules, accurate maps, trained enumerators, all were lacking. The estimates were often products of bureaucratic ritual. Honan province, for example, during much of the nineteenth century reported an increase of 1000 persons every other year.

One may guess that the Chinese population in Sung times may have been 100 million. Possibly by 1600 it was closer to 150 million. From 1741 to the outbreak of the great rebellion in 1851 the annual figures rose steadily and spectacularly, beginning with 143 million and ending with 432 million. If we accept these totals, we are confronted with a situation in which the Chinese population doubled in the fifty years from 1790 to 1840. If, with greater caution, we assume a total of 200 million in the early eighteenth century and only 400 million by 1850, we still face a startling fact: something like a doubling of the vast Chinese population in the century *before* Western contact, foreign trade, and industrialization could have much effect.

To explain this sudden increase we cannot point to factors constant in Chinese society but must find conditions or a combination of factors which were newly effective during this period. Among these the most obvious is the almost complete internal peace maintained under Manchu rule during the eighteenth century. There was also an increase in foreign trade through Canton and possibly some improvement of transportation facilities within the empire. But of critical importance was the food supply.

Confronted with a multitude of unreliable figures, economists have compared the population records with the aggregate data for cultivated land area and grain production in the six centuries since 1368. Assuming that China's population in 1400 was about 80 million, Dwight Perkins concludes that its growth to 700 million or more in the 1960's was made possible by a steady increase of the grain supply, which evidently grew five or six times between 1400 and 1800 and rose another 50 percent between 1800 and today. This increase of food supply was due perhaps half to the increase of cultivated area, particularly by migration and settlement in the central and western provinces, and half to greater productivity, the farmers' success in raising more crops per unit of land. This technological advance took many forms: most important was the continual introduction from the south of earlier ripening varieties of rice, which made possible double-cropping. New crops were also introduced from the Americas such as corn and sweet potatoes as well as peanuts and tobacco. Corn, for instance, can be grown on the dry soil and marginal hill land of North China, where it is used for food, fuel, and fodder, and provides something like one seventh of the food energy available in the area. The sweet potato, growing in sandy soil and providing more food energy per unit of land than other crops, became the poor man's food in much of the South China rice area. Productivity in agriculture was also improved by capital investments in irrigation works, farm tools, draft animals, and human fertilizer (nightsoil), to say nothing of the population growth itself, which increased half again as fast as cultivated land area and so increased the ratio of human hands and of nightsoil available per unit of land. Thus the rising population was fed by a more intensive agriculture, applying more labor and fertilizer to the land.

In this broader perspective, population growth over the last 600 years has averaged only about four tenths of one percent a year, not a rapid rate overall. But the eighteenth and early nineteenth century doubling and redoubling of numbers, something like the contemporary European population explosion triggered partly by the spread of the potato, spelled disaster for the Manchu dynasty. As the whole economy grew, the government tax rate failed to keep pace. Trade increased along with the population, but the Ch'ing administration lagged behind. All the devices so astutely contrived by the ruling class over the centuries to maintain social stability (described by Professor K. C. Hsiao) became undermanned and less effective: police control by household registration and mutual responsibility among neighborhood groups, the so-called *pao-chia* system; the corvée labor service and village tax collections according to registered quotas; famine control by maintaining reserves in official granaries; thought control by having local lecturers expound the Emperor's *Sacred Edict* of edifying precepts and by officially honoring virtuous persons and condemning heterodox writings — all were weakened by the administration's failure to keep up with the growth of population and economy. Instead, the massive enlargement of the Chinese body politic was accompanied throughout the nineteenth century by a continual increase of unsolved problems, official corruption, endemic disorder, and widespread demoralization.

This pervasive crisis greatly exacerbated the usual difficulties of dynastic decline, rebellion, and reunification. Pressure of numbers has equally menaced the whole effort at modernization. Industrialization elsewhere has generally involved a rapid population increase. But China's population greatly expanded before industrialization. This has set the stage for the most serious population problem of all time.

The People's Republic faces this problem today. The registration effort of 1953–54, still not a genuine census in our terms, gave a grand and appalling total of 586 million in mainland China. At 2 percent net increase a year, by no means an unlikely rate, the Chinese people could soon total a billion. Small wonder that, despite its Marxist contempt for Malthusianism, Peking is promoting birth control.

7 The Revolutionary Process: Rebellion and Restoration

The breakdown of the old way of life in China and the building of new ways is the least known story of modern times, and one of the most dramatic. It has been marked during the last century by a series of phases. Each phase has seen the collapse of certain old forms and the emergence of new ones. The major periods of change, considered as a single revolutionary process, may be grouped to form two main stages: a period of anti-dynastic rebellion along traditional lines which was suppressed in a traditional fashion, and a period of reform and Westernization which merged into revolution. Indeed, rebellion, reform, and revolution have been intermixed, and the division of the revolutionary process into stages is merely an analytical device, to indicate how the elements of Chinese society have been remade and reorganized during the last century. Behind them all may be seen two types of change at work, one cyclical and one permanent.

By cyclical change I mean simple pendulum-like fluctuations, for example, from unity to disunity and back to unity again. This kind of change has occurred often in Chinese history with the rise and fall of dynasties, many of which ended

154

with great rebellions provoked by the corruption of the bureaucracy, the rise of provincial warlords fighting civil wars, and the eventual reunification of the country under another strong founder of a dynasty. This process may be seen in the decline and fall of the Manchu dynasty, the warlord period which followed (1916–1928), and the rise of regimes under Chiang Kai-shek and Mao Tse-tung in succession.

By permanent (or secular) change we mean the reshaping of Chinese life through seemingly irreversible trends like the emancipation of women, inauguration of government by parties instead of dynasties, the increasing use of machines, and the spread of new ideas. Obviously, these secular changes are much the more far-reaching and fundamental. Yet they are obstructed at every turn by the persistence of old cyclical patterns, like the re-emergence of Confucianism as an ideological support for a new central government.

Here let us recall briefly that when the modern revolution began a century ago, the old China was still a society containing two main strata, the literate upper class and the illiterate mass of the peasantry. The gentry families included most of the local degree-holders. Some of their sons became scholars, some of them in turn became officials. Government was conducted by the bureaucracy selected mainly from the literate upper class, who were knit together by the Confucian ideology which they imbibed from the classics. Thus an authoritarian monarchic government had for centuries held sway over a universal empire which embraced the world of Chinese culture. But it rested upon intensive cultivation of the soil by an earthbound peasantry who did not participate in the higher life of government and the arts. The politics, economy, and ideas of old China were still dominated respectively by bureaucratic authoritarianism, the landlord, and the Confucian ethic.

The first phase of the revolutionary process consisted of re-

155

bellion in the traditional pattern against both the local elite and the alien Manchu dynasty. The fanatical religious leadership of this rebellion was anti-Confucian in ideology and failed to enlist the support of the Confucian literati, who supported a restoration of the traditional administration.

The Reform Movement at the end of the century was led by the literati, who sought to retain Confucian values while strengthening the Chinese state by adopting Western methods. But these scholar reformers sought change through the Emperor, from the top down, and had no thought of mobilizing peasant support.

The Republican revolutionary movement was led by students of the West and supported by the new merchant and military classes. The transition from the Manchu Empire to the Chinese Republic in 1912 marked both the end of a dynastic cycle in the traditional pattern and a permanent change away from monarchy. But Western ideas of parliamentary government did not take firm root and the peasantry still did not participate in politics — China relapsed into warlordism.

In the ensuing decade the student class, imbued with a new patriotism, became leaders of a true nationalist movement in politics and espoused social and cultural reform under the slogan of "Science and Democracy." The modern scholar class for almost the first time began to try to give political leadership to the illiterate populace.

This abbreviated preview of the summary which follows is offered here to indicate one thing — that political change in modern China has been part of fundamental social developments in class structure as well as in the economy and system of values. These changes have been accelerating.

The White Lotus as a Prototype

Military power in agrarian China rested on the control of the countryside, its man power and its food supply. These were the sinews of warfare, which might be mobilized to unseat the reigning dynasty. Domestic rebellions therefore saw a struggle between competing groups, as to which side could control and use the men and crops in the villages. The dynasties relied first upon their professional striking forces, like the Manchu bannermen, and ultimately upon local gentry initiative in supporting the established order. The rebels usually found their initial organization in a secret society or religious cult.

This age-old pattern emerged once again, before the expansion of Western contact, in the savage rising of the White Lotus Society, 1796–1804. This secret society went back to the Mongol period. As a religious cult, it appealed to the superstitious faith of poverty-stricken peasants by its multiple promises that the Buddha would descend into the world, that the Ming dynasty would be restored, and that disaster, disease, and personal suffering could be obviated in this life and happiness secured in the next. In the late eighteenth century the cult had spread through the border region where the provinces of Hupeh, Szechwan, and Shensi join, in the region north of the Yangtze gorges and on the upper waters of the Han River. This mountainous area, rather inhospitable to agriculture, had been opened to cultivation and settlement under official Ch'ing auspices only recently. Migration of poor settlers into these mountains, although encouraged officially, had not been accompanied by an equal development of imperial administration over them. The communities of settlers lived on the very margin of subsistence and tended to be a law unto themselves. The fanatical leaders of the White Lotus cult soon added to their popular appeal an anti-Manchu racial doctrine.

The rebellion began in 1796 as a movement of protest against the exactions of minor tax collectors. Though the imperial garrisons were able to come in and get each small uprising under control in turn, new outbreaks continued to erupt and became too numerous to control. The populace had already organized self-defense corps against the aborigines to the south and had collected arms and food. The insurgents could move into easily defensible mountain redoubts and had time to establish their positions before the imperial forces could arrive. The systematic corruption permitted by the senile Emperor Ch'ien-lung handicapped the imperial military effort. While the rebels had little strategic plan and remained merely roving bands, the imperial forces lacked supplies, morale, and incentive as well as vigorous leadership. Both sides ravaged the populace instead of fighting.*

The White Lotus Rebellion was suppressed only after the Chia-ch'ing Emperor assumed real power in 1799 and supported vigorous Manchu commanders who restored discipline to their forces. By pursuing the rebels tenaciously, on the one hand, and getting control of the man power and food supply of the area, on the other, the Manchu generals eventually achieved an old-style suppression of the rising. Their methods, which have been analyzed by Philip Kuhn, indicate certain persistent problems in the military control of a densely populated countryside.

First of all, they mobilized the villagers to build several hundred walled enclosures in which the local peasantry could be concentrated. These walled villages were then protected by newly organized local militia who could by this time more easily be enrolled because the devastation of the countryside had seriously hindered their farming and sustenance. Thus the populace was brought under imperial control. Meanwhile militia were trained to join in the campaign of extermination against the rebels, although it was found that these troops when properly trained became professional soldiers, warlike and dangerous, and subsequently an effort had to be made to

---

* A contemporary satire on this subject may be put into pidgin English as follows: "Bandits arrive, troops no trace. Troops come, bandits disappeared. How sad, the troops and the bandits! When will they ever get to meet each other?"

recover their arms from them. At the same time a policy of conciliation was pursued toward the men the rebels had impressed into their bands, so as to secure their surrender; and other measures were taken to prevent refugees from continuing to join the rebels. By this combination of force and administrative arrangements, the imperial commanders gradually starved the rebels of their new recruits and supplies. The policy of "strengthening the walls and clearing the countryside" eventually sapped the strength of the rebellion and it died out. It had cost the imperial regime the rough equivalent of five years' revenue (200 million ounces of silver).

This pattern is reminiscent of many earlier uprisings and is even relevant to North China during the Japanese invasion of the 1930's, the Chinese Communist expansion of the 1940's, and the war in South Vietnam in the 1960's. But the White Lotus, though an omen of dynastic decline, lacked one ingredient of power: the ideological and administrative leadership of scholars. In this respect it was a mere curtain raiser for the greatest struggle of the nineteenth century world, a civil war in China which in numbers dwarfed our own Civil War.

The Chinese revolution of today really goes back to the Taiping Rebellion of 1851–1864, a full lifetime before Marxism entered China. The Taiping rebels were mainly peasants. They never heard of the Communist Manifesto. Yet modern China's revolution is unintelligible without reference to the Taiping effort to destroy Confucianism, and why it failed.

The Taiping Heavenly Kingdom

This great upheaval arose from a background of population pressure, which had increased the insecurity of life and the vulnerability of the populace to drought, flood, famine, and disease. These in turn presented the creaking machinery of government with problems which it could not meet — flood control, famine relief, increased need for taxes, increased difficulty in getting them. These larger burdens combined with official self-seeking to produce inefficiency in government and loss of confidence among the people. The Emperor's inability to subdue the British barbarians in 1842 had shaken the imperial prestige. In 1846–1848 flood and famine were widespread among China's expanded population. It is not surprising that a great uprising finally began in 1850.

We can also understand why it should have begun in the southernmost provinces. The Canton region and its hinterland had been longest connected with the growing foreign trade, not only of the Western merchants at Canton but of Chinese traders with Southeast Asia. Disorder grew through the connivance of Chinese merchants and pirates with the foreigner in the import of Indian opium. This area, moreover, had been last conquered by the Ch'ing, and their military hold was relatively weak in the very region which had been most fully subjected to the upsetting effect of foreign trade. The local society, as analyzed by Fred Wakeman, Jr., was dominated by large landowning clans, whose militia bands in this era of weak government often carried on armed feuds between clan villages or groups of villages. Such local wars were fostered by ethnic fragmentation, due to the fact that South China had received infusions of migrants from the north, such as the Hakka people, whose customs set them apart both from the earlier Han Chinese inhabitants and from the tribal peoples in the hills. Finally, as population grew and conditions worsened, the foreign opium trade gave a key role to the anti-dynastic secret societies, those sworn brotherhoods that offered mutual help and a social subsystem to the alienated and adventurous, especially on the trade routes. In the traditional pattern the natural candidates to lead rebellion were the branches and offshoots of the Triad Society, whose network was already widespread among Chinese overseas and in foreign trade. The fact that the Taiping Rebellion did not join with these established agencies of revolt is one of the accidents of history and springs directly from the personality of the Taiping founder, Hung Hsiu-ch'üan.

How this disappointed scholar had visions and became a rebel Emperor of half China is a remarkable saga. Hung was born into a Hakka family in 1814. Three times he tried and failed in the provincial examinations at Canton. After one failure he suffered an illness and delirium. He believed that he saw a venerable sage who commanded him to defeat the demons and save humanity. After this vision he returned from Canton to continue as a village schoolmaster, bringing with him a Christian missionary tract entitled "Good Words to Admonish the Age." Curiously enough, Hung appears to have read this tract and its biblical quotations for the first time only six years later, in 1843. The correspondence between its teaching and his earlier vision gave him the conviction that God had called him. He became a traveling preacher and made converts in villages along the West River in Kwangsi, where his followers soon organized a sect, the God Worshipers' Society.

A subsequent visit to a Protestant missionary at Canton, in whose house he spent two months, added to Hung's store of religious tenets and confirmed him in his sense of mission. For his followers he wrote hymns and religious tracts. With them he performed the rite of baptism, broke the idols in the local temples, and prayed to God. He soon had between one and two thousand baptized converts and began to give his religious teaching an anti-Manchu tinge. Already his lieutenants had created a military organization for protection against bandits, and to fight in village feuds or against local gentry-armed militia groups, in this era of growing disorder. By this concatenation of seemingly chance elements, Hung's movement grew in strength. In 1851 the leaders gave it a dynastic title, *T'ai-p'ing t'ien-kuo,* "The Heavenly Kingdom of Great Peace," and thus raised the standard of open rebellion.

Once launched, the rebellion rapidly expanded and its leaders conducted their forces on a great northern expedition into the Yangtze valley, comparable to the later northern expedition of the Nationalist forces under Chiang Kai-shek in 1926. The troops of the established dynasty held out in the Hunan capital, Changsha, but otherwise were routed or beat strategic retreats. Their "victories," which every imperial commander was bound by custom to report to the throne, occurred closer and closer to Peking. In the beginning of 1853 the Taipings captured and burned Wuhan and started down the Yangtze by boat, half a million strong. In March 1853 they captured Nanking and made it their capital. Expeditions continued northward and got within thirty miles of Tientsin but failed to capture the symbol of dynastic authority, Peking. The Taipings thus established their base in the lower Yangtze but at first made no effort to seize Shanghai. The next decade saw much bloodshed but a continuing stalemate between the imperial and the rebel forces.

So great a rebellion has naturally demanded explanations of its rapid rise and long drawn out failure. In the present state of research more can be said about its ideology and leadership than about its actual administration or economic circumstances.

The Taiping Religion. In creating his new religion, Hung selected elements of Christianity from missionary translations mainly of the Old Testament: the uniqueness and omnipotence of God the creator, his spiritual fatherhood of all men, the efficacy of prayer, baptism, keeping the Sabbath, the Ten Commandments, the rewards of Heaven, together with stories of the creation, the flood, the flight from Egypt, and the like. But he found little use for Jesus' teaching of the spiritual power of love, forgiveness, and concern for one's neighbor. Instead, Hung set himself up as Jesus' younger brother, the second son of God, sent down by him to create a new heaven on earth. Thus he became a new fount of pseudo-Christian revelation.

Having studied the Confucian texts so long in preparation for the classical examinations, Hung in his theology inevitably expressed Confucius' values more than Christ's. As analyzed by Vincent Shih, the Taipings' sacred writings are studded with quotations from the *Analects,* the *Mencius,* and classical authors, often unacknowledged or slightly modified. They rejected the basic Christian concept of original sin in favor of the more optimistic Chinese belief in the fundamental goodness of human nature, which of course made repentance less meaningful. The Taipings stressed many traditional moral concepts: the importance of maintaining basic social distinctions and relationships, and of proper conduct according to status, the need to accept fate, the ideal of the Great Harmony.

Most interesting was their choice of the term for God, a key decision confronting all advocates of monotheism in China. The early Jesuits had settled on *t'ien* "Heaven" and *shang-ti* "Lord on High" but their opponents in the famous Rites Controversy had secured a papal decision in 1715 in favor of *t'ien-chu* "Lord of Heaven." Protestant missionaries in the mid-nineteenth century remained split between *shang-ti* and *shen* "Spirit," so irreconcilably indeed that they produced two versions of the Bible. Hung chose *t'ien* "Heaven" as his principal term and so his God at once acquired traditional attributes such as conferring the Mandate of Heaven.

Thus the Taipings' religion had an apparently Christian framework, but it was distorted to meet their needs. Their religious literature added in many bits and pieces of the Confucian classics, but played down a key element like filial piety. In short, they made their own mixture.

Fanaticism, the priceless ingredient in their sudden success, was supplied partly by another Taiping leader, a former charcoal burner, Yang Hsiu-ch'ing. Though less educated than Hung, Yang showed considerably more genius as a political organizer and military leader. Very early he developed a capacity to receive direct visitations from God, who in a crisis would speak through his lips in no uncertain terms. Hung never found this capacity and was left literally speechless. Yang became commander-in-chief, the third son of God as well as the Holy Ghost, and the chief power at Nanking until Hung got him assassinated in 1856.

All in all it seems plain, as Chinese scholars of all camps have pointed out, that the great rebellion failed primarily from inadequate leadership. In spite of their tremendous fervor and the early devotion of their followers, Hung and Yang and the other leaders were blinded by their religion and incapable of setting up an effective government. The Hakka leadership were displaced persons, from a minority group. At Nanking they soon imitated earlier dynasties in creating a nobility, Six Boards, examinations, levels of bureaucracy, and sumptuary laws to distinguish gradations among this elite according to costumes and ceremonies. But they never developed an effective civil service or administration over the countryside, and were therefore quite unable to lead a genuine social revolution in the villages. As Philip Kuhn remarks, the Taipings "remained, in effect, besieged in the cities" while their enemies, the Confucian gentry elite, continued to control and eventually to mobilize the countryside against them.

The Taipings' failure to win the adherence of any body of Confucian literati was a primary element in their political failure as a whole. Meanwhile their failure to join forces with the anti-Manchu secret societies, particularly the Triads, seems to have come partly from the antithesis between the "Christian" rites and doctrines used by Taiping fanatics and the Triad ceremonies derived from Chinese folk religion. The Triad ritual, for example, used esoteric characters not to be found in a Chinese dictionary, Triad members worshiped the Dipper, recited thirty-six incantations, stabbed their fingers to achieve a blood brotherhood, and performed ceremonies to represent the forces of heaven, earth, and man.

Since the Triad Society was widely organized in South China in five main lodges, of which the head was in Fukien and others in Kwangtung and Kwangsi, with a great number of followers among the lower military and civil officials, their aid to the Taiping cause could have been substantial. The Triads also had many members among the petty merchants and seafaring people connected with foreign trade at the southern ports. In 1853 rebels connected with the Triads actually seized the walled city of Shanghai, next door to the young Foreign Settlement, and held it for seventeen months. Yet in this time the Taiping movement at Nanking failed to join forces with them. They also failed to court the friendship of the foreign trading powers at Shanghai.

Taiping Communism. The gropings of the Taiping leaders in the direction of a social and economic reorganization of Chinese life were visible in their use of ancient utopian ideas from pre-Confucian classics like the *Rites of Chou,* schemes to which earlier Chinese reformers had also appealed. These ancient texts called for a sort of primitive communism in which each twenty-five households among the peasantry were to form one communal unit, each with its treasury and temple and two superintendents. In these communities the fields were to be tilled in common, as on a communist collective farm today. Food, clothing, and money were to be used in common. The surplus from the harvest was to revert to the communal treasury. While this system seems to have been actually put into effect only in Taiping military organization, it expressed their egalitarian interest.

In the same vein they advocated, although they could not make it effective, the redistribution of land so as to have it used according to need. Farm land was to be divided into nine classes and distributed among the people, with preference to men above sixteen and under fifty. At the same time the farming population was to be redistributed. In this way it was proposed to distribute land and people so that all would be equally well off. This was essentially a policy of equalization of land use, reminiscent of traditional reform efforts. It may be compared with the doctrine later put forth by the Chinese Communists, in the agrarian reform which preceded collectivization.

In other social teachings the Taipings advocated equality between the sexes. They inveighed against slavery, concubinage, foot binding, arranged marriage, cruel punishments, and the use of opium. These doctrines reflected popular desires which have found fuller expression in later decades.

Their military policy suffered from a lack of controlling leadership. The chief leaders usually acted on their own and became prey to feuds and jealousy. After 1854 they too often remained on the defensive and time after time squandered strategic opportunities. All the original leaders were eventually murdered or expelled, except Hung, whose fanaticism verged upon insanity. He killed himself when Nanking fell in 1864, after a revival under new leadership in the early 1860's had proved unavailing.

The final collapse of this great rebellion, with all its latent potentialities, was an inevitable result of its early failures. Securing the support neither of scholar-gentry nor of anti-Manchu secret societies, it could not achieve a dynastic revolution of the traditional type. On the other hand its religion was too thin and its social and economic doctrines inadequate to take the place of Confucianism.

The Nien Rebels. During the period of Taiping control of the lower Yangtze region there arose on their north between the Huai and the Yellow rivers another movement, of rebel bands called "Nien." Based on fortified earth-walled villages on the southern edge of the North China plain, these bands followed the White Lotus tradition. They organized cavalry forces in their own banner system for raiding abroad, and controlled their territorial base by taking over the local militia corps. Though lacking dynastic pretensions, the Nien movement from 1853 to 1868 supplanted the imperial government in a sizable region and harassed it with raids to plunder food supplies from neighboring provinces.

Imperial efforts to root the Nien out of their fortified nests repeatedly failed. Walls were leveled only to rise again. At last the scholar-generals who had defeated the Taipings developed a more-than-military strategy: to deprive the Nien of their popular support in the villages by promising security to the populace, death to the leaders, and pardon to the followers, many of whom shifted to the imperial forces. By taking over and reorganizing one village after another they cut the rebel cavalry off from their supplies of food and man power and eventually, with blockade lines and counter-cavalry, destroyed them on the plain.

In the aftermath of these revolts which convulsed Central and North China there were also sanguinary risings of Chinese Moslems in the Southwest and Northwest during the 1860's and 1870's — bitter struggles which are only now beginning to be studied. All in all, the movement for change in modern China began by following traditional patterns of peasant-based rebellion and produced little but disorder and disaster, bequeathing to later revolutionists an egregious example of intellectual failure in popular leadership.

The Restoration of Confucian Government

The constructive alternative to rebellion was to combine some degree of Western-style modernization with an old style revival of imperial administration. In 1860 the Ch'ing dynasty seemed on the point of collapse, beset by a recrudescence of Taiping military vigor in the lower Yangtze region and by the Anglo-French invasion and capture of Peking. Yet just at this point there emerged new Manchu leaders under the regency of the young Empress Dowager (Tz'u-hsi). By accepting the Western treaty system and supporting the conservative Chinese scholar-generals in the provinces, they achieved the suppression of the Taipings by 1864 and gave their dynasty a new lease on life. A small Sino-foreign mercenary army, led by an American and then a British commander (F. T. Ward of Salem, and the famous C. G. "Chinese" Gordon), helped defeat the rebels around Shanghai; but the victory was essentially a Chinese one.

As a result the 1860's saw a genuine conservative effort at a "Restoration," similar to those which had occurred after the founding of the Later Han dynasty or after the great mid-T'ang rebellion of the eighth century. During the 1860's the components of the traditional Confucian state were energized to function again: a group of high-principled civil officials, chosen by examination in the classics and loyal to the reigning dynasty, sternly suppressed rebellion and tried to minister benevolently to the agrarian economy and the popular welfare. Order was restored in the central provinces, armies were reduced, taxes remitted, land reopened to cultivation, schools founded, and men of talent recruited for the civil service. While reviving the traditional order in this fashion, the Restoration leaders also began to Westernize. They set up arsenals to supply modern arms, built steamships, translated Western textbooks in technology and international law, and created a prototype foreign office in the form of a special committee (the Tsungli Yamen) under the Grand Council. In these efforts they were aided by the cooperative policy of the Western powers, whose imperialist rivalries did not become intense until the 1870's. Yet in the end this renewed vitality within the Ch'ing administration showed both the strength and also the inertia of the traditional Chinese polity — it could not really be modernized but could function effectively only on its own terms, which were now out of date. As analyzed in a classic work by Mary Wright, this successful revival within a context of inevitable failure makes an absorbing story.

The personal embodiment of the Restoration was the scholar-general Tseng Kuo-fan (1811–1872), who has been revered or condemned ever since as the great protagonist of Chinese conservatism. Tseng was loyal to the Manchu dynasty because it was an integral part of the Chinese social order. He was not racially nationalistic in the modern fashion but was patriotically culturalistic in the old tradition of the Middle Kingdom. Although trained as a classical scholar and civil official at Peking, during the 1850's he became a general in the provinces, organizing the famous Hunan Army which suppressed the Taipings along the central Yangtze by a strategy of gradual envelopment and mobilization of provincial resources. This first regional army of modern times was officered largely by local gentry-literati who followed Tseng Kuo-fan's example in leading peasant troops by the force of their personal moral character, their paternalistic sense of duty, and their faith in the Confucian principles of social order. Both in civil war and in later reconstruction, Tseng and his colleagues stressed the pre-eminence of "human abilities" or talent and character, which were partly inborn but partly could be cultivated by individual devotion to principle. They therefore stressed the revival of the examination system as a means of choosing talent and, for this purpose, the founding of academies and reprinting of classic texts.

In spite of the influx of Western trade and the evident commercial power of the foreigners, the Restoration leaders clung conservatively to the economic principle of the pre-eminence

of agriculture as the basis of state revenue and popular livelihood. They had no conception of economic growth or development in the modern sense but were austerely anti-acquisitive
and disparaged commerce, including foreign trade, as nonproductive. Rather, they tried to set before the peasantry and bureaucracy the classical ideals of frugality and incorruptibility,
so that the product of the land could more readily suffice to
maintain the people and the government. To assist agriculture, they reduced land taxes in the lower Yangtze region,
but did not try to lower rents or prevent landlordism. They
tried to revive the necessary public works for water control,
but could not control the Yellow River any better than their
predecessors.

The Restoration lost vitality after the 1860's for many reasons. Its leaders were conscientiously reviving the past instead
of facing China's new future creatively. They could not adequately inspire the lower levels of their bureaucracy nor handle the specialized technical and intellectual problems of modernization. The very strength of their conservative and
restorative effort inhibited China's responding to Western contact in a revolutionary way.

"China's Response to the West" in Retrospect. Since "China" and
"the West" were complex variables in the nineteenth century,
both terms need careful definition if they are to help our
thinking and not hinder it. As Paul Cohen has pointed out,
Chinese leaders had to respond to the total situation confronting them, "of which the Western impact was only one ingredient." As in so many countries, the foreign menace evoked ini-
tially a nativist reaction that asserted traditional values. But
the domestic menace of rebellion was also of a traditional sort.
Basically the Taiping movement was a response to local problems of livelihood and authority. It was influenced by the West
only superficially, in its pseudo-Christianity. "The 'slowness' of

China's response was due not only to the nature of Chinese society but to the extraordinary problems facing it . . . There was no time to respond to the West." In short, we confront again the concept that China's center of gravity lay deep within the country, and the treaty ports and treaty system, though important in the eyes of their Western creators, remained for a long time peripheral and marginal to the main concerns of the Chinese people and even of the ruling class.

This view receives support from China's tardy adoption of foreign arms during the period of the great rebellion and its suppression. The Western impact had been most evident in the fire power of naval cannon. During the Opium War in 1840–1842 the British had used a shallow-bottomed paddle-wheel iron steamer, called the *Nemesis*, which became the dominant weapon of its day, the prototypical gunboat. It carried swivel cannon fore and aft and was capable of moving into the wind and against the tide in a manner disastrous to China's fortunes. Chinese officials like Commissioner Lin Tse-hsu, trying to pacify the new barbarians from the West, could not but be impressed with this mechanism. At Canton in 1840 Lin led the way in study of the West, securing translations of Western periodicals, patronizing an American missionary hospital, and experimenting in the construction of cannon and gunboats. Officials in the coastal provinces made extensive preparations for coast defense, at least on paper, and several followed Lin's example in studying Western geography and arms. But in contrast to the contemporary Japanese, these Chinese officials of the 1840's were unable to initiate changes to meet the foreign menace once the British had been pacified. During the two decades following the first war with Britain no fundamental progress was made in learning Western technology for military purposes, much less in accepting Western ideas.

Meanwhile, however, the great rebellion created profound

changes in the Chinese political structure, primarily by shifting the center of initiative from the capital to the provinces both in financial and in military affairs. With Peking cut off from its richest provinces, it was left for local Chinese gentry leaders to raise the funds and the armies with which to suppress the rebels. The result was that trade taxes began to compete with the land tax as the government's staff of life, while personally led regional armies began to supplant the effete imperial forces. As the dynasty weakened, the gentry enhanced their position.

The chief new trade tax instituted at this time was *likin* (literally, a tax of "one-thousandth"). Beginning in 1853 in the lower Yangtze, provincial officials set up *likin* stations on the main routes of domestic commerce. These soon proliferated in all the provinces as a source of local revenue, available for the support of regional armies. Meanwhile the new foreign-staffed Imperial Maritime Customs began to give the central government an increased revenue from foreign trade, which could be used partly to support the new office under the Grand Council for handling foreign affairs, the Tsungli Yamen. Once the major rebellion was brought under control, the new trade revenues could finance fresh efforts, both in the provinces and at Peking, to deal with the Western invaders.

8 The Revolutionary Process: Reform and Revolution

The Self-strengthening Movement

During the decades following the Ch'ing Restoration of the 1860's, a whole generation of leading Manchu and Chinese officials worked to strengthen the Chinese position by imitating and adapting Western devices and institutions. This movement for "self-strengthening," studied by Albert Feuerwerker, Kwang-Ching Liu, and others, was posited on the attractive though fallacious doctrine of "Chinese learning as the fundamental structure, Western learning for practical use" — as though Western arms, steamships, science, and technology could somehow be utilized to preserve Confucian values, instead of destroying them. In retrospect we can see that the latter was inevitable — gunboats and cotton looms bring their own philosophy with them. But the generation of 1860–1900 clung to the frustrating shibboleth that China could leap halfway into modernization.

Under the slogan of self-strengthening they therefore began the adoption of Western arms and machines, only to find themselves sucked into an inexorable process in which one Western borrowing led to another, from machinery to technology, from science to all learning, from acceptance of new ideas to change of institutions, eventually from constitutional reform to republican revolution. The fallacy of halfway modernization, in tools but not in values, was in fact apparent to many conservative scholars, who therefore chose the alternative of opposing all things Western. With policy discussions dominated by these die-hards and the halfway modernizers, there was little chance for a third course of drastic revolutionary change.

The leaders in self-strengthening were those who had crushed the Taipings, scholar-officials like Tseng Kuo-fan and his younger coadjutor, Li Hung-chang (1823–1901). These men set up arsenals to make Western ships and guns. They supported the translation of Western books on science and spread the idea that Western methods must be learned and used for defense. As early as 1864, Li explained to Peking that the foreigners' domination of China was based on the superiority of their weapons, that it was hopeless to try to drive them out, and that Chinese society therefore faced the greatest crisis since its unification under the First Emperor in 221 B.C. Li concluded that in order to strengthen herself China must learn to use Western machinery, which implied the training of Chinese personnel. This simple line of reasoning had been immediately self-evident to the fighting men of Japan after Perry's arrival in 1853. But the movement for modernization in China was obstructed at every turn by the ignorance and prejudice of the Confucian literati. This lack of responsiveness in China, during the decades when Japan was being rapidly modernized, provides one of the great contrasts of history.

The difficulties of China's modernization were repeatedly illustrated. To make Western learning available, for example, some eighty Jesuit missionaries during the seventeenth and eighteenth centuries had produced Chinese translations of over four hundred Western works, more than half on Christianity and about a third in science. Protestant missionaries of the early nineteenth century published about eight hundred items, but nearly all as religious tracts or translations of scripture, mainly directed in simple parlance at the common man, not the Chinese literati. At Tseng Kuo-fan's arsenal at Shanghai during the last third of the century one gifted Englishman (John Fryer) collaborated with Chinese scholars to translate more than a hundred works on science and technology, developing the necessary terminology in Chinese as they went along. But the distribution of all these works was limited, rather few Chinese scholars seem to have read them, and their production depended on the initiative of foreigners or of a few officials concerned with foreign affairs, not under guidance from the throne.

At the capital an interpreters' college had been set up in 1862 as a government institution to prepare young men for diplomatic negotiation. With an American missionary as head and nine foreign professors under him, this new college soon had over one hundred Manchu and Chinese students of foreign languages. Yet this innovation had to be defended vigorously against the attack of anti-foreign literati who objected to the teaching of Western subjects. The erroneous excuse had to be offered that "Western sciences borrowed their roots from ancient Chinese mathematics. Westerners still regard their mathematics as coming from the Orient . . . China invented the method, Westerners adopted it."

The jealousy of a scholar class whose fortunes were tied to Chinese learning was most vigorously illustrated in the case of the first Chinese returned student. This man, Yung Wing, had been taken to the United States by missionaries in 1847 and graduated from Yale in 1854. When he returned to China after eight years abroad, he had to wait almost a decade before he was used by Tseng Kuo-fan as an agent to buy machinery and as an interpreter and translator. Yung Wing's proposal to send Chinese students abroad was not acted upon until fifteen years after his return. In 1872 he headed an educational mission which brought some 120 long-gowned Chinese students to Hartford, Connecticut. Old-style Chinese teachers came with them to prepare these prospective modernizers of China for the examinations in the classics, a preparation still essential to their becoming officials. Yung Wing was also given as colleague an obscurantist scholar whose mission was to see to it that Western contact did not undermine the students' Confucian morals. In 1881 the whole project was abandoned.

Similar attitudes handicapped the early industrialization effort. Conservatives feared that mines, railroads, and telegraph lines would upset the harmony between man and nature (*feng-shui*) and create all sorts of problems — by disturbing the imperial ancestors, by assembling unruly crowds of miners, by throwing boatmen and carters out of work, by absorbing government revenues, by creating a dependence on foreign machines and technicians. Even when modernizers like Li Hung-chang could overcome such fears they still faced enormous practical difficulties such as the lack of entrepreneurial skill and capital. Major projects had to be sponsored by high officials, usually under the formula of "official supervision and merchant operation." This meant in practice that enterprises were hamstrung by bureaucratism. Merchant managers remained under the thumb of their official patrons. Both groups milked the new companies of their current profits instead of reinvesting them. An ongoing process of self-sustaining industrial growth through reinvestment was never achieved.

Thus China's late-nineteenth century industrialization proved generally abortive in spite of the early promise of many officially sponsored projects. For example, the China Merchants' Steam Navigation Company founded in 1872 was subsidized to carry the tribute rice from the Yangtze delta to feed the capital. Almost every year since 1415 long flotillas of grain junks had moved these shipments up the Grand Canal. Now they could go quickly by sea from Shanghai to Tientsin. To provide coal for the steamer fleet the Kaiping coal mines were opened north of Tientsin in 1878. To transport this coal, China's first permanent railway was inaugurated in 1881. Yet by the end of the century these mutually supporting enterprises had made comparatively little progress. The China Merchants' Company, plundered by its patrons, managers, and employees, lost ground to British steamship lines. The Kaiping mines, heavily in debt to foreigners, were taken over by Herbert Hoover and others in 1900. Railroad building was neglected by China and promoted by the imperialist powers in their spheres of influence after 1895.

How far China's slowness in modernization was due to foreign privilege and exploitation under the unequal treaties is a question awaiting impartial study. As Western imperialism in the Far East intensified in the late nineteenth century, Japan succeeded in throwing it off while China succumbed further and further. Certainly one main cause in this period was the nature of Chinese institutions, including the fact of a big country with a comparatively weak central government.

Christianity, Imperialism, and Reform

During the four decades from 1860 to 1900 China was opened increasingly to foreign commercial exploitation and missionary endeavor. Foreign trade grew though it never realized the persistent Western hope that if every "Chinaman" would only add an inch to his shirttail, the mills of Lancashire might be kept humming indefinitely. China proved less attractive to foreign capital investment than newer lands in the Americas or the British empire. Likewise the Western evangelist found China remarkably self-sufficient and spiritual converts rather few.

The opening of the country in the 1860's facilitated the great effort to Christianize China. Building on old foundations, the Roman Catholic establishment totaled by 1894 some 750 European missionaries, 400 native priests, and over half a million communicants. By 1894 the newer Protestant mission effort supported over 1300 missionaries, mainly British and American, and maintained some 500 stations — each with a church, residences, street chapels, and usually a small school and possibly a hospital or dispensary — in about 350 different cities and towns. Yet they had made less than 60,000 Chinese Christian converts. Plainly, China was not destined to become a Christian nation. But the influence of mission schools and hospitals, of missionary ideals and activities in seeking out the common man, translating Western literature, initiating women's education, assisting in ancient tasks of charity and famine relief and in new tasks of modernization, was considerable. No doubt future historians will conclude that this influence was highly disruptive to the old Chinese society, even though it was eminently helpful to the Chinese people.

On a small scale, the missionaries were the Communists' predecessors, but the Peking fashion today is to belittle the good works of the missionaries as "cultural imperialism." The argument that they were carried on by self-righteous foreigners under the protection of extraterritorial privileges backed by gunboats is undeniable. So is the fact that there were hundreds of anti-Christian riots, sometimes with loss of life, including at least fifty cases that required top-level diplomatic attention, up to the Boxer massacres of 1900. Yet the fact remains that the missionary movement, whatever its spiritual-doctrinal result in this period, was a profound stimulus to China's modernization. The riots against it seem to have been generally inspired less by the superstitious fears of the populace in the first instance than by the jealousy of the Chinese gentry, whose privileged status in society was directly threatened — socially, ideologically, and in the end politically — by the new class of privileged cultural invaders from abroad.

As long as the dynasty and its traditional institutions survived, the penalty for China's complacent self-sufficiency and inertia became apparent mainly on the frontiers where the lesser states, traditionally tributary to China, were taken over by imperialist powers. Japan took the Liu-ch'iu Islands, Russia moved for a time into the Ili region in Central Asia, France seized Annam and created French Indo-China, the British took Burma, and Korea was opened to foreign intercourse. As these ominous developments continued to whittle away the Middle Kingdom's once-proud hegemony in Eastern Asia, the pressure for drastic action gradually accumulated, but institutional reform became fashionable only when disaster was imminent. Not until Japan had unexpectedly defeated the Chinese empire in 1895 and the European powers had extorted leaseholds and concessions in the three years following were genuine institutional changes attempted. Even then, the objective was still not fundamental change but merely intensified "self-strengthening" by the use of foreign methods. The reformers still took the position that the fundamental values in Chinese society should remain unchangeable but that the laws and institutions were changeable and must be made to take account of the West.

Thus the reformers of 1898 were merely reformers and not revolutionaries. They still wanted only "change within tradition." With great courage and even greater optimism they hoped that the bearers of the Chinese tradition could renovate it to suit modern needs.

Most famous of these men was the fiery Cantonese K'ang Yu-wei, a scholar of high standing who startled the literati with his study *Confucius as a Reformer*. This iconoclastic interpretation pictured Confucius as standing for the rights of the people as a check upon the authority of the ruler. By quoting ancient texts of a minor tradition, K'ang smuggled the idea of progress into the classical heritage.

K'ang Yu-wei's chief argument was that China must reform or perish, and that moderate reform was not enough to save her. He was intensely loyal to the dynasty and knew little of the West at first hand, his knowledge of it being derived entirely from translations. In reforming, he believed China should learn particularly from Japan, whose experience was closer in time and space than that of Western countries. This led K'ang to advocate constitutionalism. He organized a rudimentary political party, the Society for the Study of Self-strengthening, to spread this point of view. His collaborator at this time was another Cantonese literary genius, Liang Ch'i-ch'ao, who edited a self-strengthening newspaper.

This group gained adherents after the disastrous defeat of China by the Japanese in 1895 and attracted the attention of the Emperor, for whose information K'ang prepared memorials and wrote two books. So convincing was his presentation that the young Emperor for a brief period of one hundred days in the summer of 1898 with his assistance issued a cataclysmic series of reform edicts.

These famous documents in the name of the Emperor ordered the remaking of the examination system, the administration, and many of the government institutions. The edicts aimed to inaugurate all the new services of a modern government and at the same time to wipe out the sinecures and corruption of the old. There were edicts dealing with medicine, agriculture, education, the penal code, the police, postal service, mining, commerce, the army, the navy, inventions, and study abroad. Seldom has the untrammeled power of an Emperor been more vividly exemplified, at least on paper.

The Hundred Days of 1898 produced consternation among

officials high and low. It mattered little that the constitution envisaged by the reformers would hardly limit the ruler's power, even though it espoused the rule of law — the fact was that too many officials felt themselves too closely endangered by these sudden changes. The Manchu Empress Dowager, Tz'u-hsi, who had been in retirement for the past decade, was able with military support to effect a coup d'état, depose the unfortunate Emperor, declare herself regent, and rescind his edicts. Six of the reformers were executed. K'ang and Liang fled to Japan.

No incident could have dramatized more effectively the hopelessness of modernizing China through gradual reform from above. The defeat of 1895 and the fiasco of 1898 together gave the first great impetus toward revolutionary change. From then on, efforts at political revolution ran parallel to those for constitutional reform.

Revolutionaries versus Reformers

Sun Yat-sen (1866–1925) came from the modernizing fringe of China and was the most Westernized of her modern leaders, educated in Western medicine, fluent in English, much traveled abroad. His career symbolized the rise of nationalism, which grew up strongest among treaty-port merchants, overseas Chinese, and students abroad, on the frontier of foreign contact where Chinese were most aware of the power and achievements of foreign nations. Operating in this no-man's-land outside the bonds of the old society, Sun was devoted to his nationalist cause and ready to try anything that would help it, a sincere opportunist. His sincerity was charismatic, his opportunism quite practical, even when he pursued inconsistent alternatives at the same moment. Perhaps equally important for his career was the fact that he early became a symbol and subsequently kept on trying. In the course of his efforts, as analyzed by Harold Schiffrin, Sun Yat-sen dealt with all the revolutionary social forces of his time: Cantonese emigrants to foreign lands, Christian missionaries in China, treaty-port compradors and journalists, reforming officials of the Manchu dynasty, anti-dynastic secret societies, overseas Chinese merchants, Japanese expansionists, Chinese students abroad, New Army officers at home.

Sun was born near Macao in the region from which so many Cantonese emigrants have gone overseas. He got his first contact with the West in 1879 when at the age of fourteen he went from Macao to Honolulu on a British steamer as an emigrant to join his elder brother there. In Honolulu his brother placed him in a Church of England boarding school for Hawaiian boys. He studied English, mathematics, and English history and even sang in the choir. When he returned to his native village at the age of seventeen, he was a radical. Partly because he attacked the images in the local temple, he was sent away from his village and became a student at Queen's College at Hong Kong. Here he became a baptized Christian in the Congregational Church, in 1884, the same year that he dutifully married in the traditional manner a girl of his native village whom he had never seen and who remained there as a proper daughter-in-law.

The crushing French defeat of China in the undeclared war of 1885 roused Sun Yat-sen's interest in reform and national salvation. He appears already to have made some contact with the Triad Society. After another visit to his brother in Hawaii, Sun decided to study medicine. For five years from 1887 to 1892 he was a student of a young British missionary doctor, (Sir) James Cantlie, at Hong Kong. He studied chemistry, botany, physics, physiology, surgery, and clinical medicine, learned to play cricket with Cantlie, and assisted him in many missionary projects. After his graduation he began to practice as a surgeon at Macao and seemed well launched upon a professional career. The Portuguese who ran Macao, however, in order to preserve their medical monopoly forbade him to practice without a diploma from Portugal. In 1893 Sun abandoned his new profession and traveled to North China. There he vainly memorialized the authorities, urging programs currently espoused by reformers to use modern technology, increase food and mineral production, and recruit men of talent.

Frustrated again, Sun finally embarked upon a revolutionary career. He had already organized a secret society of his own, the Hsing Chung Hui (lit., "Revive China Society"). Its ostensible purpose was to save China by improving the livelihood of the people through education and the press and the use of modern methods in agriculture and industry. The members were sworn to secrecy by oaths written in blood, and Sun began to organize branches of fifteen or more adherents in other centers. Thus by the time that the Japanese victory of 1895 shook the Chinese state from its lethargy and precipitated the efforts at reform as well as the heightened imperialism of the powers, Sun had already become a leader in the cause of revolution. At this early date he appears to have met and got help from a Shanghai merchant, Charles Jones Soong, who had lived in the United States as a child, become a baptized Methodist, and studied theology three years at Vanderbilt University before returning to China. (His three daughters married Sun Yat-sen, Chiang Kai-shek, and H. H. Kung. Their brother was T. V. Soong.)

Sun Yat-sen's first revolutionary effort was made in 1895. Using Hong Kong as a base, his group attempted to seize the Canton provincial government offices. The plot was discovered. Several of Sun's colleagues were executed. He himself escaped with a price on his head. It was then that he went into disguise, cutting his queue and adopting foreign dress. With a mustache he thenceforth passed easily as a Japanese. When in Japan he used the name Nakayama (meaning literally "central mountain"), pronounced in Chinese "Chung-shan," a name later applied to numerous institutions, streets, and even a style of clothing in modern China. As Marius Jansen's fascinating study makes clear, Sun during the next decade got repeated and substantial help from Japanese patrioteer expansionists, including the Black Dragon Society and politicians of the Liberal Party. This help included funds, arms, advice, and protection.

In 1896 Sun underwent in London an experience which confirmed him in his revolutionary mission. He was recognized at the Chinese legation and locked up there incommunicado for twelve days. The legation prepared to ship him back to China to be executed. During the first days of his captivity Sun says that he prayed without ceasing and then achieved a greater peace of spirit. A few days later he got word to Sir James Cantlie, who lived nearby, and through official British intervention, Sun was saved. He found himself at the age of thirty world-famous as the leader of the anti-Manchu revolutionary movement. During the next two years he studied in London and on the Continent, acquiring more background of political and social theory. From 1900 to 1905 he was on the move in the Far East organizing revolutionary activity, sometimes disguised as a coolie or a peddler, at other times as a Japanese carrying a forged Hawaiian birth certificate. He moved between Shanghai, Hanoi, Malaya, Honolulu, and Japan. In China he and his colleagues developed connections with the Triad Society and also worked among the officers of the newly modernized imperial army. However, Sun Yat-sen's political work was only one of the long-term developments that led to revolution. In the decade preceding the birth of the Chinese Republic in 1911, intensive reformist activity prepared the ground for it.

Liang Ch'i-ch'ao. After the fiasco of 1898, K'ang Yu-wei had remained a monarchist. He was left behind in the development of the reform movement while Liang Ch'i-ch'ao through his writing and editing in Japan became one of the founders of the modern Chinese liberal tradition. Liang was a classical scholar, a graduate of the provincial examinations, and a powerful writer. As Joseph Levenson's study makes clear, he was essentially a reformer of ideas rather than a political revolutionist. His pre-eminent literary abilities made him the man to reinterpret the Chinese tradition by importing Western ideas.

After travel in the West he began in 1902 in Yokohama to publish the *New Citizen,* a journal devoted to the theme of the "renovation of the people" (*hsin min*). In the first few issues were articles by himself on Hobbes, Spinoza, Montesquieu, Bentham, Rousseau, and the history of Western political thought. He extolled Anglo-Saxon individualism and pointed out that personal freedom is possible only under the disciplined acceptance of law and order, tempered by common sense. The new Chinese citizen, said Liang, should learn to be public-spirited, to have a spirit of enterprise, to assert his rights and forget the Emperor's benevolence; he should achieve and maintain his independence of social custom, take an interest in his community, and demand self-government. This was a direct attack upon the ancient dogma of the Confucian relationships.

Liang's reinterpretation of the Confucian ethic may be illustrated by his use of loyalty and filial piety. Since the state had now become the community in which the fortunes of the people were involved, it, he said, instead of the monarch, should now become the focus of loyalty. Confucian loyalty should be metamorphosed into modern patriotism through the redirection of human feeling, not by coercion.

Thinking along these evolutionary lines, Liang argued that a republican form of government in China was still impossible; the educational standard of the Chinese people was still too low to permit their participation in representative government. Moreover a revolution would bring great dangers of dictatorship and invite foreign aggression and the partition of China. He therefore advocated a benevolent constitutional monarchism under which education for the new citizenship and the establishment of provincial and national assemblies would permit gradual progress. The political group which Liang organized in Japan advocated the setting up of a national assembly with a cabinet government responsible to it, new law codes and an independent judiciary, local self-government, a division of powers between local and central government, and the achievement of diplomatic equality through abolition of the unequal treaties. This enlightened and gradual, though utopian, program represented the most humane and sophisticated political thought of the period and had wide influence, competing for the support of student youth.

Liang's gradualism lost out, in competition with the revolutionaries, because it had little program of action and could not offer immediate results or satisfy the passion of patriotic youth to smash the old order and save China overnight. The sweeping blueprints of the revolutionaries appealed to a scholar class trained in abstract principles more than in action. Republicanism was also the latest style in governments, and the child-Emperor could not possibly symbolize the new Chinese nationalism. Thus the ancient Chinese monarchy was doomed along with the Manchu dynasty, even though the monarchy showed considerable vitality and adaptability even in its last decade.

Dynastic Reform and Republican Revolution

The activity of revolutionists and reformers abroad was paralleled in the 1900's by the belated reform efforts of the dynasty at home. In this effort to save itself by changing its spots, the Manchu government was given a compelling impulse by the Boxer uprising of 1900, which had the makings of a traditional peasant rebellion but lacked even the social objectives of the Taiping movement. It was led by fanatical members of a secret society, who eventually got support from xenophobic officials and gentry. The gentry violently resented both the obvious aggressions of imperialism and the less spectacular rise of a new class of Christian converts and protégés under the wing of foreign missions and the protection of extraterritoriality. Manchu princes finally supported this bitter and superstitious effort to expel the foreigner by relying on the magic "invulnerability" of Boxer braves.

In the end armed provocation by foreign troops was partly responsible for the outbreak of violence against foreigners. In this sudden frenzy the Boxers killed some 242 missionaries and other foreign civilians in North China and Manchuria. For two months in the hot summer of 1900 they besieged the foreign community in the Peking legations, yet the attack was never pushed home because leading Manchus realized its suicidal futility. Chinese officials in the southern provinces quickly asserted that this was a domestic rebellion, not the anti-foreign war which Peking had declared it to be. By this fiction the dynasty was preserved for another decade, though further humbled by the Boxer Protocol and indemnity of 1901. But the powers egregiously failed to demand or support genuine reform. Once again they used their influence to prop up a profitable though decadent status quo.

The Empress Dowager, on her return early in 1902 from her flight on a "tour of inspection" to the western provinces, took full responsibility for the Boxer trouble and announced a reform program. During the next decade the Manchus attempted, too late, to carry out many of the reforms which had been proposed during the famous Hundred Days of 1898. But history left them behind. The net effect of their reluctant reform efforts was to prepare the ground for the revolution.

The apparent inevitability of this process, in which the incompetent leadership of the Manchu dynasty seemed capable only of leading it to disaster, is well illustrated in its program for educational reform, which succeeded just enough to undermine the established order.

In 1905 the ancient examination system was abolished, marking the end of an era. New schools and new studies were hopefully planned to take its place, though the funds and the teachers were alike inadequate. Students were sent abroad, principally to Japan, both by Peking and by the provincial governments. An elementary school system was inaugurated, modeled on that of Japan. Colleges were opened in many centers. By 1911 there were said to be 57,000 schools with 1,600,000 students (out of perhaps 65,000,000 young people of school age). In higher education the Imperial University at Peking was formally established, incorporating the interpreters' college founded in the 1860's. As of 1911 there were in the United States some 800 Chinese students and in Europe about 400. Meanwhile, however, Japan had been the chief training ground for modern China. During the decade of the 1900's and particularly after Japan's great victory over Russia in 1905, every year saw 10,000 or even 15,000 Chinese students securing a modern education in Japan. Much of the top leadership of China in the next generation came from this group. But from the point of view of the Chinese government the net effect of this decade of educational beginnings was to create in China a student class with radical ideas.

The students' dangerous thoughts came partly from their having a little learning, an awareness of China's backwardness, without any very fundamental understanding of the relation between a society and its institutions. Many of them on their return to China were appointed to official positions in the traditional manner. Others became teachers in the new colleges on which Chinese local authorities prided themselves.

188

Some were poor and others were idealists and many joined the revolutionary movement secretly.

In yielding to the pressure for reform the court accepted the idea of constitutionalism, an idea the ruling oligarchy in Japan had actively pursued a generation earlier. The constitutional commission sent abroad after 1905 quickly copied the Japanese constitution. A reorganization of the government's ministries in 1906 established a cabinet system. Reorganization of provincial government in 1907 was followed in 1908 by the proclamation of a set of principles looking toward full constitutional government at the end of a nine-year period of preparation. It was proposed to establish assemblies in the provincial and central governments, which, however, should be purely consultative. When they met in 1909 they became natural centers of agitation for change.

Many of the Manchu reform efforts got no further than the paper stage. This was particularly true in relation to the navy and the Western-type legal system, both so foreign to Chinese ways. Efforts at tariff revision as provided in the Boxer protocol were impeded by the difficulty of securing agreement among the powers. Currency reform was attempted but made little progress. Of all these efforts perhaps the most significant was the development of the New Army, the lead in which was taken by a vigorous Chinese official, Yuan Shih-k'ai. Following the precedent of Tseng Kuo-fan and Li Hung-chang, he became in effect the head of a personal army organization, the commanders of which felt loyalty to him more than to the state. But this was less true of junior officers.

The New Nationalism. The awakening of patriotism in the 1900's, roused by the acts of imperialist aggression in the decades preceding, was only one of the many processes of social change now under way. The rise of the treaty ports together with steamship and some railway travel, the telegraph, newspapers and magazines, the imperial post office, had all greatly enlarged the literate Chinese political community. Education was spreading, literacy increasing. Local citizens, often led by Christian converts, now lent support to reform movements against opium-smoking, foot-binding, servant-girl bondage, prostitution, gambling, and other evils. Urbanization and the gradual discrediting of Confucianism had weakened the "three bonds" of the old society, for as soon as the Manchu Emperor's right to rule came into question, the subordination of youth to age and of women to men was questioned equally. The emancipation of women, that great revolution quietly effected by an unsung silent majority, began to gather momentum. Youth came to the fore, and merchants responded to their agitation for boycotts of foreign goods — against the United States over exclusion of "oriental" immigration in 1905 and against Japan because of an incident in 1908.

As Mary Wright has so brilliantly shown, these social stirrings of the New China were accompanied by the demand for "recovery of sovereign rights," in effect, the rolling back of the whole unequal treaty system. Peking's vigorous reassertion of sovereignty in Manchuria, Mongolia, Tibet, and along the southern frontiers in the decade of the 1900's represented a Chinese at least as much as a Ch'ing dynasty or Manchu program. But the revolutionaries, like the dynasty, avoided stressing the theme of anti-imperialism for very practical reasons. The "foreign omnipresence" was a principal fact in the Chinese political scene: not only British and American gunboats in the ports and on the Yangtze patrol but also Anglo-American, Japanese, and European business enterprises both in the treaty-port concession areas and in the interior provinces. This was a pervasive influence. For instance, a great part of the central government revenues now went to meet just the interest payments on the foreign loans for the Japanese indemnity of 1895 and the Boxer indemnity of 1901, without reducing the principal still to be paid off. In the shadow of this semi-permanent imperialist intervention in Chinese life, the revolutionary movement could more easily concentrate on being anti-dynastic, anti-Manchu, than on being anti-imperialist. In any case, paradoxically, the revolutionary effort was in large part inspired and aided from abroad.

By using Japan as their base in the early 1900's, Sun and his corevolutionaries were well situated to enlist both the idealists and the adventurers among the thousands of Chinese students who came there. Sun's main problem, now that a new generation of student youth were flocking to Tokyo, was how to offer them intellectual leadership, something more than putschist plotting, no easy task when he was not himself a classically trained literatus. His first statement of the Three Principles of the People (*San-min chu-i*) which still form the dogma of the Kuomintang (National People's Party) was made in 1905. Roughly translated, they are Nationalism, Democracy, and the People's Livelihood, which included some rather vague ideas of non-Marxist socialism, particularly Henry George's proposal to expropriate future increases in land values, effecting an "equalization of land rights." In 1905, with Japanese help in bringing disparate Chinese student groups together in Tokyo, Sun amalgamated his own revolutionary society with others to form a secret revolutionary league (the T'ung Meng Hui). Four hundred members at the first meeting took an oath to overthrow the Manchus and establish a republic.

This new and more powerful organization continued its secret activity using traditional techniques. Members were known by number only and communicated verbally rather than in writing. They made themselves known to one another by such devices as lifting a teacup with a thumb and two fingers. Using Japan as their base, they began publication in 1905 of a monthly newspaper, *The People* (*Min Pao*), smuggling two thousand copies regularly into China to feed the discontent of the student class. By early 1911, ten revolutionary outbreaks had been engineered, all in vain.

As this subversive movement gained strength, the Ch'ing government had been able to strike against it. The revolutionary attempt of 1906 in Hunan province failed. Diplomatic representations from Peking moved the Japanese government to refuse further shelter to the revolutionists. Dissension arose within their ranks against Sun himself, who was finally expelled by the Japanese. When Sun set up headquarters in Hanoi, he was expelled by the French in turn. By 1909 the organization was in danger of disruption and demoralization. Further putsches had failed. To meet this crisis Sun Yat-sen in 1910 made another world tour to seek funds while others resorted to terrorist assassinations.

The Revolution. A revolutionary attempt at Canton in April 1911 was put down with the loss of seventy-two martyrs. This constituted the tenth failure. The next plot was planned in Hankow in October 1911. Its accidental discovery precipitated the uprising of October 10, since celebrated as the birthday of the Republic, the "double ten" (tenth day of the tenth month). This was the signal for similar risings in most of the other provinces. The Manchus' mandate had been exhausted, and the lead in declaring the independence of one province after another was taken by two principal elements: the military governors who commanded the New Army forces and the gentry-official-merchant leaders of the provincial assemblies. These elements had more power and were more conservative than the youthful revolutionists of the T'ung Meng Hui. The anti-Manchu movement swept the country with comparatively little bloodshed, but the ease with which it overthrew the dynasty was deceptive, for the various groups who joined in the movement soon proved to have little in common but their patriotic opposition to the Manchus.

Sun Yat-sen and his many revolutionary colleagues had derived their main support from the new merchant class among the overseas Chinese and from parts of the new student and officer classes within the country. In revolt, they joined with the larger movement, inside China, which sought provincial autonomy particularly in economic development. On this issue the leading landlord gentry and commercial interests active in the provincial assemblies had united in opposition to the belated efforts of the Manchu central government when it tried to reform China from the top down. The whole issue of provincial autonomy against monarchic centralization of power had been raised in the provincial assemblies and also in the provisional national assembly at Peking. It had been brought to a head by the dispute over railroad development, particularly the financing of railroads through Hankow and into Szechwan. On this railroad issue the provincial leaders had ranged themselves in public statements against the element of foreign control implicit in Peking's railway loan agreements. In actual fact they had been jealous of the prospect that central government officials would chiefly profit from the new developments.

The revolution of 1911 thus represented a good deal more than the revolutionary leadership supplied by Sun Yat-sen and his colleagues. By the same token, Sun, though the nominal leader of the revolution, had relatively little power to control the forces behind it. He was inaugurated as provisional President of the new Republic on January 1, 1912, at Nanking. But several considerations combined to make him decide to step aside within a few weeks in favor of Yuan Shih-k'ai, as a strong administrator better fitted to succeed to the top position.

Yuan, the builder of the New Army in North China, had been called to run the Peking government when the Manchu regent resigned in December 1911. With this beginning he was able to improve his position as the only man prospectively capable of maintaining order in the country. He negotiated with Sun but used delaying tactics. Time favored Yuan, for it became increasingly apparent to all that a China which continued divided would invite foreign aggression. The foreign trading powers, led by Great Britain, encouraged peace within China because they feared the possibility of intervention by her territorial neighbors, Japan or Russia. The revolutionists themselves were aware of this danger and tried to secure from Yuan assurances which would safeguard the Republic.

Agreement was soon reached in the negotiations between Yuan at Peking and Sun at Nanking. On February 12, 1912, the Manchu Emperor formally abdicated to Yuan Shih-k'ai as provisional President of the Republic of China. In this new post Yuan was to work with a parliament, and a cabinet vaguely responsible to it, under the terms of a new constitution. In this way the Chinese Republic was inaugurated to succeed the Manchu dynasty without any settlement of the fundamental institutional problems which confronted it. A political institution of 2133 years' standing had come to an end. What would take its place?

9 The Rise of the Kuomintang

The Search for a New Order

The end of the monarchy in 1912 marked the beginning of a prolonged crisis of authority and central power in the world's most ancient state. While not exactly theocratic, the Son of Heaven had been indubitably placed above mankind. The significance of the Revolution of 1911 thus lay in its negative achievement — the extinction of the monarchy, which was not just a national kingship of the European type but the universal kingship of the Son of Heaven. This abandonment of China's age-old focus of political life was possible because nationalism had arisen to provide a new loyalty to the Chinese state, culture, and people. But this new nationalism had not yet found institutional expression.

Once the Son of Heaven vanished from the scene, China's political life inevitably deteriorated because the chief of state now lacked the customary ideological sanction for the exercise of final authority. The sovereignty that resided in a dynasty had been far more concrete and tangible than the newly alleged sovereignty of the people, especially when there was as yet no election process to give it form. In the absence of either a dynastic succession or a party election, how was an administration to be legitimized? Just at the moment when nationalism had triumphed in theory, the Chinese Republic suffered a decline of central power in fact, and modern patriots in addition to the continued burden of China's semi-colonial status under the unequal treaties now had to bear the further humiliation of political chaos. First the attempt at parliamentary democracy failed and then the state degenerated into warlordism.

These developments occurred during the decade from 1911 to 1921 in the context of three circumstances. First, the central power declined and there was a lessening of efforts at reform or at repression from the top, and widespread opportunity for local change and innovation. Second, the foreign powers became absorbed in World War I, and industry in China had a breathing space in which to develop in relative freedom from the pressure of foreign commercial competition. Third, the World War gave Japan an opportunity for political aggression. After ousting the Germans from Shantung in 1914, the Japanese presented to China in 1915 the notorious Twenty-one Demands. This brazen diplomacy backed by the threat of force consolidated the Japanese position in Shantung and Manchuria but failed to achieve a Japanese protectorate over China. In the process it roused Chinese nationalist sentiment to a new height.

The Collapse of Parliamentary Democracy. The provisional president was a military leader who represented the old style in Chinese politics, a strong man who was capable of taking personal responsibility for his regime but was not concerned about legal niceties and indeed had developed a tendency to assassinate his rivals. Harnessed with him were new-style institutions of a parliament and a cabinet which were supposed to represent the people after the fashion of Western democracies. But these new institutions had little or no foundation in Chinese political practice.

The idea of political parties, for example, was contrary to the tradition by which the Emperor had ruled through his bureaucracy with a monopoly of political organization while opposition groups had had to become secret societies in order to survive. Not only were party programs a new alternative to personal leadership as a principle of group organization; the very idea of a cabinet responsible to parliament was a further anomaly, since the cabinet ministers were at the same time confronted with the Confucian tradition of the ministers' fundamental loyalty to the head of the state. The old-style landlord interest in the provinces was not accustomed to participation in the settlement of national problems, and the new commercial interests of the treaty ports were still not strong enough to dominate their society. The genuinely modern-minded revolutionists who were led by Sun Yat-sen formed but a slight leaven in the Chinese mass.

Yuan as the chief executive steadily strengthened his position. He got his own men into the cabinet, disregarded the spirit of the constitution, and attacked the newly organized Kuomintang. The Kuomintang had been created as an open, electioneering political party, out of the revolutionary T'ung Meng Hui and other groups, by a brilliant young Hunanese, Sung Chiao-jen. The Kuomintang candidates in February 1913 won China's first national election, based on a very limited franchise. Sung's campaigning in Central China showed such promise of leadership that Yuan promptly had him assassinated. This murder demonstrated a principle (that the ruler is above the law) and a tactic (that opponents can best be checked by eliminating their leader) which have strangled democracy in China ever since.

Yuan finally dissolved the parliament entirely. Led on by

his entourage, he eventually attempted in 1915 to establish himself as Emperor; he was thwarted in this by the opposition of the revolutionists, abandoned the project, and died in June 1916. After his death China broke up into rival warload areas and for more than a decade, from 1916 to 1928, suffered disunity even though the government at Peking continued to receive international recognition.

Why did the 1911 revolution fail to build a new Chinese state on Western lines? First, there was no common goal. As already noted, the elements that combined at the time of the uprising had few common objectives beyond the overthrow of the Manchus. Second, there was little body politic, little participation. The revolutionists in their secret plots had not been able and indeed had seldom attempted to mobilize mass support either in the cities or in the countryside. The conservative gentry class who cooperated against Peking were at heart the opposite of revolutionary. They soon acknowledged the superior armed force which Yuan was able to put into the field. Third, all patriotic Chinese at this time feared active foreign intervention. As an alternative to Japanese troops at Peking they were inclined to acquiesce in the stabilizing efforts of other foreign powers led by the British, who backed Yuan Shih-k'ai. The reorganization loan of £25,000,000 in 1913 (from which the United States abstained) represented the powers' inveterate support of stability, which Yuan then embodied. Against this combination of foreign finance and domestic arms, the revolutionaries could do little. Finally and most important, the ideas of political organization through a constitutional parliament and cabinet, which the Chinese Republic had borrowed from the West, could not be linked up with the Chinese political tradition.

The Republic's Decline into Warlordism. Warlordism was in part an old-style political phenomenon, regionalism carried to the level of power struggle. It was based on the fact that coolie armies were easy to conscript and feed and that most Chinese provinces have natural geographic boundaries and can be made into military satrapies relatively independent of outside authority. Shansi province with its mountain escarpment on the east, the Yellow River on the west and south, and the Great Wall on the north is a prime exemplar of a unit based on geographic boundaries. It is not surprising that it remained almost continuously from 1911 to 1949 under the domination of a single warlord, the so-called "model governor," Yen Hsi-shan. Other warlord areas were centered about key economic regions such as the Canton delta, the Chengtu plain in Szechwan, the lower Yangtze valley around Shanghai and Nanking, or southern Manchuria. Using these geographic bases it was the aim of each warlord to train and enlarge his army, secure economic resources, and defeat his rivals.

At this point, however, warlordism departed from the old pattern of a dynastic interregnum with its struggle to claim the Mandate of Heaven; for the monarchy was gone, dynasties were out, and a new basis for political unity had to be found. The warlords struggled in an ideological vacuum. To have the commanding personality of a would-be Son of Heaven was not enough. As C. M. Wilbur points out, a warlord must now claim to be acting for "the people," and if possible secure his legitimacy from a civilian parliament. His new officer corps, trained in specialties like artillery, engineering, and signals, might form a nascent, literate bureaucracy with some capacities for administration. But several factors made for continual rivalry among regional commanders. One was the foreign omnipresence, the fact that arms, funds, and even sanctuary might be obtained from treaty ports, if not actually from treaty powers like Japan, which backed the Anfu clique in North China. Another factor was the new transportation, the steamship and railway, which gave the warlord forces a new mobility and tended to uproot them from any one region. As rivals for power, they could not leave one another alone, and so their armies ended up as peripatetic scourges upon the landscape.

Many warlords were military parvenus of lowly origin — bandits, coolies, peddlers, privates risen from the ranks. The most famous was the "Christian General," Feng Yü-hsiang. He had been converted to Methodism by Dr. John R. Mott and set his men an example of puritan living, physical fitness, and strict discipline. A man of unusual height and physique, Feng prided himself on his peasant origin. He recruited and trained his troops with care, stressing vocational education, recreation clubs, and even conversion to Christianity. It may be untrue that he baptized them with a fire hose. But the folklore concerning him testifies to an unusual vigor of personality. It was symptomatic of the current bankruptcy of politics that Feng had only the vaguest political program and became a pure opportunist, switching allies and fighting first on one side and then on another among the shifting warlord factions. In 1925–26 he accepted Russian aid. In 1927 he joined Chiang Kai-shek but in 1929 was arrayed against him. In the end he became an honored captive of the Kuomintang.

During the height of the warlord period Sun Yat-sen tried repeatedly to achieve his revolutionary objectives through warlord channels. He had soon become disillusioned as to the efficacy of the Western parliamentary system. In 1914 he had withdrawn from the futile competition of the cliques in Chinese politics and had organized again a secret revolutionary party, loyal to himself personally, through which to complete the unfinished task of revolution. In 1917, accompanied by much of the Chinese navy, he went to Canton and sought to cooperate with the local warlords. Thwarted at first, he nevertheless continued his efforts to unify China through military means. In the summer of 1920 Sun was cooperating with the Kwangtung governor to fight the Kwangsi governor. In early 1922 he launched his first, but abortive, northern campaign to

200

invade Hunan, like the Taiping rebels seventy years before.

In these old-style efforts to compete with the warlords by cooperating with some against others, Sun opposed the idea of federalism which was then current. This conception has sometimes been raised in modern China, by analogy to the experience of the United States. In 1922 there was a widespread "federated provinces self-government movement." Intellectuals at this time argued that democracy in China must develop on the level of the provincial assemblies, after which a national government could be built on federal lines. Warlords supported the idea of a federal constitution as a basis for their own local autonomy. It is a striking fact, however, that the logic / and apparent expediency of this federalist movement were quite unavailing, for two main reasons. First, the great weight of tradition, that there is "one sun in Heaven, and one ruler on earth," dominated political thinking. Second, the dangers of foreign intervention mobilized all the forces of nationalism in support of unity, to be attained under a strong central government.

Nationalism and the May Fourth Movement

The New Labor Class. The rise of patriotic sentiment was fostered in this period by the spread of industry in the great Chinese cities. World War I gave Chinese industrial production an opportunity to expand. Building on earlier beginnings, China developed her own industries in cotton textiles, flour milling, and the production of matches, cigarettes, cement, canned food, and similar mass commodities. Heavy industry and highly technical processes were still retarded. But the use of cheap hand labor to tend cotton spindles or sort tobacco developed steadily. Newly important towns like Tsinan, Hsüchow, and Chengchow grew up at railroad junction points. Shanghai, Tientsin, and Wuhan (including the three cities of

Wuchang, Hanyang, and Hankow) became genuine industrial centers with a large factory labor class.

The growth of industrial cities, large and small, offered alternative opportunities of employment for the peasant masses of the countryside. The new cities and the railroads leading to them opened a way of escape from the straitjacket of peasant life. The son of a farmer, for example, no longer had to depend so completely upon his family situation and particularly upon his filial rectitude toward his father as the only road toward a good life. Similarly, peasant women, customarily dependent on male domination, were offered an alternative in the form of factory wages. The old Chinese family system began to crack.

The vital significance of this process will be apparent if we recall how the family had been not only a social but also an economic institution, each peasant household functioning ideally as a self-sufficient unit. The members of the family, tilling their soil and managing their home in common, had had to accept the personal relationships of status, in which each individual found himself placed by fate. The new life of the industrial cities, however, was based on utterly different principles of organization, on function rather than status. There the wage-earning individual could be the economic unit of subsistence, not the family. Moreover, individuals were hired and fired by impersonal criteria of the labor market without reference to personal or family connections. No one should idealize the life of unskilled laborers in an industrial city. The point is that with all its evils this new life provided an alternative to the old. More than that, it created a new class of people to whom the old loyalties and customs no longer applied, a nascent proletarian class ready to give their allegiance to mass movements such as nationalism and Communism.

The New Merchant Class. The growth of the cities had its most immediate effect upon China's merchant class, for whom the treaty ports of the nineteenth century had opened a new era of opportunity. The term comprador (of Portuguese derivation) had become well established in the pidgin English of the China coast to designate the "general manager" who represented a foreign merchant in all his operations in China. Following the example of the celebrated hong merchants who had monopolized the Chinese side of foreign trade at Canton until 1842, the compradors of foreign firms in the treaty ports soon became merchants in their own right. This new merchant class grew up under the wing of the foreigner. It was trained in his ways, and frequently protected by the operation of his laws under the system of extraterritoriality. Chinese merchant capital was amassed in the treaty ports. Absorbing Western ideas, these merchants began to share the concern for national independence and unity which have typified the modern bourgeoisie in other countries.

One evidence of this growing patriotism among Chinese merchants was the increasing use of boycotts against foreign goods. The boycott had been a widely used form of passive resistance, or nonviolent coercion, by which organized groups such as merchant guilds could exert their influence upon officialdom. In the twentieth century they began to be used as expressions of anti-foreignism. The Twenty-one Demands in 1915 provoked a nationwide movement to boycott Japanese goods and to encourage the purchase of Chinese goods and the growth of Chinese industries.

The May Fourth Movement. This is the name given in China to the intellectual movement which crystallized in the Peking student demonstration of May 4, 1919. By extension the term has come to represent the whole development of thought and activity among the Chinese scholar class in the years immediately before and after that date. This intellectual movement was a necessary preparation for the successful Nationalist revolution of the years 1925 to 1928. To be properly understood, the May Fourth Movement must therefore be seen against the background of warlordism, industrialization, and rising patriotism sketched above. In the May Fourth Movement the scholar class now for a brief time assumed the active leadership of the Chinese revolution. This reflected the fact that China's problems lay so deep that the analysis and understanding of them were more than ever prerequisite to effective action. The failure of the constitutional reform movement of 1898 and of the parliamentary movement after 1911 had demonstrated that no mere imitation of the West would suffice to remake China. Yet the national humiliations of the Japanese victory of 1895, the Boxer Protocol of 1901, and the Japanese demands of 1915 had strengthened the realization that Chinese society must be somehow revived and reorganized by the most fundamental changes.

One point of attack upon this problem of change was the classical written language. In the twentieth century a script and even a vocabulary which had been largely created by about 200 B.C. were still being used. In the minds of Western-educated Chinese it inevitably became a question whether this language, like Latin in the West, had not become outmoded and insufficient for modern needs. Like all languages, Chinese has been the creation as well as the creator of those who studied it. Like Japanese, it had begun to absorb modern technical terms. The fundamental question was not the technical one, whether the classical language could be used for modern purposes of scholarship, but the social one, whether its use could be spread among the great mass of the Chinese people as a written medium.

Since the Chinese written language has been one of the tools by which the upper class has enjoyed the fruits of Chinese culture and maintained its social dominance, language reform and the mass literacy which it might make possible have been a fundamental problem in China's revolution.

The first stage in the linguistic revolution was to use the everyday speech in written form — the step taken in Europe at the time of the Renaissance, when the national vernaculars supplanted Latin. Protestant missionaries had pioneered in this effort, to make the scriptures available to the common man. Among the new scholar class, leadership was taken by the noted writer who later became known to Americans as China's wartime ambassador, Dr. Hu Shih. While a student at Cornell and Columbia during World War I he had advocated the use of the *pai-hua,* or Chinese spoken language, as a written medium for scholarship and all purposes of communication. Many others joined in this revolutionary movement, which denied the superior value of the old literary style and made the Confucian classics into works of reference rather than textbooks to be memorized by every student. The use of *pai-hua* spread rapidly; the tyranny of the classics had been broken.

Hu Shih, a student of John Dewey and of pragmatism, also became a leader in the advocacy of scientific methods of thought and criticism. The value of science in technical studies had long been incontrovertible. Its application, as a way of thought, to Chinese literary criticism and historical scholarship now marked a further step. The new scholarship vigorously attacked the myths and legends of early Chinese history and reassessed the authenticity of the classics.

With science came democracy as the other watchword of the new learning. Leadership in the propagation of the new doctrine of Science and Democracy was taken by the son of a rich family, Ch'en Tu-hsiu. He had absorbed in France the tradition of the French Revolution and returned to found a magazine in Shanghai in 1915 called *The New Youth* (*Hsin Ch'ing Nien,* or *La Jeunesse*). In this and a score of similar journals which soon sprang up in the cities, the scholars of this revolutionary generation debated and discussed the application of Western ideas to China's ancient culture. Hu Shih stood forth for a critical attitude toward all things and the necessity of persistent, long-term effort to change Chinese thinking bit by bit, solving problems, not marching to slogans. Ch'en Tu-hsiu, in the name of human rights and social equality, attacked Confucianism. Like Liang Ch'i-ch'ao, these scholars pointed the way toward an ethical revolution at the very roots of China's ancient society.

Beginning in 1917 this intellectual ferment centered in the National University of Peking (commonly abbreviated in China as Peita), where the chancellor, Ts'ai Yuan-p'ei, a courageous advocate of freedom of thought and expression, invited Ch'en Tu-hsiu to serve as dean of literature and Hu Shih to lecture as a professor. (Mao Tse-tung for a time was an assistant in the Peita library.) With this leadership it is not surprising that the May Fourth Movement originated in Peking National University.

The Student Movement. The incident of May 4, 1919, was provoked by the decision of the peacemakers at Versailles to leave in Japanese hands the former German concessions in Shantung. After learning of this decision, some five thousand students from Peita and other Peking institutions held a mass demonstration at one of the palace gates. They burned the house of a pro-Japanese cabinet minister and seized and beat the Chinese minister to Japan. Police attacked the students. They thereupon called a student strike, sent telegrams to students elsewhere, and organized patriotic teams to distribute leaflets and make speeches among the populace. Similar demonstrations were staged in Tientsin, Shanghai, Nanking, Wuhan, Foochow, Canton, and elsewhere. A few students were killed and others were wounded. The prisons were soon full of demonstrators.

The spirit of protest spread among the merchants, who joined the movement by closing their shops in a merchants' strike which spread through the major centers in June of 1919. This developed into a boycott of Japanese goods attended by clashes with Japanese residents. For more than a year student patriots continued the agitation for the destruction of Japan's market in China, with an appreciable effect upon it. Meanwhile strikes were staged among the recently organized labor unions, which joined in the broadest demonstration of national feeling that China had ever seen.

The startling thing about this movement is the fact that while the traditional ruling class of officials and gentry had little to do with it, as might be expected, its leadership was also neither among the new militarists nor among the new politicians. It was led by intellectuals who were quickly supported by organizations of retail merchants, industrial and craft workers, and similar groups. The movement was particularly significant in that it brought both the new cultural ideas of science and democracy and the new patriotism into a common focus in an anti-imperialist program. More than ever before in modern history the student class assumed responsibility for China's fate. They began the effort through their student organizations to reach the common people in the villages, a movement to bring the Chinese scholar into touch with the peasant in a common cause.

The Nationalist Revolution

In a general way the Nationalist revolution of the 1920's combined the traditional trend toward reunification of the country under a strong leader (in this case Chiang Kai-shek) with a new trend toward modernization of the government through the use of Western administrative methods, the inculcation of a new loyalty to the nation, and the monopoly of power by a party dictatorship (rather than a dynasty). The dominant sentiment behind the revolution was a nationalism which sought both unity within China and independence from foreign domination. Its class basis was still, however, the literate upper stratum. Essentially, the Nanking government in the decade after 1927 led the way in the modernization of China's upper class institutions. But it turned against the idea of revolutionizing the life of the common peasant.

This part-way nature of the Nationalist cause, its limited aims in the reorganizing of Chinese society, emerged quite clearly in the 1920's. The occasion was provided by Sun Yat-sen's decision in 1922 to learn from, and Chiang Kai-shek's decision in 1927 to break with, Soviet Russia.

The Kuomintang-Communist Alliance. The Chinese Nationalist revolution, in its effort to shake off the unequal treaties and other bonds of imperialism, was of course deeply influenced by the doctrines of Marxism-Leninism and the example of Soviet Russia. Leninist theory put anti-imperialism on a more than national basis and made it a part of the worldwide trend of history. Since political thinking in China had always been based on universal principles, and the Chinese empire had traditionally embraced the civilized world, Chinese revolutionists readily sought to base their cause on doctrines of universal validity. Ch'en Tu-hsiu became one of the founders of the Chinese Communist Party which was organized in the summer of 1921 in Shanghai. Sun Yat-sen, while not subscribing to the Communist idea of class struggle, in the last years before his death (in March 1925) fully recognized the usefulness of Communist methods and accepted Communist collaboration in his Nationalist cause.

The Russian Bolsheviks had organized the Comintern (Communist International) out of scattered groups in various countries. Their first Comintern congress in 1919 was followed by six other international congresses before World War II. Immediately after World War I the Comintern encouraged active revolution in many countries in Europe. But after 1921, when Lenin turned the Soviet Union to his new economic policy, though the Comintern still competed with the revived socialist parties of Europe, it was less actively revolutionary, except in China.

Lenin held that Western capitalism was using the backward countries of Asia as a source of profit to bolster the capitalist system. Without imperialist exploitation of Asia, which allowed continued high wages for the workers of the West, capitalism would more rapidly collapse. Nationalist revolutions in Asia, which would deprive the imperialist powers of their profitable markets and sources of raw materials, would therefore constitute a "flank attack" on Western capitalism at its weakest point — that is, in Asian economies where imperialist domination exploited the working class most ruthlessly. From the very beginning the Bolsheviks had therefore called upon the colonial peoples to rise against their Western masters. From this time on, Lenin's explanation of imperialism was to gain increasing acceptance among Asian intellectuals.

In China the Soviet government had capitalized upon its own impotence by grandly renouncing the privileges of the Tsar's unequal treaties. But it subsequently proved a hard bargainer over the old tsarist rights in Manchuria, and its Foreign Office continued to deal diplomatically with the Peking government and warlords in North China while the Comintern worked subversively for revolution. The Comintern picked China as the chief area of foreign struggle and British imperialism as its chief target in the years from 1922 to 1927.

On his part Sun Yat-sen by 1922, after thirty years of agitation, had reached a low point in his fortunes. He had been proclaimed president of the Chinese Republic only to see his country disintegrate into warlordism. His effort to unify China through warlord means had led him into dealings with opportunist military leaders at Canton. In June 1922 a Cantonese militarist whom he had attempted to outmaneuver turned the tables upon him. Sun was forced to flee, and reached Shanghai in August. It was just at this moment, when Sun had demonstrated his pre-eminence as China's Nationalist leader but his incompetence to complete the revolution, that he joined forces with the Comintern. In September 1922 he began the reorganization of the Kuomintang on Soviet lines.

This was purely a marriage of convenience. The entente announced in a joint statement by Dr. Sun and a Soviet representative in January 1923 was a strictly limited arrangement. It stated that Sun did not favor Communism for China since conditions were not appropriate to it, that the Soviets agreed that China needed unity and independence, and were ready to aid the Chinese Nationalist revolution. As Sun Yat-sen wrote to Chiang Kai-shek at the time, he had to seek help where he could get it. The Western powers offered no aid. But although Sun now sought and accepted Soviet Russian aid, Communism in his mind did not supplant his own Three Principles of the People as the program for the Chinese revolution — even though he found it useful to incorporate in his ideas the Communist emphasis on a mass movement fired by anti-imperialism.

On the basis of this uneasy alliance, Soviet help was soon forthcoming. Chiang Kai-shek spent three months in Russia in late 1923 and returned to head the new Whampoa Military Academy at Canton in 1924. Meanwhile Michael Borodin, an able organizer who had lived in the United States, became the Kuomintang's expert on how to make a revolution. He helped to set up a political institute for the training of propagandists, to teach Kuomintang politicians how to secure mass support. On the Soviet model the Kuomintang now developed local cells which in turn elected representatives to a party congress. The first national congress was convened in January 1924, and elected a Soviet-modeled central executive committee as the chief authority in the party. Borodin wrote its new constitution.

In addition to aiding the Nationalist revolution, the ulterior objective of the Comintern was to develop the Chinese Communist Party and get it into a strategic position within the Kuomintang, so as eventually to seize control of it. Members of the Chinese Communist Party were, by agreement with the Kuomintang, admitted to membership in it as individuals, at the same time that the Chinese Communist Party continued its separate existence. This admission of Communists seemed feasible to Sun Yat-sen because they were still so few in number, the two parties were united on the basis of anti-imperialism, and the Kuomintang aimed to lead a broad, national multi-class movement avoiding class war. Sun also felt that there was little real difference between the People's Livelihood and Communism, that the Chinese Communists were only a group of "youngsters" who hoped to monopolize Russian aid, that Russia would disavow them if necessary to cooperate with the Kuomintang.

On their side the Chinese Communists were seeking definite class support among urban workers, poor peasants, and students. But they recognized that this class basis was still weak and backward. They therefore sought to go along with and utilize the Nationalist movement without antagonizing the major non-Communist elements within it. It should not be forgotten that the Communist Party in China at this time was still in its infancy. It numbered hardly more than 300 members in 1922, only 1500 or so by 1925, whereas the Kuomintang in 1923 had some 50,000 members. As in other countries the Chinese Communists of this period were significant for their ideas and methods of organization rather than their numbers.

Thus from the beginning the Kuomintang-Communist entente was a precarious thing, held together by the usefulness of each group to the other, by their common enemy, imperialism, and, while he lived, by Sun Yat-sen's predominance over the more anti-Communist elements of his party.

The Nationalist Accession to Power. After Dr. Sun's untimely death in March 1925, his followers achieved, in 1926–27, the successful northern expedition from Canton to the Yangtze valley. The newly trained propagandists of the Nationalist revolution preceded the armies of Chiang Kai-shek, who was aided by Russian arms and advisers. This military effort was the climax to the great wave of nationwide anti-imperialist sentiment which had been roused by student demonstrations and police gunfire in incidents at Shanghai and Canton (May 30 and June 23, 1925, respectively). These provocative and dramatic proofs that the unequal treaties and the foreigners' privileges still persisted had been followed by a prolonged boycott and strike against the British at Hong Kong.

Thus Chinese nationalism in the years from 1925 to 1927 had reached a new height of expression and was focused against Britain as the chief imperialist power. To defend their position the British on the one hand restored to China their concessions at Hankow and Kiukiang on the Yangtze and on the other hand, with the support of the powers, built up an international force of 40,000 troops to protect Shanghai. In fear of antiforeignism, most of the missionaries evacuated the interior. In March 1927, when the revolutionary troops reached Nanking, foreign residents were attacked, six of them killed, and the others evacuated under the protecting shellfire of foreign gunboats in the river.

It was at this point in the spring of 1927 that the latent split between the right and left wings of the revolution finally became complete. For two years the right and left within the movement had generally cooperated, although as early as March 1926 Chiang Kai-shek had arrested leftist elements at Canton to forestall a plot to kidnap him. His three-month view of Russia in 1923 had left him aware of Soviet methods and suspicious of Communist aims. The success of the Northern Expedition finally took the lid off the situation.

In brief, the left wing of the Kuomintang together with the Communists by March 1927 dominated the revolutionary government which had been moved from Canton to Wuhan. Here were collected, among other leaders, Madame Sun Yat-sen and Wang Ching-wei, the widow and the chief disciple of the founder, and Borodin, the chief adviser on revolution. Wuhan had been proclaimed the new national capital. This suited Communist strategy because it was a large industrial center. Two members of the Chinese Communist Party had actually been made cabinet ministers. But this government was weak in military strength.

Chiang Kai-shek with the support of the more conservative leaders of the Kuomintang had aimed at the rich strategic center of the lower Yangtze. Once the Shanghai-Nanking region was in his grasp, Chiang was able by military force to forestall the Communists, and consolidate his position. In April 1927 at Shanghai foreign troops and warships confronted the Communist-led labor unions which had seized local control. Under Comintern orders they awaited Chiang as their ally, only to be attacked and decimated by his forces once he had got in a position to do so. He set up his capital at Nanking and shortly afterward a local general seized power at Wuhan and broke up the left-wing government. Some of its leaders fled, like Borodin, to Moscow. The new Nanking government expelled the Chinese Communists from its ranks and instituted a nationwide terror to suppress the Communist revolution. In this effort it was, for the time being, largely successful. Small contingents of Communist-led troops revolted, and in December 1927 the Communists attempted a coup at Canton. But after this failure to seize power they withdrew to the rural mountain area of Kiangsi province in Central China.

This ignominious failure of the Comintern's laboratory experiment in revolution in China had been affected by a power struggle in Moscow. Trotsky and his followers had criticized the Comintern effort to work through the Kuomintang. They foresaw Chiang Kai-shek's "betrayal" and urged an independent program to develop workers' and peasants' soviets in China under purely Communist leadership. Stalin and his supporters, however, had argued that an independent Communist movement in so backward a country would invite suppression all the sooner. They had looked forward to the time at a later stage of the revolution when, in Stalin's phrase, the Communists could drop their Kuomintang allies as so many "squeezed-out lemons." Whatever the merits of these competing strategies, it is plain that the right-wing Kuomintang squeezed first.

Much of the Comintern's ineptitude undoubtedly came from its remoteness from the scene of action. Lacking instantaneous radio communication, Stalin and his colleagues could hardly succeed in masterminding by the aid of Marxist dialectics the confused and unprecedented stirrings of revolution in a place like Shanghai. The Comintern plot in China was also frustrated by the Comintern's own prior act in giving the Kuomintang a centralized Soviet-style party apparatus, which was much harder to infiltrate and subvert than an open Western-style parliamentary party. In the end the Comintern made Ch'en Tu-hsiu, who had been a founder and leader of the Chinese Communist Party, the scapegoat. He was expelled in 1929.

Chiang Kai-shek's break with the Communists represented an effort to consolidate the gains of the national revolution at a certain level in the revolutionary process, stopping short of class struggle, social revolution, and the remaking of peasant life in the villages. This consolidation in the Nanking government, combined with military campaigns to check revolt, enabled Chiang and the Kuomintang leaders to achieve a superficial national unity, secure the recognition of the powers, and begin the process of administrative development which would be a necessary prerequisite to the abolition of the unequal treaties. In the spring of 1928 Chiang led a further northern expedition from the Yangtze to Peking, which was occupied in June and renamed Peiping ("Northern Peace"). In November the young warlord of Manchuria completed the nominal unification of all China by recognizing the jurisdiction of the Nanking government. Meantime the foreign powers one by one made treaties with it and so gave the Nationalist revolution international recognition.

In historical perspective, these achievements can be viewed as a phase in a long process which has not even yet been finished — the gradual mobilization of the Chinese people in their national political life. The fact that the Nationalist revolution went only part way in realizing this potentiality of popular mobilization gave the Communists their later opportunity.

The Nanking Government

Party Government. The Nationalist government of China at Nanking in the decade from 1927 to 1937 was the most modern that China had known. The Nanking government was controlled by the Kuomintang on the basis of party dictatorship. The Kuomintang had inherited from Sun Yat-sen his five-power division of the government among executive, legislative, judicial, civil service, and censorial agencies (*yuan*). Of these, the Executive Yuan with its dozen ministries of Foreign Affairs, Economics, Communications, War, and the like at once became dominant and overshadowed all the others. The last two agencies, the Examination Yuan and the Control Yuan, were derived by Sun from the imperial traditions of the examinations and the censorate. In practice this censorate tradition was carried further by the extensive growth of the secret police, both of the government and of the party. Sun's theory of the three stages of the revolution (military unification, political tutelage, and constitutional democracy) was carried out by the proclamation in 1929 of the beginning of the period of political tutelage under the Kuomintang dictatorship.

Ever since the first Party Congress had met in January 1924 and adopted a Soviet-style organization, the Central Executive Committee had become the chief repository of political authority. High officials of the government were chosen by the Central Executive Committee and usually from it. Constitutional government was postponed. Party ministries, such as the Ministries of Information, Social Affairs, Overseas Affairs, or Party Organization, functioned as part of the central administration and yet were in form under the Kuomintang, not the government. Party and government thus became indistinguishable.

But in this way the Kuomintang became a wing of the bureaucracy and lost its revolutionary mission. The earlier party supervision of local administration, its political work in the army, its special criminal courts to try counterrevolutionaries, all were reduced or abandoned. So also were the mass organizations of workers, peasants, youth, merchants, and women. These mass movements had mobilized popular support for the Northern Expedition, but the Nanking power-holders now looked askance at processions, demonstrations, and mass meetings. They discouraged student movements, looking back upon all these activities of the mid-twenties as useful tools to beat the warlords but no longer of value, now that power was theirs to organize for purposes of control. With this attitude the Kuomintang suffered an actual drop in numbers. By late 1929 its membership totaled barely 550,000 of whom 280,000 were military. Members in Shanghai were mainly officials or policemen.

Rights Recovery. Nationalism received its first expression after the unification of 1928 in the "rights recovery" movement.

This was an effort to wipe out the unequal treaties bit by bit. The Washington Conference in 1922 had provided for modifications in extraterritoriality and the customs tariff. By 1930 the Nanking government had secured treaties which placed many minor foreign nationalities under Chinese legal jurisdiction. New civil and criminal codes had been issued. The old Sino-Foreign Mixed Court at Shanghai had been abolished, although the major powers, Britain, the United States, France, and Japan, had not yet given up extraterritoriality. This promising beginning came to a halt when the Japanese aggression of 1931–32 gave both the Chinese and the other foreign powers a common interest in the preservation of the powers' legal position.

Similarly the new Nationalist government sought to realize the promise of the Washington Conference regarding tariff reform. Under the unequal treaties China had been prevented from protecting her native industries or taxing foreign trade for revenue beyond nominal rates of about 5 percent. Most of the available customs revenue had become earmarked to pay foreign loans and indemnities. After 1911 the customs duties had been collected, in effect, for an international commission of bankers. The Nanking government at once moved to recover tariff autonomy and by 1930 had done so. Boxer indemnity payments by that time had also been largely remitted by the powers, on the understanding in the cases of Britain and the United States that the sums due would continue to be made available by China mainly for educational purposes.

The foreign concessions which had been the embodiment of the unequal treaties began to return to Chinese sovereignty. By the outbreak of the war with Japan in 1937 the maximum of thirty-three concession areas leased to foreign powers had been reduced to thirteen, in addition to the continuing International Settlements at Shanghai and Amoy. The rights of the foreign powers to station troops and warships in China and navigate her inland waters still persisted. But this was mainly because they had become measures of international opposition to Japanese encroachment. In general the Nanking government had begun to satisfy the demands of Chinese nationalism for the assertion of Chinese sovereignty and international equality. By 1937 the chief impairment of China's national independence came not from the unequal treaties (which were finally abolished in 1943) but from Japan.

10 Problems of National Development Under the Kuomintang

History is regularly colored by the age-old rule that any regime stands condemned by its successor. Nanking said little in favor of Yuan Shih-k'ai and the warlords. Today in the People's Republic, the Kuomintang era is seen as a dark age, the acme of feudal backwardness, imperialist aggression, and social evils. Yet in the long course of China's struggle for modernity, the Nanking decade began as the time of greatest promise since 1912. Let us view it for itself, as an interlude between the earlier evil of warlordism and the later evil of Japanese invasion.

The most poignant feature of the Nanking period as we look back at it is the superficiality of China's modernization up to that time. The modern China with which we Americans then had contact was a thin veneer spread lightly over the surface of an ancient civilization. Beneath it the old China still endured, in the peasant villages of half a continent. But it was cut off from us by barriers of language, material standards, and social taboos. Americans had no direct contact with the profuse remnants of this old culture. Our knowledge of it was mediated through modern China, which included the educated minority of the people, the routes of rail and steamship communication, books and newspapers in the modernized language, the new conceptions and interests assimilated from the West, the needs and techniques of a modern state. All this agglomeration of modern life in China — financiers, students, urban proletariat, ricksha coolies (a new profession), and trained soldiers — were participants in the new society which represented on Chinese soil the new world culture of literacy, telecommunications, factory industry, world markets, and mass movements. But beneath and behind this new China whose life interpenetrated with ours abroad lay the old Chinese society, rooted in an alien cultural tradition, which Westerners, and often the modern Chinese, failed to understand.

Our failure in understanding sprang partly from our mistaking the modern veneer of China for the whole of Chinese life. This was particularly easy because the modernized top stratum of Chinese society — the moneyed, official, and literate classes — almost monopolized the machinery of power. The government, the banking structure, education and the press, the bureaucracy, were dominated by the new generation, many of whom indeed knew English and could the more easily deal with China's alien problems in a Western way.

It was deceptively easy during this generation for a new class of Chinese scholars, merchants, and officials to use foreign techniques — financial, military, and ideological — in order to erect a modern Chinese nation on the ruins of the old Chinese society. Yet how superficial a thing this new nation was may be seen in a few statistics. In mileage of highways, China (78,850 miles in 1943) was about the size of Spain (77,574 miles in 1941). In mileage of steam railroads, China in 1942 (12,036 miles including Manchuria) was smaller than Illinois (12,967 miles) or Italy (14,384 miles). In cotton spindles China was also about the size of Italy. The telegraph lines at the disposal of an administration governing in China (59,275 miles in 1943) exceeded those available in Italy (41,354 miles in 1938) but were less than a third of those in France (229,000 miles in 1937). If we turn to less material matters, the total of 1,163,116 students in secondary schools in China (population say 450 million) hardly exceeded the total of 1,077,000 students in high schools in the two states of Illinois and New York (population roughly 23 million).

However we look at it, Kuomintang China in its equipment and modern plant was a small show. In industrial production it was smaller than Belgium, in air and sea power negligible, in the gadgets and equipment of American life not as big as a middle western state. Yet this small and relatively insignificant modern state was spread out over the protean body of a vigorous people in a vast and ancient land. Nanking's problems were therefore formidable from the start. Progress was greatest in the treaty ports, in transport, urban industry, and public finance, and least in the great agrarian sector among the peasant villages where most of the people lived.

The Modern Sector: Transport and Industry

Lack of transport was one major obstacle to agrarian development. Once a Chinese farmer had his crop, he could usually offer it for sale only within the region he could reach by carrying it on a pole or wheelbarrow. Where the United States had one mile of highway for each square mile of area, China had perhaps seventy feet — transportation was by paths, not roads. Manpower transport was the norm. Animals were in the minority. One estimate was that three fifths of all farm produce was sold locally or at nearby villages, while another investigator concluded that, even so, transportation accounted for the great part of marketing costs. Consequently every locality had to be largely self-sufficient. It seldom could specialize in production or count on outside help in time of shortage. The farmer had to sell to the merchant at hand and could not bargain in a wide market nor store his produce to await a higher price.

The major means of transport in Central and South China was still the ancient system of waterways, which make the great Yangtze River still the lifeline of the country. The old China was not able to defend herself on these routes, and the opening of China had begun with the British and American steamship invasion of the junk trade along the coasts and up the Yangtze. Foreign treaty rights of inland navigation gave British firms like Jardine Matheson and Company for a time almost a monopoly of modern waterborne commerce. Even as late as 1936 two fifths of the steam tonnage in China's domestic coastal and river trade was still under the British flag. Chinese vessels carried less of this domestic trade than did those flying the Union Jack.

Railways had been delayed as long as possible because officials of the Manchu period were fully aware of their strategic importance and wanted them, when built, to be under Chinese control. The first railroad, from Shanghai to Wusung, was proposed in 1865, constructed by foreign merchants in 1876, purchased and destroyed by Chinese authorities in 1878. By 1894 China had only 195 miles of railroad in the whole country. After the imperialist powers' scramble for concessions in 1898, this mileage was increased to 2700 by 1903 and 5800 by 1911. The decade before the Revolution saw the completion of the network from Shanghai to Nanking and thence to Tientsin and Peking and the parallel line on the west from Hankow to Peking, which provided two main north-south arteries north of the Yangtze. The first Chinese-built line had also been started along the southern border of Inner Mongolia, west from Peking. A beginning had been made on the Lunghai Railroad, the main east-west line just south of the Yellow River (see map p. 144).

Problems of National Development

After 1911 the combination of warlord rivalry, foreign absorption in the World War, and the international bankers' consortium arrangements (which tended to act as a brake on the investment both of Japanese and other foreign capital), all contributed to the retardation of railroad development. By 1926 the total mileage in China including Manchuria was only 7683 and by 1935 it was still under 10,000 miles. Railway construction in North China was far ahead of South China, yet it was equally far behind the railroad development in Manchuria. The railway accompanied the expansion of the frontier of Chinese settlement into Manchuria more easily than it could be introduced into the crowded countryside and rough terrain of South China. As a result, more than a third of all China's railways were in Manchuria, serving less than one tenth of China's population. (By 1945 Japan's heavy investment in Manchukuo's strategic and economic rail network made the total mileage roughly equal to that in China proper.)

The history of Chinese railroad construction suggests that it was retarded by the relative adequacy of the water transport network and, specifically, by lack of capital for investment. Provincial gentry demanded control over railroad construction before the Revolution of 1911 and put forward projects in fourteen provinces, but were unable to mobilize the requisite capital. The Nationalist government program after 1928 was stalemated by the patriotic aversion to foreign financial control and the foreign hesitation to invest without more definite security. In the end foreign firms were asked to finance the foreign-built equipment for new roads while Chinese sources financed the local building costs. Foreign loans, which had been in default, were refinanced and a new period of growth was just beginning when Japan struck. The major achievement of the Nationalist government in preparation for its struggle against Japan was to complete the Canton-Hankow

Railway, connecting the Yangtze with Hong Kong, and build an east-west (Chekiang-Kiangsi) line from Shanghai south of the Yangtze westward to meet the Canton-Hankow line.

Thus the railway in crowded China has not played the role for which it gained fame in the wide open spaces of the American West. Unable to supplant the established water routes, it did not precipitate a commercialization of agriculture nor did it markedly stimulate industrialization, except in the most modern economic region, Manchuria.

Industry. As a power resource for industry, China's coal reserves were conservatively estimated during the Nationalist period at 240 billion tons, three-quarters bituminous and one-quarter anthracite, with coking coal available in several places. This made China's reserves perhaps the fourth largest in the world, comparable to those of Germany and surpassed only by Canada, the United States, and the USSR. China's iron resources were variously estimated, by pessimists and optimists. The higher estimates placed them at between 1.4 and 1.8 billion tons of iron ore, of which three fifths were in Manchuria. This would make China's reserves comparable in quantity to those of the Lake Superior district in the United States or about half those of European Russia. But in quality China's ores seemed generally low-grade.

The use of coal and iron by heavy industry in China had been impeded by problems of politics, management, and capitalization. An industrial complex using coal and iron was inaugurated by Chang Chih-tung in Central China near Wuhan in the 1890's. British interests developed the Kailan coal mines north of Tientsin. But the chief industrial development was left for the Japanese in the Mukden region of Manchuria.

While Manchuria (called by Chinese "the Northeast") was unquestionably a part of China, inhabited over 95 percent by Chinese people, it was very different indeed from the more settled regions south of the Great Wall. Except for the Chinese pale south of Mukden, it had remained in large part a Manchu preserve down to the late nineteenth century and therefore became a focus of rivalry among Russia, Japan, and China. As an undeveloped area Manchuria profited by its low density of population. Its 500,000 square miles (including Jehol, the mountainous province north of Peking) are one quarter the size of China proper, yet the population as estimated in 1900 was only 17 million. Its subsequent rapid growth was aided by migration of Chinese farm labor from North China.

When the Japanese grabbed Manchuria in 1931 and made it their puppet state of "Manchukuo," it accounted for one fifth of all China's trade. The trade in soy beans and Japanese coal and iron exports had made Dairen the second port to Shanghai. This was only a beginning. The Japanese rapidly developed a communications network, reformed the currency, and pushed industrialization for strategic purposes. In the fourteen years of their occupation, they invested something like US $2 billion, a large amount considering Japan's resources. Manchuria acquired some 60,000 miles of roads in addition to about 6000 miles of railway. Dairen, Changchun (Hsin-king), and Mukden all became big cities. Coal production reached 30 million tons a year. The steel works at Anshan near Mukden could produce 2 million tons of pig iron and 1.5 million tons of steel. On the basis of an efficient coal and iron combine, great factories arose in Mukden where machinery, chemicals, automobiles, and even aircraft were produced. As an industrial base Manchuria under Japanese exploitation outstripped all the rest of China put together.

Meanwhile in China proper, textiles and light industries had concentrated in Shanghai and a few other treaty ports like Tientsin and the Yangtze cities. Here again, foreign and Chinese finance and entrepreneurship combined with cheap Chinese labor to produce a mixed Sino-foreign management of the modern economy, with "semi-colonial" features. The cotton mills, silk filatures, small shipyards, cement works, canneries, and cigarette factories of Kuomintang China did not add up to a heavy industrial base. Machines to make machines were still lacking. The nearest thing to the contemporary Soviet, German, and Japanese economic plans was a program for developing arsenals and military production under Nazi tutelage.

Banking and Fiscal Policy

China's old-style "native" banks had been local institutions, usually partnerships, which existed for the purpose of handling money — lending, saving, transmitting, or exchanging it — but not for purposes of productive investment. Although organized in guilds, the native banks were decentralized and conducted a form of small private business, mainly in supporting small merchants with unsecured personal loans. Countrywide remittances had been handled by the famous Shansi banks and their many branches. But after 1911 these traditional institutions proved inadequate. The native banks generally had depended on methods of personal contact under the wing of official patronage instead of modern legal forms, and had profited by speculation rather than investment. Their financial resources were inadequate to serve a growing economy.

The second element in the financial structure of Kuomintang China was the foreign banks that had grown up in the treaty ports under the protection of extraterritoriality to finance foreign trade and handle foreign exchange. By 1936 there were some thirty-three foreign banks in China, many of which had issued their own bank notes. The most important of them historically was the Hongkong and Shanghai Banking

Corporation, established in 1864 with a capital of Hongkong (HK) $2.5 million. By the 1930's its paid-up capital was HK $20 million with a reserve of HK $100 million and assets of HK $1 billion. Until 1927 the foreign banks had dominated the Chinese financial scene not only because they financed foreign trade and after 1911 held the official funds derived from the Chinese Maritime Customs and other sources to pay off foreign debts and indemnities, but also because they served as repositories of the private funds of politicians and militarists. Fundamentally, their position rested on their monopoly of foreign exchange and international transactions. At times they held as much as half the silver stocks in Shanghai.

Under the Kuomintang after 1927 the modern government banks led the way in modernization. This long and arduous process of fiscal reform included the introduction of new credit instruments and new business habits. It went back to 1905 when the Manchu government had finally opened a Board of Revenue Bank to issue notes and conduct modern central banking operations. This early institution became the Bank of China in 1913. Its chief competitor was the official Bank of Communications set up in 1907. During the warlord period provincial banks were also established on modern lines, often issuing great quantities of rapidly depreciating bank notes. By 1926 the total of modern government, provincial, and private banks had grown to 102 institutions, most of them mercantile in character and dealing in short-term liabilities rather than long-term investments. As part of their chief business these modern banks had begun to finance the government both by issuing loans and by direct advances.

The Kuomintang had begun in Canton in 1924 by setting up the Central Bank of China to finance the Nationalist revolution. T. V. Soong was the first manager. It was reorganized in Shanghai in 1928 to act as a central bank of issue and a government treasury. In the same year the Bank of China was reorganized in order to make it dominant in the business of foreign exchange. The Bank of China proceeded to handle about half of all the foreign business done by modern Chinese banks, although its functions were never entirely differentiated from those of the Central Bank of China. The Bank of Communications, also reorganized in 1928, was intended to foster the growth of transportation and industry but failed to develop as an industrial bank. The Farmers Bank of China was established in 1933 to facilitate agricultural credit, and set up its branches in the wake of the military campaigns against the Communists. These four government banks all issued bank notes, and the functions performed by a single central government bank in most European countries were distributed among them. The flow of silver funds to the treaty ports led to a heavy concentration of capital in Shanghai and a consequent deflation in the rural economy. By 1935 the four government banks had two fifths of the total capital and reserves of all the modern Chinese banks and more than half of the total deposits.

Thus in its first years the Nanking government, led by T. V. Soong as Minister of Finance until 1933, had succeeded in creating a government banking mechanism which greatly aided its program of unification. The readjustment of internal loans and external debts, reforms of taxation, and the suppression of the tael (the old unit of account) in 1933 were all aspects of a program whereby the modern sector of the economy was brought increasingly under the financial domination of the central government. By 1937 there was a marked concentration of the national capital resources under government influence, which could pave the way for government control of credit. The monetary reform of November 1935, with the support of Britain and the United States, was a final essential step in creating the modern banking structure. The American silver-buying program had already exacerbated the depression in China and was sucking out her currency in a most disastrous manner. This reform now nationalized all the old silver currency in China, thus taking it out of circulation, and substituted a managed currency. The foreign banks, even with extraterritoriality, were put in a position of "necessary cooperation" with the Chinese government. The latter was now able to unify and administer the financial reserves which it held against note issue. These reserves were gradually changed from silver into foreign exchange. The effort was to nationalize control of foreign exchange and build a national banking system independent of foreign powers. The notes of the four government banks were substituted for silver and other notes. In 1936–37 there was still no inflation.

This modernization of Chinese banking entailed the development of branch banking, interbank cooperation, long-term financing of industry, and the organization of bankers' associations (beginning with the Shanghai Bankers' Association in 1917).

But it must be admitted that this modernization was most rapid on the fringe of China where the money economy centered, in the treaty ports. For four fifths of the people the greater problem was agricultural credit and how the government or the modern banks could take the place of the rural moneylender. Some city banks attempted to counter the preference for financing treaty-port activities and tried to channel bank credit into rural areas through credit cooperatives. This had been aided by the China International Famine Relief Commission, which by 1927 had set up more than 500 cooperative credit associations in the province around Peking. In 1937 the government organized the Agricultural Credit Administration. Many expedients were tried. But the tendency was to use rural bank credit for seasonal short-term needs, in the same way as the loans of old-style usurers, not for long-term productive investment. Moreover, the official class who controlled bank credit flowing through government channels had many common ties at the local level with the landlord moneylenders.

Public Finance. The halfway nature of the Nationalist regime was nowhere more evident than in its fiscal policies. The central government from the first renounced its claim to the land tax, the chief potential source of revenue, and left it for provincial administrations to exploit. Instead, Nanking financed its regime by taxing the trade and industry of the modern sector of the economy, thus living off that very sector that it should have tried by all means to develop.

About 50 percent of the revenue came from the Maritime Customs (as compared with about 1 percent in the United States). The second source was consolidated excise taxes on consumer staples like tobacco, kerosene, and flour, and the government salt monopoly. This was regressive taxation, reducing the purchasing power of the masses at the lower income levels. The ancient tradition of bureaucratic revenue-grabbing still continued, for example, in the form of export duties which penalized native industry instead of subsidizing its development.

In this context, the important fiscal reforms led by T. V. Soong remained superficial and indeed took on an ambiguous air. The *likin* tax on local trade was finally abolished along with the intricate tael system, and the currency was unified. But it proved impossible to install an effective budget system or keep military expenditures anywhere within bounds. Constant deficits were met by borrowing about 25 percent of the sums expended from the four government banks, which in turn issued bonds on the domestic market. Debt payments to domestic bondholders soon exceeded those to foreigners, which had been extensive, and the service of these debts took a third of the government expenditures.

The net result was to tax the consumption goods of the poor

in order to pay interest to the rich bondholders, many of whom were Nanking bureaucrats. Productive investment at home and capital loans from abroad were both discouraged by these anti-development policies. The Nanking decade probably saw continued stagnation in the agrarian economy, with no appreciable increase of production. This was accompanied, moreover, by a stultifying growth of "bureaucratic capitalism," that is, domination of industry and finance by officials and political cliques who feathered their private nests by manipulating government monopolies, finances, development schemes, and agencies.

As a result of these aims and practices in the immemorial tradition of *sheng-kuan fa-ts'ai,* "become an official and get rich," the modernizers at Nanking were unable to achieve a healthy and solvent fiscal regime, much less a breakthrough into a genuine process of self-sustaining reinvestment and industrialization. Their unified government banking structure was used not to provide cheap credit for purposes of economic growth, but to pay high interest rates (20 to 40 percent after allowance for discounts) to government bondholders, and to finance the very heavy military expenditures. Savings were thus channeled into current government use or private speculation, while the nation's capital resources were not mobilized, even for military purposes.

Local Government

Local administration under the Kuomintang spread downward from the hsien (county or district). Under the Manchus there had been about 1400, under Nanking there were now about 2000, of these units. It was here that the Nationalist regime faced the central task of any Chinese government, how to govern a rural society from an urban base.

In imperial times the district magistrate, a seventh-rank

231

official, had borne comprehensive responsibilities, in meeting which he had been heavily dependent on the cooperation of the local elite or gentry. After the maintenance of order and necessary public works and ritual observances, his chief task was to collect the revenue: land tax, grain levies, salt revenue, customs duties, and miscellaneous duties including taxes on goods in transit. Only a small fraction of this revenue which the official collectors secured from the villages ever reached Peking. From the collections received in each provincial treasury, regular quotas went to the capital annually, and transfers were made to other provinces as Peking might require. But Peking received no more than a proportion, perhaps a quarter, of the reported tax collection; and the collection reported was no more than a part, possibly one quarter, of the revenue actually received. In short, the officials lived on their take. The magistrate was a tax-farmer who had to support himself, his collectors and personal staff, and his relatives out of the public funds passing through his hands. As times grew harder in the nineteenth century, influential gentry-landlord households could usually make better deals with the collectors, small households therefore often sought their protection, and the big gentry thus wound up as unauthorized tax-farmers themselves, collecting and turning in the taxes of commoners while taking a commission. Big landlord families might also set up bursaries to collect their rents from tenants and get the help of the local magistrate's underlings in coercing rent-defaulters. Thus the local elite and local officials joined forces to squeeze rents and taxes out of the villages, with no benefit to the government treasury and increasing damage to its image among the populace.

A similar enlargement of the gentry role in maintaining order had occurred during the suppression of the mid-century rebellions: the local elite then took the initiative to mobilize militia, first as officially authorized local defense forces and then, at a higher level of militarization, as mobile battalions of professional mercenaries or "braves" who were organized in striking forces personally recruited, trained, and led by scholar-official commanders. Tseng Kuo-fan had been only the most famous of this class of gentry-military. Their rise broke the central government's monopoly of arms and contributed to the regionalism of the late nineteenth century.

What happened to the gentry class in the twentieth century? After the ancient examination system was abolished in 1905, official degree-holders were no longer produced, while the new secondary school and college graduates flocked into city life. Absentee landlordism presumably grew and the educated elite became diversified, fragmented, and probably fewer in the countryside. Under the warlords local administration deteriorated along with peasant livelihood. The landed ruling class, no longer the top elite of the country, no longer indoctrinated in Confucian ideals of community leadership, became even more narrowly self-seeking. Secret societies like the Red Spears in Shantung or the Society of Brothers and Elders (Ko Lao Hui) in Szechwan became tools of the local families of property, helping to protect them against both popular disorder and official exaction. Organized in a network of branches, each with its secretariat, treasury, and directorate capable of mobilizing the clandestine brotherhood, such agencies could help the big family lineages dominate the villages in a rich enclave like the Chengtu plain. For a secret society had its executive arm in the person of professional thugs, as well as its income from the protection of illicit activities — gambling houses, brothels, opium dens, or illegal markets where government taxes were evaded. The combination of this darker side with the protection of respectable rank and file members in their daily pursuits, and with clandestine leadership by some of the wealthiest landlords and officials, was reminiscent of the bossism and rackets of a Western city.

Modern Centralism. When the Kuomintang inherited the central government, it was unlike its imperial predecessor in that it possessed modern facilities for bringing its control down to the village level. The telephone and telegraph, motor roads and bus routes, linking local areas with the capital gave Nanking and later Chungking the means of conveying their orders at once to the smallest hamlet. The new Nationalist government became a center for the spread of reform to the villages through agricultural extension, crop improvement, and other programs. Simultaneously it tried to choke off peasant-based rebellion by an intensified police control. But since it wanted to avoid violent social change, it was foredoomed to govern from the top down. Trained modern personnel were lacking to build local self-government up to the provincial level; moreover such an effort might open the door to popular agitation and dissident movements; so Nanking sought to build its central administration down through the provinces to the village level.

In the place of the magistrates and gentry of imperial times, the new administrators from Nanking tried to spread their reforms, and the police organized their anti-Communist net, radiating from the capital. Both came further into the local scene than had been the custom under the empire. Where the Emperor had appointed the hsien magistrate but left him under the provincial authorities, the central government now developed direct contact with him. Magistrates were a chief element among the trainees brought to the capital for indoctrination in Chiang Kai-shek's Central Training Corps. Meanwhile the central government established local administrative organs in charge of military, customs, transportation, or other matters, independent of the regular structure of district government. The Kuomintang set up its local cells under central party control, parallel to the official system. Below the hsien (now translated "county") were new levels of districts and subdistricts including groups of towns and villages, and still smaller divisions below them, leading down to the groups of households which formed the revived *pao-chia* system: families organized in units for mutual guarantee, each unit responsible for the acts of all the others — a surveillance system which set neighbor to spy upon neighbor and kith upon kin. (Ideally, one hundred families formed a *chia* and ten *chia* formed a *pao*.)

The Kuomintang theory was that through this hierarchy of subunits the government could train the people during the period of political tutelage to prepare them for local autonomy. In 1939 the Nationalist government issued a new statute to reorganize local government. Families were to be grouped more flexibly, on community lines, to form *chia* and *pao*. Villages and towns were now to become incorporated legal persons able to operate their own local administrations. Each *pao* should form an assembly and elect two representatives, who would in turn function in a village or town assembly to assist the head of the village or town government, who would himself be elected.

The result of this effort to inculcate democracy was disappointing. Wartime circumstances were highly unpropitious. The reform was confined to the political sphere, unattended by change in the local social and economic structure. On paper the law of 1939 was put into effect in nearly all the districts in Free China. Yet in the same period the military and police authorities dominated the scene. There is little record of the election process taking hold as a factor for active change.

The Rural Problem

Looking back on the Nanking decade, we can see that, ideally, the new government should have attacked the key problem of agricultural production, which gave the Chinese people their living, by inaugurating programs to improve farm technology.

Nanking early sought technical aid from the League of Nations for public health work, and from this contact was stimulated to set up in 1933 the National Economic Council as an advisory body to coordinate efforts at development. Many fine blueprints were offered in the 1930's and 1940's for China's economic regeneration. Land reclamation, reforestation, water conservancy, hydropower, crop and animal breeding, better tools, improved land use, pest control, crop storage facilities, land redistribution, rent reduction, light and heavy industrialization, rural industry and cooperatives, cheaper farm credit, mass education, public health, transportation, law and order — all had their advocates and their obvious rationale. The first and foremost object of all such efforts was to increase the productivity of the farmer. This was the crux of China's modernization effort but the government was unable to get at it. To tackle a diffused and multifarious set of interrelated problems no comprehensive plan was ever devised, much less given effect. The Nanking decade was the time for Western aid to China's vigorous economic growth. But America was absorbed in the Depression and New Deal. Kuomintang China in these years made halting and spotty progress along many lines, to no particular end.

Poverty as a Social Institution. The brilliant social anthropologist Fei Hsiao-t'ung described the quagmire of old agricultural conditions and practices as a "closed economy" or "economy of scarcity." We might also call it an economy of struggle for physical survival. Fei pointed to the social attitudes and values that maintained the inertia of this long established low-level man-power economy, perpetuated by the Chinese emphasis upon the virtue of contentment and limitation of wants. This age-old acceptance of the institutionalized penury of peasant life, for want of any alternative, was a means by which the individual could fit himself into his kinship group, sustain his lot in life, and actually achieve a high degree of "social integra-

236

tion" of himself in the community. Indeed the narrow horizon, low efficiency, poor diet, and chronic diseases of the Chinese peasant, which struck the eye of the modern investigator, were always an integral part of the old society, just as they were part of premodern society in Europe. One could expect the Chinese peasant, like his European predecessor, to join eventually in an effort to better himself. But one could not expect this process to create any less disorder, violence, and bloodshed than it did in Europe.

Not only did the old farm economy produce a relatively small surplus. The surplus, once produced, was poorly distributed — little or none of it could be invested in improvements. Here again an appreciation of Chinese social values, of the expectations and assumptions in a farmer's mind, is necessary to any understanding of how the product of the land was distributed. As already noted, landholding relationships in China were generally complex; tenantry, sharecropping, and various forms and degrees of indebtedness were intermixed. The simple terms, rent and taxation, included a great variety of payments, exactions, and charges by which the farmer was separated from his surplus, if not his actual subsistence. Landlordism was generally small-scale and there were few large baronial estates. Probably the majority of peasants were independent landowners, not tenants at all. Yet they were handicapped by the minuscule size of their holdings and by their lack of capital and were consequently vulnerable in time of stringency vis-à-vis the small-scale landlord moneylender with his extra, though meager, resources. One careful American expert concluded that rents in China took from 45 to 60 percent of the crop, not counting other payments. Indebtedness was endemic, but probably half or more of farm loans were for unproductive purposes, to buy food or repay debts, or to meet the compelling social obligation of ceremonial display and hospitality on occasions of marriage and death.

Only the firmest code of social conduct could have kept this old system operating, could have induced the peasant to make his rent, tax, and interest payments, and acquiesce in perpetual indebtedness and poverty. Plainly the sanctity of title to landed property, backed by the power of the landlord-official class, was one potent factor. But concern for social display and for filial piety, for an honest name and avoidance of conflict with the law, were other factors, to say nothing of ignorance born of illiteracy, and the ancient virtue of contentment.

Rural Reconstruction. In the early 1930's the lack of large-scale and effective central government aid for the villages was highlighted by a growing private interest in the reconstruction of village economy. Several programs were set going in selected areas where the problems of peasant life were studied and methods developed for the promotion of literacy and improvement of living standards. In many of these efforts, as J. C. Thomson, Jr., has shown, Christian missionaries had led the way. Best known to Westerners was the experiment financed partly by the Rockefeller Foundation at Ting-hsien in North China under the leadership of the dynamic Dr. Y. C. James Yen. Another model county was developed by the government near Nanking, and a pioneer effort of this type was also made by the scholar Liang Sou-ming in Shantung. Fundamentally, these were all reform efforts which tried to give the peasantry some education for citizenship, some public health service, and scientific improvements as in crop and animal breeding.

The movement for rural reconstruction discovered very soon that the problems of economic livelihood were deeply imbedded in social and political institutions. It became plain that a higher standard of living was a prerequisite for any democratic processes of a Western type. Improvements in living standards in turn depended upon social change. For example, the scientific reforms attempted at Ting-hsien needed financial support greater than the peasantry could provide, peasant organizations in support of local improvements required official permission, the improvement of crops raised questions of rent and land tenure, an increase of literacy was likely to make the populace more vocal in the pressing of grievances.

In short, any real change in one aspect of the old order on the land implied fundamental changes in the whole system. The problems of the Chinese countryside were so far-reaching and the pressure for change so great that reforms were always likely to set off a chain reaction toward revolt.

11 Authoritarianism and Liberalism during the War of Resistance

The Kuomintang Response to Japanese Aggression

One long-term factor in the Chinese Communist rise to power was Japan's continuous effort at military conquest, which roused the Chinese people for patriotic political action but weakened the Nationalist government's capacity to lead them in other than military ways.

Japan's attack, from 1931 on, obliged the Kuomintang to continue militarizing in self-defense. Its resources went into its armies, its leadership into the hands of a Generalissimo, its policies became more defensive and militaristic — "unify before resisting" rather than "unify by resisting." During the long years of warfare Whampoa generals and party organizers came to dominate its councils and control its actions as they might not otherwise have done.

The Japanese invasion of China in 1937, like the subsequent effort of the Nationalist government to quell the Communist rebellion, was dominated strategically by the problem of transport. In each case the higher striking power of modernized armies could be made effective only over a transportation network. So the Japanese campaign in China during its first year and a half was a railroad campaign. The Japanese first brought their troops in over the Peiping-Mukden line and advanced from Tientsin southward and from Peiping both south and west along the main trunk lines. They overran both Shantung and Shansi provinces. They moved from Shanghai up the railway to Nanking and then up the Yangtze to Wuhan.

Japan's war machine, conquering cities with torture and rapine, burning villages, bombing Free China, roused the student youth and the peasant populace for a movement of resist ance and national survival which went far beyond the military sphere. Millions of persons were displaced, some 14 million men conscripted, families were broken up, vested interests destroyed — the social order over wide areas was thoroughly disrupted. The student youth and the peasant populace were both subjected to violent social changes and so prepared for revolutionary programs of action.

The immediate underlying factor in the Communist rise to power was the Kuomintang's failure to lead the country in a program of creative action. Free China had the beginnings in men and ideas. The rural reconstruction movement of James Yen, the "little teacher" movement of H. C. T'ao, the Industrial Cooperatives, the plants of the National Resources Commission, the trained workers of the Public Health Administration, the army medical corps (energized by a Peiping physiology professor, Dr. Robert Lim), all these and a hundred other groups and agencies existed in Free China. They were the product of modernization through contact with the liberal West, and formed a reservoir of trained talent and public-spirited citizens, eager to participate in their country's reconstruction. But the Nationalist government lacked the vision to mobilize and lead them. Intent on holding power, its leaders distrusted the enthusiasm of private agencies and individuals.

In Chiang Kai-shek the government had a military leader who met the demands both of ancient tradition and of warlord politics. Born in 1887 in a gentry family near Ningpo, Chiang had entered China's first military academy at Paoting near Peking in 1906 and then spent four years at a military college in Tokyo. A convert of Sun Yat-sen's, he participated in the revolutionary efforts of 1911 and 1913. During the first World War he led an obscure existence as a small broker in Shanghai. His career really began when Sun sent him to Moscow in 1923. He provided the Nationalist movement, through his political astuteness and ruthless determination, with a strong man who could deal with and outdo the warlords. In this respect he was the traditional hero who founds a dynasty by skill and violence. At the same time, however, Chiang Kai-shek was a party member, austerely and fervently devoted to the cause of Chinese Nationalism, which he came to regard as indistinguishable from his own career. After sharing power in the early 1930's with Wang Ching-wei and other party stalwarts senior to him, Chiang had eventually emerged as the one indispensable man. Japan's aggressions combined with Nanking's domestic problem of suppressing warlord and Communist armies to make him essential. Chiang has been aptly characterized as a "military politician," supremely capable of holding power in a country where armies and generals, not electorates, provide the final sanction.

In the end the Generalissimo's power rested on a tripod of army, party, and government. Surviving graduates of the first classes at the Whampoa Military Academy formed a "Whampoa clique" of generals personally loyal to him, which dominated China's new armies. In 1939 he became permanent

Party Leader. Any office he held was the point of government decision-making. All this reflected not merely Chiang's ability but even more the demand of the Chinese political scene for personal rule by a modernized Son of Heaven.

Echoes of Confucianism. The growth of political controls through local gendarmerie, secret police, press censorship, subsidizing of education, the *pao-chia,* and other devices, all supervised by the local party office, was accompanied in Kuomintang China by a Confucian revival. This doctrinal metamorphosis began by stressing the principle of nationalism and from it going back to the national heritage to find political doctrines which would support central power. Even as commandant at Whampoa in 1924 Chiang Kai-shek had taken as his model the victor over the Taipings, Tseng Kuo-fan. As Mary Wright has shown in her study of the post-Taiping Restoration, the example of revived Confucian government in the 1860's had a fatal fascination for the Kuomintang leaders of the 1930's, even though the Restoration had failed to preserve that traditional Confucian order which by its nature could never have modernized. The fact was that Nanking's new leaders had not been able to modernize their own thinking. Culture-bound, they sought intellectual sanction for a new stability in the classical doctrine — rule by leaders of impeccable moral virtue, obedience by a people disciplined in personal loyalty and filial piety.

By 1934 the state cult of Confucius was nominally revived. In the same year Chiang launched his New Life Movement to instill in his people a new social consciousness and martial spirit through a revival of the ancient moral virtues: proper behavior according to status, right conduct, integrity, and the sense of shame. Since these classical concepts were now vague at best, 96 specific rules applied them to the categories of food, clothing, shelter, and action: for example, do not eat noisily, correct your posture, stop smoking, keep your gown buttoned, do not spit, kill rats and flies, be prompt, use native products. Through a nationwide network of some 1300 local associations, the movement sought paternalistically to lead each individual to practice orderliness and cleanliness. Many other activities proliferated under it in 1934–1937. Some of them were easy to ridicule but they represented nevertheless a direct attack on China's problem of social regeneration — in just the way that the commandant of a military academy might be expected to attempt it.

Chiang Kai-shek's thought was a syncretism derived from many sources: Tseng Kuo-fan's view of moral purpose as the arbiter of human affairs, Lenin's interpretation of imperialism, the Methodist piety of a practicing Christian, influences from Japan, Russia, America, and the Axis powers, all within the framework of a conservative nationalism. Much of this appears in the book that he published in Chinese, not for foreign consumption, in 1943, *China's Destiny*. This volume celebrated the abolition of the American and British unequal treaties in 1943 and became required reading for Free China's youth in the compulsory study of "party principles." It attributed China's national humiliation and other modern ills almost entirely to the unequal treaties. Foreign imperialists not merely aided but caused China's civil wars. Foreign courts in the concessions were even worse than unreformed Chinese courts. The treaties and treaty ports caused the spread of famine, stock market panics, the breakup of the family, selfishness, the use of narcotics, profit-seeking materialism, Chinese self-abasement, and the slavish copying of Western ways. While publishing this work to urge national revival by moral regeneration, Chiang also produced in 1943 a work restricted to official circles entitled *Chinese Economic Theory*. In it he derived from the ancient philosophers a sanction for the state control of economic life. Against Western free enterprise this work called for an anti-Marxist Confucian totalitarianism. It sought to direct

244

China's industrialization toward building a defense state, rather than toward mass welfare. Specifically, Chiang asserted that Western economic theory is unsuited to China and so he tried to reconstruct China's traditional economics by quoting the sages. This opened the door to several non-Western conceptions — for example, that land and labor are factors of production in China, but not capital.

The people's livelihood of Sun Yat-sen was now bracketed with national defense as the dual objective of state control of economic life. They constituted a single problem. The solution proposed for it was to conscript China's farmers onto collective farms where they would also be soldiers. If the masses were farmer-soldiers, China would be strong. In general, Chiang castigated the liberal tradition in economics as advocating government noninterference in the people's economic life. In China he believed the government should not only plan the people's livelihood but also control and restrict their wants, thus combining "benevolence" with "justice."

The revival of Confucianism was most actively promoted by Ch'en Li-fu, whose uncle had been Chiang Kai-shek's patron and who became Chiang's most loyal political organizer. Ch'en Li-fu had studied at the Pittsburgh School of Mines. He specialized in party personnel management, together with his elder brother, Ch'en Kuo-fu, the patriarch of the Central Political Institute for the training of civil servants. The Ch'en brothers led the "CC" clique which dominated the right wing of the Kuomintang. In general Ch'en Li-fu called for the fusion of Western technology and Confucian social values. "The spirit of Confucianism is the means of adjusting our culture to the modern age." He urged that the dicta of famous Confucian scholars be systematically arranged and explained to the people. "Confucianism belongs to no specific class." It is actually in keeping with Sun's Three Principles.

These ideas of Chiang and his henchman made no contribution to Chinese thought but had importance because they were held by the wielders of Kuomintang power. Modern-minded Chinese scholars could not find in their confused atavism any solution to the fundamental problems of China's adaptation to modern life. The right-wing authoritarianism of Chiang and Ch'en, though widely spread through school and party, lacked the intellectual vigor to gain the allegiance of thinking Chinese.

The New Militarism. Modern militarism, manifest in the growth of larger and larger armies, naturally supported authoritarianism. The officer corps trained under German advisers at the Central Military Academy at Nanking combined their patriotic sentiment with personal loyalty to the Generalissimo and had a new social status: for it could not be denied that military cadets were students, who after their graduation possessed a certain type of learning and deserved respect accordingly. In the 1940's the Chinese air cadets often came from the best families and universities, received a highly technical education, and after training in the United States had the status of returned students as well as soldiers. These young pilots of the nascent Chinese air force were idolized by Chinese youth and were an entirely new social phenomenon. The inertia of tradition, however, was evident in the gulf which separated them from their mechanics.

Needless to say, the fifteen long years of Japan's aggression, from 1931 to 1945, provided the need and the excuse for the growth of Chinese militarism. Eventually, in addition to the sanctions of patriotism, technical learning, and defense, the power of the new military class rested on the brute size of the military establishment. The millions of troops (Chungking claimed to have 5,000,000 mobilized at one time), with their half million officers, required thousands of military bureaucrats and all the institutions of bureaucracy. Militarism became an enormous vested interest. The gigantic Military

Affairs Commission with its congeries of subministries formed part of the real governing trinity: army, party, and civil administration. Being essentially an authoritarian institution, the army inhibited political democracy, even though, as in Japan, it provided a channel for upward social mobility.

Liberalism and Education

The scholars of Peking (Peiping) had represented a quite different tradition from the party dictatorship and militarism developing at Nanking. While not stemming from Western liberalism, which depends upon the supremacy of law to safeguard the individual in his rights of property and personal freedom, the Chinese tradition of humanism still offered certain rudiments upon which returned students from the West could try to build. The first was the ideal of the cultivated man (the "superior man" or *chün-tzu*), who through the centuries had trained himself to act correctly as a Confucian gentleman and scholar. His ideals of self-respect and propriety had been communicated to each individual farmer in national traits of politeness, concern for face, and the Chinese sense of responsibility. More important, the Confucian moral code stressed personal integrity in the pursuit of virtuous conduct, which meant that the civilized individual might be called upon to sacrifice himself for principle. With this self-discipline was associated reverence for education, which gave the learned man a responsibility not only to know the truth transmitted through Chinese literature, but also to speak out on public matters. The modern scholar continued to feel it a duty to advise the government.

In this framework the predecessor of the modern liberal was the Chinese scholar who courageously stood forth and denounced the evils of bureaucracy or tyranny. The censorate had been in fact an institution created to give learned men who were loyal officials the duty and opportunity of attacking political evils. More than one censor lost his life for it. Though in a different context, these brave scholars in Chinese history had corresponded to tribunes of the people and martyrs for personal faith in the West. Leaders of the modern student movement therefore had a native historical precedent to follow, even though it was the elitist tradition of the literate ruling class.

The modern liberal tradition in China stemmed directly from Peita (Peking National University) in the time of the May Fourth Movement. In the decade from 1917 to 1927 the spirit of criticism in scholarship and in politics flourished there with relative freedom from official control. Over the years the surge and conflict of new ideas found expression in vigorous journals of opinion. *The New Youth, The New Tide, The Modern Critic,* and *The Independent Critic* were forums of discussion. In the absence of lecture platforms, radio, or political rallies and campaigns, these journals gave men of scholarship and talent their opportunity to be heard.

Western missionary education in China also nurtured the new liberalism. Supported by Protestant constituencies mainly in the United States, Britain, and Canada, Christian education produced a great variety of schools in different parts of China which by degrees merged and developed into the Christian colleges. Before postwar reorganizations, these included the following Protestant universities: Cheeloo at Tsinan in Shantung, Yenching outside Peiping, St. John's at Shanghai, Lingnan near Canton, a trio of institutions at Hangchow, Soochow, and Shanghai, West China Union University at Chengtu in Szechwan, Nanking University and Ginling College for Women at Nanking, two institutions at Foochow, and a group of colleges forming Central China University at Wuhan. These institutions represented the cooperation of twenty-one Protestant societies and a dozen American universities. In 1936–37 their faculties totaled 652 persons including 466 Chinese; their student bodies, 6424. Chinese sources including tuition fees provided more than half their total income. Missionaries of the Catholic Church had more converts but fewer institutions of higher education, their leading universities being Fu-jen at Peiping and Aurora at Shanghai. Western missionary education was on a small scale but of wide influence.

Against this background one can understand why the old traditions and the Western example produced liberal individuals in modern China, but no liberal movement. Liberalism could not become institutionalized.

As one factor, the concept of freedom under law was not adequately developed. There was no real acknowledgment by those in power of the civil liberties and basic freedoms of speech and person, habeas corpus and jury trial, in short the supremacy of law — to which Americans are all too unconsciously accustomed. Inclusion of such guaranties in constitutions and law codes was but a first step on a long hard road. The liberally inclined individual did not enjoy the legal security of liberals in the West. Similarly there was no strong middle class of the Western type. Private property, like the individual himself, had little legal protection against an inveterately corrupt officialdom. Liberals in China generally lacked the security of private economic means which has sustained the Western liberal movement.

Lacking the defenses of law and property, the Chinese liberal found an uncertain security in the superior social status accorded the scholar. The fate of liberalism in China was therefore closely bound up with the fate of education.

The modernization of higher learning made great progress during the decade of uneasy peace from 1927 to 1937. Leading government universities like Peita and Tsing Hua at Peiping were able to dispense with foreign staff members and to set standards of scholarship in many fields superior to those of the Christian colleges. The fine new buildings in modernized Chinese architecture, the broad campuses, and the thousands of students in these new government universities dwarfed the missionary institutions. Their staffs belonged to a generation trained abroad. (By 1953, in the estimate of Y. C. Wang, at least 36,000 Chinese had studied in the United States.) The faculty of the wartime Southwest Associated University created at Kunming by the cooperation of Peita, Tsing Hua, and Nankai universities had more than 170 professors, out of 200 in all, who had received advanced training abroad. Of this 170, more than 100 had taken doctoral degrees in the United States.

The new Chinese scholarship was led by new agencies. The Geological Survey of China surveyed the natural resources and mapped the terrain of the country. Eventually, it and the other new institutions, such as those for research in Chinese architecture, the social sciences, or in various aspects of the physical sciences, became parts of China's modern national research academy, the Academia Sinica. Its dozen institutes, maintained on all too meager government funds, became leading centers of pure research in all the departments of learning.

In this period archaeological excavations uncovered the story of Peking man at Chou-k'ou-tien and found China's most ancient capital at Anyang. The palace of the Manchus was made into a national museum. Publications were made from their archives. With American help the new National Library of Peiping and the Peking Union Medical College set new standards of scientific technique and social service and stimulated, respectively, the development of other national libraries and of a national health administration. By the end of the decade the new scholarship was producing new critical editions and indexes to classical sources, and critical monographs with specific footnote references — both indexes and footnotes being modern additions to a scholarly tradition based on verbatim memory of the classics.

The Chinese scholars in the government-supported universities and research institutes had their counterparts in the Western-trained administrative staffs gathered at Nanking. They were able to build on the older parts of China's modern administration, like the Maritime Customs Service, the Post Office, and the Salt Revenue Administration, which had been inaugurated under foreign guidance. Recruiting of foreign personnel was stopped at the same time that training programs were developed for Chinese personnel.

In the 1930's, however, the new liberalism, centered in Peiping, had come under increasing pressure from the new bureaucracy at Nanking. Party agents were planted in the universities. Students who criticized the government were seized by police squads raiding their dormitories at dawn, and carted off to prison. Teachers and editors were intimidated.

Politics in Education. It was no accident that Japan began in 1937 by bombing Nankai University at Tientsin as a symbol of Chinese nationalism. But the Japanese bombings and the spectacular scorched-earth policy of the Chinese resistance were no more disastrous to the country than the undermining of liberal institutions and ideas which the war facilitated. The fine beginnings of the preceding decade came under wartime pressures, especially the twin evils of inflation and domination by political authorities.

When war came, most of the universities, in the coastal area, were either destroyed by the Japanese or abandoned by patriotic faculties and student bodies, who moved inland with the government. Institutions in Nanking and Wuhan took much of their equipment directly up the Yangtze. The Academia Sinica transported its unrivaled Sinological library via Indo-China to a village on the Yangtze in Szechwan. But the universities in Peiping suffered badly. Peita and Tsing Hua,

251

for example, moved in 1937 to a campus at Changsha which was soon bombed by the Japanese, necessitating a further removal by truck and on foot through the mountains to Kunming. There the French railway from Indo-China formed the only real link with the outer world during the first years of war, like the Burma Road at a later date.

In wartime, each institution leaned more heavily upon the central government. Meanwhile Ch'en Li-fu, Minister of Education from 1938 to 1945, presided over a wartime expansion of the university system. In 1936, there had been 108 institutions of higher education with 41,000 students. The war quickly reduced the total, but by 1941–42 there were 132 institutions with 57,000 students, and 145 by 1945. Yet after five years of war the purchasing power of the Chinese dollar was hardly more than 1 percent of what it had been in 1937. The educational system had no sooner expanded than it was left penniless.

Students and faculties survived mainly because the government rice allowances gave them something to eat. They had to sell or pawn books, clothes, and furniture in order to keep alive. The expansion of instruction, when training and equipment were lacking, was an educational inflation. From the political point of view, however, it brought a greater number of impoverished intellectuals under party influence.

The Kuomintang had always considered education to be a tool of the state. The political thinking of students was intimidated increasingly through the Kuomintang Youth Corps founded in 1938. Branches of the corps within every student body made it their business to exalt the official ideology and denounce deviant thought. Mass education was meanwhile discountenanced. As one example take the experience of Dr. T'ao Hsing-chih (Heng-chi Tao). After studying at the University of Illinois and with John Dewey at Columbia, T'ao had gone into rural education in China and helped develop the "little teacher" movement whereby school children became teachers to other illiterates. This literacy movement turned into a chain reaction, particularly during the united front of 1937–38 when the government was at Wuhan. Evidently it seemed like political dynamite. Ch'en Li-fu called T'ao in and offered him the presidency of an agricultural college. The "little teacher" movement was suppressed.

The Government's Loss of Moral Prestige

By the end of World War II the Nationalist government faced difficulties, including runaway inflation, which it lacked the resources, the methods, the personnel, and the will to overcome. The apparent wartime prosperity of some of China's farmers, during a decade which decimated the city salaried class, could not offset the overall disaster and disinvestment which warfare had brought upon the farm economy. The number of draft animals was seriously depleted over wide areas; the farms lost labor power, and the soil its necessary fertilizer. Manpower had been greatly depleted by conscription. Loss of men and animals reduced transport resources and impeded marketing and trade. The farmer's usual handicraft industries were depressed. Instead of raising modern cash crops like cotton and tobacco, he had to go back to cereals and subsistence farming. His standard of living suffered accordingly.

In retrospect it seems plain that the government at Nanking, as the first fruit of the Nationalist movement, had been caught between two forces. The one was aggressive Japanese militarism which sought to shatter its new unity and check all that it might accomplish in the building of a powerful Chinese state. The other force was that of a mass discontent which sought to remake the life of the Chinese people on the land.

Unhappily the very factors which gave Nanking its strength as a focus of nationalism seem to have prevented it from taking the leadership of the nascent mass revolution. For the spirit of patriotism had arisen first among the urban merchants and students who constituted the modern face of the traditional ruling class. Compradors, merchants, and bankers in the treaty ports used capital derived from the rents of the hinterland and the perquisites of old-style officials. Modern students who led the way in patriotism came necessarily from upper class backgrounds, rather than from the peasantry. China could not be remade in a day, and Sun Yat-sen's followers, after the overthrow of the imperial system and the warlords, concentrated on creating the superstructure of a new nation. In the long course of the revolution, Nanking represented the partial modernization of China's central government more than a broadening of its base.

By a more active rural program the Kuomintang could have competed against Communism. After expelling the Communists from Kiangsi in 1935 they had sought to make it a model province but were unable to finance and organize a dynamic peasant movement. Under the united front of 1937–38 through which the Communists were extending their influence, the Kuomintang now faced again the old alternative: whether to compete directly with the Communists by encouraging mass resistance through social revolution, or to fight on two fronts against foreign invasion and domestic revolt at the same time.

When the Nationalist government moved from the seacoast to the interior of Szechwan, there had been a corresponding shift in the nature of its support. The Shanghai bankers had been in the forefront of the Nationalist movement and had supported reform, though not revolution, in the countryside. But now the Szechwan landlords and militarists took their place. These landed magnates of the interior were conservatives of an earlier generation. In their part of China there had of course been no Japanese invasion and consequently no shattering of the local structure of authority, nor any rousing of the common people to organize in self-defense. They interpreted the wartime slogan of "Resistance and Reconstruction" to mean resistance to social change and consolidation of their position, while the Communists interpreted it to mean the acquisition of power through militant mass organization. Since the Nationalist government in its Szechwan base felt dependent upon the established order, it opposed a mass mobilization which would arm the peasantry.

To those who had seen the old China before the Kuomintang came to power and could recall the idealism, vigor, and efficiency of some of that party's early administrators, the evils which grew up within it during the Japanese war were hard to believe. The Nationalist government which in 1938 was forced into exile beyond the Yangtze gorges, among the mountains and paddy fields of Szechwan, had become a rallying point for the best talent of modern China, the first fruit of the new patriotism and technical training. Eight years later the leadership which returned down the river to Nanking and Shanghai in late 1945 was worn and demoralized. During exile in the mists of Szechwan the top personnel of the government had changed very little. Cabinet reshuffling had only brought the same faces to different windows. But by retaining personal power, the Kuomintang leaders had devitalized their organization. Politically they marked time while waiting for the war to end. The best men among them knew how to modernize China technologically. But they were unable to mobilize the back country in a continuing social revolution. The revolution consequently passed them by.

Wartime politics in China had some overtones of the passing of the Mandate of Heaven, modern style. Like the old imperial administration, the Kuomintang government, in spite of the expanded number of its officials and the greater mobility and fire power of its armed forces, was still a rather small organization for so large a country. Its grip therefore depended partly on its prestige; and one constant aim of its Chinese Communist opponents was to undermine its moral repute, through radio and press as well as by more ancient methods of rumor and propaganda. In this the Communists had the greatest help from the bad postwar record of the government itself.

Postwar Politics. The postwar take-over process, when carpet-bagging generals and politicians returned to the coastal provinces and Formosa, was as shameful a record of official looting as modern history has displayed. The inflation made official salaries shrink out of sight; graft took their place. But self-seeking and corruption were intensified by the officials' loss of confidence in the government's future. The result was a cynical *sauve qui peut.*

The government was thus obliged to shift from a reliance on its moral prestige to an increasing reliance on naked force. Faced with disaster, the whole regime relied on its organizers, as Chiang relied on the Ch'en brothers. Unfortunately the organizers were those who placed the fortunes of the regime above all other considerations, including those of principle. Men who believed in secret police, thought control, and suppression of opposition gained an ascendancy. This produced government action, like the punishment of critics, which antagonized formerly loyal elements. The consequent weakening of the regime was met with further reliance upon force. Thus public humiliation and beating of demonstrating students, who were mostly non-Communist, turned them toward Communism. In this way, the advocates of force obliged the government to rely on nothing else.

The Kuomintang, although operating a party dictatorship, had permitted the existence of several small political groups, or "minor parties," each consisting of a small nucleus of persons with a few thousand followers, quite different in kind from

256

the Kuomintang and the Communist Party. In 1941 several of them formed a Federation of Democratic Parties to oppose one-party government, party armies, secret police, and corruption. Later organized as the Democratic League, they stood primarily for a joint program: "democratization of the government, nationalization of the army." In the negotiations of 1945 and 1946 the Democratic League was recognized as a third element standing between the Kuomintang and the Communists, potentially in a position to hold a balance if a coalition government were formed. Even before the breakdown of negotiations, however, the right-wing Kuomintang began to intensify its coercion of intellectuals, particularly those of the Democratic League. One of its leaders was a poet and scholar of Chinese literature, Professor Wen I-to, a University of Chicago graduate who had led the Peiping students in their march overland from Changsha to Kunming. His open assassination in July 1946 was only the most prominent of many beatings, abductions, and assassinations aimed at the intimidation of Chinese liberals.

Two minor parties were brought into the National Assembly organized by the Kuomintang in 1948. The great part of the liberals in politics, however, remained aloof from these window-dressing efforts at multi-party government. The new constitution then adopted was a generally liberal document but it expressed worthy ideals, not political realities. In no part of China could an election process by secret ballot become established.

Given the record of corruption and terrorism which overtook the Kuomintang government in proportion as its problems multiplied and its leadership moved to the right, it is not surprising that the Chinese intelligentsia in their political thinking became steadily more estranged from it. The Chinese Communist Party was able more and more easily to recruit personnel from the student class, at the same time gaining the widespread tacit sympathy of intellectuals in education, the professions, and the lower levels of the bureaucracy. The Communist appeal to the intelligentsia was typically expressed in terms of the civil liberties and social justice so openly flouted by the Kuomintang police and bureaucrats. The result was a "desertion of the intellectuals." They abhorred the police state and were patriotically opposed to Soviet influence in China. But the Communist regime, operating entirely in the countryside, had become a functioning government with a record on which it could be judged. In this situation a Chinese liberal who as an individual subscribed to much the same ideals of freedom as his American counterpart might be more nearly on the fence than the average American would think possible. The fact was that the Kuomintang regime was very different from the United States government, and the Chinese Communist Party very different from the American Communist Party.

12 The Rise of the Communist Party

Vicissitudes of the First Decade

The Kuomintang and the Chinese Communist Party have experienced a curious parallelism in their life histories. Each party soon after its formation came close to power and then met disaster. Each spent a long period in the wilderness before reaching the top at last. After a decade in power, each ran into a major crisis.

After its formation in 1912 as successor to the revolutionary T'ung Meng Hui and its proscription by Yuan Shih-k'ai, the Kuomintang spent the next decade largely in eclipse and came to power only sixteen years after its founding. After the founding of the Chinese Communist Party in 1921 and its early effort to seize control of the Nationalist revolution, the split of 1927 drove it out of the cities into the mountains of South China. Its final triumph came twenty-two years later.

This superficial similarity in their careers is not the only common characteristic of these rival parties. Studies of their leadership indicate that in both parties the original elite were men from upper class, not peasant, backgrounds who had had some higher education. They were typically "alienated intellectuals," whose modern education pulled them out of the traditional society, restless misfits who found careers as full-time professional politicians and military or party organizers. Many got their start as specialists in violence, suited to a revolutionary era. Both groups rose to power as exponents of modern mass nationalism.

The early Kuomintang and Communist leaders differed less in social than in geographical origin. Dr. Sun's followers were city men, often from merchant families and hence from the big coastal treaty ports, particularly Canton. More of the Communists were from rural areas, particularly the central Yangtze basin. As time went on, the Communists recruited leaders of true peasant origin, the Kuomintang did not. Perhaps the main difference between them was chronological. The founding fathers of the Kuomintang grew up in that ancient time before World War I. The Communists belonged to the wartime and postwar generations of an entirely different age, responsive to new pressures and new ideas. It is not surprising that the older generation of republican revolutionists was destined to do a partway job, leaving the potentialities of change in modern China to be exploited more thoroughly by a younger group.

The Attractions of Communism. Several aspects of China's past favored the Communist approach. Confucian tradition gave the modern student the sanction and indeed the moral imperative to take the lead in public affairs as a member of the scholar-elite and in terms of ideological principles. The authoritarian tradition by which the official class monopolized all overt political activity made it natural that an opposition movement must be secretly organized. Rebellion in the past had usually been energized by utopian and messianic doctrines (usually of Buddhist derivation but in the case of the

Taipings pseudo-Christian). Rebels had usually found in their sworn brotherhood a substitute for the support given each individual, in the absence of legal safeguards, by the old family system. Chinese folklore and literature had a romantic Robin Hood tradition of banditry in the cause of the downtrodden.

China's experience in modern times reinforced traditional tendencies. As the economic plight of the farmer grew more apparent, if not in fact steadily worse, it was naturally assumed that government action should be taken to remedy it. The job was too big for individuals and must be the primary responsibility of those in power — all of which suggested some kind of state socialism. Sun Yat-sen had vaguely pointed in this direction. The Marxian social ideal in China, however, had been from the first a Communist Party monopoly. No social-democratic movement preceded it, to spread the socialist creed as in Europe on a gradualist, reformist basis. For those attracted to socialism there was nowhere to go but into a Leninist party. Leninism, finally, provided an explanation of the great fact in any Chinese patriot's political life — the foreign omnipresence, "imperialism." When it proceeded to identify those ancient twin evils of landlords and warlords as "feudalism," the Marxist-Leninist scheme of history seemed to many sufficiently applicable to China to deserve their belief and faith. It claimed to be "scientific" and strictly "modern." It would allow China to expunge her modern humiliations by leaping over the capitalist phase of universal development to stand as she should in the forefront of the nations. For the faithful believer the party would provide. A new China would result.

To offset these favorable factors there were several reasons why the Communist movement was checked and almost suppressed, before the Japanese war facilitated its resurgence. One reason was the success of the Kuomintang at Nanking in mobilizing talent and support for its new government. Another was the Kuomintang effort at suppression which killed thousands, if not tens of thousands, of leftist youth. But perhaps the most fundamental reason for retardation lay with the Chinese Communist Party (hereafter CCP) itself and the orthodox urban orientation given it by the masterminds of the Comintern in Moscow. This can be seen if we trace the early vicissitudes of the party line — that ingenious device for maintaining inner unity while choosing allies and isolating enemies by "class analysis" according to "laws of history."

The Comintern's Failure. After the Comintern agent Gregory Voitinsky in 1920 had prompted Ch'en Tu-hsiu to call together a mixed group of intellectual-revolutionaries to form a Communist party, it required some time to mold them into a genuinely Bolshevik organization. They early became active in the labor movement but, as C. M. Wilbur points out, their membership remained less than a thousand until the May Thirtieth Movement of 1925 roused a great surge of anti-imperialist feeling and gave them a tenfold increase of numbers. The greater size of the Kuomintang (KMT) intensified the Communists' persistent problem: how to seize political opportunities on a basis of theoretical principles, thereby avoiding a mere unprincipled opportunism. This necessity for rational flexibility, for reasoned opportunism, is what makes the party line so interesting a study. The Marxist-Leninist dialectic makes dry reading, but this rather tasteless fare has vital significance for the initiated. A change of line, redefinition of a term, may make or break human careers more decisively than the fluctuating statistics of a stock exchange in time of panic. Lives depend on the turn of the dialectic.

The Chinese Communists had begun by dividing Chinese society into the classes of workers (proletariat), peasants, petty bourgeoisie, national bourgeoisie (capitalists), and other, reactionary classes (militarists, "feudal" landlords, *et al.*). Their first manifesto of June 1922 (a year after the formal founding) called for a united front against the militarists in which the CCP would represent the workers (assuming with Marx that a party can really be an organ of only one class) and also poor peasants, while the "democratic party" (the KMT) would represent bourgeois elements. This concept was abruptly overruled when the Comintern shortly declared that the KMT was actually, and quite anomalously, a "bloc of four classes" (bourgeoisie, petty bourgeoisie, workers, and peasants) and that the CCP, instead of seeking a united front with it as a "bloc without" (that is, from outside), should do so as a "bloc within," that is, by having CCP members as individuals become KMT members while still remaining part of the CCP apparatus. The CCP Third Congress in June 1923, in confirming this ingenious idea, echoed the Comintern declaration that the KMT "should be the central force of the national revolution." When dual membership was accepted by the KMT in January 1924, the race began to see which party apparatus could make more use of the other. Communists gained key posts in the KMT organization.

Adhering to this approach (advocated by Stalin, criticized by Trotsky), the Comintern in December 1926 ordered the CCP to join the left wing of the KMT in the Nationalist government at Wuhan, which it now defined to be a bloc of three classes (workers, peasants, and petty bourgeoisie). The aim was to effect a transition by which the national bourgeoisie would be excluded from the revolutionary movement. As a result the CCP continued to seek power as a "bloc within," even though its subordination to Wuhan prevented its exploiting the peasant unrest of the time. The final fiasco of the Comintern's "bloc within" strategy was signalized first by the split between the left KMT at Wuhan and the right KMT at Nanking (February-April 1927) and then by Wuhan's expulsion of the Communists (July 1927).

Under Comintern orders the CCP now reoriented itself

263

(August 1927). It condemned Ch'en Tu-hsiu (who later was expelled) and "the Party's leading cadres" (who themselves participated in the condemnation) for "opportunism." "Their constant vacillation, their false, unrevolutionary theories . . . in complete contradiction to the resolutions and instructions of the Comintern . . . in reality betrayed the revolution." At the same time the CCP accepted Stalin's view that the revolution was entering a "higher" stage which must be marked by secret conspiracy and armed insurrections in city and countryside. Yet lip service was still paid to the necessity of achieving "hegemony within the Kuomintang," a statement without meaning except as support of Stalin against Trotsky.

Following this new line the CCP staged the Autumn Harvest uprising in Hunan (led by Mao Tse-tung) and seized the South China port of Swatow for a week, in September 1927. In December it contrived a four-day uprising in Canton (the "Canton Commune"). These and similar efforts all failed.

The Sixth Congress of the CCP, meeting in Moscow with eighty or more members present in June and July 1928, again condemned Ch'en Tu-hsiu for his "opportunist" right deviation, and now equally condemned his successor for the "putschist" left deviation which had resulted in unsuccessful uprisings. The new line stated that the revolution was at this time in a "trough between two waves" and the CCP must prepare for armed insurrections in view of the inevitable arrival of a new "revolutionary rising tide." This laid the basis for the disastrous "Li Li-san line" of 1929–30.

The Sixth Congress of 1928 had decreed that the agrarian revolution was the main "content" of the Chinese revolution as a whole, but that the agrarian revolution could be achieved only under "proletarian hegemony." This meant that the CCP must recapture the leadership of the urban proletariat. At the same time it must prepare armed insurrection so as to be ready for the new "rising tide" of revolution. The result was that under Li Li-san, as secretary general appointed by Moscow, the CCP apparatus had to organize city workers for political strikes and armed uprisings, exploiting the labor union members for party ends rather than representing their economic grievances. In the face of the KMT white terror and its competing "yellow" (anti-Communist) labor union movement, Li Li-san and his close ally in this period, Chou En-lai, got nowhere. No tide rose, least of all in the cities. In 1926 two thirds of the party had been classed as proletarian and another fifth as intellectuals. In 1930 Chou En-lai reported that out of 120,000 party members, only about 2,000 were industrial workers.

The climax of Li Li-san's insurrectionary effort came in July 1930 when Communist forces made front-page news by seizing Changsha, the capital of Hunan, only to be expelled a few days later. Li Li-san's downfall followed in the usual way. He was condemned for both "opportunism" and "putschism." He had struggled "against the Comintern line, disobeyed Comintern discipline, and adopted the arguments used by the leftist and rightist rebels against the Comintern by saying that the Comintern did not understand the Chinese situation," et cetera. Li Li-san recanted and went to Moscow "for study" (to reappear in Manchuria in 1946). Chou En-lai, after confessing his "cowardly rotten opportunism," remained on the Central Committee. The Central Committee was now dominated by a "returned student" group of comrades newly trained in Moscow who still assumed that the urban proletariat must lead China's revolution.

The failure of the first decade of Chinese Communism reflected the difficulty of importing and adapting a foreign faith and its institutions. Leninist party discipline included the fiction that Moscow could not err and that the faithful executor of the Comintern line, if he failed, was himself at fault. The irrationality of this latest importation from the West was not attractive to most Chinese intellectuals, though it was reminiscent of the Emperor's holding a local mandarin responsible for acts of God within his bailiwick. In Chinese politics the CCP leadership was something new, a band of professional revolutionists, disciplined and trained to concentrate in Leninist ideological terms upon the organization and seizure of power. The decisive feature of their party was that, unlike the Kuomintang which had borrowed a similar Leninist structure, it functioned as an ideological entity. The line set by the leadership on reasoned "dialectical" grounds was capable of shifts and reversals, resilient in adversity and flexible when opportunity offered, always sacrificing individuals as expendable in the total cause.

Comintern directives, often concocted with one eye on Stalin's enemies in Moscow, had been disastrously doctrinaire. Yet as political platform documents they regularly included contradictory alternatives which could later be cited to prove wrong those who, like Li Li-san, had followed their main tenor. For example, the CCP Sixth Congress of 1928 in Moscow had foreseen "a war in the Pacific for the partition of China . . . the coastal provinces . . . will become the battleground." It declared that "the reformist devices of the bourgeoisie cannot solve the agrarian problem." It called for "alliance with the petty bourgeoisie and the rich peasants" (without, however, abandoning "the class struggle against the rich peasants"). It urged support of peasant guerrilla warfare, development of the Red Army, organization of peasant women and youth, the setting up of Soviet bases. In short, like a campaign platform, it covered all eventualities and so in later retrospect could be cited to prove Moscow's foresight, even though its main directive had led to defeat.

Thus by 1931 the first decade of Communism in China had created a Leninist party, in spite of the failure of Comintern policy. The second decade was to see an indigenous adaptation of Marxism-Leninism to Chinese potentialities. (One cannot help thinking back, in a general way, to the adaptation of Buddhism some fourteen centuries before, to find points of comparison and of contrast.)

The Rise of Mao and the Yenan Period

The Maoist Strategy. The Comintern had reiterated that only the proletariat could lead the peasantry. It regarded peasants, in orthodox Marxist-Leninist fashion, as capable only of auxiliary action. But Mao Tse-tung's famous report on the peasant movement in Hunan foreshadowed what Benjamin Schwartz has called "the Maoist strategy." Written in February 1927, before the debacle of that year, this report asserted heretically that the "revolutionary vanguard" in China was not the proletariat but the "poor peasantry." When Mao's Autumn Harvest uprising of 1927 failed, he was temporarily dismissed from the CCP Politburo but he continued his work in the Hunan countryside. Convinced that mass revolution in China must be based on the peasantry, Mao learned from experience the necessity of combining mass organization with military power. Building up rural guerrilla forces, he began to create "soviets" (as Trotsky had advocated) even before the Comintern sanctioned it. With Chu Teh as military commander he took refuge in the winter of 1927–28 in the mountainous Chingkangshan region on the Hunan-Kiangsi border, collecting some 10,000 men, together with arms for perhaps 2,000.

Here developed a territorial base, to be fused with the other components — a Leninist party, support from the peasant masses, a Red Army — in the "Maoist strategy." The territorial base, Mao declared in 1928, must have a food supply and a strategic location, preferably on the rugged natural border between two provinces. Collecting here the traditional sinews of rebellion, manpower and grain, Mao kept his movement ideologically orthodox in form if not in substance. The Chinese Soviet Republic was proclaimed at Juichin, Kiangsi, in November 1931 as a "democratic dictatorship of the proletariat and peasantry," using Lenin's formula of 1905 in utterly different circumstances. The nonexistent "proletariat" were favored by excellent labor laws on paper and given greater representation than the peasantry in the system of soviets, the same as in Russia. The Red Army was specially privileged as a political class army. Land was violently redistributed, both in the time-honored fashion of peasant uprisings and also in the name of class warfare, for purposes of establishing political control. But collectivization, then the Russian fashion, was not pushed. In fact the Soviet Republic in Kiangsi was in no position to coerce all the soviets organized in and around its base area. Some rich peasants and landlords organized soviets so as to make peace with it. But Mao's rural strategy was like Lenin's: rely on the poor peasants as allies and treat the rich peasants as class enemies.

Mao Tse-tung's ascendancy was delayed when Kuomintang arrests and executions forced the Central Committee to abandon Shanghai for Kiangsi in the autumn of 1932. Chiang Kai-shek's first four extermination campaigns, in late 1931, May-June and July-October 1932, and again in 1933 were checked by guerrilla tactics which drew KMT columns into the mountains and concentrated superior force against isolated units. In late 1933–1934, however, a systematic, German-devised, KMT blockade and penetration along lines of blockhouses began to invade the Soviet base. The Red Army's efforts at positional defense proved disastrous. After receiving permission from Moscow by radio, over 100,000 CCP personnel in October broke out of their Kiangsi redoubt, moving swiftly by night on the beginning of the Long March. Only now, when Chinese Communism was out of touch with Moscow and irrevocably committed to survive in the countryside or not at all, was the Moscow-trained element in the party leadership obliged to acknowledge Mao's dominance, which CCP official history now dates from the Tsunyi conference of January 1935. Mao's rise was not decreed from the Kremlin.

Yenan and Wartime Expansion. After marching and fighting on a circuitous route of 6000 miles or more through half a dozen provinces of Southwest China, surviving perils and hardships now legendary, most of the CCP leaders and less than 20,000 troops reached northern Shensi province in the latter part of 1935, transferring their headquarters to Yenan at the end of 1936. Here in the arid, sun-baked Northwest, halfway from Nanking to the border of Soviet Outer Mongolia, a new chapter opened with the second united front, this time against Japan.

Since general Chinese resistance to Japan would serve a dual purpose, diverting Japan from attacking Russia and Nanking from attacking the CCP, it is not surprising that at the beginning of August 1935 both the CCP and the Comintern called for nationwide resistance in a new united front. With some exceptions the CCP statements now offered to join with the archenemy, Chiang Kai-shek; but he remained deaf to this proposal until after his spectacular kidnapping at Sian in December 1936 by Manchurian troops who chafed to fight Japanese invaders, not Chinese rebels. Chou En-lai on Russian orders mediated to secure the release of Generalissimo Chiang, who now reached the zenith of his career as the indomitable symbol of national resistance.

Subsequent pourparlers and Japan's attack near Peiping on July 7, 1937, led to a second KMT-CCP marriage of convenience, an uneasy armed truce which began in an atmosphere of patriotic enthusiasm but soon deteriorated. The Communists now met Nanking's demands and promised to support Sun's Three Principles, to give up overthrowing the KMT by force and abandon the soviet campaign against landlordism, to democratize their local regime, and to put their troops under Nationalist command. These were of course temporary tactical expedients by which to expand CCP power in the wholly new context of a national war of resistance.

This process of expansion was first of all military. The name of the Red Army was abolished in 1937 and it was put nominally under the orders of the central government, which named it the Eighth Route Army. By degrees its forces pushed into the mountain-ringed province of Shansi and thence out onto the North China plain. In the second year of the war the Communists organized the New Fourth Army from remnant forces left in the lower Yangtze region and extended their organization also into the seacoast province of Shantung. The war bases which they organized centered in the less accessible border areas between provinces, beginning with the Shansi-Hopei-Chahar Border Region set up in 1938, which eventually contained roughly 20 million people. By 1941 the old area of the Nien rebellion of 1853–1868 on the Shansi-Hopei-Honan-Shantung borders was unified as another such region with a population of perhaps 30 million. By war's end there were said to be 19 bases, mostly called Liberated Areas, with a total population of 70 to 90 million, protected by about 2 million militia and by Communist armies claimed to total 910,000 troops.

The Nationalist government, never locally dominant in much of North China, could not prevent this expansion. Its modernized forces, absorbed in stemming the main Japanese war effort in such areas as the Hunan rice-bowl, were trained for positional, not guerrilla, warfare. Chiang Kai-shek's troops were also handicapped by the Chinese military tradition which kept the army separate from the people.

Throughout Chinese history an armed populace had invariably endangered the established order, while the soldier had been held in low esteem, kept ignorant, used wastefully, and bought and sold as a mercenary. Armies had lived off the countryside and been the scourge of the people. Politically indoctrinated armies were a new thing in modern China. In this as in other respects it was typical of the Kuomintang that it had modernized its military machine to the point of giving social prestige to a patriotic new officer corps and giving new arms and training to their peasant soldiers, but it had not reached the point of indoctrinating the ordinary rifleman to fraternize with the farmer and fight in his behalf, because this would have been revolutionary. For that very reason Mao and Chu from the beginning had trained their troops to regard themselves as the defenders of the populace. In practice this meant paying for supplies, helping the households on whom they were quartered, and making the Eighth Route Army the friend of the people. As the Communists put it, "the soldiers are fish and the people water" — the army depended upon popular support. This slogan is an illuminating contrast to the orthodox statement of the philosopher Hsün-tzu (ca. 300–235 B.C.) that "the people are the water and the ruler is the boat; the water can support the boat but it can also sink it." The Communists, so to speak, by being immersible among the people added a dimension to their movement.

This fraternization with the populace meant that the Communist troops could dispense with the modern paraphernalia of a central commissary. By using civilian intelligence networks they could more easily decentralize their military organization. This enabled the Eighth Route Army to operate as a scattered, mobile force, appearing and disappearing in the populated farm land behind the Japanese lines. This was something that the central government forces could not do unless they combined their military operations with a more popular political program.

In their political organization the Chinese Communists expanded to fill a vacuum. Local politicians had been the first to go as the Japanese advanced, and in some cases had gone over to puppetry. New leadership had arisen locally, teachers from Peiping in some cases becoming chairmen of guerrilla governments. Into these local situations where new leadership was arising came a great influx of young students from the coastal centers. Intellectuals from Yenching and the big government universities at Peiping, inheritors of the spirit of the May Fourth Movement, packed their belongings in a bundle and joined the guerrillas. Living close to nature and the common people, they emulated the adventurous heroes of Chinese folklore, daring all with loyal comrades in a righteous cause to succor the downtrodden, like the famous characters of the picaresque novel *Shui-hu-chuan* (translated by Pearl Buck as *All Men Are Brothers*).

The migration of patriots was common to both South and North, but with different effect. In the more modern centers of the unoccupied Southwest, the students became symbols of the country's future technological development and remained in the universities-in-exile. In the Border Regions and Liberated Areas of North China, on the other hand, where universities were lacking, they were recruited to be Communist cadres, in teams of political workers. The Communist area during the early united front period attracted venturesome idealists who sought action. By degrees the Communists organized these diverse individuals into a network of decentralized government.

Organization of Popular Support. In their land policy the Communists temporarily abandoned their program of land confiscation and redistribution in favor of rent reduction. This merely carried out the Kuomintang law of 1930 which limited rent to $37\frac{1}{2}$ percent of the crop. At this time landlords were very generally left in possession, guaranteed a reduced rent, and also allowed to vote in local elections, so that there was no great flight of the propertied class from the Communist area. Instead of their former soviet system, the Communists announced direct elections by the so-called three-thirds system in which they would confine their own representation to one third and seek to retain Kuomintang and independent participation in the other two thirds of the offices. This was based on the united front theory that in a community unified against the Japanese the Communists would provide leadership most effectively by refraining from a monopoly of government. The system had the merit of apparent competition. Although the Communists had preponderant force in reserve, their local political representatives had to prove their administrative competence and political wisdom before the bar of public opinion. While this was a passive Chinese type of public opinion, expressed by tacit acquiescence and lack of protest rather than by speeches and editorials, it was still a determining factor in wartime politics. Like traditional contenders for the Mandate of Heaven, the Communists had to steer by the willingness of the populace to put up with their regime rather than turn against it. In practice the Communist movement and the Eighth Route Army in these years could prosper only in proportion as the populace actually supported them, for the war period was one of free political competition, in which the Japanese and their Chinese puppets as well as the Kuomintang offered some alternative to the Communist regime.

The key to popular support lay in the CCP leadership of a patriotic war of resistance and, at the same time, in the Communists' economic program. In the densely populated North China plain where some fifteen hundred people try to live off each square mile of cultivated land, food was more important than civil liberties. The latter had been unknown. Chinese governments had never countenanced the active participation of the farmer in politics. Privately sponsored meetings and speeches had been seditious, elections unheard of, and freedom to publish meaningless among illiterate peasants.

The CCP's economic program included production drives

both by troops and by farmers which sought to achieve the self-sufficiency of each area in food supply and, with more difficulty, in cotton production. The Communists were not well supplied with improved seeds and farming techniques such as those developed by scientific farming in the West. But they made up for this lack by their emphasis upon cooperation in land reclamation, labor exchange among farmers, mutual aid in transport, and small-scale industrial cooperatives. Since the old order had inveterately discouraged the cooperative association of peasant households in any way that might threaten authority, the immense potentialities of peasant cooperation at the village level were ready at hand for Communist exploitation. By bringing the farmers into associations for common ends and controlling these associations through leadership and propaganda, the Communists found a new road to political power.

Compared with the years of struggle and disaster in the wilderness after 1927, the Yenan decade of the united front after 1936 was full of vitality, growth, and innovation. While not renouncing their orthodox Communist aims, the CCP now stressed "agrarian reform," though far from being "mere agrarian reformers." When an enterprising American journalist, Edgar Snow, interviewed Mao and his colleagues after the Long March, he found a self-confident and even jovial band of veteran revolutionaries, whose homespun earthiness and evident devotion to the peasant's cause, brilliantly portrayed in *Red Star over China,* captured the imagination of readers around the world. During World War II the electric optimism and sunny atmosphere of Yenan impressed foreign visitors, who invariably arrived there from the clammy fog and frustration of the capital at Chungking. Communist propaganda in this period sang a liberal tune, for "national independence, democratic liberty, and the people's welfare" (paraphrasing Sun's

Three Principles), with no further stress on soviets, bolsheviza-tion, class war, dictatorship, or even the absent proletariat. This facade for outside observers, however, did not disclose the party's inner aims and methods, nor its problems of organizing central power during its wartime growth.

Wartime Ideological Development

The three goals set forth by Mao in 1940 were to pursue the united front, armed struggle, and party-building. The trick was to maintain a Leninist party with its long-term revolution-ary aims while finding as many allies as possible in the dual effort to fight Japan and reform China.

For this purpose the CCP united front tactics became so-phisticated, flexible, and efficient. As Lyman van Slyke puts it, they "defined the enemy in terms as manageable as possible and sought to isolate him," separating out all possible allies and neutrals, appealing to their interests, cultivating their friendship, caring for their specific needs almost like a ward politician, and yet never compromising the ultimate inde-pendence, power, and aims of the CCP. The United Front Work Department at Yenan had its "united front cadres" in the KMT areas pose as non-Communists, pursue overt, con-structive, liberal-type careers, make their own friends, and never expect CCP help or acknowledge any connection. Free China's cultural and political life was accordingly infiltrated by able, dedicated, and hard-working patriots who kept their secret faith in China's Communist future but had contact with the CCP only occasionally and at a high level. Similarly the "friendly armies" program penetrated the KMT forces with military men who rose by merit and acquired influence while awaiting future opportunities. But the united front was much more than secret infiltration and recruitment among the unorganized. It was also a wartime attitude of friendly cooperation and exemplary sacrifice in the common cause of Chinese patriotism.

Armed struggle was first of all against the Japanese invader. The Communists had declared war on Japan when in Kiangsi. In North China their guerrilla warfare culminated in the "Hundred Regiments" attack on Japanese forces in five provinces simultaneously by 400,000 troops in August 1940, a damaging blow which however roused savage and comprehensive Japanese retaliation in 1941. Meanwhile CCP troops on occasion fought KMT forces, for example, in North Kiangsu, north of the Yangtze from Shanghai, where the CCP was intent on establishing a base area. When Nationalist forces wiped out part of the CCP New Fourth Army south of the Yangtze in January 1941, they made them into martyrs, for as Chalmers Johnson has pointed out, the CCP had come to seem "more anti-Japanese than the government," notwithstanding their flouting of its orders. Thus the war provided the great overt sanction for the CCP's innate militancy. Armed struggle could be integrally combined with the united front, against either Japanese invaders or KMT diehards, once they had been sufficiently isolated. In united front politics, as in guerrilla warfare, one maneuvered to isolate and outnumber the enemy before attacking.

The third ingredient of CCP power was party-building, and this was essential because CCP expansion had created decentralization. Party membership grew from 40,000 (claimed by Mao in 1937) to 80,000 (claimed by Chou in 1943) to 1,200,000 (claimed by Mao in 1945). Strenuous efforts were required to keep the CCP a disciplined, centrally controlled Leninist party. Its membership was new. It was less than ever a party of the proletariat, even though peasants were now called "rural proletarians." At the same time its activities were spread over a quarter of a million square miles where travel was mainly by foot of man or beast and communication was quick only by radio. Control could be exercised only by Communists working with proper ideological coordination in the four parallel hierarchies of party, local government, army, and mass organizations (for women, youth, labor, and the like). Veterans of the Long March usually headed these hierarchies. P'eng Te-huai, Lin Piao, and others commanded armies, Liu Shao-ch'i headed the labor federation. But to retain central direction it was essential to indoctrinate the new cadres (party workers) in Leninist assumptions and principles of organization.

For this purpose party schools processed thousands of students at Yenan and in 1942 Mao inaugurated an ideological reform movement for "correcting unorthodox tendencies" (*cheng-feng*) in thought, in personal relations inside and outside the party, and in speech and writing. Borrowing heavily from Russian and Comintern sources, he and his colleagues produced a body of documents for intensive study and discussion — "How To Be a Communist Party Member," "In Opposition to Liberalism," "Liquidation of Menshevik Thought," "On the Intra-Party Struggle." Prolonged criticism and self-criticism in small groups, confessions of guilt and repentance in public meetings, became standard procedures. The aim was to maintain the party's militancy and dedication during all the distractions of a united front period, to keep its membership prepared for future tasks. Behind the jargon of "subjectivism, sectarianism, and formalism" (the three main evils attacked), one can perceive a strenuous effort to re-educate and discipline new followers still contaminated by a liberal background, an individualistic.temperament, or traditional morality.

Simultaneously the *cheng-feng* movement marked the final eclipse (though not a physical purge) of the doctrinaire "returned student" group who had behind them more training in

Moscow than work in the villages. Marxist-Leninist theory must be tested in action, applied to rural China's concrete realities: this became the basis of "Maoism." As the new CCP constitution of 1945 put it, "the ideas of Mao Tse-tung, the combined principles derived from the practical experience of the Chinese revolution" were now added to Marxism-Leninism as the party's guiding principles. While not calling for an independent national Communism like that of Tito in Yugoslavia, this growth of Maoism represented the Sinification of Communism in China, in a period of wartime nationalism and minimal Russian influence. Henceforth it was no longer an alien creed. Its principal achievement had been to build a Leninist party on a peasant base, demonstrating (contrary to its own theory) that the Communist order is in fact independent of the proletariat.

This inversion of Marxism implied that a man's ideological tendencies did not come from his class affiliation, as posited by historical materialism. His class was now determined by his ideology; a bright peasant could become a "proletarian." This triumph of subjective and political considerations over the influence of the economic mode of production marked another step in the doctrinal disintegration of Marxism-Leninism.

The New Democracy. The party line for public consumption in the Yenan period was laid down in Mao's essay *On the New Democracy* of 1940, a persuasive propaganda document which justified the united front as a temporary phase and yet reaffirmed the party's long-term mission. Mao divided the Chinese revolution into two stages: first, a "democratic revolution" (the New Democracy), and then a "socialist revolution." The New Democracy must first change the old "semi-feudal" society into an independent "democratic" society, which the Chinese people had been attempting ever since the Opium War. The 1911 Revolution, though a step in this direction, was only bourgeois-democratic, whereas the New Democracy would be part of the worldwide proletarian-socialist revolution, in which China could win her freedom from imperialism only with the aid of international socialism represented by the Soviet Union. Thus the New Democracy aimed to develop a type of "democratic" state suited to China's semi-colonial situation, ruled by an alliance of several revolutionary classes (unlike the "dictatorship of the proletariat" in Russia), before proceeding to a second stage of socialism.

In form the New Democracy should have a government of "democratic centralism" based on elections in which all participated, but graded through a hierarchy of people's assemblies from the village on up to a national congress. In economic life the new government should own and operate large-scale and monopoly activities including big banks, big industries, railways, and the like, in accord with the declaration of the first Kuomintang Congress of 1924. On the land the New Democracy would confiscate and distribute the holdings of big landlords in order to realize Sun Yat-sen's slogan, "Land to those who till it." By turning the land into the private property of the peasants, this reform, said Mao, would produce something quite different from a socialist agricultural system.

In the cultural revolution the May Fourth Movement had been chiefly significant for the introduction of Communist cultural thought. For the current phase the new culture should not try to be socialist, since socialism was not yet achieved, but should be based upon nationalism, science, and the masses of the people. Thus Mao Tse-tung toward his non-Marxist audience blandly claimed to inherit the mantle of Sun Yat-sen and the May Fourth Movement, while for Marxists he put himself on the level of Marx-Engels-Lenin-Stalin as an original contributor to Communist theory. In actual fact Mao's "innovations" had been in the realm of practice, not theory. All his dicta could be found in earlier literature. His real "contribution" had been the creation of a state within a state — a party, an army, and mass support in a territorial base. But this was not something to boast of in 1940. The ambiguity of Mao's terminology catered to the liberals' hopes while actually building a framework in which to organize them.

"Liberation." The semi-totalitarianism of wartime in any country, when life is mobilized by the state under the sanction of a common struggle for survival, may for a time create high morale in the midst of suffering. With Japanese armies in the land, the Communists' organizational know-how, their current reasonableness and moderation, their militant and messianic faith, set the stage for a new cult of the common people. "Liberation" aimed at the awakening and activation of the Chinese peasant masses. The cultural movement stressed pictorial art in the form of the woodcut, which could be cheaply reproduced by wood-block printing for mass distribution. Choral singing was another wartime development in all parts of China. In the Communist areas it was combined with an ancient type of country dance to create a new art form in the *yang-ko* ("seedling song"), an all-talking-singing-dancing poorman's opera which used simple rhythms, folk tunes, a very simple chain dance step, propaganda stories, and the subject matter of everyday life to provide entertainment which indoctrinated as it liberated. Getting the common man to express himself in public in country dancing and choral singing was part of a process of social integration of the individual.

Popular participation in cultural, economic, and political programs created a new psychological atmosphere. Participants in this wartime order were moved by a new creed, a humanitarian love of the peasant masses. This religion of the common man embraced the revolutionary ideal that modern technology and a new social organization could be used to remake and enrich the life of the peasant. This cult of the common people, the *lao-pai-hsing,* animated the cadres and the military forces. In order that the revolution might draw perpetual sustenance from the masses, the party worker was taught that he must live in the villages, work with the peasant, eat his food, lead his life, think his thoughts. Only thus could party cadres lead the peasant masses in their regeneration.

This almost spiritual concept of "liberation" became a dynamic element in the Communist movement, and by the inexorable logic of events became also the sanction for the new party dictatorship. The reasoning in this paradox proceeded on orthodox lines: (1) the revolution aimed to give the masses a new life, beginning with their economic betterment; (2) this betterment could be achieved only through the exercise of absolute political power, sufficient to change the old order; (3) political power could not be achieved by uncoordinated individuals but only through organization in a centralized party; (4) a party could be effective only if its members submitted to absolute party discipline — in party councils all might have a voice, but once the party decision was taken, all must obey it. By this logical progression the party took on the character of an ongoing, living entity with a historic mission, transcendent over individuals who expended themselves in its cause. With its alleged scientific foreknowledge of the historical process, it became (or rather its leadership became) a law unto itself.

Coalition. When the CCP held its seventh congress in April-June 1945, the first since 1928, it perfected its strategy for the postwar period by adopting the flexible line of "coalition government." After the New Fourth Army incident of January 1941, when Nationalist troops had fought a CCP force south of the Yangtze, the government had blockaded the CCP area more intensively, partly to prevent contact with Russia through Central Asia. Henceforth it had focused its attention as much on the Communists as on the Japanese, who in any event were plainly going to be dealt with by the United States. A general fear arose in China that World War II would be followed by civil war. Both Chungking and Yenan responded by promising to seek a "political" rather than military solution of their differences, and negotiations began early in 1943.

Building on his New Democracy line, Mao now declared that, being still in the stage of "bourgeois-democratic revolution," China needed a "New Democratic government of a coalition nature embracing all parties and nonpartisan representatives." Depending on expediency, this could mean a coalition including the Kuomintang, as was to be proposed in 1946, or a coalition with minor parties and liberals against the Kuomintang, as was to be achieved in 1949. Meanwhile this line appealed particularly to the modern-minded but frustrated intellectuals of Free China — professors, students, journalists, the literate and technically trained, who formed a basic resource for postwar reconstruction.

By war's end in 1945 the CCP had created a dynamic centrally controlled movement in its own areas and exerted a great attraction upon intellectuals in Free China. Having done less of the fighting against Japan than the Nationalist government and having avoided the burdens of city government and modern services, it was prepared to bid for power in the countryside. Only at this point did it become an immediate and inescapable problem for United States policy.

13   Our
Inherited
China
Policy

Vietnam has made it plain that we need a new perspective on our past relations with East Asia. Have our relations there always depended in the last analysis on bombs and bullets or at least the threat of bombs and bullets held in reserve? Or is our reliance on military firepower a new thing, a recent aberration? The answer is mixed. The Western position in East Asia during the past century was maintained by force, but the force was usually European, seldom American. And before the spread of nationalism and modern technology to East Asia, not so much force was needed to maintain a Western position, and not so much firepower was available. Our use of violence in Vietnam has not been unprecedented or aberrant so much as tragically out of date, disastrously out of proportion.

A new perspective on ourselves requires first a framework of conceptions. This, I think, must come from the academic disciplines because they represent the way our minds are organized for analytic purposes. We think in the terms of economics, politics, psychology, sociology, literature, fine arts, and so on. When we picture the past, the insights of all these approaches contribute to our historical synthesis. To an inquiring mind, no monocausal system is likely to be sufficient. Neither original sin nor the class struggle is the one key to understanding our past behavior.

A new perspective requires, second, that we recognize certain basic features of our past relations with East Asia, beginning with our own dynamism as part of the Western imperialist expansion in general.

American Expansion and Britain's Empire

In the early decades of the Republic, before the railroad and other forms of technological progress opened up the Middle West, the United States was a small nation on the western fringe of the Atlantic civilization. Its new and revolutionary doctrines of democracy were designed to give the individual maximum freedom of enterprise in trade, travel, proselytism, and general self-development within the protective framework of the Bill of Rights and rule by law. Government and special privilege were to be strictly limited, and opportunity thereby enhanced for all who could make the most of it. Our early trade was mainly by sea. James A. Field, Jr., has described how our early traders got around the British and French empires by trading in the eastern Mediterranean. Boston merchants who bought Turkey opium at Smyrna to ship to Canton were part of a three-pronged expansion of merchants, naval officers, and missionaries who were at first more active in the Mediterranean than in the Far East. The United States Navy's Mediterranean squadron, usually based on Majorca, conducted gunboat diplomacy with the "Barbary Pirates," meaning the local rulers of Morocco, Algiers, Tunis, and Tripoli, primarily to protect American traders there. Our earliest missionaries abroad were mainly in the Levant and the Ottoman empire beginning in the 1820's.

Thus developed several features of the American expansion

which were to be repeated in East Asia. First, we were country cousins of the British and righteously condemnatory of their empire; but we also relied upon their facilities, like the ports of Malta or Hong Kong, and imitated many of their methods. After all, London was the center of world trade, in which we were eager participants. Second, we were ready to demand the privileges of extraterritoriality. For example, we joined in the system of capitulations which exempted Europeans from the legal jurisdiction of the Ottoman empire. Third, we demanded equal opportunity and therefore most-favored-nation treatment, so that we could show the British and other imperialists what American enterprise and ingenuity could do in a fair field.

Finally, in dealing with local peoples, American democrats, proud of our new democracy at home, were ever ready to assist local rebels with doctrines of national independence, reform, and social equality. We felt ourselves to be on the giving end and enjoyed the feeling. Foreign missions, which grew steadily throughout the nineteenth century, were only one expression of this general attitude. Since Britain was master of India, the Ottoman empire was at first our main field of missionary enterprise. Toward the end of the century, with the decline of the "sick man of Europe," we found our chief evangelical opportunity in the Chinese empire, the sick man of Asia.

This missionary endeavor, in both Near East and Far East, was distinctly culture-bound, an expression of American home values. It used methods developed in the early missions of the seventeenth and eighteenth centuries to the American Indians. As summarized by R. Pierce Beaver, these methods "included the primary emphasis on preaching, the founding of churches, the assumed unity of evangelization and civilization, general education, Bible translation and the production of vernacular literature, the recruiting and training of native pastors, evangelists and teachers, the mission station, and to some extent the

Christian colony or community." All these features characterized our missions in the Near East and in China.

Our expansion across the Pacific had begun with the Canton trade, the whaling industry, and the fur trade of the
Northwest coast, all handled from New England and the Middle Atlantic states by sea. But as we moved westward to ex-
plore and settle the American continent, we began in the
1840's to see our trans-Pacific contact as a natural extension of
America's "manifest destiny." Orators pictured the westward
course of empire, from the ancient Near East through Greece,
Rome, Western Europe, and on across the Great Plains. Eventually in the 1880's the frontier began to disappear at home at
the same time that student youth volunteering for foreign missions felt challenged by a new frontier in China.

The American frontier in Asia was very different from that
of the Great Plains: instead of open spaces and natural resources, we found Cathay. This new and strange type of
human society aroused our curiosity and eventually our sympathy quite as much as our greed or avarice. Toward it we
proceeded to apply attitudes developed at home. These were
expansive, adventurous, and acquisitive. They included conceptions of progress, growth, and improvement as the law of
life. The American merchant in Shanghai spoke of the be-
neficent role of commerce; the missionary, of saving the heathen from their state of sin. The American expansion into
China was not solely economic, religious, or nationalist, but a
combination of them all.

This American activity was largely carried on by individuals or private agencies; the United States government seldom
led the way. Instead of the joint-stock trading companies with
their armed fleets and semi-official merchant-administrators
who had conducted the European expansion in the age of
mercantilism, the early New Englanders went as commercial
adventurers, a few boys and men in one tiny ship at a time.

286

They took with them the peculiar philosophy of the young American nation — an eye for profit, innovation, and invention; concern for the moral worth and salvation of the individual; energy and self-confidence. Beginning with Peter Parker's celebrated eye hospital in Canton in the 1830's, American missionaries soon rivaled the British in numbers and in resources, decades before the American merchant caught up with his British counterpart. Missionary constituencies have been the seedbed of our humanitarianism toward China, a sentiment that sometimes almost dominated policy and sometimes ran into serious frustration.

America's Role within Britain's Informal Empire. Our traders at Canton after 1784 had found Britain the dominant Western power there. They continued to condemn British imperialism while making use of its banking facilities. The concept of "informal empire" is of course only a semi-concept; it describes a partway situation in which a foreign power dominates some aspects but by no means the whole of a local situation. But the British-sponsored unequal treaty system in East Asia made foreigners a privileged class on a par with the local ruling class, and certainly had some attributes of empire. The system was maintained by the presence of foreign naval firepower and gunboat diplomacy. The fact that our Commodore M. C. Perry, who had risen to fame as a gunboat diplomat on the Barbary Coast, was the man who opened Japan merely proved the rule: the Americans were a minor part of Britain's informal empire but could sometimes take the lead in its expansion.

This Anglo-American relationship was at first quite unequal. Britain was a bigger and more powerful country, covering the globe. America's economic absorption after the Civil War in her own domestic growth left her quite subordinate in the China trade, and her naval power in East Asian waters remained equally small. Consequently the Americans got the fruits of informal empire without the hard work and experience of using power. British diplomacy had to learn how to make difficult decisions, calculate the consequences, and live with them afterward. For example, when Harry Parkes, the chief British negotiator, was seized under a flag of truce in 1860, Lord Elgin felt he had to retaliate against the Ch'ing government but not hurt Chinese people. His solution was to burn the Ch'ing Summer Palace outside Peking. This was only one of many thousands of British imperial decisions that had to be made, day in and day out. The Americans had little similar experience.

Historians have been misled by the fact that our junior partnership with the British in China was not always apparent in the American archives. To a student of the American end of the record, American policy in China before John Hay is poorly documented and dull as dishwater. The scanty correspondence of our diplomats was chiefly enlivened by the anti-British fulminations of doughty and oratorical amateurs like Humphrey Marshall, American Commissioner in 1853. Mr. Marshall has been often quoted by students of the American record because he asserted our duty to support the Chinese Empire against British machinations. But he was there so briefly, knew so little of the facts, and had such inadequate assistance that his dispatches express an attitude rather than a policy. British imperialism in its commercial phase on the China coast was not particularly exclusive. The real American policy in this early period was usually to acquiesce, sometimes querulously, in British policy.

When Robert Hart, in building up the Chinese Imperial Maritime Customs Service, enlisted E. B. Drew of Cambridge, Massachusetts, and Drew in turn enlisted four members of the Harvard class of 1874 to go to China and as customs commissioners superintend the foreign trade of the treaty ports, it had nothing to do with American policy. It was private American participation in British policy, mediated through Manchu policy at Peking.

After 1922, when the Anglo-Japanese alliance, that prolongation of British Far Eastern naval dominance, came to an end, American influence and activity in China began to outstrip Britain's. The Shanghai Municipal Council and the Hong Kong docks were still British preserves, but the dozen Christian colleges of the 1920's and 1930's were primarily American achievements, and some big commercial distributors like the British-American Tobacco Company were joint Anglo-American efforts. The rise of Nazi Germany in the 1930's made it plain that foreign help to stop Japanese expansion would have to come mainly from America rather than Britain. America was also becoming the chief source of Chinese returned students, superseding Japan as well as Europe. The decade of the Nanking government was the height of American peacetime influence, and it was followed by the big American military effort in China during the 1940's. The balance shifted, and the United States inherited the British position as the principal Western power active in China.

The American Ambivalence about China

The way in which we first entered the Chinese scene, on the morrow of our war of independence against the British empire, still inveighing against its evils while demanding equal enjoyment of its benefits, contributed to a curious ambivalence in our China policy, a gap between thought and reality. The principal reality was the unequal treaty system but since this had been fought for and was still maintained by British and French arms, the United States government felt little primary responsibility for it. Our principal thought was to get our share of privilege and opportunity, a me-too policy.

The United States and China

In politics, for example, by our own revolutionary tradition we were conscientiously opposed to colonialism, suspicious of European machinations, a bit holier-than-they in our early abstention from empire and even from power politics. Yet at the same time by demanding most-favored-nation treatment we were quick to enjoy all the semi-colonial fruits of extraterritoriality. In daily life, even the most undistinguished American citizens — dead beats escaping their failures, remittance men sent abroad for their families' sake, stowaways and adventurers — once they disembarked at Shanghai had upper class status thrust upon them. Like the Chinese gentry, they were set above the masses, not subject to local police coercion. Embarrassed at first to be pulled by a human horse in a ricksha, the average American soon accepted his superiority and found Oriental life and its inexpensive personal services enjoyable. Even the most egalitarian missionary had to compromise with Chinese hierarchic realities.

From this ambivalent experience, I suggest, emerged the sometimes startling contrast between the vigor of our verbal pronouncements and the limitations of our official actions. We would not abandon our ideals of national self-determination and individual freedom for the Chinese people, but somehow we could never take action to get these values realized in fact. The ideals we treasured as part of our own culture; the facts were part of China's. They remained incompatible. The result was to encourage in our traditional policy a disconcerting split between humanitarian ideals and strategic realism. The moral righteousness which long distinguished American Far Eastern policy was remarkable for its omission of any idea that war is a practical tool of policy. We were ready to pronounce vigorous moral judgments condemning Japanese aggression at the same time that we refused absolutely to contemplate going to war in support of our moral and diplomatic position. This resulted in anomalous situations, as when the Stimson doctrine after 1931 upheld our honor by refusing to recognize Manchukuo, while we still sold war supplies to Japan.

Our inability to translate our moral ideals into active policy in China, our tendency to talk grand and act small, sometimes almost irresponsibly, has been affected by another pattern, one of fluctuation between energy and apathy. The long-term fluctuations in our interest in East Asia have been a function of many complex factors in American life, including the fact that we were never as dependent as Britain upon overseas trade. We were latecomers at Canton and even later in California. Both the Spanish and for a time the Russians were on the Pacific coast ahead of us. (One incentive to the Monroe Doctrine of 1823 was the Russian ukase of 1821 which declared the Pacific coast from 51 degrees northward to be a Russian preserve.) Our efforts in the period 1818–1824 had given us a continental position stretching to the Pacific; but the Mexican War, the California gold rush, Perry's opening of Japan, and the general American westward expansion of the forties and early fifties were followed by another period of apathy. Washington remained profoundly uninterested in trans-Pacific expansion. Repeated plans and proposals by Americans in the Orient left the American home government unmoved. In Formosa, Americans from Canton explored the island, built a port, raised the American flag, loaded some seventy-eight vessels with cargoes worth half a million dollars, and got the American commissioner to China to advocate annexation. The State Department did not even reply to the proposal. When the Russians in the 1860's decided to sell Alaska as indefensible in war and unprofitable in peace, Secretary Seward had great difficulty in getting congressional approval. The area for which he was paying about two cents an acre was denounced as "an inhospitable, wretched and God-forsaken region worth nothing." The House of Representatives passed the appropriation bill only after nine months' delay and after the Russian Minister had paid out thousands of dollars in bribes.

Underlying the gap between word and deed, and the waxing and waning of interest, perhaps we can discern the intractable problem of cultural differences. Our folklore and public attitudes concerning China have included several discordant images — exotic, idealized, or disillusioned — which have coexisted but remained unreconciled in our inherited thinking.

The exotic approach used to emphasize cultural oddities — men's pigtails, women's bound feet, everyone's long fingernails, opium smoking, and other trappings of the pre-modern age. Reader interest in man-bites-dog items was satisfied by tidbits like "Chinese eat rats." The exotic approach also made much of all things "Chinesey" (an adjective denoting Westernized versions of things Chinese) like "Chinese chow," moon gates, and the cunning handicraft curios produced for the tourist trade. Emphasis was on dissimilarity. "Everything in China is opposite." The men wear gowns and the women trousers. They read from up to down and right to left. The soup comes last. Mourners wear white and brides red. The last name comes first. The compass points south. Left is the seat of honor, and so on. In more serious vein this school went in for literal translation of Chinese proper names, like the servant "Bald-the-third" in Nora Waln's inside view of a big family, *House of Exile*. Quips like "Confucius say" and "Damn clever, these Chinese" belong in this category, as well as the inscrutable Dr. Fu Manchu. Other sources of exoticism were the supposed Chinese indifference to suffering and the tradition of fiendish Oriental tortures, associated respectively with lower economic and lower political standards of living.

The idealized approach to China had more substance. It went back to the eighteenth century vision of China's rational and enlightened despotism as a model for Europe. This favorable view included our reverence for the wisdom of the East, which interested Emerson and the New England transcendentalists. Some China traders and Christian missionaries nourished the thought of a "special relationship" between Americans and Chinese, a supra-cultural friendship based on common traits and values and mutual respect. In real life our penchant for idealization was applied to such contrasting persons as Madame Chiang Kai-shek, on her famous grand tour of the United States in 1943, and the Communist guerrillas of the Eighth Route army, during the earlier stages of the anti-Japanese war — both of whom were assigned incredible virtues by the obvious predilections of the American public. Idealization of Chinese resistance against Japan, at a time when the United States was still supplying war materials to the latter, no doubt sprang from a guilty conscience; but other factors of American mass psychology also entered into our periodic enthusiasms about China — particularly our sympathy with the underdog.

In 1894 when China was still a vast archaic empire and Japan an up-and-coming pupil of the West, American opinion favored Japan in her war against China, and on the same underdog principle, also favored Japan against Russia in 1904. We began to fear Japan only after 1905 when Japan gave promise of being top dog in the Far East. In the 1930's American opinion supported the valiant but ill-equipped efforts of Chinese patriots to withstand Japanese aggression. This sentiment was particularly evident in the American support of Chiang Kai-shek during the early war years. Yet the same sentiment operated in favor of the Chinese Communists when they represented a minority cause among the peasantry, struggling against the weight of Chiang's legions. Our concern for the underdog led us to shift our emotional support from one contestant to another depending on the apparent justice of their cause and the circumstances of their relative strength. It may be doubted whether the Japanese or Chiang Kai-shek or the Chinese Communists changed as greatly as American opinion concerning them changed.

The disillusioned view of China bulks large in the record, for nineteenth century Americans as fresh apostles of progress found a China in decay, actually sunk in poverty, filth, disease, corruption, thievery, and disorder, and apparently unwilling to do anything about it. Reform-minded Americans, always ready with suggestions, were overwhelmed with the size of China's problems, annoyed by Chinese apathy concerning them. In the United States the picture of Chinese drug addiction, prostitution, footbinding, concubinage, and unspeakable vices excited the morbid, while heathen idolatry and sin appalled the devout. Chinese immigrant laborers, brought to help develop California, by 1880 formed a twelfth of the population there, and scores were killed in anti-Chinese riots in California and other western states in the 1870's and 1880's. But the Chinese exclusion acts of 1882 and later years were supported by East Coast sentiment as well. These laws expressed many fears: that Chinese were culturally and racially unassimilable, that their lower living standard was a positive menace to public health, that their presence would promote the spread of slavery, as well as the new labor unions' fear of their economic competition.

Meanwhile in China American farm boys who had received the call and become missionaries, when they met the hostility of the elite and indifference of the masses, found their Christian forebearance sorely tried. The Rev. Arthur H. Smith in his *Chinese Characteristics* (1890) expressed the tolerant but sometimes acerbic frustration of missionaries who found the Chinese villager impervious to progress and the gospel. Disillusionment was also epitomized in the "Shanghai mind" of the treaty-port businessman, whose low view of Chinese character was summed up in the 1920's in Rodney Gilbert's *What's*

Wrong with China. During World War II, this disillusionment was distilled in the GI hatred of Chinese filth and poverty ("Why can't they at least clean up this place?"), heightened by the scandalous rumors, lonely boredom, and complaints of wartime. Later the Chinese Communists' manufacture of the germ warfare charge and their treatment of American prisoners in Korea seemed to exemplify the super-evils produced by modern totalitarianism in a backward country. The Cold War made our earlier mood of patronizing enthusiasm for a land of sturdy peasants and attractive students fade into the background.

Americanists have only begun to study our ambivalent images of China. Their variety is confusing, but one thing stands out: in Sino-American relations to 1949, China was always the weaker party, in trouble, the recipient of our interest and philanthropy. America was always the superior party, not in such trouble, able to help. It was not an equal relationship, which is no doubt why we enjoyed it.

The Evolution of the Open Door Doctrine

In the circumstances of 1899 John Hay's notes take on a significance quite different from the tradition of benevolence toward China which later became associated with them. The Open Door must be viewed in connection both with our expansion in 1898 and 1899 in Hawaii, Samoa, and the Philippines and with the contemporary British predicament in China.

In July 1898 Congress annexed Hawaii. In December the treaty with Spain gave us Puerto Rico, Guam, and the Philippines. In December 1899 a tripartite treaty awarded us part of Samoa. These acquisitions in the few months preceding and following the Open Door notes of September 1899 outstripped those of the other powers in the Pacific. While the Germans were securing a naval base at Kiaochow in Shantung and the Russians at Port Arthur, we got potential bases in Hawaii, Samoa, and the Philippines. Similarly while the European powers were seeking spheres of interest for commercial exploitation in China, we annexed an Asian archipelago. This American expansion is all the more significant because it was so largely unpremeditated in the public mind.

Britain's original interest in the Open Door is clearly visible in the trade statistics In 1898 British shipping carried two thirds of the tonnage in China's ports and paid two thirds of the customs revenue. To defend this commercial empire against imperialist encroachment by other powers Britain followed at first a policy of taking compensation. In the great-power rivalry which set in after China's disastrous defeat by Japan in 1895, Britain got in on two of the three big foreign loans and secured two leased territories (Weihaiwei and Kowloon) and by far the greatest mileage of railroad concessions. But no amount of success in a partition of China could benefit British interests when they already dominated the trade of the whole country. Concessions and spheres could only reduce her area of trade.

By early 1898 the Russians had given no promise that they would not establish preferential rates for their trade in Manchuria, and the British had failed to secure all that they desired in the Yangtze valley. They therefore considered again the traditional idea of preserving an Open Door for trade in China by the "collective influence of the trading nations." This idea was broached in the House of Commons early in 1898. The Foreign Secretary proposed it to John Hay, then our Minister in London. But the British after March 1898 reverted to their more concrete program of building up a Yangtze sphere and generally keeping up with imperialism.

Hay as Secretary of State asked W. W. Rockhill, in August 1899, to draft a memorandum on the Open Door. Rockhill had studied Chinese affairs and had definite views of his own. He also got the advice of a British Commissioner of Chinese Maritime Customs, Alfred E. Hippisley, a friend who had recently come from China on leave and had a first-hand acquaintance with the problem. Hippisley had been one of the closest coworkers and assistants of Robert Hart — so much so that when Hart thought of retiring from the inspector generalship of the customs in 1896, Hippisley was then his probable successor. Robert Hart's amazing career has not yet been thoroughly studied. He was at this time the chief proponent of equal taxation of, and commercial opportunity for, the trade of all nations in China. His policy differed from that of the British Foreign Office.

Following Hart's general views, the Open Door notes of September 1899 made no reference to the integrity of China and interposed no bar to the extension of spheres of influence. The notes were primarily concerned with the customs problem. After proposing, first, that each power not interfere with the vested interests of other powers within its sphere, the notes then proposed, second, that only the Chinese government should collect customs duties, and only according to the Chinese treaty tariff, and, third, that no preferential harbor dues or railroad charges should benefit the subjects of a power having a sphere. It was not until Russia had begun to occupy Manchuria as a consequence of the Boxer Rebellion that Hay's supplementary notes of July 1900 raised the question of the integrity of China. In its origin the Open Door was intended to preserve foreign trade in China, not the Chinese state. In 1898 it was called for specifically by American business groups, but very soon it began to represent a good deal more than an economic interest.

The Integrity of China. The Open Door began as a political, not a legal, doctrine. It was expressed in the form of policy statements and in bilateral treaties on many occasions after

297

1900, but it was not until 1922 that it was stated in a legal form binding on all parties. The doctrine itself underwent growth and expansion. The second set of notes of July 1900 was much more positive, and supported Chinese "territorial and administrative entity," a phrase later supplanted by "territorial and administrative integrity." This reflected the fact that Russia had moved very rapidly into Manchuria, contrary to the interest of most of the powers. Thus by 1900 Hay had developed his doctrine actually to the point of attacking any extension of spheres of influence. The Anglo-Japanese alliance of 1902 introduced the phrase "equal opportunity." This was entirely in keeping with the British conception of the Open Door for trade. In later statements, however, "equal opportunity" was applied to "cultural" activities as well as commercial, and was also made to embrace the idea of freedom of "movement." By 1938 American policy statements were regularly including the phrases "free competition" and "fair treatment."

In this way the Open Door doctrine developed two main tenets: the integrity of China, and the equal treatment of all foreigners there. Viewed cynically, the doctrine of China's integrity was a device to prevent other powers, for example, Russia, from taking over areas of China and excluding us from them. But the independence of China has also appealed to Americans as a matter of political justice. Until recently it fitted the doctrine of the self-determination and sovereignty of weaker nations, which constituted one of our major political sentiments.

The nonrecognition doctrine of Bryan in 1915 and Stimson in 1931, by which we refused to recognize any Japanese impairment of China's integrity, was a corollary of the integrity idea itself. As a doctrine, nonrecognition proved as unavailing as our other invocations of righteousness. In the later stages of

Japan's aggression during the 1930's, Secretary Hull emphasized another aspect of the same idea, nonintervention. This became one of the chief moral thunderbolts he hurled so unavailingly at the Japanese. Today the Open Door and its attendant doctrines have chiefly historical interest, yet a certain residue from them remains in our thinking.

After World War I the United States sought to carry out its policy toward China through collective action. This was in marked contrast to our Latin American policy, in which we interpreted the Monroe Doctrine in such a way as to forbid a collective approach by the United States and European powers. It also contrasted with our European policy, in which we stayed out of the League and so in effect left Europe's problems to the British and French. Only in the Far East did we take the lead in action through the concert of powers.

The legal basis for our collective action in the Far East was established by the Washington Conference of 1921–22, particularly in the Nine Power Treaty concerning China. This was a codification of the Open Door doctrine in expanded form. In 1928 collective action was buttressed on paper by the Kellogg-Briand Pact outlawing war. The United States also joined collective action against Japan, to no avail, by associating an American representative with the League of Nations (Lytton) commission which fruitlessly investigated Japan's seizure of Manchuria in 1931. During the 1930's the foreign policy of Stimson and Hull generally followed the line of collective or at least parallel action as the best hope of mobilizing diplomatic pressure to stop Japan. This approach was a second-best and ineffective alternative at a time of isolationism, when it seemed impossible to mobilize unilateral American economic or military activity.

After World War II the United Nations became another vehicle for collective action against aggression. and we joined with it actively to repel the North Korean attack on the Republic of Korea in June 1950 and the Chinese intervention which followed.

The Nature of the American Interest. It is a truism that the American commercial interest in China has had a large admixture of imagination and hope. Actually our financial investments in China and Japan in the 1930's were about equal. American investments in China, chiefly direct investments, were less than a quarter of a billion United States dollars, while our investments in Japan, chiefly in Japanese bonds, were also something less than a quarter of a billion. In fact, our entire investment in the Far East was only about three quarters of a billion, only 5 or 6 percent of the total American investment abroad. Moreover, our financial investment in China was a very small part indeed of the total foreign stake in China, a good deal less than one tenth. British and Japanese investments were each over a billion dollars, while ours were barely one fifth of the British. Two thirds of our financial interest was concentrated in Shanghai.

If we turn to foreign trade the figures are no more encouraging to the theory of economic determinism as the sole source of our policy. In the 1930's Japan took between 8 and 9 percent of our total foreign trade, while China accounted for less than half that amount (even counting Manchuria as still part of China). Japan's large foreign trade was conducted one third with the United States, while of all our Far Eastern trade two fifths was with Japan and only about one fifth was with China. Our missionary investment in China represented about 40 million dollars in terms of money but obviously a great deal more in terms of sentiment. However we approach the problem, dollars and cents, even in the minds of businessmen, have not been an all-compelling factor in our China policy.

The operation of sentiment rather than dollar diplomacy in the State Department has been documented by Dorothy

Borg's study of the period 1925–1928. She makes it plain that Secretary Kellogg based his China policy on a "simple almost instinctive reaction" typical of the general American attitude toward China in the 1920's. He wished to get rid of the unequal treaties and make China fully independent as soon as possible. He wanted to remain neutral among factions within China and refused to be obsessed by the Bolshevik menace there. He steadfastly refused to apply sanctions after the incident in which Americans were attacked at Nanking in 1927. On the other hand he was equally determined to deal only with a Chinese government that represented a unified country. 'He did not want to facilitate in any way a division of China into two parts. The vigor of the anti-foreign feeling in China in 1925 caught the treaty powers as well as the missionaries by surprise. The Shanghai business community became convinced very soon that this Chinese anti-foreignism was a Moscow plot. Many voices were raised advocating intervention to save China from Soviet domination. Secretary Kellogg and his chief assistant, Nelson Johnson, refused to be stampeded by this hysteria.

Aid to China was by custom a private matter for the attention of the missionary profession, the public organs concerned with famine or flood relief, agencies like the Rockefeller Foundation interested in educational and medical development, and other groups and individuals. By the remission of part of the Boxer indemnity in 1908, the remainder in 1924, and similar gestures, the United States government began to take a hand in the process of helping China remake herself. In 1934 Washington inaugurated, primarily for domestic reasons, a silver purchase program which soon began to dislocate and depress the Chinese economy. It led to vast amounts of silver being smuggled out of China, which had to leave the silver standard and adopt a managed paper currency in 1935. Subsequently, however, the Treasury under Secretary Morgenthau was able to make the silver purchase program of direct though unpublicized aid to the Nationalist government by paying it gold or US dollars for some 500 million ounces of silver. In 1937–1939, for example, we paid 184 million dollars on this account.

With World War II government aid to China became the dominant form of American assistance. Beginning with loans in the months before Pearl Harbor and the clandestine development of Colonel C. L. Chennault's "Flying Tigers" (American Volunteer Group) as an air force in Burma and Yunnan, we embarked in 1942 upon a continuing government program of financial, material, and technical assistance.

This was a milestone, if not indeed a gravemarker, in our relations with the Chinese people. Before this, American philanthropy had been from person to person, group to group, small-scale but persistent, maintaining institutions or helping movements but never supporting governments. Now our aid was official as well as massive. It could go only to the recognized government of the country, which was well aware of its right to be the sole channel. Unfortunately our ally the Nationalist government was by 1942 already well advanced in that process of decline noted in a previous chapter. Our help could not remake its inner nature but served merely to make it less dependent on domestic opinion and more inclined eventually to rely upon its new American-made armaments. In fighting Japan we had no recourse, in conscience or in reality, but to support the government of Chiang Kai-shek. But our half-billion-dollar morale booster of early 1942, for example, was given with no strings attached. We never learned exactly who used it for what purposes. No country program was set up by treaty, calling for bilateral actions in planned phases. From the beginning of our wartime alliance, American officials found themselves dealing with an ineffective administration, too debilitated by its domestic problems to respond to foreign stimuli. Trying to aid it, we became entangled in its decline and fall.

The United States government finally found itself, almost involuntarily, playing a major role in China's domestic politics. The British had had this experience, but it had never been part of our traditional policy.

14 United States Policy and the Nationalist Collapse

Looking back (so much easier than looking ahead!) we can see how 1912 and 1949 marked two phases of China's political metamorphosis. In the nineteenth century the Manchu dynasty had been forced to give the treaty powers a privileged role within its East Asian empire, but as the Chinese people awakened to national life, the alien monarchy was dissolved in 1912. In its absence the treaty powers' position grew more prominent while the national revolution gathered strength only gradually. After Japan's aggression began in 1931, the Western powers proved useful against it until 1945, by which time the United States had become involved in supporting the established government. When it collapsed in 1949, Western activity and contact in China collapsed with it, and the unequal treaty century in China came to an end amid widespread recrimination.

Thus the American government's position in China, inherited from Britain, was built up in response to Japan's invasion. But as World War II progressed after December 7, 1941, China became a theater of supreme frustration. Chiang Kai-shek failed to get a coordinated allied strategy centered on himself. Britain failed to hold Singapore or the Burma Road. Joseph W. Stilwell, one of the ablest American generals, had hardly arrived to be Chiang's chief of staff when he took on the hopeless task of defending Burma. Burma fell in early 1942, amid much Anglo-Chinese-American recrimination, and Stilwell then set himself the grueling three-year task of re-opening a land route to China across the North Burma jungle. Yet even after it and its accompanying pipeline were opened in early 1945, the incredible Hump airlift still carried more tonnage. Again, our Twentieth Bomber Command got five big airfields built near Chengtu in Szechwan, of rock crushed by Chinese corvée labor. Supplying their B-29s took more Hump tonnage in 1944 than was allocated to the Chinese armies. But they had hardly begun to bomb Japan before their base was shifted to the Marianas, supplied by sea and nearer Tokyo. Entering the war as the prospective allied base for defeating Japan, Free China found that job done by naval and air power at sea and herself cut off, a low-priority sideshow. The American aim became merely to keep Free China in the war. The result was not defeat but neither was it victory.

Chinese nationalism continued to suffer frustration after Japan's defeat. Well before Pearl Harbor, in May 1941, we had offered to abandon extraterritoriality as soon as peace should come in China. In October 1942 we offered to negotiate imme-diately, and a new Sino-American treaty on equal terms was signed January 11, 1943. But within five months another agreement was made, freeing American troops in China from Chinese criminal jurisdiction. American bases, supply and transport services, radio networks, airlines, and army post offices were soon operating on Chinese soil in greater volume and with greater license than Southwest China had ever seen under the unequal treaties. At war's end Shanghai streets for many months were filled with GI's and roistering sailors far

The United States and China

beyond the memory of treaty-port days. This ill suited China's new great-power status. China's new-found sovereignty took on a quizzical character. Right-wing chauvinists, Communists, and patriotic liberals could unite in inveighing against GI incidents connected with wine, women, and jeeps.

American Aid and Mediation

Our Wartime China Policy. From late 1943 American diplomats began to glimpse the inherent danger in KMT-CCP rivalry — "civil war at some undetermined date," which might hamstring the war effort and eventually let Russia back the Communists. The Americans aimed therefore (1) to avert civil war by encouraging a political settlement, which Chiang Kai-shek advocated as early as September 1943, and (2) to strengthen the Nationalist government position, partly by building up its armies, partly by getting it to reform itself. Armies were built up but reform proved impossible, for reasons already indicated. The idea of a political settlement, however, was accepted by all parties at least verbally. KMT-CCP negotiations had been resumed early in 1943. American policy proceeded on three levels.

First, on the international stage we tried to make China a great power in form if not in substance. She was permanently excluded from the high command of the war at the British-American conference at Quebec in August 1943, but was included along with the Soviet Union in the Moscow Declaration of great-power principles in October. The British-American-Chinese Cairo Declaration of December 1943 promised to return to China all territories lost to Japan, and Roosevelt at the Teheran Conference stood firm for China's great-power status on the future United Nations Security Council. But this conferring of great-power status on the Nationalist government was an American accomplishment, not Chinese or, least of all, British or Soviet. It was seen at the time as a fine and friendly gesture toward a great and deserving people. History, however, may view it with disillusion as a doctrinaire effort at trans-Pacific masterminding of Chinese history, trying with words from abroad to strengthen a regime already in decline at home. (Peking of course now calls it simply an imperialist plot.)

Second, our idealistic support of Chungking's international prestige accompanied a realistic military effort, which produced a modernized Nationalist army and airforce. Stilwell's faith in the Chinese common soldier set in motion a program in India and China, with a thousand American instructors and advisers, to train and equip thirty-nine divisions.

Third, we tried to heal the KMT-CCP breach. The U.S. Army's single-minded concern for defeating Japan led it to question the efficacy of having 200 to 400 thousand Nationalist troops blockade the Communist area. In June 1944 Vice President Wallace visited Chungking to suggest that Nationalist and Communist forces both fight Japan rather than watch each other. He got Chiang to let an American military observer mission stay in Yenan, whither Western journalists had already been admitted in May. This opened an interesting window on the Communist scene but it remained apparent that Chungking and Yenan were each more concerned about the other than about Japan. Japanese forces meanwhile by late 1944 had pushed south through the Hunan rice bowl and west from Canton to seize the major Sino-American air base at Kweilin. During this crisis Chiang had held out against Stilwell's appointment to overall command in China, and forced his recall in October; he also held out against the projected arming and use of Communist forces in a unified Chinese war effort. Unity and reform both remained remote hopes, but

Ambassador Patrick J. Hurley, with more bravado than finesse, continued to encourage a Nationalist-Communist rapprochement.

At Yalta in February 1945 Roosevelt tried to secure Stalin's future support of the Nationalist government as the price of Russia's recovery of the tsarist position in northeast Asia. This was made known to Chiang, whose concurrence we had promised to obtain, only in June; and ratified in a Sino-Soviet treaty only as Japan surrendered, on August 14. By that date Russia was already in possession of Manchuria.

Behind all the infinitely detailed complexities of this story looms a basic fact: the Soviet Union and the Chinese Communists had the military capability to expand into Manchuria and parts of North China, respectively, and they could hardly have been controlled merely by a token show of force. Soon the Communists were further strengthened with surrendered Japanese arms which they got through Soviet connivance in Manchuria.

With peace came a great American air and sea lift of half a million Nationalist forces back to the coastal centers, a Communist race overland to expand by taking Japanese surrenders in North China, and American repatriation of 1,200,000 enemy troops to Japan. Even as the United States began to relax and demobilize, the long foreseen civil war began in the rivalry over the occupied areas. This was a moment when the American people were least prepared, emotionally and intellectually, to face a Chinese crisis. We had no intention in the winter of 1945–46 of fighting another war in East Asia.

General Marshall's Mediation. It was against this background that George C. Marshall went to Chungking in December 1945. His first months there were a hopeful chapter of American diplomacy. His aim was a political settlement of the burgeoning civil war. The only statesmanlike alternative to internecine warfare was to get the Chinese Communists into the political and military framework of a constitutional regime, in a position similar to that of Communist parties in Western Europe. The two contending parties would both be represented in a reorganized coalition government under Chiang; their armies would be merged and reduced, whereupon American economic aid would be forthcoming. In January 1946 the Political Consultative Conference in Chungking reached a political agreement. A cease-fire order was issued by both armies. In February a military merger was agreed to. Meanwhile an unprecedented tripartite agency, the Executive Headquarters, was set up to superintend the quelling of a subcontinental civil war. American planes took jeeps, radios, supplies, and truce teams, composed usually of an American colonel with Nationalist and Communist generals, to far-flung inaccessible spots where fighting was in progress. Fighting practically stopped.

This breathtaking achievement was a personal tribute to General Marshall. It involved a strenuous effort to remain neutral in China's internal political process, and simultaneously to uphold the supremacy of the recognized government without being used by it. The truce collapsed principally in Manchuria, which still remained beyond the effective cease-fire limits. Behind the renewal of civil war in 1946 lay an intransigent Nationalist confidence in their superior armament, a shrewd Communist calculation of the Nationalists' actual vulnerability. While Stalin showed little confidence in the Chinese Communists' being soon victorious over the Nationalists, the onset of his Cold War with the West gave them stimulus and opportunity to bid for power.

Might the American mediation, after all, have been successful? It is hard to prove a might-have-been: neither Chinese party trusted the other, nor was ready to give up its hope of eventual countrywide control. They had rival armies and organizations, and bitter memories of two decades of killing and being killed. In its historical context, a more irrepressible conflict can hardly be imagined. In the long view it is easy to conclude that Marshall's effort was a forlorn hope.

Yet at the time the Chinese people wanted peace, the United States felt it had enormous prestige and power to bring to bear upon the scene, the Communists stood to gain from the agreements, the Kuomintang was heavily dependent upon us. Not the least of our problems was how to get a party dictatorship to pursue democratic reforms in order to head off a revolution. Actually we had a divided objective: to press the Kuomintang leaders into reform which would diminish their autocratic power and facilitate internal peace; at the same time to strengthen the Kuomintang-controlled regime as a step toward political stability in East Asia. We became involved in continuing to build up the Kuomintang dictatorship materially at the same time that we tried to get it to tear itself down politically. But we could not control Chiang and his generals, who preferred to do things their way. They relied on their new arms.

After General Marshall became secretary of state in 1947 and we checked Communist expansion with the Greek-Turkish aid program, some felt that we should have "saved" China in the same way. China was roughly forty-five times bigger than Greece in territory and eighty-five times in population. From our bitter experience in Vietnam we now know that to have treated China like Greece would have required millions of American troops and billions of dollars and even so would have been a failure. General Marshall, of all people, best knew the magnitude of such a task. We had no alternative after 1947 but to abstain from intervention in the Chinese civil war. Whether we should have given greater aid to the Nationalists in this period was later much disputed. Responsible American generals said there was no lack of arms. Many disputants overlooked the severe limitations of our capacity to affect the outcome by means of material aid from outside.

The Nationalist Collapse

The outcome in 1949 showed not that Soviet aid had been greater than American (the reverse was true), but that the Chinese Communists had been able to mobilize and utilize the potentialities of revolution while the Nationalists had not. The Communist victory also showed that over a period of thirty years the American example had not contributed to the organization of political power in China as effectively as the Soviet example. We had no Comintern. Behind our lack of a conspiratorial revolutionary apparatus lay the more general lack of any philosophy or method for forced-draft economic development and political collectivism. Considering the suffering that rapid modernization of any sort was bound to bring upon the Chinese people, we need not entirely regret our inability to be China's model for the brutal task of remaking and industrializing her ancient society.

The Nationalist Debacle

From 1946 to 1949 China saw one of the big wars of modern times. Nationalist forces totaled at the beginning about three million men, the Communists about one million. United States aid to China between V-J Day and early 1948 cost over two billion dollars, in addition to some billion and a half committed during World War II. By sheer weight of arms Nationalist forces spread out to major cities and, when eventually permitted by Russia, into Manchuria. An infinitude of factors undid them: the military under Chiang were out of civilian control, their postwar American-style reorganization heightened the confusion, the sessile Whampoa clique discriminated against provincial commanders and armies, particularly those of Kwangsi. Their strategic doctrine was to hold strong positions defensively, their instinct was to hoard supplies and wait for others to move first, their field tactics were sometimes masterminded by the Generalissimo from a great distance. Corruption, demoralization, and desertion steadily depleted the Nationalist armies. The Communists pursued opposite tactics, maneuvering in the countryside, recruiting among the populace, destroying railroads, avoiding unfavorable terms of battle. They grew in numbers and armament, both from the Japanese Manchurian stocks and from Nationalist defections, sales, and surrenders. By June 1948 they were roughly equal in numbers of men, rifles, and cannon. Late in 1947 they had cut off the Manchurian garrisons. In October 1948 they forced their surrender — a third of a million men. This set the stage for a showdown.

The balance of power had not shifted only at the front, where the Communists steadily built up their stock of American guns and supplies. The Nationalist cause had also been degutted in the rear, in its city bases, by an economic collapse indexed by inflation.

Bombing by an enemy, like flood, fire, earthquake, or other disasters of nature, though destructive, tends to increase public morale and community effort in the face of a common danger. Hyperinflation, on the other hand, impoverishes and demoralizes each salaried individual as it gradually destroys the regime's fiscal capacity and public confidence in it. Life under hyperinflation is a slow strangulation. Salaries and wages never keep up. Furniture, books, and clothing go for food. Gradual malnutrition produces skin diseases, stomach ailments, tuberculosis. The whole society sickens, and the responsibility is put on those in power. Nationalist military collapse when it came was headlined in America, the ten-year hyperinflation which preceded it was not.

Free China's price level had risen only moderately in 1937–1939. The Nationalist currency still circulated over the whole country; Japanese puppet note issues began at Peking only in 1938 and at Nanking only in 1939. Thereafter the Japanese mounted a campaign to undermine Free China's price stability, and meanwhile Chungking steadily increased its expenditures, with income lagging far behind outlay. In 1941, when revenues provided only 15 percent of expenditures, the central government finally took over the land tax in kind. Income from it and from government monopolies and indirect taxes still provided, temporarily, only 30 percent of the budget. Government taxes, domestic loans, gold sales, and bond drives proved ineffective in mopping up the public's excess purchasing power. The situation steadily deteriorated, prices doubling every few months or weeks. In September 1945 the volume of note issue was 465 times that of July 1937.

The end of World War II gave a brief respite as the Nationalist currency spread back over all China, but large government expenditures continued, to say nothing of the buying spree by civilians returning to the coastal cities. Hyperinflation resumed. Prices doubled 67 times in the two and one-half years from January 1946 to August 1948. Counting on its military superiority to end the civil war quickly, Nanking let its foreign exchange reserve be gradually reduced to pay for consumer imports and industrial raw materials. Foreign exchange was at first not seriously rationed nor imports restricted, and so capital fled the country. Meanwhile the domestic currency began to be replaced by foreign dollars and gold.

In order to break the vicious circle a "currency reform" in August 1948 demonetized the old currency and replaced it by the "gold yuan." At the same time price ceilings were set and enforced by police methods, and private holdings of specie and foreign currencies were forcibly converted to finance the civil war. Thus the few resources remaining to the most anti-Communist element, the urban upper middle class, were tied to the "gold yuan"; when it collapsed in late 1948 (prices finally rose 85,000 times in six months), the last remnant of civilian support for the Nationalist cause went with it.

The great two-month battle of the Huai-Hai was fought in

the old Nien area of the Huai River basin, south of the Lung-hai Railway, 100 miles or so north of Nanking. Generalissimo Chiang against the best advice of his staff committed some 50 divisions, out of 200 still remaining, to form a strongpoint on the plains around Hsuchow. He himself from Nanking directed their tactical movements down to the division level in battle. The Communists, however, not only controlled the villages but by reactivating the railways as they advanced were able to deploy large forces. By mid-November, four Nationalist army groups, about 340,000 men, had been quickly cut off and encircled on the plain. A relief force of 120,000 troops, including the best American-trained divisions, was similarly blocked and encircled south of there. When the Hsuchow armies broke out to effect a junction, taking along their American trucks and cannon and the armored corps of tanks, this "mobile fortress" was blocked in turn by deep trenches and soon ripped by American-made Nationalist-surrendered heavy artillery. By late December the 130,000 surviving Nationalist forces, out of 66 divisions committed, were squeezed into six square miles, surrounded by 300,000 troops of the People's Liberation Army. They learned that Nanking proposed to destroy their treasured heavy equipment "by air bombardment — *in situ*," as Edmund Clubb (our last consul general in Peiping) puts it; they surrendered on January 10, 1949. Of 550,000 Nationalists lost, the Communists claimed 327,000 surrendered.

Typical of the entire Nationalist fiasco were Chiang Kai-shek's unwise decision to fight on the Hsuchow plain instead of the Huai River and his refusal to give command to the Kwangsi general, Pai Ch'ung-hsi, an able tactician who knew the terrain. Jealous noncooperation among the Whampoa commanders, nonuse of Nanking's monopoly of the air, inability to bring their American-made firepower to bear upon the enemy, every aspect of this great defeat underlines the old adage that armament alone cannot bring victory. Tientsin and Peking surrendered in January 1949. In April the Communists crossed the Yangtze, in May they entered Shanghai, in October Canton, in November Chungking.

The Nationalist debacle had been not only military but also economic, political, and moral. The chaos, disorders, and dangers of 1948–49 turned city dwellers irrevocably against the Nationalist government and therefore against American aid to it. Having backed that government increasingly since 1937, we could not in the Chinese view divest ourselves of responsibility for its evils even though our aid had been well-intended, often critical of those selfsame evils, and consequently limited in scope and amount. Our top generals opposed Chiang's strategy, to no avail.

Our worst disaster, however, came from the widening gulf between Chinese and American public feeling — in the postwar years when ineptitude and corruption were thoroughly discrediting the Kuomintang in China, we were experiencing intensified alarm over Soviet expansionist aims and methods, particularly over the duplicity and ruthlessness of the Communist movement. As the experience of daily life continued to diverge in China and America, Communism seemed increasingly to be the only way out for one people and the mortal enemy of the other.

The Fall of China in America

For a decade the American public had idealized Free China; now increasingly the combination of the atomic age, espionage, and the Cold War had intensified their fear of Communism. To have Free China become Communist seemed a national disaster. Like the Great Depression, it became political ammunition against the party in office. The Republicans used it in the 1948 campaign. Soon the Hiss case, the Fuchs atomic spy case, the fear of spies and conspiracies, capped by a major war against Communist China in Korea, among other complex factors, took the lid off the McCarthy era.

The open season on China specialists in 1951–52 has had pervasive repercussions on American thinking about China ever since. It was facilitated by several circumstances. The American corps of China specialists both in and outside the government had been a small group in the 1930's. Most of them knew one another professionally as Foreign Service officers, scholars, or journalists. They had nearly all been "associated" with one another, if only at social or professional gatherings. If one assumed that American aid was a determining factor in China's domestic affairs, that the Nationalists could have lost their military superiority only through treachery, that American policy-makers had been anti-Chiang and therefore pro-Communist, and that Communist conspiracy could be detected through a man's associations (a series of untrue nonsequiturs accepted by many during the McCarthy era) then it became a public duty (and a rich opportunity) to investigate.

The motives for pursuing investigations were quite various. They ranged from the conscientious concern of officers responsible for our security to the shrewd calculations of political opportunists. In the background was a mood of anti-intellectualism and insecurity in a nation of whodunit readers suddenly fascinated by the morbid thought that almost anybody who seemed innocent of conspiracy might therefore be guilty of it. Along with the congressional investigations of the time came intensified security screenings in the executive branch and industry which still continue, in a defensive imitation of totalitarianism. (This defensiveness fitted the overly pessimistic thesis that the American liberal tradition had lost its creative capacity at home, in addition to being nonexportable to Asia.)

Among China specialists the opportunity to find guilt by association was enhanced by fortuitous circumstance. The Institute of Pacific Relations (IPR) since 1925 had pursued a program of research and publication punctuated by private conferences of scholars, diplomats, and businessmen representing research bodies, like the Royal Institute of International Affairs in London, in eleven countries concerned with the Pacific area. The IPR had produced some 1200 publications — books, pamphlets, reports — many of high scholarly value. While avoiding expressions of opinion itself, it had also sought contact with persons of many views and its records had been preserved. The files of the American IPR were replete with references to China specialists high and low, as well as some Communists, pro-Communists, and numerous foreigners. By seizing and exploiting these files a senatorial subcommittee was able to make frequent headlines for almost a year, up to the eve of the Republican convention of 1952.

The committee's report claimed in sweeping terms to show an IPR conspiracy to influence State Department policymakers under Democratic administrations in favor of the Chinese Communists. The fourteen volumes of hearings disregarded almost entirely the IPR's conferences and publications and concentrated on dubious contacts and questionable or pro-Communist utterances, whether or not actually connected with the IPR. My personal view is that the investigation got the truth of the matter thoroughly mixed up with hearsay, evidence out of context, and guilt by association.* If this had been combined with executive powers and police measures, it might have resembled a totalitarian purge trial. It was based

* I was a trustee of the American Institute of Pacific Relations from 1946 until its demise a decade later. In Washington I was "identified" as a Communist (by L. Budenz) and as part of a "hard inner core" of an alleged pro-Communist conspiracy. In Peking I have been cited as an "imperialist spy" and "the number-one cultural secret-agent of American imperialism," et cetera. Critics of earlier editions of this book in Taipei, the USSR, and elsewhere have called it variously an apology for American imperialism and for Chinese Maoism.

on the necessary legislators' right of investigation, but exploited the great American tradition of playing cops and robbers and dirty politics.

The only action resulting from the IPR hearings was the indictment of one of Senator McCarthy's numerous targets, Owen Lattimore, for perjury allegedly committed during a record-breaking twelve days of public questioning. A federal court threw out this indictment in 1955.

These hearings and those on General MacArthur's recall from his command in Korea were only the visible top of the iceberg. They were paralleled by secret security investigations of Foreign Service officers and other government employees on a wide and continuing scale. The China specialists were generally transferred to other areas, some were dismissed, and some resigned. John S. Service was cleared six times in succession by the State Department Loyalty Board but was eventually dismissed at the request of the Loyalty Review Board. In June 1957 as a result of a Supreme Court order he was reinstated.

To an observer outside the government, the chief results of all these China policy investigations seem to have been security-consciousness and conformity. Very little if any Communism, espionage, or treachery was uncovered but everyone was intimidated. Fearfulness and conformity handicapped our official thinking for a long time afterward.

My own impression is that the American people responded to the Cold War and the Chinese Communist victory more fearfully than creatively. The chief significance of Joseph McCarthy was that he was tolerated for so long by those Americans who approved his stated aims but not his methods and yet out of fear were willing to countenance his methods. Fear was compounded by ignorance. After 1949 the score or more of American press correspondents formerly in China were excluded. The gigantic upheavals among the Chinese people, the metamorphosis of Chinese society, remained almost unknown in America.

Our Ally Taiwan

Our frontier of contact with the Chinese people after 1949 was Formosa, as the Europeans named it, or Taiwan, as it is called in both Chinese and Japanese. It is about 250 miles long and 60 to 80 miles wide, with a good many peaks over 10,000 feet in the mountain spine on the east and only about a quarter of the area cultivable, mainly on the west. Chinese immigration became important only in the Ming period. The Dutch and Spanish both maintained trading settlements in the seventeenth century, and the island was the last Ming refuge against the Manchu conquerors. Nineteenth century Western trade never became important, but four treaty ports were opened after 1860 and some modernization had begun before the Japanese take-over in 1895.

Japanese colonialism established order, created some material progress, and eventually became less harsh. No real political life was encouraged, although by the 1930's the regime had moved toward local self-government with a limited franchise. The Japanese land policy checked absentee landlordism and encouraged farmers' associations for agricultural improvement, as well as public health services. With a single-minded interest in increasing production, the Japanese regime got about half the children into elementary schools and established a fairly high level of literacy, although less than a hundred students a year reached the university level.

The very small top class of modern-trained Formosan leaders of Chinese background which had been permitted to develop under the Japanese was decimated by the Nationalist massacres of March 1947, carried out to suppress complaints against the corruption of the Nationalist postwar take-over. Several thousand leading Taiwanese were killed — an inauspicious beginning for the remnant of the Nationalist government that moved to Taiwan in 1949. The American attitude until 1950 was to refuse responsibility for the island, but to continue economic aid without military aid, as part of our attempted disengagement from China. The North Korean aggression of 1950 led to our Seventh Fleet patrolling the Formosa Strait, to keep the island out of the war and protected from mainland attack. In 1954 we signed an alliance treaty. An American military mission assisted in the application of our aid program, and the Nationalist forces of half a million or so eventually combatted superannuation by conscripting Taiwanese. Meanwhile the Nationalist government in exile remained superimposed upon the Taiwan provincial government which it dominated. Kuomintang reform efforts were accompanied by control measures, facilitated by a continued state of war with the mainland and martial law.

Economically, the island's earlier reliance on sugar and rice production for the Japanese market had to be followed by a considerable reorientation to achieve greater self-sufficiency and to push industrialization in the face of rapid population increase. The three million population of 1905 had approached seven million by 1940; with an influx of two million or more from the mainland, the total by 1958 was about eleven million, and by 1970 fourteen million. Compared with the mainland, however, Taiwan had a higher living standard with good prospects for economic growth. Development proceeded within a general framework of government domination or monopolies in industry. American assistance of some two billion dollars fostered growth until the mid-1960's, with such success that industrialization then continued apace without our aid, and attracted increasing amounts of Japanese investment. The Nationalist armed forces, one of the world's heaviest per capita burdens, received continued American military aid, though in diminishing amounts. Abroad, the Republic of China at Taipei with American help year after year kept its seat in the United Nations Security Council and as of 1970 maintained more embassies abroad than the People's Republic at Peking.

One creative instance of Chinese-American collaboration was the Joint Commission on Rural Reconstruction, set up by our China Aid Act of 1948. When it began operations on the mainland in October 1948, the Joint Commission aimed to increase the food supply and raise the farmers' standard of living mainly through technological assistance, following the recommendations of an expert Sino-American commission. Agricultural specialists had often argued that since land redistribution could not increase acreage, it bore little promise of increasing productivity as compared with the many improvements possible in seeds, breeding, tools, farming techniques, elimination of plant and animal diseases, and the like. As the program got started in South China and on Taiwan, it stressed development of irrigation through dike-building, but left unsolved the problem of farmer organization as a means to mobilize local resources and secure credit to finance improvements. Experience soon led the Joint Commission to turn to the actual problem of land tenure reform, specifically the reduction of rent to the statutory 37.5 percent of the crop and at the same time the extension of contracts to more than one year as a safeguard against landlord extortion. Thus an American type of farm-extension approach, beginning with technology, soon found in practice that landlord-tenant relations were an essential aspect of a rural reform program.

Once confined to operations on Taiwan, the Joint Commission secured the backing of the provincial government and was able to build on the Japanese structure of farmers' associations. It carried through a general rent reduction and eventually a program for each farmer to own his own land. All this was combined with practical demonstrations, publications, producers' and credit cooperatives, and rural handicraft development. As an institution the Joint Commission also avoided the problems of official relations between two governments by having a single administrative echelon and by using established agencies rather than building up its own apparatus. Like our own Tennessee Valley Authority, the Joint Commission on Rural Reconstruction on Taiwan has set an example of great interest to developing countries.

Since the American people in their history have created fifty states at home, dealt with twenty-one others in Latin America, fostered the Philippine Republic, and seen the postwar emergence of numerous republics in Asia, it is quite natural for us to imagine that Taiwan might also form a new state, independent of the mainland. This would be a concrete application of our own traditional principle of self-determination. It would preserve an alternative, though small, center of modern Chinese political, economic, and cultural development, outside the totalitarian monopoly of all forms of Chinese life on the mainland. On the other hand, Chinese politics for two thousand years has been focused on the unity of all Chinese under one rule. The Anglo-Saxon concept of self-determination has been denounced equally by Chou En-lai and Chiang Kai-shek.

Meanwhile the Taiwanese Chinese, the people most concerned, have acquired a distinct identity. For fifty years under Japan and twenty-five under the Nationalists, they have lived apart on their strategically situated island, relying increasingly on foreign trade and developing a higher living standard than most of the mainland. The real issue is not that of "two Chinas" but of an independent Taiwan, which in fact remains the chief fruit of our China policy since 1949. Given the flow of Japanese trade and investment into Taiwan, its future seems involved in a three-way economic-strategic relationship with China, Japan, and the United States. How to reconcile this with the political sovereignty claimed by Peking is a major problem.

15 The People's Republic: Establishing the New Order

The Chinese revolution since 1949 has been the greatest in history, measured either by the number of people involved or by the extent and rapidity of the changes made. To the outside world it has also been the least known event of modern times. Frenzies of joyful enthusiasm and vengeful hatred, of organized effort and self-sacrifice, depths of terror and exhaustion, prolonged frustration, ardent self-discipline, new hope and pride, have been experienced among a population rising from 600 to 800 millions. Yet this colossal drama has been seen only from a distance, by Peking diplomats, Hong Kong journalists, a few travelers. All broadcasts and publications have been from the regime, but it largely stopped publishing statistics in the 1960's and professional or academic journals after 1966. The private voices have been mainly those of refugees. Foreigners reading even the controlled Chinese press have numbered only a few thousand around the world. Never have such large events among so many been observed and studied by so few.

Ignorance fosters speculation, which permits prejudice. The Cold War of the 1950's between pro-Communist expansionism and anti-Communist expansionism colored everyone's thinking about China. Today anyone who feels himself quite free from bias (in the sense of having a woefully incomplete view) is obviously a fool. There are, however, different ways of being biased about the Chinese revolution. At the extreme points on a spectrum, one can simply enthuse over Mao's inspirational message for mankind, or one can abjectly fear its police-state authoritarianism. My own bias is for understanding the experience of the Chinese people, come what may. This means sympathizing but evaluating, comprehending but criticizing, trying to see the reality. Different observers of China will often see different truths in the same event there; nevertheless we must consciously seek the "truth" because history consists at rock bottom of particular acts by unique individuals, and alleged historical forces — original sin, Progress, the class struggle — are human generalizations. The reality accessible to us consists of the particular facts; the generalizations we supply ourselves, and they need constant scrutiny lest we mislead ourselves. Since man is a moralizing animal, we inevitably make moral judgments, but I distrust instant morality. It is too easy, too subjective, value-laden and culture-bound. Fortunately talented journalists and researchers have been studying China's revolution factually and systematically over many years, and we can also try to see it in historical perspective.

Our effort to comprehend China's metamorphosis, so far away and difficult to observe, must begin with certain assumptions. First, Chinese governments over the centuries, struggling to spread and maintain a unified state and a uniform culture over a vast and diverse subcontinent, became skilled at imposing centralized military, social, and ideological controls and large-scale bureaucratic administration; and the Chinese Communists inherited this great tradition of unified government from Peking. Like scholar-officials trained to apply Confucian principles on behalf of the Emperor, party members could act effectively for the CCP in far places roughly in proportion as they were trained in Marxism-Leninism and the thought of Mao Tse-tung.

Second, the ingredients of the central power that arose after 1949 had accumulated over several decades — not only in the twenty-eight-year experience of the Chinese Communist Party before its achievement of power but also in the experience of the whole Chinese people. The long era of warlordism and the Nationalist revolution, followed by the eight years of Japanese invasion and the four years of civil war, had produced a nationwide craving for central authority, firm leadership, peace and order. The forms and methods of a new order had also accumulated: the Leninist system of party dictatorship used by both parties; the organization of student youth, developed ever since the pioneer days of the Chinese YMCA and the Reform Movement of the 1890's; the techniques of material improvement in the village — famine relief, public health measures, fly-swatting, well-digging, tree-planting, crop improvement, the whole program of rural reconstruction, tracing back to nineteenth century missionary beginnings and the mass education movement. Meanwhile, inspiring the use of these new methods was the spirit of devotion to country above all — including, for example, the ideals of citizenship espoused by Liang Ch'i-ch'ao, the welfare of "the people" invoked by Sun Yat-sen, the national unity once embodied in Chiang Kai-shek.

Such perspectives may suggest that the new regime in Peking was less monolithic than it liked to think it was and less purely a product of Marxism-Leninism than it claimed to be. Its achievement was less to invent all the parts of the new order than to put them together, under an unprecedented degree of central control made possible by Communist theory and practice. The result, in any case, was something quite new in Chinese experience.

Below we look first at the measures and mechanisms by which the Chinese Communist Party built up its control over the Chinese state and people, and second at its effort to remake them. Though the two processes went hand in hand, remaking depended on first controlling.

Political Control

The military take-over occupied a year and a half, from the fall of Mukden on November 1, 1948, and of Peking and Tientsin in January 1949, until the occupation of all the mainland by May 1950. The Chinese People's Republic was proclaimed in the midst of this process on October 1, 1949. The take-over left in office most local administrators. On the surface the Communist cadres gave it a festive air, dancing the *yang-ko* in the streets, proclaiming peace and liberation. The troops generally behaved scrupulously. It was a hopeful honeymoon period, devoted to military mopping-up, economic recovery, and political organization.

Coalition Government. The policy for this period, laid down by Mao in January and confirmed by the CCP Central Committee in March 1949, amounted to a platform of getting rid of the Kuomintang, supplanting it with a coalition government, and reforming China's armies, foreign relations, and economic system. In order to mobilize a broad basis of support, the coalition government should be organized by a new People's Political Consultative Conference, reminiscent in name but not in membership of the multi-party conference at the time of General Marshall's mediation.

This line was developed in Mao's statement of July 1, 1949, "On the people's democratic dictatorship." Echoing Lenin's

327

phrase the "democratic dictatorship of workers and peasants," Mao propounded the quite un-Leninist thesis that the new government should be a democratic coalition under Communist leadership at the same time that it was a dictatorship directed against the reactionary classes or "enemies of the people." Thus the "people's democratic dictatorship" would attempt in united-front style to line up the broadest possible support for the regime and at the same time eliminate its foes within the Chinese world. The "people" were defined as composed of four classes: proletariat, peasantry, petty bourgeoisie, national bourgeoisie. For the peasantry there was a prospect of maintaining, at least temporarily, private property in land, and for the bourgeoisie, a sector of privately owned industry. This carried out the original idea of the New Democracy.

Since any individual could be transferred by a stroke of the pen to the category of reactionaries or enemies of the people, this framework was completely flexible as a basis for sifting out dissident members of the population. The power of class imputation remained with the Communist Party, and a reformed "reactionary" could be declared by it to be a member of the "people." Leaving this mechanism at first in the background, Mao Tse-tung called upon his countrymen, in this moment of hope and general relief, to take the first step on a 10,000 mile march, to wipe out domestic and repulse foreign enemies and to remake Chinese society, without help from abroad except that of the Soviet Union, using the means at hand but learning from all quarters.

After several months' preparation, the Preparatory Committee of the People's Political Consultative Conference was set up at Peking in June 1949, nominally representing twenty-three parties or groups. The PPCC itself was convened in September for ten days, with 662 delegates. It passed the Common Program, a general statement of aims of the new coalition government, and the Organic Law of the Central People's Government, which made the working class the leader of the republic. Since the CCP was the vanguard which represents the working class, this meant that the government was to be its administrative arm. The new administration was given complete executive, legislative, and judicial powers on a centralist basis. Some thirty ministries or similar agencies were set up, fifteen of them connected with economic affairs. In the top committee, thirty-one out of fifty-six seats were occupied by Communists. Chou En-lai, surely one of the great number-two men of all time, became premier.

This powerful autocratic administration by Communist desire left the minor parties in existence, though without much following, and gave posts of prominence to non-Communists in order to carry out the idea of coalition government, that the talents of all the people must be used in building the new society. It was essential for Communist China to use the training and ability of that major part of the upper class which had never been Communist. These people were not susceptible to complete remaking into Communists but nevertheless essential for the time being as part of the Communist structure and program. Liberal intellectuals were therefore catered to, given scope for their talents and placed in high position, interlarded in the new ministries with party members who lacked their abilities but were more disciplined. (One is reminded of barbarian conquerors' use of Chinese administrators.) The larger part of the Western-returned scholars, including those educated in the United States, appear to have been in this category. As patriots, they were devoted to their country's future. Long since estranged from the Kuomintang, they saw no alternative. The Communist Party also had long since developed its united-front methods for manipulating and utilizing liberal intellectuals.

The Communists, like the Kuomintang, set up a tripod of power — party, government, and army, each forming a separate echelon but all three tied together by the Communist leadership. The party grew to 2.7 million members by 1947, to 6.1 million by 1953, to fourteen million by 1959, to seventeen million by 1961. The top authority reposed in the Central Committee, which grew to include ninety-four members and ninety-three alternate members, as of 1962, but power was exercised by its Political Bureau of nineteen members and six alternates (who might participate in discussions but not vote), and ultimately by this bureau's Standing Committee of seven persons. Below the Central Committee the party structure descended through roughly eight levels, the principal ones being six regional bureaus; 28 provincial or equivalent committees; 258 special district committees; 2200 hsien or similar committees; some 26,000 commune committees after 1958; and more than one million branch committees in the villages, factories, schools, and so on. These myriad committees exercised the party's powers of leadership, supervision, patronage, and control.

The party structure was paralleled by the government structure that its members interpenetrated. Communist government reached far below the old Kuomintang level. People's Representative Congresses, like Russian soviets, were set up in a hierarchy from the village on up to the National People's Congress at Peking, which was first convened in 1954. These government congresses had quasi-legislative functions and were used mainly as sounding boards and transmission belts for policy from above. They provided an arena for popular participation in "democratic centralism" but had no real power in a Western legal sense.

The government structure was reorganized several times. In 1954 the new government constitution (to be distinguished from the new party constitution of 1956) diminished the role of non-Communists and strengthened that of the premier. Chou

En-lai now headed a State Council which included as many as sixteen vice premiers and the heads of some seventy ministries or similar bodies.

A. Doak Barnett, John W. Lewis, Franz Schurmann, and others have studied how this government was controlled by the party and operated in tandem with it. In brief, the administration was divided into major functional systems which handled all over the country certain major government functions. The major systems concerned political and legal (internal) affairs; propaganda and education (cultural matters); agriculture, forestry, and water conservancy (rural work); industry and communications; finance and trade. These various lines of administration were pursued in a vertical structure of agencies stretching down from the capital through the various territorial levels of the administrative hierarchy. Each of these systems was supervised both by an office of the State Council and by an office of the Party Central Committee. There was a direct flow of instructions from the top down and of reports from the bottom up, but this "vertical rule" extending downward through lower-level branch agencies was balanced by "dual rule" when such branch agencies were also coordinated through committees operating laterally at a given level in the hierarchy. The specialties of foreign affairs and military affairs were both handled by functional systems, and the term was applied also to united front work by the party among the people and to the programs of party work among youth and among women.

In all operations the party set the policy and the government agencies carried it out. The party not only issued directives from the top, it also had its members in most of the key administrative posts within the government hierarchy; and its regional, provincial, and local party committees could supervise as they coordinated action at the various levels. Within each government agency party members had their own organization in committees and branches, and the leading party members formed a top group or "party fraction."

The Mass Organizations. Parallel to the structures of party and government, there were the new nationwide mass organizations. These organizations had originated during the KMT-CCP collaboration of the 1920's, but the Kuomintang had let them wither away after its rise to power at Nanking. The All-China Federation of Trade Unions had been founded in 1922; in 1956 it claimed a membership of over 13 million. In 1949 there was created a full panoply of parallel bodies: an All-China Federation of Democratic Women (76 million members in 1953); of Democratic Youth (34 million in 1957); of Cooperative Workers, that is, peasants in cooperatives (162 million in 1956); and of Literature and Art, under the prolific writer Kuo Mo-jo, to mobilize intellectuals. In addition there were an All-China Students' Federation (4 million in 1955), a children's Young Pioneer corps (30 million in 1957), and many comparable bodies more specialized in nature, dealing with science, art and learning, welfare activities, or international relations — for example, the Sino-Soviet Friendship Association (68 million members in 1953) and similar associations for Sino-Indian and Sino-Burmese friendship. Finally in 1953 was established the All-China Association of Industry and Commerce, for the national bourgeoisie, who at that time still existed. (Three years later they had ceased to exist as a recognized class.)

Mass organizations reached the individual in his professional or social role, among his peers, in ways that the government could not. Each was controlled from the top by "democratic centralism" though authority was nominally vested in a national congress meeting at long intervals. Party members of course predominated in key posts but through them reached out to mobilize the general public. Each organization had broadly defined purposes and programs and an extensive administrative apparatus. Something like half the adult Chinese population were thus brought into one or another action group and involved in its program of meetings, study, and agitation.

The mass organizations developed big training programs with schools and indoctrination centers, and served as recruiting agencies for talented and activist personnel. Their welfare and cultural work included such things as labor insurance, leave and pension systems, literacy classes, maternity hospitals and midwife training, or recreational activities, accompanied by a large output of books, magazines, and pamphlets circulated through libraries. Their members could also be used in the security system or in nationwide campaigns like that against reactionaries. All this had its ultimate effect through the local units of organization, the neighborhood (street) committees and small groups at places of work.

The mass organizations performed primarily political functions as quasi-government agencies, bridging the immemorial gap between populace and officialdom. In James Townsend's phrase, they "politicized an apolitical population" as one part of the apparatus which applied the concept of the "mass line": that the CCP leadership must be guided by constant contact with the worker-peasant masses, first securing from the party workers full and accurate reports as to the masses' problems and opinions, then issuing policy directives to meet these problems, and finally getting the masses to adopt the policies as their own and carry them out. The mass organizations received government aid and even representation in the People's Congresses. In actuality, their main function was to indoctrinate. Working directly with the populace through meetings and demonstrations as well as propagandizing through mass media, they were able to manipulate the climate of opinion. Local police stations also used the street committees, whose duty it was to promote not only welfare measures but also mutual surveillance and denunciation among neighbors and within families. When coordinated in each locality, this whole apparatus could bring to bear upon every individual a pervasive and overwhelming public pressure.

The mechanism to increase this pressure was the campaign or movement. Campaigns might appear to start spontaneously, but they developed only as the Central Committee of the party decreed. Campaigns quickly set in motion the enormous new apparatus of party, state, and mass organizations and directed its hammer blows against one target after another among the various classes and their institutions. The campaign method of revolutionary development, encouraging the cadres to attack certain heterodox ideas or undesired activities, could develop a high momentum and easily overshoot the mark, achieving "excesses." Each campaign therefore gave rise to another to check, redirect, or supersede the previous one.

Standing behind this apparatus were well-paid security forces and secret services. Locally the street committees or residents' committees and their mediation officers or committees were encouraged to dispose informally of conflicts arising among individuals from day to day. Also at the local level the police stations handled cases or if necessary passed them on to the hierarchy of "people's courts," also an arm of the central administration. As Jerome A. Cohen has made plain, serious criminal cases normally came to trial only after the accused had been thoroughly interrogated, without benefit of counsel, had fully confessed, and had denounced any others concerned in the crime with which he had been charged. Since law expressed the revolutionary policy of the party, it remained largely uncodified and changeable. This uncertainty of the law for both judges and accused was, to be sure, reminiscent of the traditional Chinese system. Justice was still weighted on the side of the state, in effect personal and particular, to be secured by applying universal principles to the circumstances discerned in each case, with a minimum of procedure. Litigation was disesteemed, legislation unimportant. Codes remained unpublished, but norms of conduct were of course made known through political indoctrination.

Economic Reconstruction

The intensive program of political organization to set up the apparatus sketched above was carried on concomitantly with a vigorous economic program. Early in 1949 Mao announced a "shift to the cities" as the focus of effort, reaffirming the primacy of the urban proletariat in a party which was now about 90 percent of peasant origin. The CCP had inherited three economic sectors: the circular-flow subsistence economy of the countryside, the separately based, foreign-trade-and-industry economy of the treaty ports, and finally Manchuria as a heavy industry base created by the Japanese in an undeveloped area. The problem was to organize these three economies into one.

The first industrial objective set in 1949 was to get production back to its prewar level within about three years. Japan's industrial build-up in Manchuria had been reduced in 1945 by Russian removal of more than half the capital equipment, with an estimated replacement value of at least two billion American dollars. In China proper, railroads had been torn up by civil war, urban labor demoralized by hyperinflation. After the Communist victory it took some time to convince the city worker that Liberation had brought him first of all the opportunity to work harder. Wartime blockades between city and country had increased rural self-sufficiency; market crops like cotton had to be revived. Meanwhile inflation was still a major problem. Military operations were still continuing in

1949–50 and some 9 million persons were on government rations or payrolls (including minor Nationalist administrative and military personnel who had been taken over). The substitution of a new "people's currency" for the Nationalist banknotes, even at favorable rates, left the regime still obliged to expand its note issue steadily to meet a budget deficit of perhaps 75 percent. Shanghai prices rose 70 times in nine months, from May 1949 to February 1950. All this demanded strenuous measures.

The first move toward quelling the inflation was to get the budget more or less balanced by increasing revenue, first in the countryside by collecting agricultural taxes in kind, then in the cities through devices like a sales tax on each major commodity and business taxes set by "democratic appraisal" of trade associations to meet quotas previously set by government. The result of the sales and business taxation was to squeeze money out of the more monetized sector of the economy. Secondly, the entire fiscal administration was reorganized and rationalized to give the central government control over formerly local taxes, to eliminate private banks' handling of official funds, and generally to reduce expenditures, licit and illicit. The regime gradually made the collection process more efficient, controlling it for the first time directly down to the village level. Through the banks the government got control of money and credit, and set up six government trading corporations to dominate prices in major cunsumer commodities.

One device for restoring confidence was to express wages, salaries, bank deposits, some government payments, and bond issues in terms of commodity units (commodity basket values), defined in quantities of goods of daily use rather than in monetary prices. A typical unit might be composed of 6 catties (8 lbs.) of rice, 1½ catties of flour, 16 catties of coal, and 4 feet of white shirting. As prices rose, the commodity-based unit would rise accordingly in money terms. Paid in this unit, one could save by making bank deposits or buying bonds in similar units; either way, one was protected against further inflation. Thus by a variety of methods designed to achieve a balance between the supply of goods and the flow of money income, the inflation was conquered by mid-1950, an impressive achievement.

Another achievement of the first year was an extensive reopening of railway track, to get most of China's 13,500 miles back into operation. Economic recovery was aided by three good harvests in 1950, 1951, and 1952. By 1952, the pre-1949 peaks of production had been equaled or surpassed in pig iron, cement, steel, and oil (all very modest in China), and in coal, electric power, flour, and cotton cloth, but production was still short of the pre-1949 peak in some consumer goods such as sugar. Most important, by 1952 the three sectors of the old economy had been given greater national unity than ever before. Railway track had expanded to 15,000 and highways to 75,000 miles. A centralized banking system and single uniform currency now covered the country. Budgeting could be attempted realistically for the first time.

Peking's long-term economic aim was to mobilize China's resources and reallocate them for purposes of industrialization. This required a gradual extension of government control over all segments of the economy. Private enterprise was permitted to continue in form but in fact it was brought increasingly under state control through numerous devices — taxation and capital levies, rationing of credit, competition by state enterprise, demands of labor unions — so that businessmen practically became bureaucrats. By controlling credit and raw materials and monopolizing key commodities, the state could now dominate production and commerce, in addition to its outright control of most heavy industry, railways, and foreign trade. The other requirement was a traditional one brought up-to-date — control of the surplus product of the land.

Land Reform. In the history of Chinese Communism there had been several shifts of land policy, exemplified by the severity of the Kiangsi period, when many landlords were exterminated, and the moderation of the Yenan period, when they were guaranteed a sizable rent. As Communist power expanded after 1946, land reform had proceeded on a piecemeal and often violent basis, sometimes with more peasant violence than the party claimed to have desired.

The nationwide land reform, begun in mid-1950 and completed by late 1952 or early 1953, was not merely economic but also social and political in aim. A work team of cadres coming to a village first identified out-and-out enemies, if necessary got them out of the way, and then explained the desirability of land reform to the poor peasantry in particular, who would theoretically be the main beneficiaries. By this means active elements were selected who had the motivation and the capacity to lead the forthcoming movement. After this preparation a period of "class struggle" was inaugurated. In a series of "struggle meetings" the accumulated grievances of the populace could be brought forth in "speaking bitterness" or "settling accounts." Hatred could be fanned into mob violence in public "trials." Unpopular landlords or "local despots" chosen for public denunciation were either killed, expelled, or brought to confess and reform, while the entire community by taking violent measures committed themselves to the new order.

The next phase was to create peasants' associations which by a process of community assent could work out the definition of class status for each individual as landlord, rich peasant, middle peasant, poor peasant, or farm laborer and could carry on the classification, confiscation, and redistribution of landholdings. The resulting "equalization of land tenure" was in the old tradition of peasant rebellions. Through Communist direction of this process, the activists were usually favored, the well-to-do reduced, and the remnants of the landlord gentry wiped out either in person or in status, while the party representatives established their authority over the village. The tiller now had title to his land, at least for the moment.

This New Democracy phase of private ownership had been advertised in 1950 to last for a "rather long time," but in fact it lasted no longer for the farmer than it had for the capitalist. To supplant the old order the Communist regime moved without delay toward the construction of the new collectivist agrarian system, beginning with a first stage of cooperatives.

Cooperation could achieve greater efficiency of production: six donkeys could go to market with one donkey-driver, not six. One housewife at a time could cook for several families. Since there were fewer draft animals than households, their use could be shared. Joint savings could buy a pump or a tool no individual could afford. In particular, handicraft cooperatives could use scattered local materials and unemployed farm labor in the off season to increase the production of consumer goods with rather little state investment. As larger units of operation, they could create a division of labor, with specialization. With organization might come literacy, health, technology, and higher productivity. Rural supply and marketing cooperatives meanwhile promoted exchange between farm and factory, handling state purchases and making available a wider variety of manufactures than the villages had seen before.

In agriculture the reform program for increased production, as it was termed, moved gradually from north to south through a series of planned phases, first setting up temporary, usually seasonal, small-scale mutual-aid teams, then larger permanent ones, and then agricultural producers' cooperatives. In the cooperatives the peasants began to cultivate in common and share a common product in proportion to their pooled contributions of land, equipment, and labor. The cooperatives were still posited on private ownership of land and voluntary cooperation for mutual benefit. However, the goal began to shift. The regime had heretofore argued that land redistribution in itself, by eliminating landlordism (though without much increase of acreage), would release the peasantry's "productive energy." Now it was admitted that only eventual collectivization could effect the increase in agricultural product necessary to pay for industrialization. The effort was to lead the inveterately property-conscious peasant, through propaganda, practice, and steady pressure, to become (as the French agronomist René Dumont put it) "a socialist without knowing it."

Social Reorganization

China's traditional ancestor reverence, family-clan cohesiveness, and filial piety had long been eroding. Communist "liberation" furthered the process. By the new marriage law of 1950, women were given full equality with men in rights of marriage, divorce, and property ownership. In the various campaigns of the 1950's, children were commended for denouncing their parents, thus spectacularly reversing the ancient stress on filial piety as the highest virtue. Extended family ties were disparaged as feudal, and romantic love as bourgeois. The new state with its ubiquitous branches tried to displace the Chinese patrilineal family system, leaving the nuclear family as the norm.

The totalitarian mobilization of the populace was made easier in late 1950 by the Korean War. Reports of China's early victories and later of alleged germ warfare by the United States provided a useful sanction for intensifying anti-American sentiment and destroying the generally favorable Chinese image of America. War was also an opportunity to get rid of irreconcilables. Two major campaigns were mounted, to "Resist America, aid Korea," and to "Suppress counterrevolutionaries." They called for patriotic spying on relatives and neighbors, public denunciation even of parents, and consignment of enemies of the people, reactionaries, and counterrevolutionaries to "reform through labor." Execution of such enemies, together with persons condemned by "people's courts" in the land reform, were in the hundreds of thousands, some say many millions. The honeymoon was over. The regime destroyed the remnants of the landlord gentry and benefited by extensive confiscations of property. It showed its claws and teeth, and the effect was not lost upon the populace, who became more amenable to discipline and direction.

In this context of terror on the one hand and patriotism on the other, foreign missionaries were denounced as spies and jailed or expelled. A "three-self" movement was set going, for "self-government, self-support, and self-propagation" of the Christian church in China, free of the missionaries' alleged "cultural imperialism." Uncooperative church leaders were gradually eliminated from positions of leadership, and "national churches" free of foreign ties were finally set up to give Chinese Christians a religion subservient to the Communist state. In 1958, having cut off foreign support and pressured Chinese Christian leaders to join up, the three-self movement unified the worship of all denominations in each locality. A Chinese Catholic church was also created, independent of the Pope, who responded with excommunication. All these efforts tried to reverse China's Western orientation.

Minor campaigns were pursued to secure a more effective payment of taxes and greater regularity in economic life. Victory bond and war donation drives mopped up public funds in order to counteract inflation. Another program was designed to raise the social status of the soldier, another to increase output and labor efficiency through the Stakhanovite system of work quotas and team competition.

The pressures and dangers of a war with the United States, whose power had bulked so large in the Chinese mind, were thus turned to purposes of social reorganization and industrial efficiency. The germ warfare hoax was also elaborately fabricated and publicized, with the approval of an international board of left-wing scientists and a mass of circumstantial evidence, to blacken the American name. Yet even here a subsidiary aim was also realized, since the germ warfare theme stimulated public health measures all over the country.

The mechanisms for mobilizing public pressure against designated types of individuals were used more and more plainly for refashioning China's social structure. A new height in this effort came with the Three-anti and Five-anti movements of 1951-52. These were organized very thoroughly and proceeded through well defined phases with standardized methods.

The Three-anti campaign was directed against officialdom, in the government, in state industries, and in the party. The movement was anti-corruption, anti-waste, and anti-bureaucratism — plainly an attempt to weed out and invigorate the vast administrative apparatus inherited from the Kuomintang and rapidly added to since 1949. The Three-anti movement permitted replacement of administrative personnel by new blood, as fast as it could be developed for the purpose, and brought the enlarged bureaucracy more thoroughly under central control by keeping the bureaucrat insecure in his new power. Like many major drives, it began in Manchuria, the most advanced area under the new regime. Special committees and an apparatus were soon formed to promote the movement countrywide with spectacular denunciations, public "trials," and great publicity.

The Five-anti movement was a similarly well organized and concerted attack on merchants and manufacturers, the bourgeoisie in general. Nominally it was against bribery, tax evasion, theft of state assets, cheating in labor or materials, and stealing of state economic intelligence. Employees were inspired to accuse employers, customers accused shopowners, and there was a general screening of all persons in urban trade and industry. As in all campaigns, the public were mobilized, committees established, and appearances created of great popular initiative, righteous anger, and enthusiasm for the triumph of virtue. Confessions, apologies, and the reform or elimination of culprits by suicide, execution, or labor camp followed. But it is evident that one immediate aim in this anti-middle class program was financial. Large sums were squeezed out of the business class, probably worth between one and two billion United States dollars. From this time the "national bourgeoisie," those small-scale businessmen and industrialists not allied with foreigners, existed on sufferance; those who remained in business were thereafter thoroughly amenable to the continued pressure for socialization of private enterprise. (Eventually they were all expropriated and in January 1956 dutifully celebrated, with firecrackers and dancing, their own demise as a social class.)

All these manipulations of the body politic got rid of numerous enemies of the regime. Forced labor camps were the natural result, built both on the Soviet model and on the ancient corvée tradition of China. Muscle power had always been the country's chief natural resource. The modern use of labor armies of 4 million persons on one project of public works, like the much-publicized Huai River dikes and dams, was no great innovation except for its increased scope and the edifying moral exhortation which accompanied it. Whether the millions of Chinese who now performed forced labor on short rations were more numerous than the millions who had normally starved while farming every year, no one could say. The difference was that the grinding down and slow extinction of life through prolonged and ill-equipped labor, always a part of the Chinese scene whether planned or purely circumstantial, was now well organized.

Pre-Communist China was pre-modern and particularistic in many ways — in the neglect of punctuality, the lack of civic consciousness and public neatness, in putting family before community and personal interests before national, in all those attitudes and habits that the futile New Life Movement had condemned in 1935. The Confucian order having been eroded away, China was truly "a sheet of loose sand" as Dr. Sun complained, a country that American GI's felt ought to be "cleaned up." In the old days, everyone haggled over prices, took note of manners, and treated every situation ad hoc and every person according to the circumstances if not on his merits. All this was quite contrary to the efficient impersonality of modern, universalistic market relations. This pre-modern character of Chinese society, its "medieval" traits, had fascinated foreigners and humiliated patriots for a century. The Confucian scholars who sought a panacea in gunboats, then technology, and finally in the reform of institutions had now been succeeded by revolutionists who condemned old ways as "feudal" and sought to remake their cosmos by applying the allegedly universal, abstract principles of a new Marxist-Leninist "science" of society. With reforming zeal their Leninist party, once thoroughly in control, applied itself to remaking not only the economy and social order but also the individual.

Thought Reform

The Communist achievement in organization, among a people so recently famous for their lack of it, depended upon the inspiring, coercing, or manipulating of individual personalities. Building upon methods used in Yenan to Leninize the party (as well as to convert Japanese war prisoners), Liu Shao-ch'i and other organizers developed empirical procedures to deal with every type of enemy or supporter. When American POW's in Korea "confessed" to germ warfare and collaborated with their Chinese captors, they were responding to techniques developed through use with Chinese of all sorts, including party members. As a result of these methods capitalists and rich peasants smilingly gave their property to the state, professors scathingly denounced their Western bourgeois education, secondary school students devotedly gave their lives to party work.

These diverse phenomena represented the real Communist effort at revolution, to change Chinese thinking and behavior. Though very diverse, thought reform generally had certain common features: control of the environment, both of the person physically and of the information available to him (this was now true of the whole country); the stimuli both of idealism and of terror, intermixed; and a grim psychological experience, undergone with guidance through successive phases and intensified by the manipulation of one's sense of guilt and shame. The Chinese slang term "brainwashing" imparted perhaps too much mystery to a process faintly visible elsewhere in religious crusades of the past, only now more thoroughly organized. Modern psychologists can explain how privation, prolonged insecurity, and tension, combined with extended fatigue and repetitive indoctrination, can shatter the individual's sense of inner identity and create pressures from which the only escape for many is submission to authority and acceptance at least temporarily of new attitudes and concepts. This coercing of the human mind, quite different in degree from the mild voluntary form of American advertising methods, is still only partially understood and exploited. Spread over the world it would create the ultimate crisis of individualism. Perhaps it is not surprising that in China, where the practical art of human relations has been more fully developed than anywhere else, these psychological methods should be so advanced.

For the Chinese student class, from whom the CCP had to get its cadres, this intellectual-emotional reconditioning was carried out in the big revolutionary colleges set up through the reorganization and expansion of the educational system. Thousands of trainees went through indoctrination courses of several months' duration. A center of this type containing 4,000 students might be subdivided into classes of one or two hundred and then into study groups of six to ten persons. A psychiatrist who analyzed the procedure, Robert Lifton, divided a typical six-month course of thought reform into three stages — first, group identification, a period of togetherness and considerable freedom and enthusiasm. During this stage major Marxist-Leninist-Maoist concepts were studied and systematic rational indoctrination was delivered, partly in lectures but mainly in small group discussions. A free exchange of views, with a high esprit de corps and feeling of common effort, led the trainee to expose himself freely and engage wholeheartedly in a "thought mobilization."

The second phase was one of induced emotional conflict within each individual. The daily schedule continued to be physically exhausting. The milieu, carefully controlled behind the scenes, now seemed to close in. The individual submitted his first summary of his own life and thought. He began to feel under pressure as criticism and self-criticism intensified and the dangers of being rejected became apparent. The evils within the old individual were now attacked, not merely the old society in the abstract, and the student strove to dig up his failings and correct them. Group pressures were focused by experienced leaders so that each individual became heavily involved emotionally, under assault. His failings might be labeled with any one of dozens of terms. He might struggle with himself and be "struggled with" by his group-mates over an excess of subjectivism or objectivism, of opportunism or dogmatism, bureaucratism or individual heroism, and so forth. The individual who attempted to hold back and resist the process could not win and took a psychological beating. Each participant, whether or not he resisted, was completely alone, isolated within himself like all his fellows. Under this pressure, similar to that used against prisoners, the individual soon felt guilt (he had sinned and should be punished) and also a sense of shame (he had lost face and self-esteem), which created intense humiliation. In attacking himself, he was thus prepared to achieve through confession and self-condemnation a psychological catharsis, feeling as though he were mentally ill and needed a cure.

The third phase was that of submission and rebirth. When his final thought summary or confession had been gone over from every angle and was accepted by the group and the authorities, the individual was likely to feel exhilarated, cleansed, a new person. This months-long process constituted on a larger scale a sort of induced religious conversion, like those of our own revival meetings, but with added elements of pressure and psychotherapy. The individual had been manipulated so that the wellsprings of his own nature had put him under intense emotional pressure, and the relief from this self-induced tension was associated with the external authority of the group and the party, on whom he should henceforth be dependent. For the party's aim was not only to secure control over disciplined activists but also to raise the quality of their performance by changing their idea of themselves, their goals and values. They renounced family and father, and accepted the party and the revolution in their place.

This process was most successful with malleable young minds. In the case of older intellectuals, particularly returned students from the West, criticism, self-criticism, and confession could only be an overlay of the formative experience of a mature person. Many statements put out by Peking professors seemed to be pro forma. They denounced the corrupting influence of the bourgeois West and their former subjection to it, possibly with some sense of guilt at having been seduced or alienated from their native culture. But the net effect of their self-criticism was probably less to change these individuals than to align them properly in the public eye as supporters of the new order. Thus the one class who might represent a Western non-Communist influence neutralized themselves and presented no model for youth.

Communism and Confucianism. Few who have lived in China will assume that a revolution, however irresistible, can quickly remake the immovable Middle Kingdom. The ambitious project to substitute the ancient ideographic script by an alphabet — the greatest literary project in all history — has been held up and modified, perhaps abandoned. Our schematic account of thought reform should not imply that it could easily remake the Chinese personality. However, the strategy was long-term, to maintain a controlled environment of lip service if not love for the regime until the new socialist generation could take over.

Out of the Chinese inheritance, moreover, authoritarian traditions could be invoked for modern purposes. Thus Confucianism in one of its aspects has a certain resonance with Marxism. This is not an identity, only a partial overlap; nor is it surprising, for Confucianism is almost as broad and various as Christianity.

One point of resonance was in the important concept of the unity of theory and practice. The Bolshevik emphasis on putting theory into revolutionary practice contended that theory was no good in itself but must be applied in activity, as part of an effort not only to understand the world but to change it.

Marxism as a "science of history" when put into practice must become an ethic, a personal philosophy animating one's entire thought and conduct. Self-criticism was a necessary part of discipline for this purpose. It was also a Communist doctrine that Marxist-Leninist theory should be applied according to the content of each national background, blending Communist ideas with the local tradition. As Mao said, "We must unify appropriately the general truth of Marxism with the concrete practice of the Chinese revolution."

Now it happened that Communist self-criticism was in some degree reminiscent of the Confucian doctrine of self-cultivation in the form associated particularly with the sixteenth century philosopher Wang Yang-ming (1472–1529). Wang attacked the dualism of knowledge and action. In Wang's view, as David Nivison puts it, "To know is to know how and to know that one ought." The completely sincere man must express his moral perceptions in equally moral conduct. Wang and others therefore urged self-cultivation as a process by which the true philosopher can bring his thought and conduct into consonance, so that knowledge is realized in action and action contributes to knowledge. This idea was echoed in Sun Yat-sen's "Knowledge is difficult, action is easy" and later by Chiang Kai-shek.

While Confucian self-cultivation was not a group affair, it stressed the moral improvability of human nature, the ancient Chinese belief that through proper ethical instruction and exhortation, man can be made into a more social being. The gap between individual self-cultivation and group self-criticism is a very broad one in fact but the two have somethng in common. Thought reform at Yenan made use of traditional Chinese terminology and invoked Confucian sanctions. The good Communist, according to Liu Shao-ch'i, must discipline himself through self-cultivation, through "watching himself when alone," so as to become flexibly and resourcefully obedient to the party's leadership. Through greater consciousness of the historical influences playing upon him, it was argued, he might indeed achieve a certain feeling of freedom within the confines of the historical process. Thus where Confucianism instilled loyalty to family, father, and Emperor, Maoism now diverted it to the people, the party, and the leader. The classics were quoted for this purpose. Marxism-Leninism seemed less outlandish.

Criticism, literary and political. In the process of thought reform, the Chinese intellectual and literary world was repeatedly agitated by ideological struggles, in which Mao Tse-tung's dictum on literature and art of 1942, that literature is a political tool in the class struggle and thoroughly subordinate to politics, provided a major premise. The full force of meetings, denunciations, and special publications was assembled to attack Hu Shih as the symbol of "decadent American bourgeois pragmatism." One campaign was against his interpretation of the famous eighteenth century novel *The Dream of the Red Chamber* as an autobiographical work. Communists preferred to see in it the inner collapse of China's feudal society, thus salvaging this fascinating book from China's heritage as belonging to "the people," like other selected heroes, poets, and cultural inheritances. The campaign simultaneously discredited Western-type literary criticism based on historical research, as part of the attack upon Chinese liberalism and its foreign allies.

But the Communist Party's creative writers still tended occasionally to be critics, the same as in the Soviet Union. Some who had gained fame attacking the evils of the old order now criticized imperfections in the new, particularly the Central Committee's claim through its literary commissar, Chou Yang, to be the final arbiter of artistic excellence. A rebellious disciple of the great satirist Lu Hsun (1881–1936) named Hu Feng was pilloried for this in a nationwide campaign. Eventually his denunciators, like the revolutionary woman novelist Ting Ling, were also denounced and purged by Chou Yang, who was himself to be purged in 1966.

Just as thought reform and other campaigns winnowed the population, separating out potential enemies and recruits, so the great corpus of China's historical inheritance had to be reappraised in Marxist-Leninist terms and integrated into the new state-and-culture. "Applying the universal principles of Marxism-Leninism to the concrete realities of China" was a never-ending process. Most of China's glorious past, for example, had to be put by definition within the Marxian period of "feudalism." Precisely when "capitalism" had begun in China was disputed; but since 1840, it was argued, foreign "capitalist imperialism," allied with domestic "feudal reaction," had checked and distorted China's "normal" capitalist development. Such formulas, imposed upon academic learning for political purposes, raised some new questions and absorbed scholarly attention.

Soviet Aid and the Soviet Model

Having early in 1949 proclaimed his policy of "leaning to one side" against "capitalist imperialism," Mao Tse-tung spent nine weeks of hard bargaining in Moscow (December 1949–February 1950). Finally he signed a thirty-year Sino-Soviet alliance treaty against aggression by Japan or any power (meaning the United States) joined with Japan. Soviet power thenceforth provided a shield behind which the Chinese Communists could pursue their domestic revolution, get rid of the last vestiges of "imperialist" rights and privileges in the former treaty ports and in the economy, religion, and education, and try to reassert China's control over border areas.

It is unlikely that Peking expected to join in the Soviet-armed North Korean aggression of June 1950 against South

Korea. Instead, the CCP evidently hoped to seize Taiwan from Nationalist hands, but this was prevented when President Truman ordered the American Seventh Fleet to stop invasion either way across the Taiwan Strait. Impelled by strategic concern for the industrial base in Manchuria, Peking entered the Korean War in force only after the UN–American forces had advanced northward across the 38th parallel. Crack divisions of Lin Piao's Fourth Field Army, labeled as "volunteers," crossed the Yalu in late 1950 and by advancing southward by night along the "impassable" mountain spine were able to catch the Yalu-bound American columns in the flank and force their great retreat from North Korea. The Chinese were light-armed, mobile forces, and when their May 1951 offensive failed to route the more heavily armed American armies, the latter counterattacked vigorously before the Chinese could regroup and rest in their usual fashion. The result was a route and the surrender of 11,000 prisoners, some in large groups. This Chinese defeat was called off by the beginning of the two-year truce negotiations in July 1951. Until the final truce of July 1953, the forces in Korea, now under General P'eng Te-huai, were built up with heavy Soviet weapons and an air force.

The People's Liberation Army also invaded Tibet in October 1950 and reasserted Chinese control in a year-long campaign of "liberation" and subjugation. Despite their cost, these campaigns built up China's military power. Afterward, military modernization used Soviet models and assistance. In 1955 compulsory military service began to draw on the five or six million young men reaching the age of eighteen each year, to create an enormous reservoir of manpower. A professional officer corps was created with Soviet-style ranks, uniforms, and differential pay as the top level of a regular army of about 2.5 million men. But jet planes and their fuel, for example, still had to be procured from the USSR.

From the start, Soviet aid came only at a price. In 1950 Sino-Soviet "joint-stock" companies were set up, on the model used in Eastern Europe, for the development of mining in Sinkiang and similar purposes potentially beneficial to the USSR. However, after the death of Stalin (announced in March 1953) these companies were liquidated. Similarly the Soviets gradually gave up their special position in Manchuria, ending joint control of the main railway in early 1953 and withdrawing from the Port Arthur naval base in 1955.

In industrialization the Soviet example and expertise were at first the Chinese Communists' greatest inspiration. Thousands of Chinese trainees went to the USSR, and thousands of Russian technicians armed with blueprints came to help renovate or build the 211 old and new projects that led the industrial program (125 more projects were added in 1958–59). Starting in 1950, the Soviet Union loaned China $60 million a year in economic aid for five years, to be repaid by Chinese exports of raw materials. China's prewar pattern of foreign trade was reversed, flowing to the Soviet bloc instead of to the West and Japan. A second loan in 1954 provided $26 million a year for five years, though by that time such a sum would hardly cover the repayments due the USSR on the first loan. China received essential help in technology, unknown amounts of military hardware, and capital equipment but went into debt accordingly.

Though the limitations of the Soviet example were not at first apparent to Peking, China's capacity to follow the Stalinist Russian industrial model was inhibited by certain specific conditions. China had extensive coal and iron ore reserves, and other mineral and oil resources greater than had been realized, but utilizing them would require a costly investment in power and transport. As Alexander Eckstein has shown, China at her level of industrial development in the early 1950's was actually closer to the Russia of 1900 than to the Soviet Union of 1928 when the five-year plans began the Soviet industrialization. Russia in 1900 already had a higher per capita production of pig iron, steel, and cotton goods, and more railroad track per square mile, than China in 1952 — and only one quarter the rural population density. By 1928 Russia had a much more extensive rail network and her production of coal, iron, steel, power, textile products, and the like in per capita terms was far greater than China's in 1952. Again, Russia had a far larger corps of modern-educated technical and professional manpower and a more developed education system. The Soviet model of industrialization, which stressed heavy industry at the expense of the peasant, was thus not really suited to China's situation. Yet the CCP at first was determined to stress heavy industry even more than the Soviets had.

Viewed against the population increase and the balance between population and food resources in the two countries, China's prospects of emulating Russia grew perceptibly dimmer. The superabundance of people (estimated by the census of 1953 at 583 million and increasing about 12 to 14 million yearly), together with the comparative lack of new land for cultivation, meant that China's population must press upon the food supply even more than Russia's had. The standard of living therefore could not be modernized very far, in the sense of raising it from the bamboo-and-rice/millet level, within the foreseeable future. Even though the centralized Chinese state might build up a superstructure of heavy industry and military power, it would remain a colossus weak in the stomach, vulnerable to natural calamity.

Mao and his colleagues were loath to accept any limits on their hopes. Consequently the ineradicable limitations in China's material resources, combined with the CCP's success in consolidating its power and mobilizing the country's human resources, set the stage by the mid-1950's for one of the great national efforts and frustrations of history.

16 The People's Republic: The Struggle for Socialist Transformation

We Americans were formerly privileged observers of the Chinese drama. Since 1949, we have been distant outsiders. The massive Chairman Mao, Chou En-lai of the handsome black eyebrows, and their seemingly interchangeable associates have tangled on a far horizon, debating strange issues in an esoteric jargon. Like actors on a screen without a soundtrack, they mouth intense feelings, but the exact import eludes us.

Yet troubles have come upon us too, in America, due to rapid growth and change. We too have suffered for our past mistakes, met problems we cannot shake off, doubted our leaders, lost our complacency and self-respect. With a little imagination we can sympathize with the Chinese experience even though from a great distance.

The revolution has tried, most basically, to make peasants into citizens, to bring the masses into politics. But the Chinese village is not yet part of automobile civilization. Not sharing in our technology, it does not suffer from traffic congestion, air pollution or highway accidents, or even from television commercials, delinquency, drug abuse, anomie, or homosexuality. Its concerns have come down from a simpler age: how to produce enough and how to distribute it. After famine and disease, the ancient enemy has been the ruling class — the privileged few whose education and connections gave them access to land and office. Ruling class status and all its trappings were posited on the classical dictum that muscle workers naturally are governed by brain workers. Since the ruling class generally governed the countryside from the cities, Mao's problem after taking power was how to reach the village to revolutionize it. If he could not, the villagers would retain the ancient ideas that sanctioned the ruling class — for example, that education qualifies one to rule others — and thus the old village would remain ready to accept a new ruling class.

The Maoist revolution, to remake the society by remaking the people, thus became a semi-controlled process of struggle, between ideas, behavior patterns, and the interests of classes, regions, and individuals. While much of this struggle has been carried on face to face in meetings large and small — five-hour reports by party secretaries, abashed self-criticisms in study-groups — it has also been reflected in reams of print. A small but able corps of American specialists has followed the Chinese output and analyzed the course of events. This brief chapter, though built upon their work (see bibliography), can only begin to represent its range and insight. From such studies we can know little of personal lives in China — the hopes and woes of individuals, who loved whom, and whatever happened to old Wang and Chang after they were publicly humiliated — but we get nevertheless vivid case histories, an impression of the issues and anxieties in public life, and also of the meagerness of private life among political activists.

One striking feature of the revolution has been the continued fusion of morality and politics, such that a policy mistake is a moral crime, on the ancient Confucian assumption that conduct is character made manifest, that theory and practice should be one, and whoever acted with good intent but bad results was in the wrong. This unitary system has worked in the People's Republic as under imperial Confucianism because moral-ideological authority and political power have been combined at the top — first in the party Central Committee and then in the great leader, Mao himself.

Theory and practice, thought and behavior, in this Chinese view interpenetrate and interreact, and ideology is constantly shifting in its application to events. It is a complex structure. Class struggle is the basic assumption, class status therefore a basic criterion. Contradictions are the stuff of dialectical conflict: contradictions of socialism against imperialism in the outer world, of the needs of industry against agriculture within China, of proletarian against bourgeois tendencies within oneself, and so on in endless profusion and in all aspects of life. Contradictions when perceived lead to struggle, eventual polarization, and resolution in a new unity, or so it is hoped. But in fact one struggle has led only to another on slightly different terms, without any end to the process, which Mao has aptly called "permanent revolution," a way of life. What a contrast with the old ideal of harmony!

Collectivization of Agriculture

The practical completion of land reform by the end of 1952, together with the tightening of controls over the urban and industrial sector of the economy, put Peking by 1953 in a position to plan joint programs for industrialization and for the collectivization of agriculture. Catching up with the West materially would require a harsh regimentation of economic effort over a prolonged period. The process would lead to urbanization: Shanghai, for example, instead of withering away as first proposed, was already approaching seven million. The swelling cities would increase their demand for agricultural products. Industrialization would also necessitate imports of Soviet-bloc capital goods, which could be paid for only by exporting, again, agricultural products. To extract more from the farm economy, a squeezing mechanism must be created in the form of true collectives. While these might lower incentives among agricultural workers, they seemed the only sure way to enforce saving and check the revival of a "rich peasant" class based on private landowning. Collectives were also the most efficient means for agronomic technical development.

Collectivization required what Alexander Eckstein has called "high-pressure gradualism," using coercion short of violence and manifold forms of persuasion on the farming populace. The initial decision to move toward collectivization, announced in December 1953 after some intra-party debate, had got results much faster than anticipated. Fifteen percent of the farm land and farming families were in agricultural producers' cooperatives (which were already called "semi-socialist collectives") by mid-1955, with many reports of 10 percent or even higher increases in production. Mao Tse-tung spent several weeks touring the major provinces, testing local sentiment. Encouraged by a bumper harvest, the CCP Central Committee, though apparently not without misgivings and objections, accepted his startling proposal for accelerated collectivization, with the final elimination of the rich peasant, the merchant-speculator, land rent, and all capitalistic tendencies in rural life. Mao called for 250 million peasants to form 2 million agricultural producers' cooperatives of fifty families each (making on the average two cooperatives in each of a million or so villages) by 1958. This bold plan, pushed by eager cadres, again went faster than expected — within less than a year, by May 1956, nine tenths of the peasantry were reported to have joined agricultural producers' cooperatives. They were quickly asked to move on to the higher level of socialized agriculture by giving up their shares in the cooperatives and becoming wage laborers on full collective farms. How had this been accomplished?

The experienced French agronomist René Dumont, who visited forty-three villages in late 1955, pointed to a number of factors. Unlike the disastrous Soviet collectivization of 1929–1932, the process in China did not lead directly to state ownership of the land but to ownership by the individual cooperatives, which formally bought the land from the peasant owners. The process moved from temporary mutual aid teams by successive stages to permanent full-scale cooperatives, from small groups to large ones: the two million agricultural producers' cooperatives would soon be reduced to one million or less, each one larger. Most important, the program at its successive stages had evidently produced results enough to obviate resistance — at least very little was reported. A sufficient proportion of China's peasantry saw no alternative but to have faith in Chairman Mao and the party. The celebrated burning of landlords' title deeds was still fresh in memory even though the New Democracy had now run its course in only five years. Unlike Lenin, Mao had begun with the villages, and all anti-Communist leadership had been eliminated.

In the new structure, state farms (3300 at the end of 1955) served only as pilot operations to lead local development, meeting technical problems of the region, setting an example, absorbing technical graduates of some twenty-six agricultural colleges. Mechanized agriculture, except on the new lands of Manchuria, remained for the distant future. Instead of the machine tractor stations of the Soviet Union, the center of gravity in the Chinese rural program remained the cooperatives, which developed forthwith into fully collective farms. One or two to a village, they now served as the new focus of village life, undertaking the local public works and welfare activities which under the empire had been the province of gentry leadership. Where the local Confucian degree-holders of the big families — a conservative-minded and often exploitative elite — had traditionally taken the initiative to repair temples and bridges or maintain schools and charities, it was now the local cooperative or collective farm chairman, usually an enthusiastic party appointee, who initiated projects for reforestation, combatting erosion, care of the aged, or improving the local dispensary. While the directives came down from above, the actual measure must be worked out at this level — introduction of pumps or new plows, literacy classes, campaign meetings.

At this level also the ambitious twelve-year rural plan for 1956–1967 set forth bright promises: to see cultural amenities introduced (radios, libraries, movie theaters), the multitude of diseases and all flood and drought eliminated, forests widely planted, labor fully employed. Mainly by full employment (never achieved in the past), the plan hopefully envisioned 400 man-days of work applied annually to every hectare of land, doubling production in South China, increasing it by half nationally. Equally ambitious was the long-term plan to control the Yellow River by a "staircase" of forty-six dams on the main stream, plus hydropower and multi-purpose projects, so as to irrigate much of North China.

For the farm boy just learning to read, this confident vision was undoubtedly inspiring. For doubters and dissenters there was plainly announced "reform through labor." Meantime food was rationed and quotas were set for compulsory delivery of commercial crops.

The First Five-Year Plan. Preparation for a Soviet-type forced-draft industrial development had gone forward with the nationalization of banking, industry, and trade, with the state buying shares in enterprises to make them joint state-private concerns, and with campaigns to exhaust the entrepreneur and make him in effect a state employee. The first five-year plan for 1953–1957 was not finally published until two and a half years had elapsed for testing it, training technicians and building up statistical services. In July 1955, it was heralded as inaugurating the "transition to socialism," which had formally superseded the New Democracy as of 1953. Among some 1600 major projects in all fields, half would be in industry (including 156 announced in 1953–54 to be commenced with Soviet aid). The new plants would make tractors, trucks, automobiles, generators, ships, and all the materials and equipment for heavy industry. University graduates would be one-third engineers, produced at the rate of 20,000 a year.

The conflict between the development of agriculture and industry, and the consequent subordination of the former, was apparent in the first five-year plan targets announced in 1955; steel to be quadrupled, power and cement doubled, machine tools more than tripled, but cotton piece goods to be increased by less than one half and food grains by less than one fifth. In other words, industry could grow only as the farmer kept his consumption down. Collectivization had put him in a box: through price manipulation in favor of industry, his product could be taken from him indirectly as well as by outright collection of crops and taxes. Textile goods would be manufactured to exchange for rural products. But just as men had been cheaper than armament in Chinese warfare, so in her agricultural development China would have to stress capital-cheap, labor-intensive projects like flood control dikes and irrigation ditches. Pigs could be multiplied to provide both food and manure, but artificial fertilizer manufacture, for example, was likely to be limited. Meanwhile capital investment was to be concentrated in heavy industry, which would receive seven or eight times the investment in light, consumer-goods industry.

The Maoist enthusiasts who now dominated the CCP Central Committee beat down the "rightist conservatism" of their policy opponents by calling for a "leap forward" in which the people's productive energies would be psychologically liberated and incentive devices such as emulation campaigns among competing workers' groups would achieve "quantity, speed, quality, and economy" of production all at once. This forced-draft industrialization eventually channeled something like 30 percent of the Chinese people's gross national product through the government, which used it approximately one fourth for defense, one fourth for administration and social services, and one half for investment. China's industrial growth in this period seemed rapid and formidable — as of 1957, the fastest of any underdeveloped Asian country.

The railroad network was extended to the northwest, to Outer Mongolia so as to connect with the trans-Siberian (done in 1956), and over the desert road to Turkestan to reach Russian Central Asia (though the final connection was not made). These lines, accompanied by migration, opened up the arid northwest frontier for mineral exploitation and also had political-strategic importance, strengthening the revived Chinese grip on Inner Mongolia and Sinkiang.

China's economic dependence on Russia meanwhile had led to the reversal of her foreign trade pattern. Formerly Japan and the West had taken her soybeans, tung oil, and other farm products, and the Communist-bloc area took hardly 2 percent of the total. Now China's trade was mainly with the latter and stressed capital goods imports.

The Struggles with Intellectuals and with Cadres

"Socialist construction" required the mobilization of all the nation's energies, including those of the thin stratum of about 100,000 technical, professional, and academic "higher intellectuals" who were still mainly Western-oriented. The party heads believed, optimistically, that their leadership and doctrines had by this time re-educated, "spiritually transformed," and won allegiance from this group; but they were evidently concerned that the new party apparatus with its host of young cadres had stifled intellectual life and tyrannized over the older intellectuals. Campaigns were therefore mounted in 1956–57 to manipulate these two strategic elements, intellectuals and cadres.

The party early in 1956 initiated a campaign among the urban intellectuals in order to ensure their fullest contribution to the tasks of socialist transformation. This was to be achieved by improving the intellectuals' working conditions, giving them more access to foreign publications, more free time, more scope for initiative, and at the same time getting them to "remold" themselves ideologically and qualify in large numbers for party membership. A campaign for freer criticism of the cadres and bureaucracy was also begun in May 1956 under the classical slogan "Let a hundred flowers bloom together, let the hundred schools of thought contend." This was not a clarion call for free speech. Criticism must not overstep the implicitly assumed limits of complete devotion to the party's final authority. This would be in the imperial censor's tradition of "loyal remonstrance," not like a "loyal opposition" in the West, which could attack a regime's policies while remaining loyal to the state.

It is a neat trick to foster intellectual vitality within a framework of uncritical loyalty. In the aftermath of the Hungarian rising of October–November 1956 and Russia's suppression of it, which coincided with signs of discontent in China, Mao announced in 1957 his doctrine of contradictions — some "antagonistic" as between the regime and its "enemies" abroad or at home, and some "nonantagonistic," normal and arguable, as between the bureaucracy and "the people." Within this framework he evidently hoped that a continuing "struggle" over the execution of policy, using his method of "unity-criticism-unity," could be healthily pursued and yet contained. As in the *cheng-feng* reform movement of the Yenan period, this dialectical process would call forth criticism and then would meet it, letting extreme views emerge to be dealt with through open argument, in order to discover faults and correct them and also to discover fault-finders and reform them. Any of "the people" who seemed hypercritical and disloyal could be classed as "enemies" to be coerced.

Repeated invitations eventually released a surprising torrent of publicly expressed dissatisfaction on the part of intellectuals and the professionally trained elite with the CCP's totalitarian political system, its ideas, aims, and methods. This widespread and basic criticism startled the party in the late spring of 1957 and was harshly suppressed. The recent critics were soon obliged to accuse themselves publicly and condemn one another in an "Anti-rightist" campaign.

Meanwhile the party's Central Committee faced the even more serious problem of controlling the enormous apparatus of cadres that executed its policies. The twin drives in agriculture and industry had achieved spectacular results. The face of the country was changed with new roads, factories, cities, dikes, dams, lakes, afforestation, and new cultivation, for which the 650 millions of China, at least a fifth of mankind, had been mobilized in nationwide efforts of unparalleled intensity and magnitude. Yet this vast "surging tide of socialism" had entailed a struggle not only against material conditions but also against recalcitrant personalities and human nature under the guidance and urging of the party cadres.

The rapid growth of this apparatus of activists was indexed by the rise in party membership — from 4.4 million in 1949 to 17 million in 1961. In addition, there were the Young Communist League (about 25 million in 1959) and the Young Pioneers (about 50 million in 1962). This multitude was needed to do the party's work, yet it was largely unseasoned and inexperienced. Four-fifths of the party members probably lacked a high school education. Young cadres fresh from their indoctrination, though given the prestige of learning and a code of leadership through self-sacrifice, might easily fall into the evils of "blind optimism," "dogmatism," and "commandism," or of "conservatism," "empiricism," and "blind opportunism," instead of manipulating the peasantry through discussion, logic, and persuasion. Cadres could be stimulated by Mao's ideological pronouncements and the party line more easily than they could be restrained and given wisdom, or saved from the corruption and false reporting that had inveterately characterized peasant-official relations in the past. Agricultural collectivization had in fact proceeded unevenly, with considerable friction on the spot and overoptimistic reporting to superiors. The Eighth Party Congress, meeting in September 1956, found that the peasantry had been widely misled by the cadres' false promises. Industrial projects had similarly been overambitious. The masses had actually suffered a lowering of their standard of living.

Roused by the dangers of excessive "commandism" and of being "out of touch with the masses," an evil that also seemed to be exemplified in the Hungarian revolt, the CCP inaugurated in April 1957 a great ideological campaign for "Rectification" of the party cadres' working style, parallel to the campaign to induce criticism from the intellectuals. Both groups were also brought into a big campaign for "downward transfer," *hsia-fang,* to move teachers, students, and city cadres and functionaries into the countryside so that by manual labor among the villagers they could avoid "separation from the masses" and could also help agricultural production.

But it proved easier to discipline the small number of intellectuals than to curb the overenthusiasm of the millions of cadres — or indeed to remain uninfected by it. The fanaticism of the revolution soon rose to a new height and the top leadership fell victim to its own enthusiasm, in a climate of feeling inspired partly by the apparent success of Communism world-wide.

China in the World Scene

Revolution at home had been accompanied by a militant attitude toward the outside world, and CCP thinking became fixed upon the universalistic theme of "American imperialism" as the enemy and China's "liberation" as the model for all colonial and semi-colonial peoples. Circumstance imposed upon Peking the traditional aim of strong dynasties: to dominate contiguous areas in defense of the Middle Kingdom. But this practical aim of conventional power politics was seen as part of a great worldwide struggle of the progressive "socialist camp" against the reactionary "imperialist camp." In these terms China's newly heightened nationalism found expression in a broader universalism, in which People's China relied upon the Soviet Union as its "elder brother." In this spirit, Peking during the 1950's utilized both coercion and persuasion in foreign policy, as on the home front.

The first phase, 1950 to 1954, began belligerently in an interaction with American belligerence, which was triggered specifically by the Soviet-backed North Korean invasion of South Korea in June 1950. As we have noted, this precipitated the American-backed United Nations defense of South Korea and a resumption of American military-naval support of the Nationalist government on Taiwan. Soon after Chinese troops intervened in Korea and entered Tibet, Chinese military support aided the Viet Minh in Indo-China. But after two years of negotiation, the Korean armistice was signed in July 1953; and after the defeat of the French at Dien Bien Phu, France's withdrawal from Indo-China was agreed upon, with China participating as a great power, at Geneva in July 1954. This expansion of Peking's influence, however, was paralleled by an expansion of American commitments. On this front of the Cold War, both sides sought security through militant action. In September 1954 a joint defense system, the Southeast Asia Treaty Organization (SEATO), was created by the United States to include Britain, France, Australia, New Zealand, the Philippines, Thailand, and Pakistan. Washington also signed defensive alliances with Seoul (October 1953) and Taipei (December 1954). Thus, by the time the Communist-Nationalist confrontation over the offshore island of Quemoy in Amoy harbor led to a crisis in early 1955, China's activity concerning four contiguous areas was matched by an American-led and -financed anti-Communist effort at "containment."

After the militancy of these early years came a phase of greater reliance on diplomatic persuasion. At the Geneva conference of April–July 1954, Chou En-lai joined the foreign ministers of the other powers in an effort to create stability in Indo-China as France withdrew. In negotiating at this time with India and Burma, Chou enunciated five principles of "peaceful coexistence." These also formed his main theme at the conference held in April 1955 at Bandung in western Java by leaders of twenty Asian and African states. In tune with the "Bandung spirit," the American and Chinese ambassadors at Warsaw began in August 1955 to hold periodic talks.

Yet this "soft" line soon yielded to a "hard" one. Imperialism seemed to be on the defensive after Russia launched the first intercontinental ballistic missile (ICBM) in August 1957 and its first satellite orbited the earth in October. In November Mao went to Moscow, leaving China for the second time, to celebrate the fortieth anniversary of the Bolshevik revolution. Declaring that "the east wind prevails over the west wind," he called for a new belligerency in East-West relations. This soon became evident in the Taiwan Straits, where the American build-up of Nationalist military power had been resumed in 1951. The Nationalists increasingly harassed the mainland by espionage, reconnaissance and leaflet-dropping flights, and commando raids. They also strengthened the fortification of "the front" on Quemoy, committing to it a third of the Nationalist forces. Eventually, Communist bombardment in August–September 1958 created a second Quemoy crisis, which subsided but left Quemoy a bone of contention, still held by the Nationalists as a recognized part of the mainland.

Another area of renewed belligerency was Tibet, whose people were pressed toward a socialist revolution that would amount to Sinicization. A rising at Lhasa in March 1959, when the Dalai Lama fled to India, led to harsh repression by the Chinese and to Tibetan charges of genocide. During the following summer Sino-Indian friction increased on both ends of the Himalayan frontier. (It finally erupted in hostilities in October 1962.) China got control of the strategic route between Tibet and Sinkiang through the Aksai-Chin region and shattered the Indian dream of peaceful coexistence. Intensified efforts were now made to absorb the Tibetans into the Chinese state as a minority nationality in an Autonomous Region, like the Inner Mongolian Autonomous Region founded in 1947 and the Sinkiang Uighur Autonomous Region founded in 1955. Accordingly Han (Chinese) settlers as well as troops and officials were sent into Tibet, while Tibetans were taken into the People's Liberation Army and their old social groupings broken up. Tibet ceased to be a buffer state.

Similarly Chinese had expanded into the thinly populated border regions of northern Manchuria, Inner Mongolia, Kansu, Ch'ing-hai, Sinkiang, and even Hainan Island. Settlers, prisoners, and volunteers brought in to cultivate virgin lands or develop mineral resources tended to dominate the local minority peoples. The vast area once ruled by the Ch'ing dynasty as a multi-racial empire was now largely occupied by the new Chinese nation.

To the south, North Vietnam continued its tradition of local independence of Chinese rule while imitating Chinese institutions. North Vietnam's attack on South Vietnam after 1959, first supporting guerrilla warfare, sabotage, and terrorism, then sending in troops, made full use of CCP techniques and assistance. This application of Chinese methods capitalized on the long-established gulf between city and countryside, between the urban upper class and the peasant village, where a new and tighter Vietnamese social and political order could be based on nationalist feeling and Communist doctrine. All this struggle in the late 1950's on China's frontiers seemed to be winning the day. It encouraged in these years an even greater effort on the domestic scene.

The Great Leap Forward and the Communes, 1957–1960

The Third Plenum of the Central Committee (elected at the Eighth Party Congress of 1956) met in September–October 1957 and faced a crucial problem. The completion of "socialist transformation" had given the new state-and-party apparatus an effective control over the economy, and party committees at all levels now made economic decisions. Mass mobilization to pressure businessmen or rich peasants was no longer necessary, and mass organizations had begun to atrophy. But, as Ezra Vogel puts it, "the appetite of Communist leaders for control over the economy had been greater than their knowledge, experience, and judgment." Red tape had grown faster than production. Collectivization had not actually increased the agricultural product received by the regime, which faced a dire problem of agricultural stagnation. During 1952–1957 rural population had increased by about 9 percent while the city population grew about 30 percent, but the government grain collection hardly grew at all, and meanwhile China had to begin repaying Soviet loans out of agricultural products. The Soviet model of taxing agriculture to build industry was facing a dead end.

The development strategy of the Great Leap Forward in 1958 was the sort of thing guerrilla warriors could put together. They had learned how to mount campaigns and mobilize the populace to obtain specific social objectives, much like capturing positions in warfare — indeed military terminology was commonly used. The whole apparatus of campaign mechanisms was now directed to an economic transformation, the simultaneous development of agriculture and industry, a strategy of dualism or as Mao said, "Walking on two legs," to achieve development in the modern industrial sector and the rural agricultural sector as two distinct though related processes. Mass mobilization would make use of rural labor never before fully employed: first, to use labor intensively for irrigation and flood control works and land reclamation; second to raise agricultural productivity per unit of land by using more hands to plant, weed, and cultivate; and third, to expand small-scale industry locally with materials and equipment at hand in order to produce consumer goods and equipment for the farmers. It was hoped that there would be no increase of rural consumption above the current, more or less subsistence level, and that rural development would not need much help from the modern industrial sector, but on the contrary could provide a surplus to it through taxes and requisitions.

Meanwhile the modern industrial sector of the economy would put its product into exports for securing capital goods from abroad or into investment in further plant construction, thus permitting the modern sector's expansion. (One cannot help being reminded of the contrast between the treaty port and rural sectors of China's economy in the imperialist era.) The CCP effort was to take advantage of China's rural backwardness and manpower surplus by realizing the Maoist faith that ideological incentives could get economic results, that a new spirit could unlock hitherto untapped sources of human energy without the use of material incentives.

This utopian reliance on the exhortations of the Chairman was combined with institutional reform reminiscent of the old statecraft tradition. The effort was made easier in 1958 because collectivization of agriculture had proceeded so successfully in the preceding years, whereas the professional experts and economists, like other intellectuals, had suffered downgrading as a result of the Hundred Flowers Campaign and the rectification movement that followed. The new stress on the mass line envisioned the unleashing of productive energies simply through mass mobilization. For this purpose there was a general decentralization of economic management in late 1957. Many enterprises and even monetary controls were decentralized down to the local level. The central statistical bureau was broken up and localized together with functions of economic planning. This was the context in which the overambitious targets of the Great Leap were formulated in each locality, not by economists but by cadres inspired by emulation who were contemptuous of experts but intensely loyal to the cause.

As a result, the state statistical bureau claimed that in 1958 production of food crops and cotton had nearly doubled in one year, and on this basis the Central Committee set ambitious targets for 1959 to increase again by 50 percent. The shortages in 1958 and 1959 were blamed on transport bottlenecks due to an unprecedentedly large harvest. The leadership apparently became a captive of its own claims. In fact 1958 was a good crop year and production rose perhaps 10 or 15 percent, while experimental plots also got very high increases. But since the statistical bureau had been decentralized, it could not check on estimates passed up to it.

The incredible figures that the Central Committee* trumpeted abroad had to be humiliatingly withdrawn in the late summer of 1959. The next years saw poor harvests due to bad weather. Food shortages continued and rationing also. Given an annual population growth of between $1\frac{1}{2}$ and $2\frac{1}{2}$ percent and a decline in food production in the five years after 1958, one can only conclude that the food supply suffered by as much as 20 percent in the year of greatest stringency, 1960–61. Given a normal intake of only about 2000 or 2200 calories a day per person, this drop was disastrous. The substitution of sweet potatoes for rice and a shortage of animal products were both evident. After 1961 the re-introduction of private plots and subsequent good harvests helped the situation. But since fertilizer production is capital-intensive, it could not solve the food problem. By 1962 fertilizer production was around two million tons, a bare beginning.

The Communes. The commune was an integral part of the Great Leap, based on the mass line idea of the release of the "spontaneous initiative of the masses." This mass mobilization was also accompanied by decentralized economic management. A typical commune was formed by amalgamating a number of agricultural producers cooperatives of the higher state, that is, collective farms. Some communes were as large as districts (*ch'ü*) while smaller communes with a membership of four to five thousand households, say 20,000 people, were roughly coincident with the administrative village or *hsiang*. The commune included local government functions, both military and security, as well as local trade, finance, taxation, accounting, statistics, and planning, all under party control. It was divided into production brigades and teams, a production

---

* Thus the CCP claims and hopes for grain production were announced as follows: production in 1957, 185 million metric tons; production in 1958 (as claimed in December 1958 and April 1959), 357 million tons; forecast (in December 1958) for 1959, 525 million tons; revised claim for 1958 (as of August 1959), 250 million tons.

team more or less corresponding to the old agricultural producers cooperative, perhaps half a village. Private plots were taken over, as well as private possessions down to the level of pots and pans, chairs and tables. Peasants ate in large mess halls, and all labor was controlled. Everyone was to work twenty-eight days of the month, while children went into day nurseries. This would bring large-scale efficiency to the village and get all its labor, including its womanpower, into full employment. This grandiose concept was pursued with great fanfare and utopian fervor — for example, by trying to set up a free supply of food and other necessities "according to need." The result, it was hoped, would be agricultural cities with the peasants proletarianized and uprooted from their own land. This would give better central control and change the peasants' attitudes.

This revolution collapsed from general overwork and exhaustion, the damaging of incentives and the incapacities of management. The egalitarian wage system, paying each according to his needs, lowered productivity. So did shifting labor about like military platoons within the commune. China's intensive hand-gardening agriculture could not be organized on the big scale of the Russian kolkhoz, especially in the absence of mechanization.

In December 1958 the Central Committee, at its Sixth Plenum in Wuhan, had to transfer the center of decision making from the commune down to the level of the production brigade as the basic unit for accounting, taxing, and distributing income. The free supply system was de-emphasized and wages were paid again according to labor done and work points acquired. As the agricultural crisis worsened in 1960, the commune was further decentralized and the production team with an average membership of about forty households that could work together became the basic unit. Private garden plots were re-introduced and mess halls often given up. Agricultural organization fell back to the collectivization stage of 1955–56.

China's original land reform had avoided the destructive evils of the Soviet collectivization because the CCP proceeded slowly, by stages and with persuasion. Yet in the end they ran into the problem of incentives just the same, and they faced agricultural stagnation. But when they began to innovate through decentralization, mass mobilization, and communes, they also met failure. Their economic recession and industrial standstill after 1960 were greater than any that had occurred in the better-off Soviet economy at any time. The decade of the 1950's had benefited from one-time economies of rehabilitation and from Soviet aid and credits. The early 1960's suffered from adverse weather and withdrawal of Soviet technicians and aid.

After overleaping itself in 1958–60, with "politics in command" and the party almost merged with the government, China underwent several years of serious economic dislocation. Gross national product declined by perhaps one third in 1960. Malnutrition was widespread and some starvation occurred. The people were exhausted and apathetic. Transportation broke down. Industry stagnated, as in a severe economic depression. Many plants closed, and statistics were no longer published. The regime acknowledged that agriculture, shortchanged for a decade, must now receive top priority. Though nature was blamed, it became apparent that Mao and the CCP, using their political power, had made economic errors on a truly gigantic scale. The cadres were demoralized, the people disillusioned.

The mounting extremism of the Chinese revolution during the 1950's, the feverish tendency to accelerate campaigns and revise targets upward, is reminiscent of other great social upheavals. This tendency was continually encouraged by Mao and the Central Committee in the faith that the masses would respond to a Marxist-Leninist leadership that knew how to unleash the latent "productive forces" of the society and free the "creative capacity" of the Chinese working class that had previously, it was believed, been held in check by domestic and foreign exploiting classes. Seldom has faith been frustrated on so vast a scale. By the 1960's the Chinese people had learned how to coexist with the CCP regime, as they had with autocracies in the past, but the initial enthusiasm of the revolution had long since been spent. Meanwhile the party leaders, who had risen to power through their "love for the masses" and "to serve the people," found themselves in the position of new rulers in hard times, feared and distrusted accordingly.

17 The Continuing Revolution

The Gradual Emergence of the Struggle between Two Lines

Socialist transformation had bureaucratized Chinese life, but neither it nor the Great Leap and communes had met the people's economic expectations. As popular dissatisfaction mounted, it inspired within party counsels a struggle between alternative lines of policy. Choosing between alternatives is the essence of politics anywhere, and the CCP had gone through several phases of choice during the two periods of united front and two periods of civil war. But whereas Mao and the Central Committee had maintained considerable unity in making these earlier shifts of line while on the way up, once in control of China after the mid-1950's their unity began to suffer from the strain of decision making, and the alternative lines inherent in the situation began to be represented by protagonists, Mao on one side and eventually Liu Shao-ch'i on the other.

Once the elephantine struggle between these two lines broke into print in the Cultural Revolution in 1966, outside analysts hastened to define the issues in retrospect. Their problem was

376

not unlike that of the blind men characterizing an elephant as pillar-like, snake-like, or wall-like, according to the part they could feel. The struggle for power was plain to see after it erupted in 1966. But what lay behind it? Let us begin by looking back on Mao's early career, whether or not we assume that revolutions commonly produce dictators, in order to see this man's special trait of independence and concern for the common peasant.

Mao's Independent Style. Mao came from Hunan, a seedbed of Chinese nationalism that produced not only the scholar-gentry-generals who suppressed the Taiping rebellion and led the Restoration of the 1860's but also several leaders of the 1911 revolution — Huang Hsing, the military commander under Sun Yat-sen, and Sung Chiao-jen, who organized the Kuomintang, among others. Mao's father, with two years of schooling, became a middle peasant owning two acres of land, eventually a rich peasant owning more than three acres. After five years of primary school from ages eight to thirteen, Mao had to work full time on the farm, where he fought with his father. By the time he got to a higher primary school, he was sixteen, and the Revolution of 1911 was at hand. To his early reading of Chinese novels like *All Men Are Brothers*, he now added the writers of the reform movement, especially Liang Ch'i-ch'ao and the ideas of nationalism. In 1911 he entered middle school in Changsha, older than his classmates, already a leader and a rebel. After six months as a common soldier, Mao got his real education between the ages of twenty and twenty-five at a provincial normal school. His first article published in *The New Youth* in 1917 was on the necessity of physical culture through systematic exercise and firmness of will.

Mao spent six months at Peking National University in the winter of 1918–19, not as a regular student but as an assistant to the librarian, Li Ta-chao, in whose Marxist study group he participated. Li's Marxism was colored by his own populist belief in the greatness of the Chinese people. After Mao returned to Changsha early in 1919 and became a leader of the May Fourth Movement there, his article on "The Great Union of the Popular Masses" stressed the revolutionary role of the whole Chinese people. He was not yet thinking in Marxist categories but was an eclectic espousing a broad range of ideas then current. By the time Mao participated in the organization meeting of the CCP in July 1921, he was twenty-eight years old, had organized labor unions and led strikes, edited journals and written articles. He was a vigorous leader but lacked a systematic grounding in Marxism and had never been abroad or received Soviet indoctrination. He was very much a nationalist-Marxist from the beginning.

During the first United Front of 1923–27, Mao was a leading collaborator with the Kuomintang. Already outstanding as an organizer, for a time he worked in the Shanghai bureau of the KMT with leaders like Wang Ching-wei and Hu Han-min. After recovering from an illness in Hunan in the winter of 1924–25, he went again to Canton and became the executive head under Wang Ching-wei of the KMT propaganda department and even presented its report to the second KMT Congress in January 1926. Mao became an alternate member of the KMT central executive committee as well as editor of a party weekly. He served as principal of the Kuomintang's Peasant Movement Training Institute from May to October 1926, long after tension had increased between the KMT and the CCP organizations and long after the Northern Expedition had commenced under Chiang Kai-shek's command. In this period, in short, Chiang and Mao were working in parallel organizations in the same general cause of national revolution. When Mao investigated the peasant movement in Hunan early in 1927, he addressed his report to the Kuomintang at Wuhan. In this report, at age thirty-four, Mao put forward his vision that the revolutionary passion and energies of the common people could be harnessed to liberate the peasantry and overthrow the old ruling class. Under the United Front government at Wuhan, he became the chief advocate of land reform. After the KMT-CCP split, Mao commanded the CCP attack on Changsha but was defeated and took his surviving forces into the mountains. He was dropped from the CCP central committee because of his "military opportunism."

From his collaboration with the Kuomintang, Mao had learned a great deal; after the split he learned the importance of military force and guerrilla tactics.* In neither period was he an organization man working primarily within the Communist Party.

The twenty years of his undisputed leadership after 1938

* Mao's guerrilla style had ancient roots. The *Sun-tzu* says, "By discovering the enemy's dispositions and remaining invisible ourselves, we can keep our forces concentrated while the enemy must be divided. We can form a single united body, while the enemy must be split into fractions." Mao in 1936: "We can turn a big 'encirclement and suppression' campaign waged by the enemy against us into a number of small, separate campaigns of encirclement and suppression waged by us against the enemy . . . This is what we call exterior-line operations within interior-line operations, encirclement and suppression within 'encirclement and suppression,' blockade within blockade, the offensive within the defensive, superiority within inferiority, strength within weakness, advantage within disadvantage, and initiative within passivity. The winning of victory in the strategic defensive depends basically on this measure — concentration of troops . . . We use the few to defeat the many — this we say to the rulers of China as a whole. We use the many to defeat the few — this we say to the enemy on the battle field."

The *Sun-tzu* had said: "All warfare is based upon deception. Hence, when able to attack, we must seem unable; when using our forces, we must seem inactive; when we are near, we must make the enemy believe that we are far away; when far away, we must make him believe we are near . . . If he is superior in strength, evade him. If your opponent is of choleric temper, seek to irritate him. Pretend to be weak that he may grow arrogant. If he is inactive, give him no rest . . . Attack him where he is unprepared; appear where you are not expected." In Kiangsi the Red Army developed defensive principles from a position of weakness: "The enemy advances, we retreat. The enemy camps, we harass. The enemy tires, we attack. The enemy retreats, we pursue." See Stuart Schram's basic study, *Mao Tse-tung*, pp. 142–145.

had seen success on a scale to warp even the finest judgment. To be at the top in Chinese politics, where tenure is unlimited, commonly gives the power holder a self-image of identity with "China," which the monolithic power structure in fact demands. Without claiming to understand the interaction between a great man and his people — who moves whom — we can still imagine that a hundred Sons of Heaven whispered somewhere behind Mao's back, and the repeated success of his style of militant struggle had made it a habit. In short, his unassailable position confirmed the correctness of his ideas and impulses. The personal dominance of Mao Tse-tung was steadily built up by the needs of the movement he headed, yet within the spectrum of alternatives he was distinctly the protagonist of one line against another.

The Two Approaches to China's Revolution. In the historical background, first of all, were the two views of revolution inherent in the European origins of Marxism. As Benjamin Schwartz has remarked, one stems from Rousseau and views history as a moral drama and revolution as a moral crusade to achieve the reign of virtue. The other stems from the physiocrats and sees the progress of the arts, especially technological development in material terms, as the agent of revolution enabling new forces of production to create new classes to lead the way. Pursuing these cognate themes, Mao could stress the moral pursuit of justice and virtue while Liu Shao-ch'i could stress the need of planning and material progress.

In modern China this latter strain of "scientific Marxism" was espoused, for example, by Ch'en Tu-hsiu. It assumed that a society's "superstructure" of political, social, and cultural life reflects its material base, the relations of production; and these must be changed before the superstructure can be changed. In contrast, the voluntarism (willfulness, not "volunteering") and populism espoused by Li Ta-chao asserted that the will of the masses, once energized, could conquer all. In Mao's background one can also see the anarchist view that had appealed to so many Chinese idealists early in the century, to abolish all government and all capitalism, and create a free society based on mutual cooperation.*

Mao also got sustenance from a certain degree of convergence between Rousseauism and the moral self-cultivation urged in the Chinese classics, particularly in the *Mencius* — the idea that all men are potentially good and only need teaching to realize their potentialities, and that leadership must be taken by an ethical elite whose moral superiority can transcend their environment and transform the populace. This residual strain in Confucianism fostered the supreme role of a sage hero, whereas the Soviet-trained Liu Shao-ch'i and his colleagues omitted in the new CCP constitution of 1956 the "thought of Mao" and opposed a cult of Mao's personality. Comrade Liu, writing on the party and stressing its equal discipline for all, could declare that "Comrade Mao Tse-tung is the leader of the whole party but he, too, obeys the party"; in contrast Mao could ask quite early in praising Stalin, "If we did not have a Stalin, who would give the orders?"

The dualism of these inherent alternatives may be sketched under several rubrics: *Leader versus commissar.* In the guerrilla warfare era after 1936, Mao was the distant, charismatic leader, a symbol of paternal compassion, whereas the party commissars under Liu Shao-ch'i had to exercise local power and demand discipline. Mao stood above his colleagues, a figure apart. *The mass line versus party building.* During the Yenan decade, Mao stood for struggle. He wanted the cadres to serve the people, guide their liberation, stir them up and re-

* Anarchists hoped to create a society where "there are no landowners, no capitalists, no parasites, no leaders, no officials, no deputies, no family heads, no armies, no prisons, no police, no courts of justice, no law, no religion, no marriage." Chinese anarchist manifesto, July 1914, quoted by Olga Lang.

spond to their stirrings in the spirit of the mass line. Liu and the other party builders preferred to keep struggle in its proper place, subordinate to party unity, and stressed the training of cadres and party members to be a new elite that could guide China's transformation. *Village versus city.* After 1949, Mao's concerns harked back to his peasant background and the simple existence of the Yenan era. He disdained city life, distrusted its evils, thought rather of the peasant mass whose vast energies, once liberated, could be harnessed to move mountains. His ideal was the omnicompetent man of the soil, a combined farmer, craftsman, and militia soldier in a self-sufficient countryside. Practical organizers in the Central Committee, in contrast, saw the need of talent and skills for industrialization, the importance therefore of the urban elite of educated and professional people, the necessity of technical education to produce specialists who could contribute to a modern state. *Voluntarism versus planning.* Most of Mao's contemporaries, confronting enormous tasks, favored the systematic effort of Five-Year Plans, the steady accumulation of investment capital and up-building of industry, as inescapable needs. Mao was less concerned with economics than with politics because he believed that with the correct attitude and determination, man could overcome all obstacles. This reliance on the will, voluntarism, was an article of Mao's personal faith, confirmed by his experience. It led him to favor local initiative versus central control, the people versus bureaucratism, the peasantry versus any revival of a ruling class, and in the most general terms politics versus economics. The most publicized of all these contrasts was that of *Red versus expert,* the politically trained versus the professionally trained. Invoking this slogan, doctrinaire activists harried the old intellectuals left over from before 1949 and contemned their foreign learning.

These different paths to China's future had not always been mutually exclusive but had been advocated as cognate principles in many Central Committee pronouncements. Commissars like Liu Shao-ch'i had backed the utopianism of the distinctly Maoist Great Leap. But its failure precipitated a hardening of attitudes over the pace of change, the degree of effort, and also its direction. After the Wuhan Plenum of December 1958, Mao "voluntarily" gave up his position as chief of state to Liu Shao-ch'i. Debate continued, but the CCP leadership now confronted the question that comes to every revolution: When should it die away? When are its gains to be consolidated? When should change give way to stability? Alternatively, how can the revolutionary spirit be kept alive? How can Mao ensure, as Robert Lifton puts it, his own "revolutionary immortality" through successors committed to his vision? In the final analysis, this was the problem of revisionism, whether to revise the goals of the movement, a dilemma which the Soviet Union had also faced. This made the impact of Soviet revisionism on Chinese politics all the greater.

The Sino-Soviet Split

Anyone who has looked back from the observation car of a railroad train will recall how the landscape changes as it recedes into the distance. Looking back today at the Sino-Soviet relationship of the early 1950's, it is easy to see the many ways in which these two great states were on divergent courses.

During the Cold War of the late 1940's and early 1950's, however, "monolithic international Communism" seemed to be unified by a single dominant ideology as well as by the final authority of Stalin. So strong was this appearance that the burden of proof was on those who doubted it. For several years after the death of Stalin in 1953, the facade of unity was maintained as an obvious asset in the general Communist cause. When we try to diagnose the failings of contemporary observers (just as we may expect the observers of the 1980's to fault those of the 1970's), the American cold warriors of the 1950's appear fallible not so much in their judgment of international Communism and its seeming unity as in their nonrecognition of their own ideological animus, as they expanded defensively and sometimes responded prematurely and therefore provocatively to the dangers they perceived.

The Sino-Soviet split developed on several levels at once. The Chinese and Russian peoples were separate nations with different histories, self-images, needs, and goals. Memory made them suspicious each of the other: the Mongol horde of the thirteenth century had enslaved South Russia, tsarist imperialists had encroached on Manchuria, Mongolia, and Turkestan. Behind the facade of communist rhetoric, history provided few bonds of mutual admiration or successful cooperation. Their recent collaboration, chiefly in the form of Soviet aid paid for by China, had followed the desires of their leaders, who could as easily disrupt it. Just as the ideology of Communist revolution had been the original bond, so it became the point of fracture.

Mao knew no foreign languages. By the time he acquired a Marxist concept it had often been a bit Sinicized in the mere process of translation.* Moreover, Mao had begun with revolutionary action; he acquired ideology as he went along. It is customary to say he applied or adapted Marxism-Leninism to "the concrete realities of China." One can also say the concrete realities of his experience dictated what ideology he found useful.

---

* "Proletariat," for example, certainly a key term, meant originally the lowest class of the Roman people and in Marx, wage-earners, working men without capital. Its Chinese translation *wu-ch'an chieh-chi* means "class without property" (since *ch'an* means "to give birth, to produce, to manufacture," there is even an implication that the "proletariat" is not only "propertyless" but even "product-less, lacking in goods"). Thus the term proletariat in Chinese means literally not the wage-earners but the poor. The correct Marxist meaning has to be superimposed on this Chinese literal meaning.

On the verbal level Mao's homely exhortations are studded with Chinese proverb and metaphor, both classical and colloquial. He castigates neutralists who would "sit on top of a mountain to watch the tigers fight" as well as supercilious cadres who think arguing with peasants is like "playing music to a cow." No one who has skirted a pit of nightsoil covered with maggots can fail to understand Mao's abhorrence of what he calls "the deep, stinking cesspool of Chinese reaction." To quote Confucius' sage advice, "think twice," does not necessarily promote Confucianism, but it helps to fit Communism into the Chinese landscape.

On the level of theory, Mao continued to warp and bend Communist doctrine to fit it to local needs. Stalin had asserted that the Soviet experience which reached socialism through the "dictatorship of the proletariat" offered the only path to socialism, which must be followed by the people's democracies of eastern Europe and presumably by all others. But the CCP after 1949 set up a "people's democratic dictatorship" and claimed that a mere "hegemony of the proletariat" at the head of a united front and a coalition government representing the whole "people," a combination of all "revolutionary classes," could lead China to socialism, and moreover could do it by a gradual, persuasive, nonviolent transformation, quite unlike the abrupt and violent change postulated by Lenin and Stalin.

After Stalin's death in late February or early March 1953, N. S. Khrushchev became (until 1964) the principal Soviet leader. His denunciation of Stalin's multiple crimes at the Soviet party's Twentieth Congress in February 1956, the beginning of Soviet "de-Stalinization," surprised and embarrassed the CCP at a time when it was still invoking Stalin's name. To be sure, the Twentieth Congress doctrine of "many paths to socialism" gave ground to the Maoist as well as the Titoist modifications of Marxism-Leninism and also accepted Peking's claim to be the model for Asia to follow; Sino-Soviet ideological solidarity was preserved, but only at the price of concessions which cut the ground from under Marxist-Leninist doctrine. From this time forward, the split widened, at first below the surface and by 1963 in full public polemics. The CCP had asserted both its organizational and its ideological autonomy. Peking like Moscow was now an autonomous center of doctrinal authority. International Communism was no longer monolithic, and under the pull of national interests, friction, if not rupture, was inevitable.

On the personal plane, though Mao could acknowledge Stalin's seniority, Khrushchev should now by rights acknowledge Mao's. But Khrushchev was on the crest of the Soviet success in launching the first sputnik and did not approach Mao as an inferior. On the contrary, he denounced and ridiculed the Great Leap and the communes, with which Mao claimed to be surpassing Moscow, as left deviations, dangerous fanaticism. In return, Soviet "revisionism" under Khrushchev seemed to Peking an opportunist deviation, a sell-out to capitalism. Although Moscow had promised Peking nuclear weapons assistance in 1957, it was subsequently stopped. As relations grew worse, the whole force of Soviet technicians with their blueprints were suddenly withdrawn from China in August 1960. All this provided concrete grievances.

National interests soon came into conflict on the world's longest frontier. The two multi-racial states governed Turkic minorities in Central Asia, and nomadic peoples like the Kazakhs and Kirghiz, who lived on both sides of the border and might support whichever side catered to their interests. In the 1960's a lively fear of Chinese fanaticism and expansion grew up in the Soviet Union, and by 1969 armed border clashes arose both along the Amur in the northeast and in Central Asia.

Viewed historically, the Soviet paramountcy in China's foreign affairs during the 1950's may be compared with earlier decades of foreign influence — for example, of the British in the 1860's, the Japanese after 1900, or the Americans in the 1940's. Many outside peoples have had their day in aiding the transformation of the Middle Kingdom, but none permanently. All have been cast off.

As the Sino-Soviet split widened, Peking sought to capture the leadership of the Communist world revolution, exporting cultural missions, exhibitions, and militant propaganda, giving aid to new nations and supporting "national liberation movements," especially in Asia and Africa. Mao's policy formulation for this period was stated in a speech of his heir apparent, Lin Piao, in September 1965 on "People's Wars of Liberation." Expanding China's experience to the world scene, Lin pictured the Chinese model of revolution applied to the underdeveloped two thirds of mankind against the industrialized imperialist powers. The metaphor was to "surround the cities from the countryside," but its concrete practicality was not assessed. It was not a Hitlerite blueprint for conquest. The advocacy of self-reliance for all people's revolutions meant that China could point the way and offer aid but not itself achieve the world revolution by its own expansion. (One is reminded of the ancient theory of tributary relations: China was a model which other countries should follow but on their own initiative.)

This do-it-yourself prescription for world revolution was issued at a time of setback in Peking's foreign relations. In February 1965, the United States began continuous bombing of North Vietnam; this aggression on China's doorstep was accompanied by promises not to invade North Vietnam on the ground; and Peking suffered the humiliation of impotence, unable to protect a neighboring ally. The effort to organize an Afro-Asian conference excluding the Soviet Union failed in

June. And in October, an abortive coup in Indonesia was followed by the slaughter of the pro-Peking Indonesian Communist Party. These and other failures abroad turned China inward.

The Growth of Bureaucratic Evils

Behind the civil strife of the late 1960's were deep strains
and stresses. The first was the gap between China's poverty
and the expectations of her citizens, newly active in politics.
To destroy the old order, the CCP had roused a whirlwind
and now had to ride it. Where the Kuomintang had been a
small, superficial regime, not active in China's million villages,
the CCP had asserted its authority down to the very rice roots.
Shortages before, in the old free market economy, had been no
one's fault. Now they reflected poor planning.

Having taken on this staggering burden, the CCP had built
enormous structures of administration. We know little as yet of
the widespread dissatisfactions of the masses but have some
idea of the bureaucratism which seemed increasingly to be the
source of their discontent. Once established, it appears that the
administrators of collective units had tended to become bureaucrats, increasingly occupied with paperwork and committees, less concerned with common labor, closer to being an
upper class. Careerists and familists reappeared, seeking connections and privileges, better education for their children,
private property. The work point system was corrupted by in-
siders, bonuses were paid to some and not others, piece-work
was creeping into the village labor system.

Among a people still only half literate, whose ancestors for
3000 years had looked up to a ruling class that had special
skills and prerogatives of education and status, government
was still going to be by an elite. "Liberation" of the common
peasant, making him a citizen, had not diminished but greatly

intensified the competition for elite status. In place of the million or so gentry degree-holders of the imperial era, there were now on the order of a hundred million active members of mass organizations, aware of politics, and many millions of able youth anxious to rise in the world, seeking education, jobs, and official status.

The CCP dilemma, common in developing countries, was that expectations could be created so much faster than they could be realized. The new party-government-army power structure was an elite organization, intensely status- and security-conscious, controlled from the top downward. Once its ranks filled up, the upper incumbents became more cautious and less revolutionary while the lower levels felt boxed in and frustrated.

The axiom that revolutionaries supplant an *ancien régime* only to inherit its evils was evidenced in the wide gap between the cadres and the Chinese public. Within this new cadre ruling class were many gradations — first of all, between the "local cadres" in communes or collectives and the "state cadres" paid by the government, party, or mass organizations. Instead of the eighteen grades of officialdom under the Empire, the People's Republic had twenty-four salary grades in urban areas and twenty-six in rural areas. The top salary was about nine times that of the bottom. Since these ratings carried with them prerogatives and privileges, they constituted a ladder of success and prestige. By the time this system was standardized in 1956 a distinct pecking order had emerged: at the top were cadres from the Long March period of the mid-1930's, then those from the Yenan decade 1936–1945. Lower down were the "liberation war cadres" who joined the party after 1945, and the "uprising cadres" who joined at the end of the civil war in 1948–49.

Of a thousand cadres assigned to a typical Peking ministry studied by A. D. Barnett, about a third were party members,

389

organized in a complex structure of small groups under branches at all levels of the ministry. The personnel bureau worked closely and secretly with the ministry's party committee. This party structure was responsible for the thought and behavior, loyalty and discipline, of all party members, who were set apart from non-party members and deeply involved in the "party life" of constant meetings, criticism and self-criticism, reporting on subordinates, and trying to maintain a good record in the secret files of the personnel, control, and supervisory offices. Non-party members, while less strenuously occupied, were also involved in small study groups that met regularly for political discussion, as well as in mass organizations such as their labor union or women's association or the Young Communist League. Party branches met every Friday evening and might be given classified materials to study, not to be discussed with non-party members. Every Saturday afternoon saw compulsory, directed reading and discussion by all party and non-party personnel in the ministry, in study groups of ten to twenty persons at levels appropriate to their educational background.

To enter the party, one had to submit a long personal history with the endorsement of two party members. The party might secretly appoint a member to get to know the applicant unobtrusively. A worthy applicant might then have to argue for his admission before a special party meeting in order to become a candidate member. A candidate might go through this application procedure two or three times before winning acceptance, not unlike the repeated efforts of scholars to pass the examinations in the old days.

Whether in the party or not, a cadre's personal dossier was almost more important than himself. He never saw it, but he knew that it contained his own statement of his personal history and background, his experience and ideological views, and all his family and other associations. At the end of every year and every campaign, the cadre wrote a personal summary of all his activities and ideas. This was scrutinized and criticized in a group meeting, the group leader added his own assessment together with that of the group, and all this went into the secret dossier. Dubious individuals would be systematically investigated, and in campaigns, of course, a vulnerable individual might become a target. Where the ancient examination system had made for self-indoctrination, the Communist system made for self-intimidation. Even the most able man's career could be torpedoed by his class background; for he could never get rid of a "bourgeois taint."

The ministry was periodically convulsed by campaigns and since these might threaten anyone's career, anxiety gripped the community. Quite aside from the specific evils attacked by a campaign, the eventual selection of certain human targets for systematic denunciation and public humiliation was sufficient to remind all observers that, but for the grace of the party, they too might be pilloried. These unnerving public spectacles strikingly reaffirmed the party's authority. Typically they moved individuals who felt threatened to denounce their pilloried colleagues with unusual vehemence, an activity which could not increase any individual's self-respect.

The privileges of cadres, in addition to their prestige and power vis-à-vis the masses, included a degree of financial security, free medical care, low-rent housing, cheap food, and better schooling for their children. But staying in one place was not among these privileges; and a husband and wife might be transferred to different cities. The worst fate was to be "transferred downward" to the countryside, a program developed in 1957 with multiple aims — to build up local leadership, to educate cadres or punish them through farm labor, or to reduce central government personnel and city populations.

Graham Peck, describing the Chinese public's disenchantment with the Kuomintang in the 1940's, wrote of "that secret smile" he saw among those who passively let the status quo collapse. A researcher in Hong Kong, Michel Oksenberg, has analyzed how campaigns, the engines of social change, could lose their efficacy in the 1960's. Cadres learned how to go through the proper forms. In criticism sessions an ambitious activist would speak early but not go beyond the limits set by the leader. A trouble avoider would speak in the middle of the session, offering the minimum expected comments. A friend determined to be a "sympathetic critic" of the person under fire would probably speak toward the end of the session and mix in some favorable comments. But cadres learned to avoid close friendships lest they involve subsequent denunciations in intimate detail. In addition to coping with small-group criticism, an activist learned how to ride out campaigns, feigning a progressive enthusiasm in the mobilization phase, anticipating the campaign's next stage, and becoming properly prudent and self-critical in the consolidation phase. The party establishment, in short, had learned how to protect itself against Mao's methods of "permanent revolution," and was thereby losing its capacity really to mobilize the people.

The Cultural Revolution, 1966–1969

The issue of revisionism arose from the fact that too many party members had lost faith in Mao's romantic, Heaven-storming approach to China's problems. Experienced party bureaucrats like Liu Shao-ch'i and the secretary general, Teng Hsiao-p'ing, opposed the Maoists' fanaticism, zealotry, and purism because they would only hinder economic recovery. Wrestling with practical problems, the bureaucrats dragged their feet when Mao, who had removed himself from administration after 1958, called in late 1962 for yet another campaign, for "socialist education." The inadequate response to this campaign among both the public and the bureaucracy led Mao to turn increasingly to the army for support.

Re-politicizing the Army. The military equivalent of government and party bureaucratism appeared in the Soviet-type professional officer corps, established in February 1955. Ranks and uniforms, differential pay, and the many regulations and new military academies, all diminished comradely relations between officers and men. Persuasion gave way to punishment. The professional officers challenged the political commissar system and attacked "politics in command." Against the People's Liberation Army (PLA) tradition of dual command they favored the Soviet principle of unity of command. As a result party committees in the armed forces declined until by 1960 one third of all companies had no party committee. Party membership also declined.

But after Defense Minister P'eng Te-huai was ousted in September 1959, apparently for criticizing the Great Leap and having had contact with the Soviets, he was succeeded by General Lin Piao, who now worked closely with Mao. A quarter of a million new party members were recruited into the armed forces in short order, and company party committees re-established. New military manuals and regulations were issued to combat the indiscriminate borrowing of foreign, that is, Soviet, methods. The army problem of "red versus expert" was met by reimposing the more pervasive political apparatus which had been diluted by the Soviet model. Within the army a separate echelon of party members had its own organization at successive levels down to the company and the squad, and its members were in positions of leadership. Indoctrination and surveillance were both part of this institutional structure. For example, an army squad of nine was typically divided into three teams of three each. The three men in such a team were responsible for each other, and the leader was probably connected with the party. They watched and supported each other both in combat and out. Indoctrination gave an authoritative interpretation of events. All these measures maintained troop morale. There was little stress on rank and less corporal punishment or abuse. The political officers in the army, down to the company level, kept this system functioning and prevented the formation of groups of like-minded dissidents. Criticism and self-criticism were part of a system to repress undesirable thoughts as well as deviant behavior. The army was thoroughly indoctrinated, so well that by 1964 it was possible to launch a nationwide emulation campaign to "learn from the experience of the PLA in political and ideological work." Meanwhile the economic administration was increasingly staffed with political and military personnel borrowed from the PLA.

By May 1965 it was possible again to abolish military ranks, with no distinction in mode of dress, uniform, or insignia. Meanwhile from among the six million youths reaching the age of eighteen every year, some 750,000 were being inducted into the army. The doctrine of man's superiority over weapons was revived, and P'eng Te-huai was attacked in retrospect for his bourgeois thinking. Thus the PLA in the fall of 1965 provided the base of strength from which Mao was able to move toward his Great Proletarian Cultural Revolution. In doing so he even used the PLA newspaper as his organ.

Mao versus the CCP. The Chairman at age 72 was concerned not for himself but for his revolution. He was determined to root out and destroy his people's tendencies to selfishness and materialism, those "bourgeois" and "revisionist" traits which he saw reappearing among the masses and within the government and party apparatus up to the very top. It is too soon to decide whether this old man achieved a colossal disaster that set China back by many years, or an essential forward step that opened up a better future. But one can note his manipulative skill.

The Cultural Revolution was a super-campaign that ran roughly from May 1966 to April 1969. But it was more a happening than a controlled program. As Mao moved against outspoken critics in the fall of 1965, he evidently found more party support for them than he had foreseen. As with the "hundred flowers" criticisms of 1956, opposition proved surprisingly widespread, but this time it was within the party. Mao responded with a vast new effort to mobilize support from outside the party. The public scene was soon filled with mass meetings, parades, and propaganda displays exalting Mao as "the red sun in our hearts." Tremendous excitement, even hysteria, among millions of youth led to exhaustion, apathy, and further surges of effort. Out of it all came a purge of the party by the leader. But where Stalin had purged the CPSU from within, secretly and using the party apparatus, Mao purged the CCP from without, publicly and using mass organizations, such as the Red Guard youth. Where Stalin used his secret police and killed millions of people, Mao relied on the PLA and used methods of public humiliation. Violence erupted chiefly as civil strife in competitions for local power.

Mao's campaign, like a guerrilla operation, followed a rhythm of attack and pause, destruction and consolidation. His first move was to assure his control of the mass media at the center by attacking cultural and educational commissars and the Peking Party Committee. His eventual targets, Liu Shao-ch'i, the chief of state, and Teng Hsiao-p'ing, the secretary general of the party, cooperated in this phase by sending out campaign teams which Mao later accused of impeding his efforts. In August 1966 he gained ground by packing the membership of the Eleventh Plenum of the Central Committee. He had already gone outside the party apparatus to field groups of teenagers as Red Guards, calling upon them in a big-character poster in his own hand to "bombard the headquarters." They were to "learn revolution by making revolution." Also outside party channels, he had set up a nationwide Cultural Revolution organization headed by a special committee that included his wife. In the fall of 1966 with logistic support from the PLA, some eleven million Red Guards came to Peking for a succession of mass rallies and then dispersed over the country to carry out their own "Long Marches" and to attack the "four olds" (old ideology, thought, habits, and customs). These were found first among the educated upper class, who were also attacked for possessing foreign books or clothing or even foreign-style haircuts. In January 1967, Mao escalated the Revolution still further to attack the party structure itself, inciting the "revolutionary masses" to seize power from below as in the Paris Commune of 1870. Many million copies of the little red booklet *Quotations from Chairman Mao Tse-tung** brought every activist a wide range of axioms to ponder — for example, that "the revolution must rely on the masses of the people, on everybody's taking a hand," and "the masses have a potentially inexhaustible enthusiasm for socialism." The cult of Mao dominated the media and grew to the point of mass hysteria among youthful demonstrators.

Working with only a minority faction of the CCP but from his unassailable position as the "Great Helmsman" backed by

* The homiletic flavor of this compilation can be seen even in its thirty-three section headings: The Communist Party, Classes and Class Struggle, Socialism and Communism, The Correct Handling of Contradictions among the People, War and Peace, Imperialism and All Reactionaries Are Paper Tigers, Dare To Struggle and Dare To Win, People's War, The People's Army, Leadership of Party Committees, The Mass Line, Political Work, Relations between Officers and Men, Relations between the Army and the People, Democracy in the Three Main Fields, Education and the Training of Troops, Serving the People, Patriotism and Internationalism, Revolutionary Heroism, Building Our Country through Diligence and Frugality, Self-Reliance and Arduous Struggle, Methods of Thinking and Methods of Work, Investigation and Study, Ideological Self-Cultivation, Unity, Discipline, Criticism and Self-Criticism, Communists, Cadres, Youth, Women, Culture and Art, Study.

the PLA, Mao thus precipitated an unprecedented degree of struggle, indeed a sort of urban guerrilla warfare, first of dissident groups against individuals in power who were "taking the capitalist road" and secondly between groups. The party power holders were attacked piecemeal and had no way to organize among themselves. As in all campaigns, there was a call for local initiative and a great build-up of ad hoc organizations and their membership. The process of struggle was by no means controlled or predetermined except as the Maoists could excite it, damp it down, or redirect it. In the result, the party establishment was thoroughly shaken up, if not shattered.

The rural impact of the Cultural Revolution in an area of optimal potentialities was reported by a Swedish journalist, Jan Myrdal. He had been allowed to spend a month in a village near Yenan in 1962, in the region longest under Communist rule, comparatively poor and simple in its subsistence economy but presumably well organized to attack its problems. Going back for a fortnight in 1969, he found that Red Guard youth in 1966 had first brought the villagers Mao's *Quotations,* calling for scrutiny of those in authority. In discussion meetings the *Quotations* thereafter were used like biblical texts. The Cultural Revolution had brought these changes: a guaranteed grain stipend for all instead of aid administered to those in need, less stress on work points (which had encouraged piece-work), less keeping of accounts, less stress on schoolwork and examinations to go on to higher education, less concern for private plots and more for collective investment, more pig-raising for food and manure, more reliance on local hygiene and simple remedies and less on stand-in-line city clinics, more active participation in the mass meetings to guide the collective's action. The leading cadres — secretary, treasurer, and teacher — once criticized had been retained.

Since the homogeneous, long-communized Yenan area was far more amenable to Mao's teaching than coastal cities could ever be, this sympathetic report suggests both the ideals in view and the inherent difficulties.

To take the place of the old structure of authority, Mao eventually called for "revolutionary committees" at all the levels of government to consist of a "three-way alliance" of, first, representatives of the Red Guards and "revolutionary rebels" (that is, mature workers and cadres), who were now all together called "revolutionary masses," and who would be new blood; second, representatives of the People's Liberation Army; and third, party cadres who had been adequately revolutionized. The party establishment fought back bitterly in one place after another by fielding their own Red Guards and executing what Mao denounced as "false power seizures," proclaiming their loyalty to him but defeating his forces and keeping their own grip on power. These defensive actions and the rebels' seizure of arms produced pitched battles between armed groups. But even after major officials had been denounced and jailed, fighting continued between the more radical and more conservative groupings of organizations. The CCP ceased to function. After a new phase of violent attacks by the "revolutionary masses" in the summer of 1967, civil strife had reached a point where the army had to be called in more and more to restore order. Meanwhile, Mao and Lin reorganized nearly half the local military commands and held training classes for senior officers.

By January 1968 revolutionary committees had been set up in all the twenty-nine provinces and major cities, but an effective core of party members, skilled in administration, had not been built up within them. It was easier to bring together army officers and zealous newcomers than it was to create effective administrations. By the summer of 1968, renewed attacks on senior personnel led to further violence and still more authority being given to the PLA. The attack on the party had given civil power to the army.

In the midst of all this frenzied turmoil, the universities and schools had remained closed while intellectuals and experts were being attacked and students revolutionized in factional fighting. Rebellious protest through armed factionalism had come in large part from graduates dissatisfied with the jobs, particularly in the countryside, to which they had been assigned; and from discharged soldiers and casual workers who lacked the skills to support themselves adequately. Their job opportunities had fallen behind their hopes. But the "political revivalism" of the Cultural Revolution, to use Ezra Vogel's phrase, could not solve the basic problems of economic and political growth. In the fall of 1968, millions of student youth including erstwhile Red Guards were sent down to communes. With them went many urban cadres, as the opportunity was seized to reduce the government bureaucracy and drive unemployed city dwellers back to the countryside.

In October 1968 Mao again packed the Twelfth Plenum of the Central Committee, and "China's Khrushchev," Liu Shao-ch'i, was finally read out of the party. The Ninth Party Congress of April 1969 was prepared for in many meetings throughout the provinces, while proposed membership lists were screened at the center. The 1500 selected delegates elected a new Central Committee, whereupon this new committee itself elected the Politburo and its standing committee of five, among whom Chou En-lai, still premier, was the only nonzealot. The new party constitution named Lin Piao as Mao's successor, while the new Central Committee of 279 full and alternate members had a preponderance of military personnel, and only 52 members left over from the previous committee. In effect, the Cultural Revolution transferred power to the military leaders; they were the only portion of the party structure who had their own separate basis of survival.

The Cultural Revolution was said to be for "consolidating the dictatorship of the proletariat, preventing capitalist restoration, and building socialism." In Leninist theory, the proletariat had been represented by the Communist Party, but in adapting this idea to China, Mao had long since decreed that a proletarian attitude might be attained by anyone who tried hard enough. The implication of this had now been achieved: the CCP was no longer the infallible bearer of the wisdom of revolution. The Chinese proletariat now consisted of those who, in Mao's view, thought like Mao, and the "dictatorship" of this amorphous body was in practice indistinguishable from that of Mao himself. When Mao reverted to the term "dictatorship of the proletariat" during the Cultural Revolution, in order to mobilize his "proletarian revolutionaries," he had pushed his ideology a step further toward meaninglessness. The evils that he sought to overcome were not the product of social relationships and objective conditions, but rather a taint in the human personality. As Benjamin Schwartz has put it, " 'bourgeoisie' and 'proletariat' have been transmuted in the Maoist universe into something like two pervasive fluids, one noxious and the other beneficial, which can find their lodgments anywhere. The source of the proletarian truth resides in no group or even organization but in the thought of Mao Tsetung." These progressive modifications of doctrine have in fact further disintegrated the CCP ideological system and ended the infallibility of the Communist Party.

18 Perspectives on China and Ourselves

The first century of contact between America and China had great significance for both peoples. But it ended in the final dissolution of the old order — both of traditional Chinese civilization and of the unequal treaty system which had ushered it into contact with the modern world. Our traditional China policy and the attitudes which underlay it were bankrupted and in fact reversed by the rise of the People's Republic.

Where before 1949 we had supported the Open Door for trade, for twenty years thereafter we embargoed American relations with the mainland. Where we had formerly defended China's administrative and territorial integrity, after 1949 we impaired it by our steadfast support of Taiwan in a continuing state of civil war.

To say that this rupture of relations between the Chinese and American peoples was all our fault would be as purblind as to say it was all their fault. It is time for us to get beyond making righteous moral judgments and seek at all costs a realistic perspective, for now all peoples are in trouble together.

Yet the first step toward a realistic perspective is surely to recognize that it was the West that invaded China, not China the West; and the chief lesson the Chinese learned from the Western invasion (as from all earlier invasions of China) was that China had to become strong in self-defense, which today implies nationalism, a mobilized populace.

In short, if we acknowledge that the West brought modern ways to China, we must accept the great Chinese revolution of the twentieth century as something we helped to start. In the end the Chinese Communist Party undertook to carry out in fact a whole host of changes that foreign administrators and missionaries, as well as patriotic reformers and revolutionaries, had advocated and attempted with increasing vigor for a century past.

Unfortunately for us, a proud people when weak do not enjoy receiving help. The American attitude toward China during the century of the unequal treaties was consciously acquisitive but also benevolent, seeking to give as well as get. We were proud of our record, indeed a bit patronizing toward the imperialist powers, of lesser virtue. Inevitably, however, the Chinese experience of Sino-American relations was different from the American experience. We found our contact with China adventurous, exhilarating, rewarding in material or spiritual terms. Americans who did not like it could avoid it. China, on the other hand, found this contact forced upon her. It was a foreign invasion, humiliating, disruptive, and in the end catastrophic. The Western menace to the traditional Chinese way of life often seemed, in the nineteenth century, every bit as dire, evil, and ominous as the totalitarian Nazi and Stalinist threats to the American way in the 1940's. The Chinese, behind their polite exterior, did not fully share our national enthusiasm for Sino-American friendship.

Out of the mix of past Sino-American relations, Chinese today can stress American imperialism where we see mainly our philanthropy, exploitation where we see American aid to the Chinese people; and of course both views will be true and documentable as far as they go. But a conscientious observer, even an unconscionable realist, cannot rest content with the view of one side alone. In order to survive together in mankind's uncertain future, Americans and Chinese will have to find some common ground in their understanding of their common history, as to how they dealt with each other in times past.

As we continue to construct our image of Sino-American relations, we can be sure of one thing: our thinking will tend to favor our side. This will be so even if, with moral feelings of guilt, we righteously denounce our past sins. I mean that to decry the evil influence of American imperialism on China may still be a very American thing to do; for example, it may self-righteously exaggerate the extent of the American influence on China. For as we abandon the American nostalgia for that treaty-port China that is no more, we must increasingly recognize the extreme self-sufficiency of Chinese life as well as its ideal of self-reliance. As foreigners, our historical grasp is strongest on the exterior, in respect of China's foreign relations; and next strongest at the top, in respect of the old ruling class. We still have far to go to plumb the life of the people.

China Today in the Light of Her Past

Continuity and discontinuity go together as the warp and weft of history. Consider how, in our own lives, every day is brand new to us, yet we live it as creatures of habit. China's great revolution is a similar blend of tradition and innovation. Looking first at certain continuities of form may help us to see what is new in fact.

Echoes of the Dynastic Cycle. The decline and fall of the Ch'ing Empire and the rebellions of the nineteenth century had many

403

classic features, which we have noted above and need not recapitulate. In the interregnum which followed 1911, Yuan Shih-k'ai, Sun Yat-sen, Chiang Kai-shek, and Mao Tse-tung with increasing success strove to reunify the Middle Kingdom. The Kuomintang was the precursor of the Chinese Communist Party in seeking to train a new type of scholar-bureaucrat in a new ideology, so as to revive the functions once performed by the Confucian scholar-gentry and the classics.

Generalissimo Chiang sought to quell the warlords by his personal rectitude as well as by bigger armies and smarter politics. Like Emperors of the T'ang and Sung, he traveled widely over the provinces on tours of inspection and performed ritual acts, climbed T'ai Shan, the sacred mountain, conducted sacrifices at the tombs of the Han Emperors near the Yellow River north of Loyang. Beginning his rule by the military conquest or hamstringing of his rivals, he proceeded in the 1930's to draw scholars into his civil administration while himself setting a moral example as the paternal head of the state. His strength lay in these traditional qualifications: courage and determination to retain power, ethical fervor and austerity that gave him personal prestige, loyalty to those who were loyal to him, ruthlessness and subtlety in balancing his rivals against one another. It was entirely in keeping with this ancient pattern that Chiang Kai-shek, a prisoner of the past, should seek to progress from the status of Hero to that of Sage, a transformation symbolized in 1943 when he became head of the National Central University at Chungking and published *China's Destiny* as a textbook.

Mao Tse-tung in his turn unified the country as a hero risen from the people, like the founders of the Han and Ming. He went them one better and swam the Yangtze to encourage his people to use and overcome nature. Mao's armies in the 1940's were not a scourge upon the peasantry but avenged their wrongs. He "won the hearts of the people" sufficiently to secure food and soldiers from territorial bases. He attracted college students to staff his administration. His ideology claimed the Mandate of History, if not of Heaven. Once in power, his regime surveyed, classified, and redistributed both the land and the populace. His example mightily affected the peripheral states. Rising to power with barbarian help, he yet patronized Chinese culture and employed scholars to document the record of the previous regime and point the lesson of its fall. In Peking in front of the great palace built by the Ming Emperors of the fifteenth century he built a great square, whither came delegations from Southeast Asia and the Western Regions to watch the great processions.

The reader can continue for himself to recognize echoes of the past in China today. C. P. Fitzgerald, for example, summarized the traditional Chinese social concepts as embracing (1) a single authority coterminous with civilization, (2) a balanced economy basically managed by the state, (3) an orthodox doctrine which harmonizes and guides all forms of human activity, including the selection of intellectuals for state service. As of 1952, he suggested that these concepts, destroyed during modern times in their traditional forms, had found expression again under Communism. Yet at the time of writing he foresaw the New Democracy persisting for some time and collectivization remaining afar off. Events have now outstripped the historian's precedents. Institutional changes have broken the cadence, and the differences between past and present are as great as the similarities.

Values have changed as well as institutions. The K'ang-hsi Emperor never watched the calisthenics of ten thousand selected maidens wearing shorts, nor commended sons for denouncing their fathers. He did no physical jerks to the noon radio. His succession was provided for in the bedchamber where he begat thirty-five sons, and was fought out among them, within a family, not a party. K'ang-hsi wooed the scholars, who had nowhere else to turn, but they had only to criticize the classics textually, not themselves in every act and thought. He paid no honors to peasants who exceeded norms nor to the idea of progress or the dialectic, though he would have acknowledged the sequence of *yang* and *yin*.

Since the patterns of the past cannot be entirely expunged, they remain curiously intertwined with new motifs. Peking today has a Marxist-Leninist-Maoist ideological orthodoxy as vigorous as Confucianism used to be; but it believes in progress toward a future millennium, not cyclical repetition descending from a golden age. Dynastic absolutism has been replaced by party dictatorship, the Son of Heaven by the Great Helmsman, the imperial family-clan council by the central executive committee, the scholar elite by a party elite, tax-gatherers by cadres in the countryside, Confucian classics by Communist classics, written examination by group discussion, scholarly self-cultivation by guilt-ridden self-criticism. Merchants continue to be disesteemed, being undoubtedly bourgeois, but soldiers are now glorified. The sages are class-angled and re-evaluated. Labor and army heroes are the new models to emulate. Women do not aspire to lily feet but approach their romantic nadir, functional interchangeability with men. Responsibility for good conduct is still mutually shared among family and neighborhood groups, but now this ancient automatic check on deviance is extended to include the neighbors' thoughts. The *pao-chia* is replaced by the street committee. Villages still are mobilized for public works, but the state philosophy of seeking harmony with nature has given way to the industrial urge to conquer nature. Government used to be thinly spread out and superficial and the peasant passive, a subpolitical animal. Today the government penetrates every hut, and peasants are people, unless they misbehave.

Processes of Modernization. In trying to explain China's modern history, the chief alternative to the traditional Chinese pattern is, of course, a traditional Western one. Where the Chinese pattern was cyclical, the Western view of history is based on the idea of linear progress (the two can be combined in a spiral). The expansion of the Atlantic community underlies this Western pattern. (Since the Marxist-Leninist scheme was drawn up mainly with the expansion of Europe in mind, much of China's modern history, seen as a product of this expansion, can be fitted into the categories of the Communist interpretation.) When we apply the Western view, certain phases may be distinguished, even though they overlap in time.

In *Phase One*, the traditional Chinese state, being incompatible with and weaker than the modern world, is attacked and mortally wounded. Over a period of a century, from the 1840's to the 1940's, the old order is progressively destroyed as a result of contact with the West. The imperial military system is discredited by Western firepower. The agrarian economy and the imperial fiscal system, based on rural tax-gathering, are disrupted by the influx of Western trade and the eventual rise of modern industry. The Emperor's prestige is dimmed by successful foreign aggression against the peripheral vassal states and eventually within spheres of influence in China proper. Efforts at self-defense on the part of the Confucian scholar-administrators — such as by adoption of Western arms, technology, and industry — prove unavailing because the agrarian-bureaucratic society of China cannot modernize as rapidly as the Western nations are modernizing. China's old order is out of date, maladjusted, and unable to respond adequately and in time. Efforts to reform the administration while retaining its Confucian values are attempted, but they are foredoomed to failure.

Phase Two begins during this process of decline. New dynamic elements of modernization are absorbed into the traditional Chinese society and begin to work their transformation.

One of these is the Western type of nationalism — loyalty to state and country as sovereign symbols in an international order of similar nations. This undermines the old faith in the Confucian relationships under the Emperor. Naturally, the new nationalism has behind it a large backlog of ethnocentrism and xenophobia, suspicion of foreigners and devotion to things Chinese. The transformation from a Sino-centric culturalism to a more modern nationalism requires the destruction of the alien Manchu dynasty and leads eventually to a Chinese cultural-nationalism more solid than Western nationalism, for it is coterminous with the entire culture, not merely with the state.

Another new element injected into the Chinese scene is the idea of economic development, particularly under official supervision and leadership. Economic growth has, of course, been a fact even before the early Western trade entered into China's domestic universe of commerce. China's great increase in population since the eighteenth century has been a permanent and not a cyclical change. The ingress of foreign transport in the form of coastal and river steamships, followed by railroads, mines, and textile mills, all demonstrate the growth capacities of modern industrialization based on science and technology. The early reformers themselves attempt to achieve economic development under the banner of the traditional idea of strengthening the state. In the process, a new type of scholar, the scientific technician, emerges, and more specialized administrators are required to guide the multiform types of industrial effort.

Modern technology also fosters militarization, beginning with provincial arsenals that mass-produce modern arms. The new officer class is technically trained, and patriotic youths flock to it. In the 1930's resistance to Japan's aggression is led by a generalissimo, while his chief adversary survives as a strategist of guerrilla warfare. The technologies of arms production, steam transport, and electronic communication all prepare the way for mass mobilization.

By the 1930's there develops the concept of rural reconstruction, the application of modern technology to the agrarian economy, a part of the worldwide effort at rural development. While the Nanking government achieves relatively little in this regard, during its period of rule the concept takes firm shape among Chinese patriots. As in so many other lines of modernization, the Western missionaries' interest in village reconstruction points the way to a new China in which missionaries will have no part.

Other new elements from abroad which revolutionize the Chinese social order in the early part of this century are Christianity and Western liberalism — a body of concepts and practices from which China makes a rather fastidious but nonetheless important selection. For example, the freedom of the individual from family controls goes hand in hand with the denial of the authority of the sages in intellectual matters and of the Son of Heaven in politics. In some degree we may speak of the influx of the ideals of the French Revolution, flowing into China a century afterward and undermining the old order before the subsequent wave of Marxism. Startling upsets and reversals of values now occur, often the result of Christian missionary teachings. Youth is honored over age, or at least youth is able to acquire the prestige of scholarship which age formerly monopolized. Egalitarianism likewise extols the common man, and the modern leader is able to convert the paternalistic Confucian concern for the populace into the Marxist cult of the people, who now supplant Heaven's mandate as the source of legitimacy. Chinese Marxist thinking stresses the populist strain, and Mao Tse-tung extols the power of the will, voluntarism, to change man's social environment and behavior. The edifying example of that paragon, the Confucian Emperor, is substituted by the cult of the Chairman's personality.

In this welter of changes, women as individuals are freed from the severe inequalities of their former status and their quiet but rapid emancipation is one of the greatest unrecorded revolutions of the century. Under the general banner of liberalism, democracy, laissez-faire, and humanitarianism, there emerge new values and new social groups, which have yet to be integrated into a new order.

Phase Three sees the putting together of some of these elements, in a new revolutionary dispensation. Looking back over the last century, one can see in retrospect the emergence of those new forces, methods, ideals, and social classes which served as raw material for the Nationalist and the Communist organizers in turn. Patriotic youth are ready to sacrifice themselves to wipe out China's past humiliations and build a new nation. New classes of factory workers and treaty-port merchant capitalists have been created by economic growth. New social groups — emancipated women, soldiers possessed of a new social status, peasants ready to participate in political life, students ready to join a party — are now in being. The very multiplicity of these new elements creates a great need for a new unity under the banner of nationalism and industrialism.

If one follows this Western-type pattern of unilinear social change in modern China, one may imperceptibly work one's historical interpretation around to the dubious conclusion that Chinese Communism represents an inevitable phase of China's "modernization." This would be just as simple-minded as to conclude that it is merely another in a long succession of dynasties. Neither view seems to me adequate.

In actual fact, of course, historical trends seldom develop in straight lines and Mao Tse-tung's being in power today depends on at least two particular circumstances among others: first, that Japan attacked and destroyed the more modern area of Kuomintang China; second, that Chiang Kai-shek, indomitable and uninstructible, developed in his long years on the mainland no rural reconstruction program such as was later achieved on Taiwan. Peking naturally contends that historical necessity made Japan aggressive and Chiang blind to agrarian reform, but this hindsight overlooks the fact that historical trends are no one's monopoly and may be ridden by alternative power groups.

In some ways (but not others) the Kuomintang period may now be viewed, at the peril of distortion, as a part-way stage toward the present regime. At least in respect of party government, the creation of a party army, the mobilization of youth, and the modernization of the economy, the Kuomintang took faltering steps down the road which the Communists have since traveled. Yet there is another element of the Kuomintang period which it would be a distortion to overlook — namely, the influx of Western ways and values under a government oriented primarily toward the Western democratic world, which I have tried to characterize above under the general term of liberalism. Thus if China under the Kuomintang seemed sometimes to move down the totalitarian road in politics, its cultural activity remained on the whole far different.

The People's Republic may also be viewed as an end-product of many accumulated elements surveyed above. Just as Nanking in the 1930's was indebted to the pioneer reform efforts of Western missionaries and was led partly by returned students from the West, so Peking in the early 1950's relied on Soviet models and party leaders who had been trained in the USSR. But to say that Chinese Communism is the latest phase of China's response to the Western impact, though true enough, would omit the heart of the matter, which is that China's mass and inertial momentum put her in her own orbit, and no one's else.

The first edition of this book in 1948 concluded that "the disintegration of the old order in China leaves that country open to reorganization under the dominant influence" of ei-

411

ther the USSR or the United States as superpowers. What nonsense! China has gone her own way.

The New Order and Its Problems

The Chinese revolution has engulfed so many people in such an ancient society that its new order cannot be anything but unique. While many aspects of Chinese life are of course comparable to life elsewhere, the Chinese way has always been distinctive, and to this difference in culture, already hard to grasp, has been added the ineffable aura of revolution, which stirs up passions and asserts values even harder for outsiders to comprehend. Thus the "struggle between two lines" that surfaced in the Cultural Revolution was over the speed and direction in which China's great organized effort should be pursued. But the alternatives within the Chinese scene, the banks within which the flow of events must find its channel, are narrower and more constricting than we can easily imagine. For example, the pressure of numbers, new to us, is an old experience in China. Bureaucratic organization, at which we chafe, was invented there. The new order, though still in process of taking shape, will inevitably have many police-state features: the new central power revives the imperial despotism at the top but gives it a new grip on the masses; five-year plans for industrialization echo the bureaucratic tradition of monopoly over large-scale economic activity but inject a new demand for forced-draft increase of production. The new order seeks not only a rapid shortcut to industrialization, but also a shortcut to modern nationalism, to the forced-draft participation of the masses in political life, even against their will as individuals. They no longer have the freedom of silence. Thus the potentialities of modern technology and organization, both economic and political, are used to create national power.

All this can be perceived in terms recognizable from the Eu-

412

ropean experience with which we are not unfamiliar. Our real problem is to encompass the new faith, Mao Tse-tung's kinetic vision that all the people should participate in a collective economic-political life in which moral conduct is enthroned and lesser materialistic motives cast down. Where foreign missionaries once worked long years to "save" a few souls, Mao has struggled to remake the personality of his entire people forthwith.

How can we appreciate the great speed of recent changes? Because of the long isolation of the Chinese culture and social order and their solid inertia in their own channels, the past century has seen more drastic changes than any other major people has ever experienced. It included among other things, five major rebellions and five wars involving every world power within the seventy years *before* World War I. The Chinese had a prouder and more distinctive tradition, responded more slowly to its collapse, suffered the humiliations of backwardness longer than any other major people. We in America have moved fast in our material culture, from the horse, buggy, and kerosene lamp to television, jet planes, and missiles, but we have not scrapped and rebuilt in the same short period our system of government and foreign relations, our language and the content of our learning, our whole society. We have not felt the same proud urge to catch up, nor tried to do it in great leaps.

This frenetic pressure for change makes one wonder if Mao Tse-tung is to figure in history like the First Emperor of the Ch'in and the founder of the Sui, men who created a new order by violent activity during a brief span of despotism and were followed respectively by the long-lived regimes of Han and T'ang. When may we expect the Chinese revolution to slow down and consolidate its new order? Will the world crisis of today permit it? Precedents can give us no assurance as to China's future, but certain major problems can be foreseen.

413

The first is the problem of morale, which derives from the extraordinary size of the Chinese polity. Never before have 800 million people lived under one regime. The secret of this feat, and whether it can persist, are not clear to us. Certainly a degree of regionalism is essential to it, together with an equilibrium between regional material interests and central military and ideological interests, presumably balancing regional profit and central prestige. Equally extraordinary in this enormous polity is the peculiarly Chinese reliance upon ethics more than law, upon moral consensus more than judicial procedure. In Western terms we might say that an element of religious belief lends strength to the Maoist orthodoxy. As a result, the cult of Mao has flourished, while the law codes have remained unpublished.

It follows that ancient evils of bureaucratism lie in wait for Peking's mammoth administration at any time its morale declines. Past bureaucracies in China have been peculiarly susceptible to long-term changes of attitude affecting the prestige of the regime in power, partly because administration was so largely personal, according to the character and sense of responsibility of the administrators. Once a regime became contemptible in the public view, personal relations in the government process lent themselves to collusion and corruption, which could be organized the more thoroughly because the old society was less dependent for its survival on the vitality of its legal institutions. Officials and commoners could still remain moral family pillars while they connived at defrauding the Emperor. The Emperor's only ultimate safeguard was to ensure that they retained a correct attitude toward his regime. Mao Tse-tung and his successors are still relying less on laws and procedures than on moral exhortation and personal example. Consequently, bureaucrats with the wrong attitude can defeat their ends and destroy their power.

To stave off a decline of morale, Communist methods today

for ensuring universal conformity in attitude are far more complete and intensive than anything the old China ever devised. The organized pressure upon the individual personality, neighbor reporting on neighbor, child watching parent, friend "struggling" with friend, and everyone isolated, is the experiential essence of a new totalitarian situation. This is the more threatening to values of individual integrity because it seems so thoroughly sanctioned in many Chinese minds by feats of material construction, public welfare and hygiene, technical training and patriotic devotion, which loom on every side in a period of rapid national growth.

Finally, the rate of population increase seems to lock the Chinese people irrevocably into their struggle to increase production through conformity and at the expense of personal choice. Pressure of numbers is still the most grievous part of China's inheritance. Every year, famine waits around the corner. Like it or not, the Chinese populace will have to put up with some kind of centralized and dictatorial planning and controls for the foreseeable future simply because there is no alternative in prospect by which to feed them, employ the youth, and satisfy the national pride.

Tradition in Foreign Relations. The strength of China's modern nationalism seems likely to reinforce the deeply ingrained attitude which views foreign relations as a problem in the balancing of foreign powers against each other to China's advantage. The ancient dictum, "use barbarians to control barbarians," was followed by dynasty after dynasty in dealing with militarily stronger alien powers. The Han dynasty sought the help of the Yüeh-chih people against the Hsiung-nu. Fifteen hundred years later the Ming used the western Mongols to crush the eastern Mongols and also used the eastern Mongols to crush the western Mongols. The chief recourse of modern China has been to play off one imperialist against another, the Americans against the British, the British against the Russians, and

415

then the League of Nations and the United States against Japan. This principle of Chinese diplomacy crops up in the writings of every official of consequence in century after century. It is no surprise that the Kuomintang in the 1940's looked to the United States to take care of its Soviet problem or that Peking, at odds with the USSR, was willing to talk to Washington. After all, China's most famous strategists date from its own classic triangle, the Three Kingdoms at the close of the Han. Today Peking has similar opportunities for triangular politics in the relations between China, the Soviet Union, and Japan, and between China, Japan, and the United States.

One urgent question both for Pentagon planners and for the American people is the degree of China's future expansiveness. Nationalistic sentiment and industrial growth, for example, led Germany and Japan as latecomers into paths of conquest. Will China follow suit? History cannot foretell, but the probabilities seem to me poor. The Chinese tradition of self-sufficiency and the virtue of self-reliance have made a comeback under the Communists. Consider this broad historical sequence. China's tradition of being a world unto herself and of minimizing foreign contact was expressed in the Canton system established in 1760: foreign merchants could reside in Macao, come to Canton for the trading season, but not enter the city walls nor come to Peking except as tribute-paying guests of the state and without diplomatic immunity. By 1860 Anglo-French arms had set up the treaty system of foreign privilege and opportunity for diplomatic contact, trade, travel, and proselytism. But by the 1960's the century of foreign contact had given way again to minimal intercourse: foreigners could come from Hong Kong to the annual trade fair at Canton but could not ordinarily travel inland except as paying guests of the state travel service, while diplomats in Peking found themselves not immune to the "people's" organized demonstrations and even violence. (The British embassy was sacked in 1967.)

China's foreign relations can still flow in either of two channels — the Western international one of trade, travel, exchanges, and diplomatic protocol, or the ancient Chinese one of accepting foreigners on sufferance, only insofar as they subscribe to Chinese aims or suit Chinese needs. Exclusion of the People's Republic from the United Nations for twenty years has no doubt fostered this ancient exclusiveness in retaliation, but meanwhile the Republic of China on Taiwan has demonstrated the Chinese capacity for cosmopolitan participation.

The People's Republic has been a nuclear power since 1964. It lacks the economic capacity to rival the American and Soviet stockpiles and delivery systems, but the ultimate worth of these things is still uncertain — they may turn out to have been liabilities. In any case, China may be expected to get prestige and influence from her nuclear weapons. Since a few hundred can probably knock us all out, a thousand warheads in China may in time counter tens of thousands elsewhere. What we need, aside from universal disarmament, is a sound perspective on China's proclivities to expand or stay at home. The historical record cited in preceding chapters suggests that China's broad expanse provided a self-sufficiency that fostered self-absorption, and Maoist thinking is still in this tradition. Too, the sheer size of China's domestic political problem, how to maintain the central power, gives it priority. The American attack on North Vietnam was not met by Chinese intervention. In this respect Mao Tse-tung in 1965 acted like Prince Kung in 1861, when he chose to fight the Taiping rebels rather than the British and French, or like Chiang Kai-shek in 1931, who opted to fight the Chinese Communists before the Japanese. All of them felt they had to put *nei* before *wai*, the internal enemy before the external menace.

On the other hand, a foreign menace if long continued can

417

rouse any nation. I conclude that Americans can expect from the Chinese roughly the degree and kind of response that we provoke. We, not they, have been the most expansive power of recent times.

Our China Policy in the Light of Vietnam

North Vietnam was part of the Chinese empire before Julius Caesar conquered Gaul. A country as old as France, it won its independence of Chinese rule a thousand years ago. But, as with Korea, its culture and institutions remained a variant of the Chinese model, using Chinese characters, the Confucian classics and family system, and the Chinese forms of bureaucratic government. Vietnam was known to the West by its Chinese name, Annam ("the pacified south"), but it was absorbed by force into French Indo-China by the 1880's and neither American merchants nor missionaries had much contact with it. Vietnam was historically part of the Chinese culture area, and modern Vietnamese patriots followed the Chinese example in both their reform efforts, dating from the 1890's, and their revolutionary efforts from the 1920's. But the United States regarded Vietnam as part of France. After World War II, during which the French had surrendered to Japan in Indo-China, we supported their effort to make Vietnam a colony again. It failed in 1954. The American public knew little more of the area than its name, but we then became gradually involved in a power politics intervention to save South Vietnam from Communism by using our superior resources and firepower.

Since no informed American can think of Vietnam without shame, it is essential that we try to understand the mainsprings of our intervention there. It is not enough to assert the platitudes of original sin (that great powers still have a propensity to use their arms) or imperialism (that the United States, thanks to modern technology, is the most expansive power of all time). We are still far from a specific understanding of our conduct in Vietnam; but it is indubitably linked to our earlier experience in East Asia and especially in China.

In the background, first of all, is our aversion to the domination of East Asia by a hostile power, whether the militarist Japan of the 1940's or the assumed international Communist monolith of the Cold War era. This sentiment echoes the aversion felt by Britian, as a sea — and trading — power, to the continental expansion of the Russian colossus in the nineteenth century.

Unfortunately our experience in East Asia to 1940 had been long on rhetoric and short on political experience. From 1840 on, Britain intervened in China and elsewhere, did the dirty work, and bore the burden of maintaining the treaty system. Participating only in the benefits, we retained our ideals. We sent our black ships to Japan with Perry in 1853–54 and to Korea in 1871, but never fought a war. The century of gunboat diplomacy — intervening with greater firepower to impose political arrangements — bequeathed to us many precedents but little direct experience. Others successfully applied pressure upon rulers — for instance, those of China, Japan, Vietnam, Siam, and Burma — in the mid-nineteenth century. But we Americans did not go in for power politics. When the intensified imperialist rivalry of the 1890's threatened China, our Open Door policy championed her national integrity but without any means of enforcement, even after it was formalized in the Washington Conference Nine-Power Treaty of 1922.

Only in 1941 did we really enter upon the few decades of our strategic hegemony in the Western Pacific and face the hard choices of how to use our power. By the 1940's we had succeeded to the British position as the principal Western country active in China. But after World War II, we decided very wisely not to intervene with troops in the KMT-CCP civil war. Yet our interests suffered from its outcome. Where China had formerly seemed condemned by fate to a quaint if sometimes exasperating backwardness in all things economic, political, and social, we now faced a strong government in a still backward country. Nationalism, though long retarded, had achieved maturity. Our thinking, in conservative America, could not keep pace with China's revolution. The first reaction of many Americans, suddenly confronted by a China strong, chauvinist, and anti-Western (instead of weak and pro-American) was to seize upon international Communism as the explanation and attribute our reverse to Kremlin plots and State Department treachery.

The Chinese Communist rise to power in 1949 called into question our own view of ourselves and our place in the world process. Insofar as the missionary conversion and general uplift of the Chinese people had expressed our conviction that we led the march of human progress, our self-confidence was dealt a grievous blow. One fourth of mankind in China spurned not only Christianity but also the supremacy of law, the ideals of individualism, the multi-party election process, civil liberties, and the self-determination of peoples, indeed, our entire political order and its concepts of freedom and security through due process. We felt our basic values directly menaced. *If* the Chinese people willingly chose Communism, it could be concluded that a majority of mankind was not going our way — at least, not for the present.

One consolation in this crisis, therefore, was to think that the new Chinese Communist dictatorship did not represent the interests of a large enough proportion of the Chinese people, that it maintained itself only by force and manipulation, that, in fine, it was too evil to last, and in any case must be opposed as a matter of principle and duty. This ideological stance of the Cold War seemed thoroughly justified by the bitter European experience under totalitarianism.

We therefore set ourselves at least to "contain" the expansion of the Sino-Soviet monolith outside its borders, and this we did in the Korean War, in our alliance with Taiwan, and by supporting the French in Indo-China until 1954 and South Vietnam after that date.

Yet a policy of containment could not be the same in East Asia as in Europe. There, containment as a policy to check the Soviet Union could stress the industrial recovery and political health of the Western European democracies that joined us in the NATO military alliance. In East Asia too we fostered industrial recovery in Japan and development in South Korea and Taiwan, but the military power had to be supplied more purely from the United States and, as it turned out, it had to be used in actual warfare. When South Korea was invaded by North Korea in 1950, we led the United Nations intervention against this aggression, on the whole successfully.

Future research should show that we intervened in Vietnam in the 1960's partly because we had *not* intervened in China in the late 1940's but *had* intervened in Korea in 1950. The "loss" of China had been used against the Democratic administration in American politics, whereas the Korean War had been accepted as an unavoidable defense of collective security and occupied Japan.

Our intervention in the 1960's to support South Vietnam was cast in the same moral framework as in Korea — to repel aggression and support self-determination. However, the circumstances proved to be different: the north had a firmer claim to embody the people's nationalism; our technologically advanced firepower proved immensely destructive, but the more things and people we destroyed materially, the more we inspired patriotic resistance. We discovered, moreover, that

Communism was not really monolithic, that Vietnamese national interests differed from Chinese national interests, as well as Chinese from Soviet. We had intervened in still another civil war, against another revolution, not the Chinese revolution, much less a movement led from Moscow.

Curiously, the Chinese People's Republic under Mao Tsetung's leadership had not proved to be very expansive. It withdrew its forces from Korea, put up with the Chinese Nationalist "front" on Quemoy, fought with Indian forces in 1962 only to assert boundary claims, and did not intervene against us in Vietnam.

What were we to conclude from all this? — that our "containment" of China had successfully prevented its expansion? or that the Chinese revolution was destined to expand, as Mao claimed, only by example (and in fact only in parts of the Chinese culture area)? Is it possible that we did not really understand what we were dealing with?

This, I think, will be the verdict of history. The old ways no longer serve, the old ideas have lost their efficacy. To coexist and survive, we have to seek a new understanding both of Asian realities and of our own aggressiveness.

Suggested Reading

1. **General Works of Reference**
Bibliographies / Geography / Historical surveys / The arts / Technology
2. **China's Traditional Civilization**
Archaeological origins / The Classics / Chinese philosophy / Early histories and historiography / Studies of early history / The Middle Period / Buddhism in China / Sino-barbarian relations / Marco Polo and others / Ming and early Ch'ing
3. **Chinese Culture and Society**
Literature in general / Poetry / The novel / Life seen through literati / Chinese thought / Social structure / Village community and family / Village economy and society / Population / Law and Administration
4. **Modern China**
General / Early European contact / China in the Enlightenment / The Canton trade / Opium War and treaty system / The mid-century rebellions / Restoration and self-strengthening / Economic developments / Late Ch'ing foreign relations / Christian missions / Reform / Revolution and warlordism / The intellectual revolution / The Nationalist revolution and government / Early history of the Chinese Communist movement / Cultural and religious life under the Republic / Foreigners' accounts
5. **The People's Republic**
Reference / Translations / Early first-hand impressions / Reports of later visitors / General appraisals from outside / Society and polity under the CCP / The economy: general appraisals and national income / The economy: special aspects / Science and professional manpower / Law / Education / Thought reform / Ideology, culture, and religion / The Cultural Revolution / The military / Arms control / The Sino-Soviet split / China's foreign policy
6. **Chinese-American Relations**
The Old China Trade / Chinese in America and American images of China / The American missionary movement and China / History of United States policy toward China / The United States in China in the 1940's / The Republic of China on Taiwan / United States policy toward the People's Republic

Suggested Reading

China used to be a journalist's dream and a statistician's nightmare, with more human drama and fewer verifiable facts per square mile than anywhere else in the world. For the American reader it is essential to penetrate the past and get a long-run view of China's recent transformation. As successful revolutionaries the Chinese Communists see evil in the past and good in the present, and want to rewrite history accordingly, to a greater degree than historians are likely to do. Yet the historical perspective of non-Communist foreign observers is also constantly menaced by the subjective hopes and fears of both the historians and their readers.

Research in libraries and observation in the field are both indispensable in the study of another society, but I believe the latter has a special value in the case of China. The present volume probably owes as much to seven years spent in various parts of China as it does to thirty-three years devoted to study of China in the West. This is because the ways of an alien land have to be experienced to be understood or even believed. Western man since Marco Polo has not stopped trying to comprehend Chinese ways. Yet the writers of each generation, whether philosophers of the eighteenth-century Enlightenment or exemplars of the treaty-port mind, have viewed Chinese civilization with a large degree of subjectivity. I doubt that social scientists can avoid doing so today, for the final portrait that one makes of an entire culture or society is a work of art, not of measurement.

Suggested Reading

The only recourse in this situation is for the reader to become in part a student, comparing one book with another, and in part a statesman, remembering that life is never quite encompassed in print, least of all Chinese life.

The world is seeing multiple explosions in population, technology, and learning, with problems multiplying faster than solutions. In this frenetic expansion, Chinese studies have not been left behind. So much has been published in the 1960's that this bibliography has greatly increased in length, even though I have omitted many works cited in the first two editions, as well as works not in English. On the other hand, the flow of academic publication from the Chinese mainland almost ceased in the latter half of the 1960's during the Cultural Revolution. While we try harder to understand the Chinese people, they hardly try to explain themselves.

Sections 1 through 4 below indicate major studies or recent works on various aspects of China — traditional and modern. The aim here is not to list all the important works, which would take half a volume, but to note certain outstanding landmarks and then add recent works, which naturally refer to earlier ones. On the problem of maintaining an informed and critical view of the Chinese People's Republic and American policy, see Sections 5 and 6.

Unless otherwise noted, publishers are in New York. HUP signifies the Harvard University Press in Cambridge, Mass.

Since the knowledge explosion has been accompanied by a tidal wave of reprinting, the reader is warned that publishers when they reprint a work may update its title page, on the specious grounds that the date of reprinting deserves such recognition. This overlooks the fact, and does not warn the reader, that the reprinted text is precisely the same as that published some time before. Thanks to this commercial chicanery, you must nowadays look overleaf at the copyright date to be sure when a work was really completed. The title page date may be quite deceiving. Even the title may be changed, as though the book were entirely new.

1. General Works of Reference

BIBLIOGRAPHIES. The best introduction to the literature on China is provided by Charles O. Hucker, *China. A Critical Bibliography* (Tucson: University of Arizona Press, 1962), an annotated listing of more than a thousand books and articles under topics, including some items in French and German. Professor Hucker has also done a pamphlet for the American Historical Association, *Chinese History: A Bibliographic Review* (Washington, D.C.: A.H.A. Service Center for Teachers of History, 1958).

The most comprehensive work, also arranged by topics, is Tung-li Yuan, *China in Western Literature* (New Haven: Far Eastern Publications, Yale University, 1958), which lists 18,000 books and pamphlets published between 1921 and 1957 in English, French, and German. A selected list in all languages is in *The American Historical Association's Guide to Historical Literature*. (Macmillan, 1963). The *Journal of Asian Studies* publishes a comprehensive annual volume.

GEOGRAPHY. The most informative first-hand survey based on extensive travel is George B. Cressey, *Land of the 500 Million* (McGraw-Hill, 1955). Norton Ginsburg, ed., *The Pattern of Asia* (Prentice-Hall, 1958), has a useful 118-page section on China. For historical maps consult the new edition, edited by Norton Ginsburg, of Albert Herrmann, *An Historical Atlas of China* (Chicago: Aldine, 1966; based on *Historical and Commercial Atlas of China*, Harvard-Yenching Institute, 1935). One of the few works in historical geography is Herold J. Wiens, *China's March toward the Tropics: A Discussion of the Southward Penetration of China's Culture, Peoples and Political Control* (Hamden, Conn.: Shoe String Press, 1954, reprinted by the same publisher in 1967 under the new title of *Han Expansion in South China*). A recent survey of regions and problems with a chapter on "Historical Geography" is by T. R. Tregear (London: University of London Press; Chicago: Aldine, 1965). Theodore Shabad, *China's Changing Map: A Political and Economic Geography of the Chinese People's Republic* (Praeger, 1956), is a systematic survey based on Moscow and Peking data.

HISTORICAL SURVEYS. For a summary of the facts known about China, the most comprehensive general source is Kenneth Scott Latourette, *The Chinese: Their History and Culture* (Macmillan, 4th ed., rev., 2 vols. in one, 1964), which has chapters on Chinese history and

427

Suggested Reading

society from nearly all angles, with very useful bibliographical sections. Although not exciting reading, it represents a lifetime of careful work. A more analytical survey is in two volumes: Edwin O. Reischauer and John K. Fairbank, *East Asia: The Great Tradition* (Boston: Houghton Mifflin, 1960), and John K. Fairbank, Edwin O. Reischauer, and Albert M. Craig, *East Asia: The Modern Transformation* (Boston: Houghton Mifflin, 1965). One of the best surveys in brief compass is L. Carrington Goodrich, *A Short History of the Chinese People* (Harper, 3rd ed., 1959), especially on the growth of China's material culture and foreign contacts. C. P. Fitzgerald, *China: A Short Cultural History* (Praeger, 3rd ed., 1961), contains well-informed essays. A readable but detailed summary grounded in French sinology is René Grousset, *The Rise and Splendour of the Chinese Empire* (Berkeley: University of California Press, 1953; paperback ed., 1965). Michael Loewe, *Imperial China. The Historical Background to the Modern Age* (Praeger, 1966), offers interesting analytic notes by a classicist. Werner Eichhorn, *Chinese Civilization. An Introduction* (Praeger paperback, 1969, transl. from German ed. of 1964), combines an intimate use of the record with a concern for the life of the people. Raymond Dawson, ed., *The Legacy of China* (Oxford: Clarendon Press, 1964), contains survey chapters by experts on thought, religion, literature, art, science, government, and the like. An English translation from the French, Marcel Granet, *Chinese Civilization,* an early classic of French sinological interpretation which had wide influence and still retains great vitality, was published by Alfred A. Knopf in 1930. A reprint is now sold by Meridian Books, World Publishing Company, dated "First Meridian printing April 1958," with date of original publication omitted.

A useful volume of selected readings to accompany any survey is by Wm. Theodore de Bary, Wing-tsit Chan, and Burton Watson, comp., *Sources of Chinese Tradition* (Columbia University Press, 1960), 950 pages of carefully selected translations — many new — with interpretive comments on the whole sweep of philosophical, religious, and political ideas from Confucius to Communism.

For comparative *chronology,* the broadest guide is of course William L. Langer, *An Encyclopedia of World History* (Boston: Houghton Mifflin, 4th ed., 1968).

Suggested Reading

THE ARTS. There is a wealth of handsomely illustrated volumes from several continents, too many to list here. For an expert survey aimed at the general reader see Laurence Sickman and Alexander Soper, *The Art and Architecture of China* (Baltimore: Penguin Books, 1956), with excellent plates and references to other works. William Willetts, *Chinese Art* (Penguin Books, 1958, 2 vols.), takes special note of artistic techniques; see also his *Foundations of Chinese Art* (London: McGraw Hill, 1965), and Michael Sullivan, *An Introduction to Chinese Art* (Berkeley: University of California Press, 1961).

TECHNOLOGY. Our view of China's contributions to world science and technology, traditionally confined to paper, printing, the compass, gunpowder, and similar great inventions, has been revolutionized by the work of Joseph Needham and his collaborators, Wang Ling and others, who are producing a multi-tomed, seven-volume series, *Science and Civilization in China* (Cambridge: Cambridge University Press): vol. 1, *Introductory Orientations* (1954); vol. 2, *History of Scientific Thought* (1956); vol. 3, *Mathematics and the Sciences of the Heavens and the Earth* (1959); vol. 4, *Physics and Physical Technology, Part I, Physics* (1962); vol. 4, *Part II, Mechanical Engineering* (1965); vol. 4, *Part III, Civil Engineering and Nautics* (1970). Selections of incidental papers and addresses have also been published, for example, Joseph Needham, *Clerks and Craftsmen in China and the West* (Cambridge University Press, 1970); Joseph Needham, *The Grand Titration. Science and Society in East and West* (Toronto: University of Toronto Press, 1969), reprints eight pieces that parallel the larger series of volumes. A major Chinese encyclopedia of technology by Sung Ying-hsing compiled in 1638 has been translated by E-tu Zen Sun and Shiou-chuan Sun, *T'ien-kung k'ai-wu, Chinese Technology in the Seventeenth Century* (University Park and London: Pennsylvania State University Press, 1966).

On the early technical developments that produced inscriptions, writing, paper, and eventually the Chinese book, see Tsuen-hsuin Tsien, *Written on Bamboo and Silk. The Beginnings of Chinese Books and Inscriptions* (University of Chicago Press, 1962). A classic monograph is by Thomas Francis Carter, *The Invention of Printing in China and Its Spread Westward*, revised and updated by L. Carrington Goodrich

Suggested Reading

(2nd ed., Ronald Press, 1955 [1925]). On calligraphic technique, Chiang Yee, *Chinese Calligraphy* (London, 1954); and on painting, Alison Stilwell Cameron, *Chinese Painting Techniques* (Tokyo: Charles E. Tuttle, 1968).

As part of China's erotic technology, note should also be taken of Howard S. Levy, *Chinese Footbinding, The History of a Curious Erotic Custom* (Walton Rawls, 1966). On traditional medicine, see Pierre Huard and Ming Wong, *Chinese Medicine,* translated from the French (McGraw-Hill, 1968), illustrated; and Heinrich Wallnoefer and Anna von Rottauscher, *Chinese Folk Medicine* (Crown, 1965). On another new field, Nathan Sivin, *Chinese Alchemy: Preliminary Studies* (HUP, 1968).

2. China's Traditional Civilization

ARCHAEOLOGICAL ORIGINS. Chang Kwang-chih, *The Archaeology of Ancient China* (New Haven: Yale University Press, 1963), synthesizes and interprets the now extensive record. Recent finds are surveyed by Cheng Te-k'un, *Archaeology in China* (vol. I, *Prehistoric China,* Cambridge: Heffer, 1959; vol. II, *Shang China,* Toronto: University of Toronto Press, 1960; vol. III, *Chou China,* the same, 1963). For an early and very readable report on Anyang see Herrlee G. Creel, *The Birth of China* (London: Cape, 1936). Professor Creel's latest study is *The Origins of Statecraft in China,* vol. 1, *The Western Chou Empire* (Chicago and London: University of Chicago Press, 1970); see also his article "The Beginnings of Bureaucracy in China: The Origin of the *Hsien*," *Journal of Asian Studies* 23.2 (Feb. 1964): 155–184. For a brief account by a distinguished pioneer see Li Chi, *The Beginnings of Chinese Civilization* (Seattle: University of Washington Press, 1957). William Watson, *China before the Han Dynasty* (Praeger, 1961), is a graphic survey of archaeological finds with 77 photographs and many drawings.

THE CLASSICS. These are above all works of literature, and one of the best introductions, sponsored by the Columbia University Committee on Oriental Studies, is Burton Watson, *Early Chinese Literature*

(Columbia University Press, 1962): survey essays on the classical Chinese works of history, philosophy, and poetry down to c. A.D. 100, with many translated passages. The principal texts have long been available in standard translations, principally by James Legge, *The Chinese Classics* (Oxford: Clarendon Press, 2nd ed., 8 vols., 1893–1895; Hong Kong: Hong Kong University Press, 3rd ed., 5 vols., 1961). Among many others, Arthur Waley in his long career as a translator contributed a number of very attractive versions — *The Analects of Confucius* (London: G. Allen and Unwin, 1938); *The Way and Its Power* (London: G. Allen and Unwin, 1934; paperback, 1958), which is the Taoist classic *Tao te ching*. See also his *Three Ways of Thought in Ancient China* (London: G. Allen and Unwin, 1939; Doubleday Anchor Books, 1956) for a comparative study of the early philosophies with extensive quotations from the *Chuang-tzu,* the *Mencius,* and the Legalists. Among other new translations by Burton Watson is *Mo Tzu: Basic Writings* (Columbia University Press, 1963). For Taoism two principal texts are J. J. L. Duyvendak, *Tao Te Ching. The Book of the Way and Its Virtue* (London: John Murray, 1954), more recent than Waley's version; and A. C. Graham, *The Book of Lieh-tzu* (London: John Murray, 1960), another Taoist classic. For a work claimed by the Legalist as well as other schools, see W. Allyn Rickett, *Kuan-tzu. A Repository of Early Chinese Thought* (Hong Kong: Hong Kong University Press, 1965). W. K. Liao (Liao Wen-kuei), tr., *The Complete Works of Han Fei Tzu. A Classic of Chinese Political Science* (London: Arthur Probsthain, 2 vols., 1939, 1959), makes available a major text of the Legalist school.

The ancient but still pertinent classic on warfare has been translated by Samuel B. Griffith, *Sun Tzu: The Art of War* (Oxford University Press, 1963).

CHINESE PHILOSOPHY. The leading general survey is the translation by Derk Bodde of Fung Yu-lan, *A History of Chinese Philosophy* (vol. I, Peiping: H. Vetch, 1937; reissued together with the publication of vol. II, Princeton: Princeton University Press, 1952). Fung Yu-lan, *A Short History of Chinese Philosophy* (Macmillan, 1948), though edited by Professor Bodde, is a separate study. The greatest of the sages is

Suggested Reading

restudied in detail by H. G. Creel, *Confucius: The Man and the Myth* (John Day, 1949). Professor Creel has also done a readable nontechnical survey, *Chinese Thought from Confucius to Mao Tse-tung* (Chicago: University of Chicago Press, 1953). See also Wing-tsit Chan, *A Source Book in Chinese Philosophy* (Princeton: Princeton University Press, 1963), and deBary et al., *Sources of Chinese Tradition,* cited above. A fascinating, fresh account of Taoism is presented in Holmes Welch, *The Parting of the Way: Lao Tzu and the Taoist Movement* (Boston: Beacon Press, 1957). A recent study of classical values is by Donald J. Munro, *The Concept of Man in Early China* (Stanford: Stanford University sity Press, 1969).

EARLY HISTORIES AND HISTORIOGRAPHY. Among the translations of sources, two works by Burton Watson bring us close to the great pioneer historian Ssu-ma Ch'ien: *Records of the Grand Historian of China* (Columbia University Press, 2 vols., 1961), a translation of the *Shih-chi,* and *Ssu-ma Ch'ien, Grand Historian of China* (Columbia University Press, 1958). On the Han, Homer Dubs has translated the annals section of the official history, *The History of the Former Han Dynasty by Pan Ku* (Baltimore: Waverly Press, vol. 1, 1938; vol. 2, 1944; vol. 3, 1955). Key economic sections from the Former Han history by Pan Ku have been translated by Nancy Lee Swann, *Food and Money in Ancient China* (Princeton: Princeton University Press, 1950). For the post-Han disunion see the translation by Achilles Fang, *The Chronicle of the Three Kingdoms (220–265)* (HUP, 2 vols., 1952, 1965), which is actually chapters 69–78 from the comprehensive history, *Tzu-chih t'ung-chien,* by Ssu-ma Kuang (1019–1086).

For a basic, brief introduction to the craft of Chinese history writing see Charles S. Gardner, *Chinese Traditional Historiography* (HUP, 1938, reprinted with additions by L. S. Yang, 1961). A notable series of articles by leading scholars is in W. G. Beasley and E. G. Pulleyblank, eds., *Historians of China and Japan* (London: Oxford University Press, 1961).

STUDIES OF EARLY HISTORY. The political institutions of the Warring States period are analyzed by Richard L. Walker, *The Multi-*

Suggested Reading

State System of Ancient China (Hamden, Conn.: Shoe String Press, 1953); Cho-yun Hsü, *Ancient China in Transition: An Analysis of Social Mobility, 722–222 B.C.* (Stanford: Stanford University Press, 1965), deals with the social history of this period in general. On the problem of ancient China's social structure, see also Derk Bodde's chapter "Feudalism in China" in Rushton Coulborn, ed., *Feudalism in History* (Princeton: Princeton University Press, 1956). On the Ch'in unification, Derk Bodde, *China's First Unifier. A Study of the Ch'in Dynasty as Seen in the Life of Li Ssu 280?–208 B.C.* (Leiden: E. J. Brill, 1938), has been reprinted with a new foreword (Hong Kong: Hong Kong University Press, 1967). A notable monograph on the Han economy is by Ying-shih Yü, *Trade and Expansion in Han China. A Study in the Structure of Sino-Barbarian Economic Relations* (Berkeley and Los Angeles: University of California Press, 1967). On the political transition from Early to Later Han, Hans Bielenstein has studied *The Restoration of the Han Dynasty* (Stockholm: Museum of Far Eastern Antiquities, vol. 1, 1954; vol. 2, 1959). On law see A. F. P. Hulsewe, *Remnants of Han Law* (Leiden: Brill, 1955).

THE MIDDLE PERIOD. So strong was the hold of the Chinese classical tradition that until 1950 relatively few monographic studies had appeared on the long period from A.D. 220 to 1644. This lack is now being rapidly made up and a number of important works are available. Edwin O. Reischauer, *Ennin's Diary: The Record of a Pilgrimage to China in Search of the Law* (Ronald Press, 1955), translates a unique first-person account of T'ang China. The companion volume, *Ennin's Travels in T'ang China* (Ronald Press, 1955), is an absorbing summary and commentary, rounding out this ninth-century Marco Polo's picture of China at the apex of world civilization. Other recent monographs on successive periods include Edwin G. Pulleyblank, *The Background of the Rebellion of An Lu-shan* (London: Oxford University Press, 1955); Denis C. Twitchett, *Financial Administration under the T'ang Dynasty* (Cambridge: Cambridge University Press, 1963); Wang Gungwu, *The Structure of Power in North China during the Five Dynasties* (Kuala Lumpur: University of Malaya Press, 1963, distributed by Oxford University Press), dealing with the interregnum be-

433

Suggested Reading

tween T'ang and Sung; E. A. Kracke, Jr., *Civil Service in Early Sung China, 960–1067* (HUP, 1953); James T. C. Liu, *Reform in Sung China: Wang An-shih (1021–1086) and His New Policies* (HUP, 1959); and Herbert Franz Schurmann, *Economic Structure of the Yuan Dynasty* (HUP, 1956, Harvard-Yenching Institute Studies XVI). One of the most vivid re-creations of Chinese life in an earlier age is H. M. Wright's translation from the French of Jacques Gernet, *Daily Life in China on the Eve of the Mongol Invasion, 1250–1276* (Macmillan, 1962). Edward H. Schafer, *The Golden Peaches of Samarkand. A Study of T'ang Exotics* (Berkeley and Los Angeles: University of California Press, 1963), is actually a mine of information on the material culture of the period. Lien-sheng Yang, *Studies in Chinese Institutional History* (HUP, 1961), reprints nine articles by this leading institutional sinologist, from the *Harvard Journal of Asiatic Studies*. See also his *Money and Credit in China: A Short History* (HUP, 1952). John L. Bishop, ed., *Studies of Governmental Institutions in Chinese History* (HUP, 1968), reprints half a dozen major articles from the *Harvard Journal of Asiatic Studies*.

BUDDHISM IN CHINA. For an interesting survey of this vast subject see Arthur F. Wright, *Buddhism in Chinese History* (Stanford: Stanford University Press, 1959); for a longer monograph, E. Zürcher, *The Buddhist Conquest of China. The Spread and Adaptation of Buddhism in Early Medieval China* (Leiden: E. J. Brill, 2 vols., 1959); for a general account, Kenneth Ch'en, *Buddhism in China, A Historical Survey* (Princeton: Princeton University Press, 1964); and for a graphic eye-witness description of monastic life in recent times, Holmes Welch, *The Practice of Chinese Buddhism, 1900–1950* (HUP, 1967). Arthur Waley's volume, *The Real Tripitaka and Other Pieces* (London: Allen and Unwin, 1952), is mainly on the Chinese Buddhist pilgrim Hsuan-tsang who went to India in 629–645. On one aspect of Buddhism now in vogue, a convenient popular collection is *The Essentials of Zen Buddhism. Selected from the Writings of Daisetz T. Suzuki,* edited by Bernard Phillips (E. P. Dutton, 1962).

SINO-BARBARIAN RELATIONS. Study of Chinese border relations with

434

Suggested Reading

Manchuria, Mongolia, and Sinkiang have been illumined and greatly stimulated by Owen Lattimore, *Inner Asian Frontiers of China* (American Geographical Society, 2nd ed., 1951 [1940]), which builds on the author's earlier publications and field experience — for example, his *Manchuria, Cradle of Conflict* (Macmillan, 1932). See his *Studies in Frontier History. Collected Papers, 1928–1958* (Oxford University Press, 1962). Wolfram Eberhard, *Conquerors and Rulers, Social Forces in Medieval China* (Leiden: Brill, 2nd ed., 1965), pursues the same themes historically, differing with certain views of K. A. Wittfogel. For data on the regime of the Khitan Mongols, see K. A. Wittfogel and Feng Chia-sheng, *History of Chinese Society: Liao (907–1125)* (Philadelphia: American Philosophical Society, 1949). Conceptions of Chinese-nomad relations are also developed in Franz Michael, *The Origin of Manchu Rule in China, Frontier and Bureaucracy as Interacting Forces in the Chinese Empire* (Baltimore: Johns Hopkins Press, 1942). On the tribute system as the vehicle of China's early modern foreign relations, see J. K. Fairbank, ed., *The Chinese World Order. Traditional China's Foreign Relations* (HUP, 1968).

The most thorough work on the Mongols in history has been done in Europe, particularly in France. On the Mongol conquests in Central Asia, see V. V. Barthold, *Turkestan down to the Mongol Invasion*, transl. by H. A. R. Gibb (London: Luzac, 2nd ed., 1958). A detailed study of the Mongols' trans-Asian imperial structure is given in George Vernadsky, *The Mongols and Russia* (New Haven: Yale University Press, 1953). Among many studies that have appeared, one of the most readable and authoritative is the English translation (from the French edition of 1944), by Denis Sinor and Marian MacKellar, of René Grousset, *Conqueror of the World: The Life of Chingis-Khan* (Toronto: Clarke, Irwin, 1967), which Professor Sinor has updated on points of scholarship to 1965.

MARCO POLO AND OTHERS. This is a field in itself. Polo's better-known precursors and contemporaries are recorded in Christopher Dawson, *The Mongol Mission. Narratives and Letters of the Franciscan Missionaries in Mongolia and China in the Thirteenth and Fourteenth Centuries* (Sheed and Ward, 1955). Leonardo Olschki, *Marco Polo's Asia. An In-*

Suggested Reading

troduction to His "Description of the World" called "Il milione" (Berkeley: University of California Press, 1960), has worked out a fascinating topical analysis of the content of Polo's great account. For the authoritative English translation, see A. C. Moule and P. Pelliot, *Marco Polo: The Description of the World* (London: Routledge, 2 vols., 1938). Of the many popular versions, several are in paperback. Henry Hart, *Venetian Adventurer* (Palo Alto: Stanford University Press, 1942; Bantam Books, 1956), is a readable biography.

MING AND EARLY CH'ING. This early modern era is now under intensive study. It is too soon for works of synthesis. Many works of institutional history are noted in other sections. One principal stimulus and aid to research has been A. W. Hummel, ed., *Eminent Chinese of the Ch'ing Period (1644–1912)* (Washington, D.C.: Government Printing Office, 2 vols., 1943, 1944). L. Carrington Goodrich is editor of a corresponding Ming Biographical History, not yet published. Both projects owe much to Chao-ying Fang and Lien-che Tu Fang as major compilers. On Ming administration, see Charles O. Hucker, *The Traditional Chinese State in Ming Times, 1368–1644* (Tucson: University of Arizona Press, 1961); and Charles O. Hucker, ed., *Chinese Government in Ming Times: Seven Studies* (Columbia University Press, 1969). The dynastic decline is dealt with by James Bunyan Parsons, *The Peasant Rebellions of the Late Ming Dynasty* (Tucson: University of Arizona Press, 1970).

On the early Ch'ing there are two studies concerning the major sixty-year reigns: Jonathan D. Spence, *Ts'ao Yin and the K'ang-hsi Emperor, Bondservant and Master* (New Haven: Yale University Press, 1966); and Harold L. Kahn, *Monarchy in the Emperor's Eyes: Image and Reality in the Ch'ien-lung Reign* (HUP, 1971).

On one facet of the Ch'ing empire, see L. Petech, *China and Tibet in the Early 18th Century. History of the Establishment of Chinese Protectorate in Tibet* (Leiden: E. J. Brill, 1950).

3. Chinese Culture and Society

This section is intended to suggest how studies of early literature, recent social structure, thought and values may interpenetrate and reinforce one another.

436

Suggested Reading

LITERATURE IN GENERAL. This category of course overlaps several of those above. For a general introduction to the different genres, see James Robert Hightower, *Topics in Chinese Literature. Outlines and Bibliographies* (HUP, 2nd ed., 1953; the fourth printing is dated "1966"), which provides extensive lists of translations and studies in this vast field down to the modern era. Cyril Birch, comp. and ed., *Anthology of Chinese Literature from Early Times to the Fourteenth Century* (Grove Press, 1965), offers brilliant selections from Chou to Yuan by a score of translators. Jaroslav Prusek, *Chinese History and Literature* (Prague: Academia, 1970), presents the studies of a leading European sinologist. Vincent Yu-chung Shih, transl., with introduction and notes, *The Literary Mind and the Carving of Dragons by Liu Hsieh, A Study of Thought and Pattern in Chinese Literature* (Columbia University Press, 1959), makes available a seminal work of c. A.D. 500.

POETRY. For a clear and concrete introduction to this universe, see James J. Y. Liu, *The Art of Chinese Poetry* (Chicago: University of Chicago Press, 1962). Among recent translations are David Hawkes, *Ch'u Tz'u, the Songs of the South; An Ancient Chinese Anthology* (Oxford: Clarendon Press, 1959); Arthur Waley, *Ballads and Stories from Tunhuang. An Anthology* (London: George Allen and Unwin, 1960), a selection of popular literature from before A.D. 1000; and Kojiro Yoshikawa, transl. by Burton Watson, *An Introduction to Sung Poetry* (HUP, 1967), the intimately detailed essays of a major scholar.

THE NOVEL. One neglected shortcut to understanding China is the corpus of novels now available in translation, including Arthur Waley's translation of *Hsi-yu chi* entitled *Monkey* (John Day, 1943; Grove Press reprint); Pearl Buck's of *Shui-hu chuan* entitled *All Men Are Brothers* (John Day, 1933; Grove Press reprint); Wang Chi-chen's of *Hung-lou meng* entitled *Dream of the Red Chamber* (Twayne Publishers, condensed edition, 1958 [1929]; a further abridged paperback, Doubleday Anchor Books, 1958); and Clement Egerton's translation of *Chin-p'ing-mei* entitled *The Golden Lotus* (London: G. Routledge, 4 vols., 1939, with passages in Latin). There is also an expurgated edition entitled *Chin P'ing Mei* (G. P. Putnam's Sons, 1940). A late Ch'ing novel is translated by Harold Shadick, *The Travels of Lao Ts'an* by Liu T'ieh-yün (Ithaca: Cornell University Press, 1952). Among the historical researches on major novels are Richard Gregg Irwin, *The Evolution of a Chinese Novel, Shui-hu-chuan* (HUP, 1953); and Wu Shih-ch'ang, *On the Red Chamber Dream, A Critical Study of Two Annotated Manuscripts of the XVIIIth Century* (Oxford: Clarendon Press, 1961).

Among many translations of literature made by Yang Hsien-yi and Gladys Yang and published by the Foreign Languages Press in Peking are *The Courtesan's Jewel Box. Chinese Stories of the X-XVII Centuries* (1957); and Wu Ching-tzu (1701–1754), *The Scholars* (1957), a translation of *Ju-lin wai-shih*. See also Cyril Birch, *Stories from a Ming Collection* (London: Bodley Head, 1958); and Wolfram Eberhard, *Folktales of China* (Chicago: University of Chicago Press, 1965). On the drama, note the recent introduction by A. C. Scott, *The Classical Theatre of China* (Macmillan, 1959).

Life seen through literati. Poets through their works lend themselves to biographical treatment, and a notable series of studies has resulted: Arthur Waley, *The Poetry and Career of Li Po, 701–762 A.D.* (London: George Allen and Unwin, 1950); Arthur Waley, *The Life and Times of Po Chü-i, 772–846* (London: George Allen and Unwin, 1949); Lin Yutang, *The Gay Genius. The Life and Times of Su Tungpo* (1036–1101) (London: William Heinemann, 1948); F. W. Mote, *The Poet Kao Ch'i, 1336–1374* (Princeton: Princeton University Press, 1962), which re-creates the atmosphere of the founding of the Ming dynasty; and Arthur Waley, *Yuan Mei, Eighteenth-Century Chinese Poet* (London: George Allen and Unwin, 1956; Grove Press reprint).

Chinese thought. Under the sponsorship of a committee of the Association for Asian Studies, a series of research-conference symposia have presented a wide range of some fifty-seven articles by specialists from several countries: Arthur F. Wright, ed., *Studies in Chi-*

Suggested Reading

nese Thought (Chicago: University of Chicago Press, 1953); J. K. Fairbank, ed., *Chinese Thought and Institutions* (the same, 1957); David S. Nivison and A. F. Wright, eds., *Confucianism in Action* (Stanford: Stanford University Press, 1959); A. F. Wright, ed., *The Confucian Persuasion* (the same, 1960); and A. F. Wright and D. C. Twitchett, eds., *Confucian Personalities* (the same, 1962). A. F. Wright, ed. and introd., *Confucianism and Chinese Civilization* (Atheneum paperback, 1964), is a selection from the last three of these volumes on Chinese thought. Further symposia have now appeared under the sponsorship of the American Council of Learned Societies' Committee on Studies of Chinese Civilization; the first of these is by Wm. Theodore deBary and the Conference on Ming Thought, *Self and Society in Ming Thought* (Columbia University Press, 1970). A major study of a historian is by David S. Nivison, *The Life and Thought of Chang Hsueh-ch'eng (1738–1801)* (Stanford: Stanford University Press, 1966).

SOCIAL STRUCTURE. Chinese ways have been more often described than analyzed. A great impetus came from the German sociologist Max Weber, whose pioneer work on China has been largely translated by Hans Gerth as *The Religion of China: Confucianism and Taoism* (Glencoe: The Free Press, 1951). Note that the paperback edition (Macmillan, 1964) has an invaluable thirty-page introduction by C. K Yang (Yang Ch'ing-k'un) who puts Weber's work in context and evaluates his contribution, including its unavoidable shortcomings. Another broad impetus through a neo-Marxist approach has come from Karl A. Wittfogel, *Oriental Despotism: A Comparative Study of Total Power* (New Haven: Yale University Press, 1957). For historical studies of social structure and bureaucracy, see Etienne Balazs, *Chinese Civilization and Bureaucracy* (New Haven and London: Yale University Press, 1964), which brings together trenchant essays by a leading European scholar, brilliantly translated. Nearly everyone, of course, touches on this subject in some fashion. For statistical research on the gentry class, in the sense of degree-holders, see Chung-li Chang, *The Chinese Gentry, Studies on Their Role in Nineteenth-Century Chinese Society* (Seattle: University of Washington Press, 1955). This analysis has been further developed and modified by Ping-ti Ho, *The*

Suggested Reading

Ladder of Success in Imperial China, Aspects of Social Mobility (Columbia University Press, 1962).

VILLAGE COMMUNITY AND FAMILY. Village studies were just getting started in the 1940's following the work of a few pioneers. One of the earliest was the American missionary, Arthur H. Smith, whose *Chinese Characteristics* (2nd ed., 1894) and *Village Life in China. A Study in Sociology* (1899) were very influential, even in Japan. Other descriptions of village and family life, including those in the novels of Pearl Buck, are listed in Latourette, pp. 602f, and in the Hucker bibliography. Among social anthropologists, one creative modern writer is Hsiao-t'ung Fei, whose works in English include *Peasant Life in China: A Field Study of Country Life in the Yangtze Valley* (Dutton, 1939); with Chih-i Chang, *Earthbound China, A Study of Rural Economy in Yunnan* (Chicago: University of Chicago Press, 1945); and "Peasantry and Gentry, an Interpretation of Chinese Social Structure and Its Changes," an article in *The American Journal of Sociology* (52.1, July 1946). A volume of Fei's essays, *China's Gentry* (Chicago: University of Chicago Press, 1953), was published after his absorption into the new order in Peking.

For work on the family and clan (or lineage) by a leader in this field, see Maurice Freedman, *Chinese Lineage and Society: Fukien and Kwangtung* (London: Athlone, 1966). Note also Hui-chen Wang Liu, *The Traditional Chinese Clan Rules* (Locust Valley, N.Y.: Augustin, 1959). The family system at work in a village may be seen in a number of case studies: Martin Yang, *A Chinese Village: Taitou, Shantung Province* (Columbia University Press, 1945); Lin Yüeh-hua, *The Golden Wing: A Sociological Study of Chinese Familism* (London: Kegan Paul, Trench, Trubner, 1948); Francis L. K. Hsu, *Under the Ancestors' Shadow: Chinese Culture and Personality* (Columbia University Press, 1948); Sidney D. Gamble, *Ting Hsien, a North China Rural Community* (Institute of Pacific Relations, 1954; reissued, Stanford: Stanford University Press, 1968); Morton H. Fried, *Fabric of Chinese Society: A Study of the Social Life of a Chinese County Seat* (Praeger, 1953); and Margery Wolf, *The House of Lim, A Study of a Chinese Farm Family* (Appleton-Century-Crofts, 1968). An early theoretical work is by Mar-

Suggested Reading

ion J. Levy, *The Family Revolution in Modern China* (HUP, 1949; Atheneum paperback, 1968). Recent work is represented in Maurice Freedman, ed., *Family and Kinship in Chinese Society* (Stanford: Stanford University Press, 1970), papers by ten specialists from an SSRC conference of 1966. See also I. C. Jarvie, ed., *Hong Kong: A Society in Transition. Contributions to the Study of Hong Kong Society* (London: Routledge and Kegan Paul, 1969), fourteen sociological studies, with photos.

VILLAGE ECONOMY AND SOCIETY. Another vital stimulus, leading toward the study of "local systems," has come from G. William Skinner's three-part article, "Marketing and Social Structure in Rural China," *Journal of Asian Studies* (vol. 24, 1964–65). The incidence of landlordism at the end of the Ch'ing period has been illuminated by Yuji Muramatsu, "A Documentary Study of Chinese Landlordism in the Late Ch'ing and the Early Republican Kiangnan," *Bulletin of the School of Oriental and African Studies* (University of London, vol. XXIX, part 3, 1966). R. H. Tawney, *Land and Labor in China* (Harcourt, Brace, 1932), is still a classic analysis of the farm economy about 1930, by a leading specialist on late medieval Europe. A recent analysis is Jack M. Potter, *Capitalism and the Chinese Peasant. Social and Economic Change in a Hong Kong Village* (Berkeley and Los Angeles: University of California Press, 1968), which questions whether foreign economic influence was as disastrous as many like Fei Hsiaot'ung once assumed. Modern Japanese as well as Chinese studies of the North China farm economy, village and market, are appraised by Ramon H. Myers, *The Chinese Peasant Economy. Agricultural Development in Hopei and Shantung, 1890–1949* (HUP, 1970).

POPULATION. The enigma of population growth is attacked by Ping-ti Ho, *Studies on the Population of China, 1368–1953* (HUP, 1959); also by Irene B. Taeuber and Wang Nai-chi, "Population Reports in the Ch'ing Dynasty," *Journal of Asian Studies* (vol. 29, 1959–60, pp. 403–417); and by John S. Aird, *The Size, Composition and Growth of the Population of Mainland China* (Washington, D.C.: Bureau of the Census, 1961). An arresting historical analysis of the growth of people

441

Suggested Reading

and food supply is in Dwight H. Perkins, with the assistance of Yeh-chien Wang and others, *Agricultural Development in China, 1368–1968* (Chicago: Aldine, 1969).

LAW AND ADMINISTRATION. T'ung-tsu Ch'ü, *Law and Society in Traditional China* (Paris and The Hague: Mouton, 1961), provides vivid details of the uses of law to regulate the social order. Sybille van der Sprenkel, *Legal Institutions in Manchu China, A Sociological Analysis* (London: Athlone Press, 1962), surveys the traditional means of conflict resolution. Derk Bodde and Clarence Morris, *Law in Imperial China, Exemplified by 190 Ch'ing Dynasty Cases* (HUP, 1967) describes the operation of the imperial legal system and its characteristics, with illustrative cases. The most concrete study of one of China's primary administrative institutions is by Charles O. Hucker, *The Censorial System of Ming China* (Stanford: Stanford University Press, 1966). T'ung-tsu Ch'ü, *Local Government in China under the Ch'ing* (HUP, 1962; Stanford University Press paperback, 1969), is a classic analysis of what goes on inside a hsien magistrate's yamen. Kung-chuan Hsiao, *Rural China: Imperial Control in the Nineteenth Century* (Seattle: University of Washington Press, 1960), describes the whole range of control mechanisms and policies. On the Manchus' control and use of their homeland, see Robert H. G. Lee, *The Manchurian Frontier in Ch'ing History* (HUP, 1970). The most recent study of administration is by Silas H. L. Wu, *Communication and Imperial Control in China. Evolution of the Palace Memorial System, 1693–1735* (HUP, 1970). For a guide to materials and their use in research on the Ch'ing administration, see John K. Fairbank, *Ch'ing Documents: An Introductory Syllabus* (HUP, 2 vols., 3rd ed. with index added, 1970).

4. Modern China

GENERAL. The chief recent survey is by Immanuel C. Y. Hsü, *The Rise of Modern China* (Oxford University Press, 1970). Among many other earlier surveys there is a translation by S. Y. Teng and J. Ingalls of Li Chien-nung, *The Political History of China, 1840–1928* (Van Nostrand, 1956). General East Asian surveys include George E. Tay-

442

lor and Franz H. Michael, *The Far East in the Modern World* (Holt, rev. ed. 1964 [1956]); Paul H. Clyde and Burton F. Beers, *The Far East, A History of the Western Impact and the Eastern Response (1830–1965)* (Prentice-Hall, 4th ed., 1966 [earlier editions by Paul H. Clyde, 1948, 1952, 1958]); George M. Beckmann, *The Modernization of China and Japan* (Harper and Row, 1962); and Harold M. Vinacke, *A History of the Far East in Modern Times* (Appleton-Century-Crofts, 6th ed., 1961). Note should be taken of the grandfather of American compendia on China, S. Wells Williams, *The Middle Kingdom, A Survey of the Geography, Government, Literature, Social Life, Arts, and History of the Chinese Empire* (Wiley and Halsted, 1848; rev. ed. Scribners, 1883), and of a summary from Peking by Chien Po-tsan, Shao Hsun-cheng, and Hu Hua, *Concise History of China* (Peking: Foreign Languages Press, 1964) — which may be taken as opposite ends of a wide spectrum.

Selected readings are provided in a volume of translations with commentary by Ssu-yu Teng and John K. Fairbank, *China's Response to the West: A Documentary Survey, 1839–1923* (HUP, 1954; Atheneum paperback); and in Franz Schurmann and Orville Schell, *The China Reader* (Random House, 3 vols., 1967: vol. 1, *Imperial China;* vol. 2, *Republican China;* and vol. 3, *Communist China*), a selection mainly of extracts from observers and historians. For an ingenious and entrancing sequence of excerpts from some 280 first-person narratives during a century and a half, from all sides, see Roger Pelissier, *The Awakening of China, 1793–1949* (G. P. Putnam's Sons, 1967; translated from French ed., *La Chine entre en scene,* 1963). H. F. MacNair, *Modern Chinese History: Selected Readings* (Shanghai: Commercial Press, 1923; reprinted Taipei, 1957; Paragon reprint, 1967), dates from an earlier era but is still of value. Its documentation parallels the basic survey, mainly from the British record, by Hosea Ballou Morse, *The International Relations of the Chinese Empire* (London: Longmans Green, 3 vols., 1910, 1918; reprinted in Taipei). This was condensed and developed as a text by H. B. Morse and Harley F. MacNair, *Far Eastern International Relations* (Boston: Houghton Mifflin, 1931). See also H. F. MacNair and Donald Lach, *Modern Far Eastern International Relations* (Van Nostrand, 2nd ed., 1955 [1950]).

For the Republican period, a very useful survey is by O. Edmund

Suggested Reading

Clubb, *20th Century China* (Columbia University Press, 1964). The chief biographical reference work for the period 1911–1949 is by Howard L. Boorman and Richard C. Howard, eds., *Biographical Dictionary of Republican China* (Columbia University Press, 5 vols.: vol. 1, Ai-Ch'ü, 1967; vol. 2, Dalai-Ma, 1968; vol. 3, Mao-Wu, 1970).

EARLY EUROPEAN CONTACT. For a general survey of European expansion, see John H. Parry, *The Age of Reconnaissance* (London: Weidenfeld and Nicolson; Cleveland: World Publishing Company, 1963). A small paperback of extracts from some two-score authors, selected by Joseph R. Levenson, ed., *European Expansion and the Counter-Example of Asia, 1300–1600* (Prentice-Hall, 1967), conveys very well the extraordinary vitality and intellectual enthusiasm of the editor. The Portuguese pioneers in China have been illumined in a series of notable studies by C. R. Boxer, including, on Macao, *Fidalgos in the Far East, 1550–1770* (The Hague: Nijhoff, 1948); and C. R. Boxer, ed., *South China in the Sixteenth Century* (London: Hakluyt Society, 1953), three narratives of adventures in 1550–1575. The broad outlines of the early European contact with China are discussed in the early sections of G. B. Sansom, *The Western World and Japan, A Study in the Interaction of European and Asiatic Cultures* (Knopf, 1950).

Like Marco Polo, the Jesuit pioneers at Peking form an entire field in themselves. Their own record has been newly appraised in a well-informed study by George H. Dunne, S.J., *Generation of Giants. The Story of the Jesuits in China in the Last Decades of the Ming Dynasty* (Notre Dame, Ind.: University of Notre Dame Press, 1962). For a somewhat different view see Columba Cary-Elwes, O.S.B., *China and the Cross. Studies in Missionary History* (Longmans Green, 1957). For a popularly written account of Matteo Ricci, see Vincent Cronin, *The Wise Man from the West* (London: Rupert-Hart-Davis, 1955). For a version of his own account, see Louis J. Gallagher, S.J., transl., *China in the Sixteenth Century: The Journals of Matthew Ricci: 1583–1610* (Random House, 1953). A recent analysis is by George L. Harris, "The Mission of Matteo Ricci, S.J. A Case Study of an Effort at Guided Culture Change in China in the Sixteenth Century," *Monumenta Serica* (Tokyo), XXV, 1966.

444

Suggested Reading

On the early Ch'ing contact with Russia, see Mark Mancall, *Russia and China: Their Diplomatic Relations to 1728* (HUP, 1971).

CHINA IN THE ENLIGHTENMENT. A multi-volume review of western literature and art on China is being made by Donald Lach, *Asia in the Making of Europe* (Chicago and London: University of Chicago Press, vol. I, *The Century of Discovery*, in 2 books, 1965; vol. 2, *A Century of Wonder, Book One. The Visual Arts*, 1970). These volumes deal with the sixteenth and seventeenth centuries, respectively. At present the broadest brief survey of the eighteenth century is still Adolf Reichwein, *China and Europe* (Alfred A. Knopf, 1925). The most trenchant researches are in French. Recent studies of Chinoiserie are W. W. Appleton, *A Cycle of Cathay. The Chinese Vogue in England* (Columbia University Press, 1951); and Hugh Honour, *Chinoiserie: The Vision of Cathay* (London: J. Murray, 1961). A general view of successive ages is in Raymond Dawson, *The Chinese Chameleon, An Analysis of European Conceptions of Chinese Civilization* (London: Oxford University Press, 1967).

THE CANTON TRADE. The major source on this is still H. B. Morse, *The Chronicles of the East India Company Trading to China* (London: Oxford University Press, 5 vols., 1926–1929). The most recent and massive study is by Louis Dermigny, *La Chine et l'Occident. Le Commerce à Canton au XVIIIe siècle, 1719–1833* (Paris: S.E.V.P.E.N., 3 vols., and vol. 4 album, 1964). For Chinese documentation in general, see Lo-shu Fu, *A Documentary Chronicle of Sino-Western Relations (1644–1820)* (Tucson: University of Arizona Press, 1966, 2 vols.); and in particular, J. L. Cranmer-Byng, "Lord Macartney's Embassy to Peking in 1793 from Official Chinese Documents," *Journal of Oriental Studies* (University of Hong Kong), 4. 1–2 (1957–1958): 117–187. The classic, roseate account of Sino-foreign contact is by William C. Hunter, *The 'Fan Kwae' at Canton before Treaty Days, 1825–44* (London, 1882; 2nd ed., Shanghai, 1911, reprinted 1949). See also Michael Greenberg, *British Trade and the Opening of China, 1800–42* (Cambridge: Cambridge University Press, 1951).

Suggested Reading

Opium War and treaty system. On the opium trade the principal study is still that of David Edward Owen, *British Opium Policy in India and China* (New Haven: Yale University Press, 1934). The major study of the war's origins is by Hsin-pao Chang, *Commissioner Lin and the Opium War* (HUP, 1964). For Chinese accounts, see Arthur Waley, *The Opium War through Chinese Eyes* (London: George Allen and Unwin, 1958). For the social milieu, Frederic Wakeman, Jr., *Strangers at the Gate. Social Disorder in South China, 1839–1861* (Berkeley: University of California Press, 1966). For the British, American, and French efforts to set up the new system of treaty relations, see John K. Fairbank, *Trade and Diplomacy on the China Coast: The Opening of the Treaty Ports, 1842–1854* (HUP, 1953, 2 vols.; Stanford University Press paperback); Earl Swisher, *China's Management of the American Barbarians. A Study of Sino-American Relations, 1841–1861, with Documents* (New Haven: Far Eastern Publications for the Far Eastern Association, 1951); and John F. Cady, *The Roots of French Imperialism in Eastern Asia* (Ithaca: Cornell University Press, 1954, for the American Historical Association). The latest study of the second war from the British side is Douglas Hurd, *The Arrow War, An Anglo-Chinese Confusion, 1856–1860* (Macmillan, 1967). For the Ch'ing side of the military-constitutional crisis, see Masataka Banno, *China and the West, 1858–1861: The Origins of the Tsungli Yamen* (HUP, 1964).

On the development of Hong Kong, see G. B. Endacott, *Government and People in Hong Kong, 1841–1962. A Constitutional History* (Hong Kong: Hong Kong University Press, 1964). The eventual scope of the treaty system may be traced in W. W. Willoughby, *Foreign Rights and Interests in China* (Baltimore: 2nd ed., 2 vols., 1927 [1920]).

The mid-century rebellions. A volume of studies of secret societies is being edited by Professor Jean Chesneaux in Paris. A recent volume is by Leon Comber, *Chinese Secret Societies in Malaya: A Survey of the Triad Society from 1800-1900* (Locust Valey, N.Y.: J. J. Augustin for the Association for Asian Studies, 1959). An early classic on rebellion in China was by the British consul Thomas Taylor Meadows, *The Chinese and Their Rebellions* (London, 1856; reprinted, Stanford: Academic Reprints, 1953). The place of peasant risings in Chinese history and current theory is analyzed by James P. Harrison, *The Communists and Chinese Peasant Rebellions, A Study in the Rewriting of Chinese History* (Atheneum, 1969).

On the Taipings, the extensive literature is appraised by Ssu-yü Teng, *Historiography of the Taiping Rebellion* (HUP, 1962). The most recent narrative is by Franz Michael in collaboration with Chung-li Chang, *The Taiping Rebellion: History and Documents* in three volumes, vol. I: *History* (Seattle: University of Washington Press, 1966). See also Vincent Y. C. Shih, *The Taiping Ideology: Its sources, Interpretations, and Influences* (Seattle: University of Washington Press, 1967). Taiping foreign relations are studied in J. S. Gregory, *Great Britain and the Taipings* (Praeger, 1969). On the Nien there are two works, Siang-tseh Chiang, *The Nien Rebellion* (Seattle: University of Washington Press, 1954); and S. Y. Teng, *The Nien Army and Their Guerrilla Warfare, 1851–1868* (Paris and The Hague: Mouton, 1961). On the Moslem rebellion in the Northwest, see Wen-djang Chu, *The Moslem Rebellion in Northwest China, 1862–1878. A Study of Government Minority Policy* (The Hague and Paris: Mouton, 1966). Less has been published on the rebellion in Southwest China. The social and institutional repercussions of all this disorder are masterfully analyzed in Philip A. Kuhn, *Rebellion and Its Enemies in Late Imperial China: Militarization and Social Structure, 1796–1864* (HUP, 1970).

RESTORATION AND SELF-STRENGTHENING. The major study of Ch'ing policy in the 1860's is by Mary Clabaugh Wright, *The Last Stand of Chinese Conservatism, the T'ung-chih Restoration, 1862–1872* (Stanford: Stanford University Press, 1957, also paperback). The interaction of restoration and westernization is surveyed in Kwang-Ching Liu, "Nineteenth-Century China: The Disintegration of the Old Order and the Impact of the West," in Ping-ti Ho and Tang Tsou, eds., *China's Heritage and the Communist Political System*, vol. 1 of *China in Crisis* (University of Chicago Press, 1968, in two books — that is, *China in Crisis* is in 3 vols., the first two of which are called vol. 1, book 1 and book 2, respectively). See also the same author's "Li Hung-chang in Chihli: The Emergence of a Policy, 1870–1875," in Albert Feuerwerker, Rhoads Murphey, and Mary C. Wright, eds., *Ap-*

Suggested Reading

proaches to Modern Chinese History (Berkeley: University of California Press, 1967), pp. 68–104; Stanley Spector, *Li Hung-chang and the Huai Army* (Seattle: University of Washington Press, 1964); and Kenneth E. Folsom, *Friends, Guests, and Colleagues. The Mu-fu System in the Late Ch'ing Period* (Berkeley: University of California Press, 1968). On the navy, John L. Rawlinson, *China's Struggle for Naval Development, 1839–1895* (HUP, 1967). On the acquisition of Western technology, Knight Biggerstaff, *The Earliest Modern Government Schools in China* (Ithaca: Cornell University Press, 1961); and Adrian Arthur Bennett, *John Fryer, The Introduction of Western Science and Technology into Nineteenth-Century China* (HUP, 1967). On postal reform, Ying-wan Cheng, *Postal Communication in China and Its Modernization, 1860–1896* (HUP, 1970).

ECONOMIC DEVELOPMENTS. On the "official-control and merchant-operation" system of development, the main study is by Albert Feuerwerker, *China's Early Industrialization: Sheng Hsuan-huai (1844–1916) and Mandarin Enterprise* (HUP, 1958). See also his systematic study *The Chinese Economy ca. 1870–1911* (Ann Arbor: Michigan Papers in Chinese Studies, no. 5, 1969). On enterprise generally see Kwang-Ching Liu, *Anglo-American Steamship Rivalry in China, 1862–1874* (HUP, 1962); and Edward Le Fevour, *Western Enterprise in Late Ch'ing China. A Selective Survey of Jardine, Matheson and Company's Operations, 1842–1895* (HUP, 1968). On the foreign activity in the chief modern mining enterprise, Ellsworth C. Carlson, *The Kaiping Mines (1877–1912)* (HUP, 2nd ed., enlarged, 1971); and in railway building, E-tu Zen Sun, *Chinese Railways and British Interests, 1898–1911* (Columbia University Press, 1954).

The whole question of foreign investment and imperialist exploitation is discussed in Chi-ming Hou, *Foreign Investment and Economic Development in China, 1840–1937* (HUP, 1965). The comprador class is similarly researched by Yen-p'ing Hao, *The Comprador in Nineteenth Century China: Bridge between East and West* (HUP, 1970). For stimulating discussions, see Rhoads Murphey, *The Treaty Ports and China's Modernization. What Went Wrong?* (Ann Arbor: Michigan Papers in Chinese Studies, no. 7, 1970), a preprint from Mark Elvin and G.

448

Suggested Reading

William Skinner, eds., *The Chinese City between Two Worlds* (Stanford: Stanford University Press, 1971); and Paul A. Cohen, "Ch'ing China: Confrontation with the West, 1850–1900," in James B. Crowley, ed., *Modern East Asia: Essays in Interpretation* (Harcourt, Brace and World, 1970).

LATE CH'ING FOREIGN RELATIONS. One inside view of the working of the treaty system is provided in Stanley F. Wright, *Hart and the Chinese Customs* (Belfast: Mullan, 1950). On the inauguration of diplomatic relations, see Immanuel C. Y. Hsü, *China's Entrance into the Family of Nations: The Diplomatic Phase, 1858–1880* (HUP, 1960); the same author's *The Ili Crisis, A Study of Sino-Russian Diplomacy, 1871–1881* (Oxford: Clarendon Press, 1965); and Lloyd E. Eastman, *Throne and Mandarins. China's Search for a Policy during the Sino-French Controversy, 1880–1885* (HUP, 1967).

Imperialist rivalry is most cogently surveyed in William L. Langer, *The Diplomacy of Imperialism* (Knopf, 2 vols., 2nd ed., 1950 [1935]). Recent background studies include R. K. I. Quested, *The Expansion of Russia in East Asia, 1857–1860* (Kuala Lumpur, Singapore: University of Malaya Press, 1968); Andrew Malozemoff, *Russian Far Eastern Policy, 1881–1904* (Berkeley: University of California Press, 1958); and Alastair Lamb, *Britain and Chinese Central Asia. The Road to Lhasa, 1767 to 1905* (London: Kegan Paul, 1960). On British policy, among many studies see Nathan A. Pelcovits, *Old China Hands and the Foreign Office* (American Institute of Pacific Relations, 1948; reprinted, Octagon Books, 1967); and Ceryl Pearl, *Morrison of China* (Sydney: Angus and Robertson, 1967), on the famous London *Times* correspondent. For a recent Chinese account of nineteenth century imperialism in China see Hu Sheng, *Imperialism and Chinese Politics* (Peking: Foreign Languages Press, 1955; first published in Chinese, 1948). Three recent studies on 1900 are Chester C. Tan, *The Boxer Catastrophe* (Columbia University Press, 1955); Victor Purcell, *The Boxer Uprising, A Background Study* (Cambridge University Press, 1963); and a popular narrative, Peter Fleming, *The Seige at Peking* (Harper, 1959). On Manchuria see George Alexander Lensen, *The Russo-Chinese War* (Tallahassee: The Diplomatic Press, 1967). On

Suggested Reading

Germany, John E. Schrecker, *Imperialism and Chinese Nationalism: Germany in Shantung* (HUP, 1971).

CHRISTIAN MISSIONS. The basic factual survey is still that of Kenneth Scott Latourette, *A History of Christian Missions in China* (London: Society for Promoting Christian Knowledge, 1929; reprint Ch'engwen Publishing Company, Taipei, 1966). In briefer compass, missions in nineteenth century China are surveyed in K. S. Latourette, *A History of the Expansion of Christianity,* vol. 6, *The Great Century in Northern Africa and Asia, A.D. 1800–A.D. 1914* (see chapter 5 "The Chinese Empire"). Study of Christian missions as part of China's institutional and intellectual history is just beginning. One pathbreaking work on the anti-Christian movement is by Paul A. Cohen, *China and Christianity: The Missionary Movement and the Growth of Chinese Antiforeignism, 1860–1870* (HUP, 1963). The role of missions in international relations is also just beginning to be investigated. Two recent studies are by Paul A. Varg, *Missionaries, Chinese, and Diplomats: The American Protestant Missionary Movement in China, 1890–1952* (Princeton: Princeton University Press, 1958), and Edmund S. Wehrle, *Britain, China, and Antimissionary Riots, 1891–1900* (Minneapolis: University of Minnesota Press, 1966). Brief histories of most of the Christian colleges have been published by the United Board for Christian Higher Education in Asia, New York City. See also Reuben Holden, *Yale in China: The Mainland, 1901–1951* (New Haven: Yale in China Association, Inc., 1964). On the YMCA, see Shirley S. Garrett, *Social Reformers in Urban China. The Chinese Y.M.C.A., 1895–1926* (HUP, 1970). Other facets of missionary activity are explored in a collection edited by Kwang-Ching Liu, *American Missionaries in China. Papers from Harvard Seminars* (HUP, 1966). The vast literature on individuals, from Robert Morrison and Peter Parker to Timothy Richard, is now being explored, but Chinese Christian leaders and institutions are still generally neglected. See also pp. 470–471 below.

REFORM. Background on the Western effort to stimulate reform is given in Jonathan Spence's fascinating bird's-eye view, *To Change China: Western Advisors to China, 1620–1960* (Boston, Toronto: Little

450

Brown, 1969). The sending of students abroad is canvassed broadly but with detailed data in Y. C. Wang, *Chinese Intellectuals and the West: 1872–1949* (Chapel Hill: University of North Carolina Press, 1966). On the conservative reform program, see William Ayers, *Chang Chih-tung and Educational Reform in China* (HUP, 1971). On the radical reformers, a notable series of articles by Kung-ch'uan Hsiao has analyzed the thought of K'ang Yu-wei; among others, see his "K'ang Yu-wei and Confucianism," *Monumenta Serica*, 18 (1959): 96–212. Lawrence G. Thompson has translated and summarized *Ta T'ung Shu: The One-World Philosophy of K'ang Yu-wei* (London: Allen and Unwin, 1958); while Jung-pang Lo, *K'ang Yu-wei. A Biography and a Symposium* (Tucson: University of Arizona Press, 1967), gives a life history. On Kang's younger colleague see Joseph R. Levenson, *Liang Ch'i-ch'ao and the Mind of Modern China* (University of California paperback [HUP, 1953]); and Hao Chang, *Liang Ch'i-ch'ao and Cultural Transition in China, 1890–1907* (HUP, 1971). The broadest factual summary of the subject is still that of Meribeth E. Cameron, *The Reform Movement in China, 1898–1912* (Palo Alto: Stanford University Press, 1931; reprinted, Octagon Books, 1963).

The principal work on the late Ch'ing attempt to profit from Western thought is the study by Benjamin I. Schwartz, *In Search of Wealth and Power: Yen Fu and the West* (HUP, 1964). See also Wolfgang Franke, *The Reform and Abolition of the Traditional Chinese Examination System* (HUP, 1968 [1960]); and two studies of legal reform: Marinus J. Meijer, *The Introduction of Modern Criminal Law in China* (Batavia: De Unie, 1950) and M. H. van der Valk, *Conservatism in Modern Chinese Family Law* (Leiden: Brill, 1956). For a leading figure of the period, see Samuel C. Chu, *Reformer in Modern China: Chang Chien, 1853–1926* (Columbia University Press, 1965).

REVOLUTION AND WARLORDISM. The principal conspectus of the origins of the 1911 Revolution is by Mary Clabaugh Wright, ed. and introd., *China in Revolution: The First Phase, 1900–1913* (New Haven: Yale University Press, 1968). A number of monographs round out the picture: Harold Z. Schiffrin, *Sun Yat-sen and the Origins of the Chinese Revolution* (Berkeley and Los Angeles: University of California

Suggested Reading

Press, 1968); Marius B. Jansen, *The Japanese and Sun Yat-sen* (HUP, 1954); Lyon Sharman, *Sun Yat-sen. His Life and its Meaning. A Critical Biography* (John Day, 1934; reissued, Stanford: Stanford University Press, 1968), on the many phases of Sun's career and the uses of him after his death; Chün-tu Hsüeh, *Huang Hsing and the Chinese Revolution* (Stanford: Stanford University Press, 1961); Mary Backus Rankin, *Early Chinese Revolutionaries. Radical Intellectuals in Shanghai and Chekiang, 1902–1911* (HUP, 1971); and Michael Gasster, *Chinese Intellectuals and the Revolution of 1911: The Birth of Modern Chinese Radicalism* (Seattle: University of Washington Press, 1969). For a critical review of the historical problems, Ernest P. Young, "Nationalism, Reform, and Republican Revolution: China in the Early Twentieth Century," in James B. Crowley, ed., *Modern East Asia: Essays in Interpretation* (Harcourt, Brace and World, 1970).

The concomitant rise of the military is traced by Ralph L. Powell, *The Rise of Chinese Military Power, 1895–1912* (Princeton: Princeton University Press, 1955); and Jerome Chen, *Yuan Shih-k'ai, 1859–1916* (Stanford: Stanford University Press, 1961). On the subsequent warlord period, see James E. Sheridan, *Chinese Warlord, The Career of Feng Yü-hsiang* (Stanford: Stanford University Press, 1966); and Donald Gillin, *Warlord. Yen Hsi-shan in Shansi Province 1911–1949* (Princeton: Princeton University Press, 1967).

THE INTELLECTUAL REVOLUTION. The major survey is that of Chow Tse-tsung, *The May Fourth Movement: Intellectual Revolution in Modern China* (HUP, 1960); see also his *Research Guide to the May Fourth Movement* (1963). Two principal monographs on non-Marxist figures are Jerome B. Grieder, *Hu Shih and the Chinese Renaissance. Liberalism in the Chinese Revolution, 1917–1937* (HUP, 1970); and Charlotte Furth, *Ting Wen-chiang. Science and China's New Culture* (HUP, 1970). On this same period, note the studies by D. W. Y. Kwok, *Scientism in Chinese Thought, 1900–1950* (New Haven: Yale University Press, 1965); and its antithesis, Stephen N. Hay, *Asian Ideas of East and West. Tagore and His Critics in Japan, China, and India* (HUP, 1970). O. Brière, S.J., *Fifty Years of Chinese Philosophy, 1898–1950* (Shanghai, 1949; London: Allen and Unwin, 1956; reprinted with new introduction and bibliography, Praeger, 1965), identifies movements of ideas and "systems" derived from oriental or occidental sources. On a leading founder of the Communist movement, see Maurice Meisner, *Li Ta-chao and the Origins of Chinese Marxism* (HUP, 1967), a basic study.

Analysis of this whole era has been greatly stimulated by the writings of Joseph R. Levenson, *Confucian China and Its Modern Fate:* vol. I, *The Problem of Intellectual Continuity;* vol. II, *The Problem of Monarchial Decay;* vol. III, *The Problem of Historical Significance* (Berkeley, University of California Press, 1958, 1964, 1965). For an illuminating application of Levensonian conceptions, see Ralph C. Croizier, *Traditional Medicine in Modern China. Science, Nationalism, and the Tensions of Cultural Change* (HUP, 1968). Monographs on contemporary developments include John de Francis, *Nationalism and Language Reform in China* (Princeton: Princeton University Press, 1950); and S. A. M. Adshead, *The Modernization of the Chinese Salt Administration, 1900–1920* (HUP, 1970).

THE NATIONALIST REVOLUTION AND GOVERNMENT. On this era research is just getting started. On the power politics of the 1920's, see Akira Iriye, *After Imperialism: The Search for a New Order in the Far East, 1921–1931* (HUP, 1965). Werner Levi, *Modern China's Foreign Policy* (Minneapolis: University of Minnesota Press, 1953), is a pioneer survey of a neglected subject. A rather various collection of essays edited by Jack Gray is on *Modern China's Search for a Political Form* (Oxford University Press, 1969). On the Kuomintang see George T. Yu, *Party Politics in Republican China. The Kuomintang, 1912–1924* (Berkeley: University of California Press, 1966); and William L. Tung, *The Political Institutions of Modern China* (The Hague: Nijhoff, 1964). The most realistic and informed study of the Kuomintang in power is by Ch'ien Tuan-sheng, *The Government and Politics of China, 1912–1949* (HUP, 1950; Stanford University Press paperback, 1970). An uncritical collection of documents is reprinted in Milton J. T. Shieh, *The Kuomintang: Selected Historical Documents, 1894–1969* (St. John's University Press, 1970). On the military under Chiang Kai-shek one of the few accounts is by F. F. Liu, *A Military History of Modern China, 1924–1949* (Princeton: Princeton University Press, 1956). On the student move-

Suggested Reading

ment: John Israel, *Student Nationalism in China, 1927–1937* (Stanford: Stanford University Press, 1966). Three works by Chiang Kai-shek are *China's Destiny* (Macmillan, 1947, trans. by Wang Ch'ung-hui); *China's Destiny and Chinese Economic Theory* (Roy Publishers, 1947, trans. by Philip Jaffe); and Chiang Chung-cheng (Chiang Kai-shek), *Soviet Russia in China, A Summing-up at Seventy* (Farrar, Straus and Cudahy, 1957).

Studies of the Nationalist revolution have thus far stressed the Communist aspect more than the Kuomintang. But help is on the way; see C. Martin Wilbur, "Military Separatism and the Process of Reunification under the Nationalist Regime, 1922–1937," in Ping-ti Ho and Tang Tsou, eds., *China's Heritage and the Communist Political System* (Chicago: University of Chicago Press, 1968), pp. 203–263; and other writings by the same author. Economic development under the Republic is analyzed by Albert Feuerwerker, *The Chinese Economy, 1912–1949* (Ann Arbor: Michigan Papers in Chinese Studies, no. 1, 1968); and Cheng Yu-kwei, *Foreign Trade and Industrial Development in China: An Historical and Integrated Analysis through 1948* (Washington, D.C.: University Press of Washington, 1956). On Nationalist economic policies in wartime see Chang Kia-ngau, *The Inflationary Spiral: The Experience in China, 1939–1950* (John Wiley, 1958); Chou Shun-hsin, *The Chinese Inflation, 1937–1949* (Columbia University Press, 1963); and Arthur N. Young, *China's Wartime Finance and Inflation, 1937–1945* (HUP, 1965).

EARLY HISTORY OF THE CHINESE COMMUNIST MOVEMENT. Here there is already a vast literature, most of it recent. On the Soviet intervention and its complications, see C. Martin Wilbur and Julie Lien-ying Howe, *Documents on Communism, Nationalism, and Soviet Advisors in China, 1918–1927* (Columbia University Press, 1956); Allen S. Whiting, *Soviet Policies in China, 1917–1924* (Columbia University Press, 1954); Peter S. H. Tang, *Russian and Soviet Policy in Manchuria and Outer Mongolia, 1911–1931* (Durham, N.C.: Duke University Press, 1959); Xenia J. Eudin and Robert C. North, *Soviet Russia and the East, 1920–1927* (Stanford: Stanford University Press for the Hoover Library, 1957), with documents; Conrad Brandt, *Stalin's Failure in*

China, 1924–1927 (HUP, 1958); Jean Chesneaux, *Le Mouvement ouvrier chinois de 1919 à 1927* (Paris, The Hague: Mouton, 1962), translated by H. M. Wright as *The Chinese Labor Movement, 1919–1927* (Stanford: Stanford University Press, 1968); and Harold Isaacs, *The Tragedy of the Chinese Revolution* (Stanford: Stanford University Press, rev. ed., 1951 [1938]). On the early development of the party line: Conrad Brandt, Benjamin Schwartz, and John K. Fairbank, *A Documentary History of Chinese Communism* (Atheneum paperback, 1966 [HUP, 1952]); and Boyd Compton, transl., *Mao's China: Party Reform Documents, 1942–44* (Seattle: University of Washington Press, 1952). On the later Soviet relationship, Charles B. McLane, *Soviet Policy and the Chinese Communists, 1931–1946* (Columbia University Press, 1958).

On the rise of Mao and Maoism: the classic account, by Mao himself, is in Edgar Snow, *Red Star over China* (Random House, 1938; first revised and enlarged edition, Grove Press, 1968). Lively, full-length biographies are by Stuart Schram, *Mao Tse-tung* (Simon and Schuster, 1966); and Jerome Ch'en, *Mao and the Chinese Revolution* (Oxford University Press, 1967). Studies are by Benjamin I. Schwartz, *Chinese Communism and the Rise of Mao* (HUP, 1951); Stuart Schram, *The Political Thought of Mao Tse-tung* (Praeger, 1963); Robert C. North, *Kuomintang and Chinese Communist Elites* (Stanford: Stanford University Press, 2nd ed., 1963 [1952]); Shanti Swarup, *A Study of the Chinese Communist Movement, 1927–1934* (Oxford: Clarendon Press, 1966); Richard C. Thornton, *The Comintern and the Chinese Communists, 1928–1931* (Seattle and London: University of Washington Press, 1969); John E. Rue, *Mao Tse-tung in Opposition, 1927–1935* (Stanford: Stanford University Press, 1966); Tso-liang Hsiao, *The Land Revolution in China, 1930–1934. A Study of Documents* (Seattle: University of Washington Press, 1969); and Edgar Snow, *Random Notes on Red China, 1936–1945* (HUP, 1957, 2nd printing, 1968). For ideological perspective: Donald M. Lowe, *The Function of "China" in Marx, Lenin, and Mao* (Berkeley and Los Angeles: University of California Press, 1966); and H. Carrère d'Encausse and Stuart R. Schram, *Marxism and Asia: An Introduction with Readings* (London: Allen Lane, The Penguin Press, 1969).

The Chinese Communist rise to power is analyzed in Chalmers A.

Suggested Reading

Johnson, *Peasant Nationalism and Communist Power, The Emergence of Revolutionary China, 1937–1945* (Stanford: Stanford University Press, 1962); Lyman P. Van Slyke, *Enemies and Friends. The United Front in Chinese Communist History* (Stanford University Press, 1967); and Lionel M. Chassin, *The Communist Conquest of China. A History of the Civil War, 1945–1949* (HUP, 1965).

For CCP accounts in English see Hu Ch'iao-mu, *Thirty Years of the Communist Party of China* (Peking: Foreign Languages Press, 1951); and Ho Kan-chih, *A History of the Modern Chinese Revolution* (Peking: Foreign Languages Press, 1959). Biographies of principal leaders include Agnes Smedley, *The Great Road: The Life and Times of Chu Teh* (Monthly Review Press, 1956), by an American radical correspondent who marched with the Red Army and knew its leaders personally; and Kai-yu Hsu, *Chou En-lai: China's Gray Eminence* (Doubleday, 1968), valuable because based on Taipei archives as well as the miscellaneous Chinese literature and 46 informants. A. Doak Barnett, *China on the Eve of Communist Takeover* (Praeger, 1963), reprints 23 first-hand field reports by a skilled journalist-observer in the years 1947–49.

CULTURAL AND RELIGIOUS LIFE UNDER THE REPUBLIC. This area is largely untouched. The broadest, quick overview is by A. C. Scott, *Literature and the Arts in Twentieth Century China* (Doubleday Anchor Books, 1963), with a bibliography. For specialized surveys, see Michael Sullivan, *Chinese Art in the Twentieth Century* (London: Faber, 1959); C. T. Hsia, *A History of Modern Chinese Fiction, 1917–1957* (New Haven: Yale University Press, 1961); and Hsu Kai-yu, trans. and ed., *Twentieth Century Chinese Poetry, An Anthology* (Doubleday, 1963). Monographs have been written by Olga Lang, on *Pa Chin and His Writings. Chinese Youth between the Two Revolutions* (HUP, 1967); by Huang Sung-k'ang on *Lu Hsün and the New Culture Movement of Modern China* (Amsterdam: Djambatan, 1957); and by Tsi-an Hsia, *The Gate of Darkness. Studies on the Leftist Literary Movement in China* (Seattle: University of Washington Press, 1968). Among many volumes of translation see Chi-chen Wang, transl., *Contemporary Chinese Stories* (Columbia University Press, 1953).

Suggested Reading

On the subject of religion the main analysis is by C. K. Yang, *Religion in Chinese Society. A Study of Contemporary Social Functions of Religion and Some of their Historical Factors* (University of California Press, 1961). See also Wing-tsit Chan, *Religious Trends in Modern China* (Columbia University Press, 1953); and Holmes Welch, *The Buddhist Revival in China* (HUP, 1968). On religion since 1949, see below.

FOREIGNERS' ACCOUNTS. Almost every foreigner who lives in China writes about it, sooner or later. Here are a very few examples from an enormous genre: Rodney Gilbert, *What's Wrong with China* (London: John Murray, 1926), expressing the Shanghai mind; John Leighton Stuart, *Fifty Years in China* (Random House, 1954), by the chief figure at Yenching University, later ambassador; Pearl S. Buck, *My Several Worlds* (John Day, 1954), an autobiography; Edgar Snow, *Journey to the Beginning* (Random House, 1958), illuminating reminiscences; and Han Suyin, *Birdless Summer* (Putnam, 1968), part of a trilogy, autobiographic and passionately patriotic.

5. The People's Republic

REFERENCE. The research explosion is nowhere better demonstrated than in the major guide to materials for research on Mainland China since 1949 and on Taiwan since 1945, Peter Berton and Eugene Wu, *Contemporary China: A Research Guide* (Stanford: Hoover Institution, 1967), which describes some 2200 items up through 1963 in Chinese, Japanese, English, and Russian; but these items include only bibliographies, reference works, documents, serials, and dissertations, and exclude most secondary works! For research biographies of leading personnel, see Donald Klein and Anne B. Clark, *Biographic Dictionary of Chinese Communism, 1921–1965* (HUP, 2 vols., 1971); less reliable, *Who's Who in Communist China* (Hong Kong: Union Research Institute, 2nd ed. rev. and enl., 2 vols., 1969), expanded from 1966 edition to include over 3000 biographical entries. For general reference, Chang-tu Hu and collaborators, *China: Its People, Its Society, Its Culture* (New Haven: HRAF Press, 1960), is a useful compendium of information on all aspects of China under the CCP as synthesized in the Human Relations Area Files at Yale.

457

Suggested Reading

TRANSLATIONS. The most substantial series of translations comes from the United States Consulate General, Hong Kong: *Survey of the China Mainland Press, Selections from China Mainland Magazines, Current Background;* and from the Joint Publications Research Service, Washington, D.C. Also from Hong Kong are publications of the Union Research Institute; as well as *China News Analysis* and *Current Scene.* The leading academic journal is *The China Quarterly,* London. The main outflow of books from the mainland in English is from the Foreign Languages Press, Peking. The chief Peking periodicals in English are *Peking Review* (successor to *People's China*), *China Reconstructs, China Pictorial,* and *China Literature.* An American outlet for Peking publications is at China Books and Periodicals, 2929 Twenty-fourth Street, San Francisco. Translations of the *Selected Works of Mao Tse-tung,* which were first published in Chinese in 4 volumes (Peking: People's Publishing Co., 1951, 1952, 1953, 1960), were published in English in 5 volumes (International Publishers, 1954–1962). For English translations of the little red book, *Mao Chu-hsi yü-lu,* see *Quotations from Chairman Mao Tse-tung* (Peking: Foreign Languages Press, 1966; reprinted, Bantam Books, 1967).

EARLY FIRST-HAND IMPRESSIONS. The two extremes in this contemporary literature, works by enthusiasts for the ideals of a new day, on the one hand, and by horrified victims of revolutionary coercion, on the other, confront the reader with unresolved anomalies — no regime could be either so good or so bad, *over all,* as some observers' writings would suggest. On the Communist take-over, a small volume by Otto B. van der Sprenkel, Robert Guillain, and Michael Lindsay, *New China: Three Views* (London: Turnstile Press, 1950), gives the informed first-hand impressions in 1949 of a sinologist, a journalist, and an economist, respectively. Derk Bodde, *Peking Diary. A Year of Revolution* (H. Schuman, 1950), by a leading American sinologist who was in Peking before and after the take-over; and Lynn and Amos Landman, *Profile of Red China* (Simon and Schuster, 1951), by two American correspondents, mainly in Shanghai, reflect the initial sense of relief and the mixed impressions of the honeymoon period. Two books by Indian correspondents raise critical questions: Frank Moraes, *Report on Mao's China* (Macmillan, 1953), and Raja Hutheesing, *The Great Peace* (Harper, 1953). Liu Shawtong, *Out of Red China* (Duell, Sloane and Pearce, 1953), and Maria Yen, *The Umbrella Garden: A Picture of Student Life in Red China* (Macmillan, 1954), are two of the disillusioned writings by intellectuals who came out. Two other works, by a Protestant and a Catholic missionary, exemplify a large body of such writings: E. Olin Stockwell, *With God in Red China* (Harper, 1953), and Mark Tennien, *No Secret Is Safe Behind the Bamboo Curtain* (Farrar, Straus and Young, 1952). A personal account by another victim, Harold W. Rigney, *Four Years in a Red Hell: the Story of Father Rigney* (Chicago: Regnery, 1956), is bitterly hostile. Allyn and Adele Rickett, *Prisoners of Liberation* (Cameron Associates, 1957), based on a similarly long incarceration, is comparatively sympathetic to the regime. All these witnesses testify sincerely and there are many more like them. They vary both in their respective experiences and in the criteria and assumptions in their own minds.

Among the more detached journalists, one of the most easy to read is a British correspondent, James Cameron, *Mandarin Red* (London: Michael Joseph, 1955); one of the most penetrating impressions is that of a Frenchman, Robert Guillain, *600 Million Chinese* (Criterion, 1957). Michael Lindsay, *China and the Cold War: A Study in International Politics* (Carlton, Victoria: Melbourne University Press, 1955), gives the criticisms of an English scholar who saw the Yenan period at first hand and later visited the People's Republic.

REPORTS OF LATER VISITORS. These vary not only according to the visitor but according to the year of his visit. Authors and publishers often conspire to hide the facts as to how long the author was actually in China and whether he ever got off the standard visitors' route and routine. The most valuable observers are those who saw China before 1949 and have a before-and-after perspective. Pre-eminent among them is Mao's biographer (in *Red Star over China*, 1937) Edgar Snow, who returned for an extensive look in 1960 and wrote an absorbing account, *The Other Side of the River: Red China Today* (Random House, n.d., copyrighted 1961, 1962). Out of the copious flow of

Suggested Reading

first-person accounts, the following stem from the most immediate contact with the people. William Hinton, *Fanshen. A Documentary of Revolution in a Chinese Village* (Monthly Review Press, 1966), an extremely well-written dramatization of village dynamics in the land-reform program of 1948 by an American who stayed in North China after the war. Isabel and David Crook, *Revolution in a Chinese Village. Ten Mile Inn* (London: Routledge and Kegan Paul, 1959), a reconstruction of a village history from the Japanese invasion to Communist liberation by two teachers of English in Peking. Isabel and David Crook, *The First Years of Yangyi Commune* (the same, 1966), based on summer visits in 1959 and 1960. Mu Fu-sheng, *The Wilting of the Hundred Flowers: The Chinese Intelligentsia under Mao* (Praeger, 1962), by a scholar who after twelve years abroad returned to China in the late 1950's but came out a year later. Jacques Marcuse, *The Peking Papers, Leaves from the Notebook of a China Correspondent* (Dutton, 1967), the new China as seen in 1962–1964 by a long-time French correspondent who had been resident in Peking in the 1930's and 1940's. Stuart and Roma Gelder, *Memories for a Chinese Granddaughter* (Stein and Day, 1968), by a British journalist who was in China in the 1940's and again in 1960 and 1966. Another before-and-after visitor with the perspective of a historian was C. P. Fitzgerald, *Flood Tide in China* (London: Cresset Press, 1958), by a resident of Peking in the early 1930's, after his return to China again in 1956.

Other travelers of special competence include Dick Wilson, *Anatomy of China. An Introduction to One Quarter of Mankind* (Weybright and Talley, 1968; first published in England in 1966 as *A Quarter of Mankind: An Anatomy of China Today*), by a former editor of the *Far Eastern Economic Review*, Hong Kong, 1958–1964, who visited the mainland in 1964 — well informed and well balanced; Jan Myrdal, *Report from a Chinese Village* (Pantheon Books, 1965), translated from Swedish ed. of 1963, based on a month in a village in the Yenan area in 1962; Jan Myrdal and Gun Kessle, *China: The Revolution Continued* (Pantheon Books, 1970), based on two weeks in 1969 in the same village seen in 1962; Tibor Mende, *China and Her Shadow* (Coward-McCann, 1962), by a Parisian political scientist-commentator who traveled in China in 1959 (the same author's *The Chinese Revolution*, London:

Thames and Hudson, 1961, is a rerun of modern history to 1949); K. S. Karol, *China, the Other Communism* (Hill and Wang, 1967; transl. from French ed. of 1966), by an observer well acquainted with the Soviet system; Hugo Portisch, *Red China Today* (Chicago: Quadrangle Books, 1966), translated from German ed. of 1965, by a Viennese journalist, based on a visit evidently in 1964. Eric Chou, *A Man Must Choose* (Knopf, 1963), is by an escapee of 1956.

GENERAL APPRAISALS FROM OUTSIDE. Nearly all the research studies listed in the sections below have been made from outside China, where one may sometimes forget that Chinese life today is generally not conditioned by plumbing, telephones, and automobiles. Early appraisals from outside included W, W. Rostow, with R. W. Hatch, F. A. Kierman, Jr., and A. Eckstein, *The Prospects for Communist China* (J. Wiley, 1954); a menacing picture by Richard L. Walker, *China under Communism: The First Five Years* (New Haven: Yale University Press, 1955); A. Doak Barnett, *Communist China: The Early Years, 1949-55* (Praeger, 1964), reports written from the vantage point of Hong Kong. Among the more recent general accounts, Klaus Mehnert, *Peking and Moscow* (Putnam's, 1963, transl. from German ed. of 1962), is by a German specialist who spent some five years each in Russia and in China; Peter S. H. Tang and Joan M. Maloney, *Communist China: The Domestic Scene, 1949-1967* (South Orange, N.J.: Seton Hall University Press, 1967), developed from Tang's *Communist China Today: Domestic and Foreign Policies* (Praeger, 1957, rev. ed., 1961); and Jan S. Prybyla, *The Political Economy of Communist China* (Scranton, Pa.: International Textbook Co., 1970), a survey with extensive bibliography. One example of a large genre of refugee reports is Valentin Chu, *Ta Ta, Tan Tan* (*"fight fight, talk talk"*). *The Inside Story of Communist China* (Norton, 1963), with horrible details compiled from escapees.

SOCIETY AND POLITY UNDER THE CCP. In the general American and Western effort to understand the revolution the specialized talents of highly trained sociologists, political scientists, and historians have been pooled, first of all to appraise the great structural changes

Suggested Reading

of the period. C. K. Yang (Yang Ch'ing-k'un), *The Chinese Family in the Chinese Communist Revolution* (Cambridge, Mass.: Technology Press, 1959), benefits from experience in China before and after 1949. C. K. Yang, *A Chinese Village in Early Communist Transition* (Cambridge, Mass.: Technology Press, 1959), is on a village near Canton. Ezra F. Vogel, *Canton under Communism: Programs and Politics in a Provincial Capital, 1949–1968* (HUP, 1969), uses the data of one area to reflect vividly the main phases and problems in the revolutionary process as a whole. Franz Schurmann, *Ideology and Organization in Communist China* (Berkeley and Los Angeles: University of California Press, 1966), is an across-the-board analysis in social science terms. John W. Lewis, ed., *Party Leadership and Revolutionary Power in China* (Cambridge: Cambridge University Press, 1970), brings together a dozen papers from a 1968 conference, a first volume from the Contemporary China Institute in London. A. Doak Barnett, with a contribution by Ezra Vogel, *Cadres, Bureaucracy, and Political Power in Communist China* (Columbia University Press, 1967), is based partly on Hong Kong interviews. John Wilson Lewis, *Major Doctrines of Communist China* (W. W. Norton, 1964), reprints extracts from CCP sources to illustrate aspects of CCP theory and practice. William T. Liu, ed., *Chinese Society under Communism: A Reader* (John Wiley, 1967), presents forty-two writings by a wide range of specialists, selected by a Catholic sociologist.

Studies of special topics include John W. Lewis, *Leadership in Communist China* (Ithaca: Cornell University Press, 1963), mainly on the party; James R. Townsend, *Political Participation in Communist China* (Berkeley and Los Angeles: University of California Press, 1968), mainly on mass mobilization; A. Doak Barnett, ed., *Chinese Communist Politics in Action* (Seattle: University of Washington Press, 1969), eleven articles resulting from a conference sponsored by the Joint Committee on Contemporary China on "microsocietal study of the Chinese political system"; Anon., *Communist China, 1955–1959: Policy Documents with Analysis* (HUP, 1963), by a well-informed observer of the period; Roderick MacFarquhar, ed., *China under Mao: Politics Takes Command. A Selection of Articles from The China Quarterly* (Cambridge, Mass.: The M.I.T. Press, 1966), twenty-four articles selected

462

Suggested Reading

from *The China Quarterly,* 1960–1965, by the then editor. Lucian W. Pye, *The Spirit of Chinese Politics: A Psycho-cultural Study of the Authority Crisis in Political Development* (Cambridge, Mass.: M.I.T. Press, 1968) is a bold characterization by a political scientist.

THE ECONOMY: GENERAL APPRAISALS AND NATIONAL INCOME. Alexander Eckstein, Walter Galenson, and Ta-chung Liu, eds., *Economic Trends in Communist China* (Chicago: Aldine, 1968), presents a dozen papers on major aspects, developed from a 1965 conference sponsored by the Social Science Research Council, Committee on the Economy of China. Other volumes sponsored by this committee include Nai-Ruenn Chen, *Chinese Economic Statistics* (Chicago: Aldine, 1967); Nai-Ruenn Chen, *The Economy of Mainland China, 1949–1963: A Bibliography of Materials in English* (Berkeley: SSRC Committee on the Economy of China, 1963); and Nai-Ruenn Chen and Walter Galenson, *The Chinese Economy under Communism* (Chicago: Aldine, 1969).

Two pioneer studies of national income, made in the 1950's when a modicum of statistics was available, are William W. Hollister, *China's Gross National Product and Social Accounts, 1950–1957* (Glencoe, Ill.: The Free Press, 1958); and Alexander Eckstein, *The National Income of Communist China* (The Free Press of Glencoe, 1961). A later study by Ta-chung Liu and Kung-chia Yeh, *The Economy of the Chinese Mainland: National Income and Economic Development, 1933–1959* (Princeton: Princeton University Press, 1965), made for the Rand Corporation, compares 1952–1957 with 1933 and finds a lowering of per capita consumption.

Other general works include Audrey Donnithorne, *China's Economic System* (Praeger, 1967); Yuan-li Wu, *The Economy of Communist China: An Introduction* (Praeger, 1965); Chao Kuo-chun, *Agrarian Policy of the Chinese Communist Party, 1921–1959* (Asia Publishing House, 1960), a well-documented survey of land reform policies from the 1920's to 1959; Choh-ming Li, *Economic Development of Communist China. An Appraisal of the First Five Years of Industrialization* (Berkeley: University of California Press, 1959); T. J. Hughes and D. E. T. Luard, *The Economic Development of Communist China, 1949–1958* (Oxford University Press, 1959; 2nd ed. of 1961 adds 8 pp.); and United

Suggested Reading

States Congress, Joint Economic Committee, *An Economic Profile of Mainland China* (Washington, D.C.: U.S. Government Printing Office, 2 vols., 1967). For a more optimistic early account by an English economist long resident in Peking, see Solomon Adler, *The Chinese Economy* (Monthly Review Press, 1957).

THE ECONOMY: SPECIAL ASPECTS. Dwight H. Perkins, *Market Control and Planning in Communist China* (HUP, 1966), analyzes CCP efforts to guide the economy and maintain its stability down to 1963. George N. Ecklund, *Financing the Chinese Government Budget: Mainland China, 1950–1959* (Chicago: Aldine, 1966), is another study sponsored by the SSRC Committee on the Economy of China. René Dumont, *Révolution dans les campagnes chinoises* (Paris: Editions du Seuil, 1957), is by a broadly experienced agronomist who investigated Chinese farm conditions at first-hand in the early 1950's. René Dumont, *Chine surpeuplé: Tiers-monde affamé* (Paris: Editions du Seuil, 1965), is both well informed and alarming on China's struggle to feed her growing population. On agriculture see also Owen L. Dawson, *Communist China's Agriculture. Its Development and Future Potential* (Praeger Publishers, 1970), well-informed estimates by the former U.S. agricultural attaché in China; and Kenneth R. Walker, *Planning in Chinese Agriculture, Socialisation and the Private Sector, 1956–1962* (London: Frank Cass and Co., 1965). On aspects of industry, see Chao Kang, *The Rate and Pattern of Industrial Production in Communist China* (Ann Arbor: University of Michigan Press, 1965); Kang Chao, *The Construction Industry in Communist China* (Chicago: Aldine, 1968); Yuan-li Wu, *The Spatial Economy of Communist China. A Study on Industrial Location and Transportation* (Praeger, for the Hoover Institution on War, Revolution and Peace, 1967); and Choh-ming Li, ed., *Industrial Development in Communist China* (Praeger, 1964), a dozen articles that formed a special issue of *The China Quarterly*, 1964. Barry M. Richman, *Industrial Society in Communist China* (Random House, 1969), is by a Canadian specialist in management technology who saw his opposite numbers during two months in 1966.

SCIENCE AND PROFESSIONAL MANPOWER. Several factual studies have

464

been prepared in Washington: Leo A. Orleans, *Professional Manpower and Education in Communist China* (Washington, D.C.: National Science Foundation, 1961); Sidney H. Gould, ed., *Sciences in Communist China* (Washington, D.C.: American Association for the Advancement of Science, 1961), appraisals by some thirty contributors to a symposium of 1960; Chu-yuan Cheng, *Scientific and Engineering Manpower in Communist China, 1949–1963* (Washington, D.C.: U. S. Government Printing Office for the National Science Foundation, 1965); and Yuan-li Wu and Robert B. Sheeks, *The Organization and Support of Scientific Research and Development in Mainland China* (Praeger, for the National Science Foundation, 1970). Robert Chin and Ai-li S. Chin, *Psychological Research in Communist China: 1949–1966* (Cambridge, Mass.: M.I.T. Press, 1969), surveys mainland work in this field, with glossary and bibliography. Mikhail A. Klochko, *Soviet Scientist in Red China* (Praeger, 1964), offers first-hand observations on scientific work by a specialist who was in China in 1958 and 1960, and defected in 1961.

LAW. For a survey of this area, see Jerome Alan Cohen, ed., *Contemporary Chinese Law: Research Problems and Perspectives* (HUP, 1970). For an exemplary monograph, see Jerome Alan Cohen, *The Criminal Process in the People's Republic of China, 1949–1963. An Introduction* (HUP, 1968). Douglas M. Johnston and Hungdah Chiu, *Agreements of the People's Republic of China, 1949–1967: A Calendar* (HUP, 1968), lists some 2000 international agreements of all kinds. For documents and bibliography, see Albert P. Blaustein, ed., *Fundamental Legal Documents of Communist China* (South Hackensack, N.J.: Rothman, 1962); and Tao-Tai Hsia, *Guide to Selected Legal Sources of Mainland China* (Washington, D.C.: Library of Congress, 1967).

EDUCATION. This topic is almost lost between scientific training (above) and ideological indoctrination (below). R. F. Price, *Education in Communist China* (Praeger, 1970), is a systematic study; the author taught in Peking in 1965–67. Stewart Fraser, ed., *Chinese Communist Education: Records of the First Decade* (Nashville: Vanderbilt University Press, 1965), a 69-page introduction plus 340 pages of documents

Suggested Reading

and 83 of bibliography. Frederick T. C. Yu, *Mass Persuasion in Communist China* (Praeger, 1964), a survey by media.

THOUGHT REFORM. For an analysis of the process in psychological terms, see Robert Jay Lifton, *Thought Reform and the Psychology of Totalism. A Study of "Brainwashing" in China* (W. W. Norton, 1961). Also Theodore H. E. Chen, *Thought Reform of the Chinese Intellectuals* (Hong Kong: Hong Kong University Press, 1960); Roderick MacFarquhar, *The Hundred Flowers Campaign and the Chinese Intellectuals* (Praeger, 1960); and Franklin W. Houn, *To Change a Nation. Propaganda and Indoctrination in Communist China* (The Free Press of Glencoe, 1961). On the particular fate of creative writers, see Merle Goldman, *Literary Dissent in Communist China* (HUP, 1967); and D. W. Fokkema, *Literary Doctrine in China and Soviet Influence, 1956–1960* (The Hague: Mouton, 1965).

IDEOLOGY, CULTURE, AND RELIGION. Ideological considerations of course permeate most studies of contemporary China. Special studies include Benjamin I. Schwartz, *Communism and China: Ideology in Flux* (HUP, 1968), trenchant essays by a leading scholar in this field. Albert Feuerwerker, ed., *History in Communist China* (Cambridge, Mass.: M.I.T. Press, 1968), analyzes the CCP treatment of various periods and aspects as studied by a dozen Western historians, originally for a *China Quarterly* conference of 1964. Ralph C. Croizier, ed., *China's Cultural Legacy and Communism* (Praeger, 1970), gives a broad selection on the arts, literature, thought, and so forth, from both CCP and Western sources, arranged topically and with useful bibliography. It is a striking fact that culture and the arts, because they have been subordinated to the state ideology, have been rather neglected by outside scholarship. Arthur A. Cohen, *The Communism of Mao Tse-tung* (Chicago: University of Chicago Press, 1964), appraises Mao's ideology in relation to Marxism-Leninism as of the early 1960's. Among many writings on Christianity under the Communists, Francis Price Jones, *The Church in Communist China. A Protestant Appraisal* (Friendship Press, 1962), with bibliography, is by the editor of the newsletter *China Bulletin* (subsequently *China Notes*). Richard C. Bush, Jr., *Reli-*

466

Suggested Reading

gion in Communist China (Abingdon Press, 1970), is a careful study of CCP policy and actions and the repercussions on Christianity, both Protestant and Catholic, also on Islam and Buddhism.

THE CULTURAL REVOLUTION. Among reports and studies of this recent phase are Robert Trumbull, ed., *This Is Communist China* (David McKay Co., 1968), reports of a team of nine Japanese journalists sent by *Yomiuri Shimbun* (Tokyo) for three months in 1966–67; Colin Mackerras and Neale Hunter, *China Observed* (Praeger, 1967), by two Australians who taught in Peking, 1964–66 (Mackerras) and in Shanghai, 1965–67 (Hunter); and Neale Hunter, *Shanghai Journal, an Eyewitness Account of the Cultural Revolution* (Praeger, 1969). See also a selection from the *Bulletin of the Atomic Scientists,* entitled *China After the Cultural Revolution* (Random House, 1969), articles by a dozen specialists, mainly British; and Robert Jay Lifton, *Revolutionary Immortality: Mao Tse-tung and the Chinese Cultural Revolution* (Random House, 1968).

THE MILITARY. On the literature, see Edward J. M. Rhoads, *The Chinese Red Army, 1927–1963: An Annotated Bibliography* (HUP, 1964). Two studies are outstanding: Samuel B. Griffith, II, *The Chinese People's Liberation Army* (McGraw-Hill, 1967), a general historical and topical account; and John Gittings, *The Role of the Chinese Army* (Oxford University Press, 1967), an analytic history of its growth and relation to the regime as a whole. Of narrower scope is the case study by Alexander L. George, *The Chinese Communist Army in Action: The Korean War and Its Aftermath* (Columbia University Press, 1967). Michael Elliott-Bateman, *Defeat in the East. The Mark of Mao Tse-tung on War* (Oxford University Press, 1967), is a theoretical work. Samuel B. Griffith, transl., *Mao Tse-tung on Guerrilla Warfare* (Praeger, 1961; also published with a work of Che Guevara and a foreword of Liddell Hart, London: Cassell, 1962); this is Mao's essay on *Yu Chi Chan* of 1937. Stuart R. Schram, transl. and introd., *Mao Tse-tung. Basic Tactics* (Praeger, 1966), reproduces Mao's lectures of 1938, a different work from the foregoing.

ARMS CONTROL. There are several American studies of the prob-

Suggested Reading

lem: Alice Langley Hsieh, *Communist China's Strategy in the Nuclear Era* (Prentice Hall, 1962); Morton H. Halperin, *China and the Bomb* (Praeger, 1965); Morton H. Halperin and Dwight H. Perkins, *Communist China and Arms Control* (Praeger, 1965); and Morton H. Halperin, ed., *Sino-Soviet Relations and Arms Control* (Cambridge, Mass.: M.I.T. Press, 1967), papers developed from a 1965 conference.

THE SINO-SOVIET SPLIT. Before this momentous development, the Sino-Soviet relationship was appraised in a symposium by H. L. Boorman, A. Eckstein, P. E. Mosely, and B. Schwartz, *Moscow-Peking Axis: Strengths and Strains* (Harper and Brothers for the Council on Foreign Relations, 1957). Its historical background was surveyed by Aitchen K. Wu, *China and the Soviet Union* (John Day, 1950), and by Henry Wei, *China and Soviet Russia* (Van Nostrand, 1956). Both used Chinese as well as foreign sources, the former over a broader period; the latter with more bibliography. Tien-Fong Cheng, *A History of Sino-Russian Relations* (Washington, D.C.: Public Affairs Press, 1957), by a Kuomintang official, dealt generally with the last four decades. A more concentrated scholarly study of Russia's postwar China policy was in Max Beloff, *Soviet Policy in the Far East, 1944–1951* (Oxford University Press, 1953).

For recent after-the-event studies, see Donald S. Zagoria, *The Sino-Soviet Conflict, 1956–1961* (Princeton: Princeton University Press, 1962); Donald W. Treadgold, ed., *Soviet and Chinese Communism: Similarities and Differences* (Seattle: University of Washington Press, 1967), papers by a score of specialists on China or the USSR from a conference of 1965; William E. Griffith, *The Sino-Soviet Rift* (Cambridge, Mass.: The M.I.T. Press, 1964), narrative and documents to late 1963; and Dennis J. Doolin, *Territorial Claims in the Sino-Soviet Conflict: Documents and Analysis* (Stanford: Hoover Institution, 1965). The most recent works are John Gittings, *Survey of the Sino-Soviet Dispute: A Commentary and Extracts from the Recent Polemics, 1963–1967* (Oxford University Press, 1968); and Walter C. Clemens, Jr., *The Arms Race and Sino-Soviet Relations* (Stanford: Hoover Institute Publications, 1968).

CHINA'S FOREIGN POLICY. Harold C. Hinton, *China's Turbulent Quest*

(Macmillan, 1970), surveys the phases in China's foreign relations since 1950. Harold C. Hinton, *Communist China in World Politics* (Boston: Houghton Mifflin, 1966), is a systematic account by areas and aspects. A. Doak Barnett, ed., *Communist Strategies in Asia. A Comparative Analysis of Governments and Parties* (Praeger, 1963), presents papers by eight area specialists, from a 1962 symposium of the Association for Asian Studies. Alastair Buchan, *China and the Peace of Asia* (Praeger, 1965), includes several papers on China, from a 1964 conference of the Institute for Strategic Studies on Asia in general. Among more specialized studies are Allen S. Whiting, *China Crosses the Yalu: The Decision to Enter the Korean War* (Macmillan, 1960); George Ginsburgs and Michael Mathos, *Communist China and Tibet. The First Dozen Years* (The Hague: Martinus Nijhoff, 1964); Alastair Lamb, *The China-India Border. The Origins of the Disputed Boundaries* (Oxford University Press, 1964), on the McMahon Line, and so forth; and Peter Van Ness, *Revolution and Chinese Foreign Policy. Peking's Support for Wars of National Liberation* (Berkeley and Los Angeles: University of California Press, 1970).

6. Chinese-American Relations

This is a badly neglected subject. The best general guide to research topics and materials is by Kwang-Ching Liu, *Americans and Chinese. A Historical Essay and a Bibliography* (HUP, 1963). For a thematic and bibliographic appraisal of the scholarly literature in English, period by period, see James C. Thomson, Jr., and Ernest R. May, eds., *American-East Asian Relations: A Survey* (HUP, 1971).

THE OLD CHINA TRADE. Leading studies on this date from half a century ago: Samuel Eliot Morison, *The Maritime History of Massachusetts, 1783–1860* (Boston: Houghton Mifflin, 1921); Kenneth Wiggins Porter, *John Jacob Astor* (HUP, 1931; reprinted by Russell), an exhaustive monograph; Foster Rea Dulles, *The Old China Trade* (Boston: Houghton Mifflin, 1930), a popular survey. Another pioneer study was George H. Danton, *The Culture Contacts of the United States and China, 1784–1844* (Columbia University Press, 1931). One recent

Suggested Reading

contribution on the investment of Russell and Company's China trade funds in mid-western railways, is in Arthur M. Johnson and Barry E. Supple, *Boston Capitalists and Western Railroads. A Study in the Nineteenth-Century Railroad Investment Process* (HUP, 1967), see pp. 19–32.

CHINESE IN AMERICA AND AMERICAN IMAGES OF CHINA. An important new study is by Stuart Creighton Miller, *The Unwelcome Immigrant. The American Image of the Chinese, 1785–1882* (Berkeley and Los Angeles: University of California Press, 1969), which examines the background of the Chinese exclusion policy in the Eastern United States as well as the West Coast. The principal monograph on the origin of the Chinese community in California is by Gunther Barth, *Bitter Strength. A History of the Chinese in the United States, 1850–1870* (HUP, 1964). A great deal of data on the Chinese community and legislation affecting it is given by S. W. Kung, *Chinese in American Life. Some Aspects of Their History, Status, Problems, and Contributions* (Seattle: University of Washington Press, 1962). The chief study of the Chinese Educational Mission to Hartford in the 1870's is still Thomas E. LaFargue, *China's First Hundred* (Pullman: State College of Washington, 1942).

There is of course a large literature on the westward expansion of the American people, in which "China" often figures but in purely rhetorical terms. A path-breaking investigation of present-day images by a scholar-journalist is Harold R. Isaacs, *Scratches on Our Minds. American Images of China and India* (John Day, 1958; paperback ed. entitled *Images of Asia: American Views of China and India,* Capricorn Books, 1962). See also Dorothy B. Jones, *The Portrayal of China and India on the American Screen 1896–1955* (Cambridge, Mass.: M.I.T. Center for International Affairs, 1955); Robert McClellan, *Heathen Chinee: The American Image of China* (Columbus, Ohio: Ohio State University Press, 1971). For background on the phases of the European view of China, see Raymond Dawson, *The Chinese Chameleon. An Analysis of European Conceptions of Chinese Civilization* (Oxford University Press, 1967).

THE AMERICAN MISSIONARY MOVEMENT AND CHINA. For the general

470

context of China missions, see Kenneth Scott Latourette, *A History of the Expansion of Christianity* (Harpers, 7 vols., 1938–45; vols. 4–6 are on the period 1800–1914; vol. 6 includes China). On one principal organization, Clifton Jackson Phillips, *Protestant America and the Pagan World. The First Half Century of the American Board of Commissioners for Foreign Missions, 1810–1860* (HUP, 1969). For comparative purposes, note that two recent studies of America in the Near East take account of missionaries there: James A. Field, Jr., *America and the Mediterranean World 1776–1882* (Princeton: Princeton University Press, 1969); and David H. Finnie, *Pioneers East. The Early American Experience in the Middle East* (HUP, 1967). China is included in general histories of church expansion: for example, Wade Crawford Barclay, *History of Methodist Missions* (Board of Missions of the Methodist Church, 6 vols.); see especially vol. III, *Widening Horizons, 1845–95* (1957), pp. 365–448. But little has been published on the American side of China missions.

The principal survey, mainly on the twentieth century, is by Paul A. Varg, *Missionaries, Chinese, and Diplomats, The American Protestant Missionary Movement in China, 1890–1952* (Princeton: Princeton University Press, 1958).

History of United States policy toward China. This is a very spotty field. The two chief surveys of "Far Eastern policy" are long since out of date: Tyler Dennett, *Americans in Eastern Asia, A Critical Study of the Policy of the United States with Reference to China, Japan and Korea in the 19th Century* (Macmillan, 1922; reprinted, Gloucester, Mass.: Peter Smith, 1959); and A. Whitney Griswold, *The Far Eastern Policy of the United States* (Harcourt, Brace, 1938). For a recent critique of our "traditional" historiography in this area, see Dorothy Borg, comp., *Historians and American Far Eastern Policy* (Columbia University East Asian Institute Occasional Papers, 1966). For a general perspective, Akira Iriye, *Across the Pacific. An Inner History of American East Asian Relations* (Harcourt, Brace and World, 1967), with a useful bibliography.

China of course figures in a great number of general works dealing with American foreign policy and expansion. Recent examples are

Suggested Reading

Ernest R. May, *Imperial Democracy: The Emergence of America as a Great Power* (Harcourt, Brace and World, 1961); and Walter LaFeber, *The New Empire. An Interpretation of American Expansion, 1860–1898* (Ithaca: Cornell University Press, 1963). This list could be greatly extended.

There is a considerable sequence of monographic studies. On the Open Door and the reappraisal of it, Paul A. Varg, *Open Door Diplomat: The Life of W. W. Rockhill* (Urbana, Ill.: University of Illinois Press, 1952); Charles S. Campbell, *Special Business Interests and the Open Door Policy* (New Haven: Yale University Press, 1951); Thomas McCormick, *China Market, America's Quest for Informal Empire, 1893–1901* (Chicago: Quadrangle Books, 1967); and Marilyn B. Young, *The Rhetoric of Empire. American China Policy, 1895–1901* (HUP, 1968). On the era of dollar diplomacy, Charles Vevier, *The United States and China 1906–1913. A Study of Finance and Diplomacy* (New Brunswick, N. J.: Rutgers University Press, 1955); and Paul A. Varg, *The Making of a Myth: The United States and China 1897–1912* (East Lansing: Michigan State University Press, 1968). On the Wilsonian era see Tien-yi Li, *Woodrow Wilson's China Policy 1913–1917* (Twayne, 1952); Russell H. Fifield, *Woodrow Wilson and the Far East, The Diplomacy of the Shantung Question* (Crowell, 1952); and Roy W. Curry, *Woodrow Wilson and Far Eastern Policy 1913–1921* (Bookman Associates, 1957). On the Twenty-one Demands, see in Arthur S. Link, *Wilson: The Struggle for Neutrality, 1914–1915* (Princeton: Princeton University Press, 1960). On the Nationalist era, Dorothy Borg, *American Policy and the Chinese Revolution 1925–1928* (American Institute of Pacific Relations and Macmillan, 1947); Sara M. Smith, *The Manchurian Crisis 1931–1932* (Columbia University Press, 1948); Robert H. Ferrell, *American Diplomacy in the Great Depression. Hoover-Stimson Foreign Policy, 1929–1933* (New Haven: Yale University Press, 1957); and Dorothy Borg, *The United States and the Far Eastern Crisis of 1933–1938* (HUP, 1964). On the contemporary policy of our closest friends, Nicholas Clifford, *Retreat from China: British Policy in the Far East, 1937–1941* (Seattle: University of Washington Press, 1967). On the era of World War II, W. L. Langer, and S. E. Gleason, *The World Crisis and American Foreign Policy:* vol. 1, *The Challenge to Isolation 1937–1940,* vol. II, *The Undeclared War 1940–41* (Harper, 1952, 1953); and W. R. Fishel, *The End*

472

of Extraterritoriality in China (Berkeley and Los Angeles: University of California Press, 1952).

On the large question of American participation in domestic reform and social change under the Kuomintang, James C. Thomson, Jr., *While China Faced West: American Reformers in Nationalist China, 1928–1937* (HUP, 1969). The solid achievements of a Rockefeller Foundation program in medicine are recorded by Mary E. Ferguson, *China Medical Board and Peking Union Medical College. A Chronicle of Fruitful Collaboration 1914–1951* (China Medical Board of New York, 1970).

THE UNITED STATES IN CHINA IN THE 1940's. An enthralling introduction to this contentious topic is Barbara Tuchman, *Stilwell and the American Experience in China 1911–1945* (Macmillan, 1971), a well-researched best-seller. The diplomatic policy record is traced out by Herbert Feis, *The China Tangle. The American Effort in China from Pearl Harbor to the Marshall Mission* (Princeton: Princeton University Press, 1953); and Tang Tsou, *America's Failure in China 1941–1950* (Chicago: University of Chicago Press, 1963). For documentation, see U. S. Department of State, *United States Relations with China with Special Reference to the Period 1944–1949* (Washington, D.C.: Government Printing Office, 1949; reprinted, Stanford: Stanford University Press, 1967), the famous China White Paper of recently confidential documents, published in advance of the usual volumes in *Foreign Relations of the United States: 1942 China* (1956); *1943 China* (1957); *1944 China* (1967). On the military record and the Stilwell saga, Charles F. Romanus and Riley Sunderland, *United States Army in World War II: China-Burma-India Theater,* 3 vols. (Washington, D.C.: Office of the Chief of Military History, Department of the Army): vol. 1, *Stilwell's Mission to China* (1953); vol. 2, *Stilwell's Command Problems* (1956); vol. 3, *Time Runs Out in CBI* (1959). For one vivid, mud-slogging aspect, see Leslie Anders, *The Ledo Road. General Joseph W. Stilwell's Highway to China* (Norman: University of Oklahoma Press, 1965). David D. Barrett, *Dixie Mission: The United States Army Observer Group in Yenan, 1944* (Berkeley: University of California Center for Chinese Studies, 1970) is by our wartime military attaché who headed the mission. On the

473

Suggested Reading

airforce, W. F. Craven, and J. L. Cate, *The Army Air Forces in World War II:* Vol. 5, *Pacific: Matterhorn to Nagasaki* (Chicago: University of Chicago Press, 1953). On the United States aid program, Arthur N. Young, *China and the Helping Hand, 1937–1945* (HUP, 1963). For personal notes by a principal officer of the American Embassy during and after the Marshall mediation, see John F. Melby, *The Mandate of Heaven. Record of a Civil War. China, 1945–49* (Toronto: University of Toronto Press, 1968).

As examples of vivid, eye-witness reporting of the Chinese scene in wartime, see Theodore H. White and Annalee Jacoby, *Thunder Out of China* (Sloane Associates, 1946); Jack Belden, *China Shakes the World* (Harper, 1949; reprinted, Monthly Review Press, 1970); and Graham Peck, *Two Kinds of Time* (Boston: Houghton Mifflin, 1950; first half reprinted, 1968).

On the who-lost-China controversy in American politics, a straightforward study by Ross Y. Koen, *The China Lobby* (Macmillan, 1960), was printed, distributed for publication, and then withdrawn by the publishers. The Joseph McCarthy view is well represented by Dr. Anthony Kubek, *How the Far East was Lost, American Policy and the Creation of Communist China, 1941–1949* (Chicago: Regnery, 1963). For an analysis of the McCarthy era, see Earl Latham, *The Communist Controversy in Washington. From the New Deal to McCarthy* (HUP, 1966).

THE REPUBLIC OF CHINA ON TAIWAN. An under-studied and under-reported subject. A few general surveys were made in the early 1950's: J. W. Ballantine, *Formosa: a Problem for United States Foreign Policy* (Washington, D.C.: Brookings Institution, 1952), by a former officer of the State Department; H. M. Bate, *Report from Formosa* (London: Eyre and Spottiswoode, 1952); and F. W. Riggs, *Formosa under Chinese Nationalist Rule* (Macmillan, 1952). A special study is by George W. Barclay, *Colonial Development and Population in Taiwan* (Princeton: Princeton University Press, 1954). Recent works include, on the Nationalist massacres of 1947, George H. Kerr, *Formosa Betrayed* (Boston: Houghton Mifflin, 1965), researched by an eye-witness. On the substantial achievements in rural reconstruction, the authoritative work is by T. H. Shen (Shen Tsung-han), *The Sino-*

474

American Joint Commission on Rural Reconstruction. Twenty Years of Cooperation for Agricultural Development (Ithaca: Cornell University Press, 1970). For a general survey, Neil H. Jacoby, *U. S. Aid to Taiwan. A Study of Foreign Aid, Self-Help, and Development* (Praeger, 1966). On the birth control program, see Ronald Freedman and John Y. Takeshita, *Family Planning in Taiwan. An Experiment in Social Change* (Princeton: Princeton University Press, 1969). On attitudes affecting Taiwan independence, Douglas Mendel, *The Politics of Formosan Nationalism* (Berkeley and Los Angeles: University of California Press, 1970), based on extensive interviews in Taiwan and elsewhere by a public opinion specialist. Lung-chu Chen and Harold Lasswell, *Formosa, China, and the United Nations. Formosa in the World Community* (St. Martin's Press, 1967), gives an analysis of factors affecting the independence of Taiwan.

UNITED STATES POLICY TOWARD THE PEOPLE'S REPUBLIC. This topic is treated, explicitly or implicitly, in much of the American writing on China. Among systematic studies, A. Doak Barnett, *Communist China and Asia: Challenge to American Policy* (Harper and Brothers, for the Council on Foreign Relations, 1960), surveyed China's evolving international role in the 1950's. Subsequently, Robert Blum organized a series and wrote a volume (edited after his untimely death by A. Doak Barnett) on *The United States and China in World Affairs* (McGraw Hill for the Council on Foreign Relations, 1966). Among the other volumes in this series are Archibald T. Steele, *The American People and China* (McGraw-Hill, 1966), a field survey of public opinion; Alexander Eckstein, *Communist China's Economic Growth and Foreign Trade: Implications for U.S. Policy* (McGraw-Hill, 1966); A. M. Halpern, *Policies toward China: Views from Six Continents* (McGraw-Hill, 1965), on attitudes of other nations; and Fred Greene, *U. S. Policy and the Security of Asia* (McGraw-Hill, 1968), treating security interests, treaties, Communist threats, the nuclear factor. Historical perspectives are attempted in a collection of articles, John K. Fairbank, *China: The People's Middle Kingdom and the U. S. A.* (HUP, 1967). For the prescient observations of a correspondent, Harold R. Isaacs, *No Peace for Asia* (Macmillan, 1947; reprinted with added introduction,

Suggested Reading

Cambridge, Mass.: M. I. T. Press, 1967). For a useful chronology of events and documentation, see Congressional Quarterly Service, *China and U.S. Far East Policy 1945–1966* (Washington, D.C.: Congressional Quarterly, April, 1967). A recent symposium edited by Tang Tsou is on *China's Policies in Asia and America's Alternatives* (Chicago: University of Chicago Press, 1968). Alexander Eckstein, ed., *China Trade Prospects and U.S. Policy* (Praeger, for the National Committee on United States–China Relations, 1971), offers a useful appraisal by experts. Finally, for vigorous even strident criticism of most previous work see Edward Friedman and Mark Selden, eds., *America's Asia: Dissenting Essays on Asian-American Relations* (Pantheon Books, 1971), with contributions by a dozen young scholars.

Index

477

Index

Index

of agriculture, 358; and Five-year plan, 361–362; Third Plenum of Eighth, 369; Sixth Plenum of Eighth, 372; Eleventh Plenum of Eighth, 395; Twelfth Plenum of Eighth, 399

Central controls: of imperial government, 100–103; under Nationalist government, 233–235; an inheritance of CCP, 325–326

Central Executive Committee, KMT, 216

Central Military Academy, of Nanking government, 246

Central People's Government, Organic Law of, 328–329

Central Political Institute, of KMT, 245

Central Training Corps, of KMT, 234

Ch'an (Zen), 117

Chang Chih-tung, 224

Chang Kwang-chih, 9, 430

Ch'ang-an (modern Sian), T'ang capital, 60

Changchun (Hsin-king), Manchuria, 225

Changsha, 162, 265, 377, 379

Cheeloo University, 248

Chekiang-Kiangsi Railway, 224

Ch'en Kuo-fu, Nationalist leader, 245

Ch'en Li-fu, Nationalist leader, 245; Minister of Education, 252, 253

Ch'en Tu-hsiu, leader in May Fourth movement, 205, 206; founder of CCP, 208, 262; scapegoat of Comintern, 214, 264; as "scientific Marxist," 380

Cheng-feng ("correcting unorthodox tendencies"), thought reform movement of CCP, 277, 364

Cheng Ho, in charge of Ming explorations, 128, 133

Ch'eng ("complete sincerity"), 63

Chengchow, 201

Chengtu, Manchu garrison in, 86

Chennault, Col. C. L., and "Flying Tigers," 302

Ch'i (primordial ether), 62

Chia-ch'ing Emperor (1796–1820), 158

Chiang Kai-shek, 155, 349, 404; detained at Sian (1936), 50; quoted, on influence of example, 51, 55; on livelihood and defense, 59; on treaty system, 137; marriage of, 183; in Nationalist Revolution, 210, 212–213, 378; as wartime leader, 242; echoes of Confucianism in, 243–246; *China's Destiny,* 51, 55, 63, 137, 244, 404; *Chinese Economic Theory,* 59, 244; anti-Communist campaigns, 268, 417; American support of, 302, 310–311; in Nationalist-Communist civil war, 314; echoes of past in behavior of, 404; failure to develop rural reconstruction on mainland, 410–411

Chiang Kai-shek, Madame, 293

Ch'ien-lung Emperor (reigned 1736–1796), 8, 85, 140, 158

Chih (Confucian virtue), 69

Chin ("Golden") dynasty, of the Jurchen people, 77, 78

Ch'in dynasty, 56, 92

China-Aid Act (1948), 321

China Inland Mission, 147

China International Famine Relief Commission, 229

China Merchants' Steam Navigation Company, 176–177

China's Destiny, by Chiang Kai-shek, 51, 55, 63, 137, 244, 404

China's impact on Europe, 134–137

Chinese Catholic Church, 341

Chinese Characteristics, by A. H. Smith, 294, 440

Chinese Communist Party (CCP; in Chinese, Kungchantang): founding of (1921), 208; alliance with KMT (1923–1927), 210, 263, recruitment of intelligentsia, 257–258; first decade of, 259–267; early history compared with KMT, 259–260; failure of Comintern advice, 262–267; Yenan period, 267–275; Maoist strategy, 267–269; second alliance with KMT (1937), 269, wartime

Index

Index

Cyclical change, 154. *See also* Dynastic cycle

Da Gama, Vasco, 130
Dairen, 225
Dalai Lama, the, 368
De Bary, W. T., 64–65, 66, 428, 439
Decentralization: as accompaniment of the Great Leap, 371; and Cultural Revolution, 397–400
Degree-holders, 28
Democracy: a new concept in China, 156; in Sun's doctrines, 191; under KMT's tutelage, 233–235; in rural reconstruction, 238–239; "democratic centralism," 279; in Mao's "mass line," 332–333
"Democratic centralism": of KMT as Leninist-style party, 233–235; of mass organizations, 332–333
"Democratic dictatorship of workers and peasants," 328, 385
Democratic League, 257
Despotism of China, by Quesnay, 136
De-Stalinization, 385
Development problems of modern China, 221–239; transport, 221–224; industry, 224–226; banking and fiscal policy, 226–231; local government, 231–235; rural program, 235–239
Dewey, John, 205, 252
Dharmas, in Buddhist thought, 114
Dialectic, Marxist-Leninist: crucial nature of, 262; flexibility of, 266
"Dictatorship of the proletariat," 385, 400
Dien Bien Phu, 366
District, see *Ch'ü; Hsien*
Doctrine of the Mean, 59, 63
Dominican friars, 132–133
"Double ten" (October 10, 1911), 192
"Downward transfer" (*hsia-fang*), 365
Dream of the Red Chamber (Hung-lou meng), 350
Drew, E. B., 288
Dualism: of *yang* and *yin,* 20; inherent in Party struggle, 381–383
Dumont, René, 340, 359, 364

Dynastic cycle, 72–95; modern echoes of, 403–406

East India Companies, 130
"Eastern Forest" (Tung-lin) academy, 118
Eckstein, Alexander, 353, 358, 461, 463, 468, 475, 476
Ecology, influence of on culture, 4
Economic depression, of early 1960's, 374
Economic development: in "self-strengthening," 173–177; under the KMT, 221–226; under CCP, 273–274; in People's Republic, 335–340; as dynamic element of modernization, 408
Economic reconstruction, under CCP, 335–340
Economy: traditional, 12–14; under Nationalist government, 220–239; in Free China, 253–258; in People's Republic, 335–340. *See also* Agriculture; Banking; Industrialization; Railroads
"Economy of scarcity," 236
Education: traditional system, 69–70; Western influence, 174; Yung Wing mission to Hartford, Conn., 175–176; of women by missionaries, 178; late Ch'ing reforms of, 188; as source of modern liberalism, 248–253
Eight-legged essay, 64
Eighth Party Congress (1956), 365, 369
Eighth Route Army, 270, 271, 273; American idealization of, 293. *See also* Armies
Elections: first national (1913), 197; lack of under KMT, 233–235; under CCP, 273
Eleventh Plenum of the Central Committee (1966), 395
Elite: role of under Confucianism, 25, 28–30, 102–103; in suppression of mid-century rebellions, 232; development of by CCP, 389
Emerson, R. W., 293
Emperor: role of in Confucian system,

Index

55; Manchu, 84–85; K'ang-hsi, 85, 87, 133; Ch'ien-lung, 85, 140, 158

Empress Dowager (Tz'u-hsi), 96, 168, 181, 187

Encyclopedists, in France, 87

Engels, Friedrich, 279

Enlightenment, China in the European, 134

"Equal opportunity," in Open Door doctrine, 298

"Equalization of land tenure," 339

Erosion, 11–12; combatted in People's Republic, 360

Essay on Morals, by Voltaire, 135

Ethnocentricity, 61, 408

Europe, China's impact on, 134–137

Examination system, 34–35, 80; origin of, 58; as Chinese invention, 67; used by Manchus, 87; reform of, 169; abolition of, 188

Examination Yuan, Nationalist, 215

Exclusion of foreigners, 416

Exclusion acts, anti-Chinese (1882 and later), 294

Executive Headquarters, in Peking (1946), 309

Executive Yuan, Nationalist, 215

Exoticism of Chinese customs, American belief in, 292

Expansion, European vs. Chinese, 124–134; of CCP, 270, 276; American, 284–287, 291, 296; of People's Republic, 422

Explorations, Ming, 127–130

Extermination campaigns, against CCP, 268

Extraterritoriality: established, 145–148; value of, to missionaries, 178; to merchants, 203; movement to end, 217–218; abandoned, 305

"Face," 119

Family system: in social structure, 18–21; and the dynastic cycle, 93; modern revolution in, 202; CCP attack on, 340, 347

Fan-kuei ("foreign devils"), 142

Farmers Bank of China, 228

Farmers' associations: on Taiwan, 321–322; under CCP, 358–360

Father: traditional prerogatives of, 18; "father and mother officials," 98; changed status under CCP, 340

Federalism, failure of movement for, 201

Federation of Democratic Parties, 257

Fei Hsiao-t'ung, 236, 440

Feng-shui ("wind and water"), 54, 176

Feng Yü-hsiang, warlord, 200

Feudalism: in ancient China, 24–25; effect of abolition of, 41, 46, 56; in the West, 41; in CCP doctrine, 261, 344, 351

Feuerwerker, Albert, 173, 448, 454, 466

Field, James A., Jr., 284, 471

Filial piety, Confucian virtue, 108–109; reversed by CCP, 340

Finance, *see* Banking

First Emperor of the Ch'in (Shih Huang Ti), 74, 91

Fiscal policy of the KMT, 227–231

Fitzgerald, C. P., 405, 460

Five-antimovement, 342, 343

Five Classics, 58, 64

Five-year plan, first CCP, 360–362

Flood, problem of, 12; CCP efforts to control, 360

"Flying Tigers," 302

Foochow: Manchu garrison at, 86; as treaty port, 145

Food supply: as demographic factor, 151–152; as problem for CCP, 354; and the Great Leap Forward, 371–372

Foot-binding: old custom, 19–20; forbidden by Manchus, 86; condemned by Taipings, 166; modern movement against, 190; Americans shocked by, 294

Forbidden City, 97

Forced labor camps, 343. *See also* Corvée labor

Foreign banks, 226–227

Foreign courts, 244

Index

Index

Index

Index

sian withdrawal from, 353; Chinese expansion in, 368
Mandarin (Peking) dialect, 100
Mandate of Heaven: origin of concept, 53; KMT loss of, 255–256; CCP as contenders for, 273
Manichaeism, 60
Manifesto of CCP, first, 262–263
Manila, 131
Manual skills, disdained by Chinese scholar, 70
Mao Tse-tung, 121, 155, 349, 404; at Peita, 206; Autumn Harvest uprising led by, 264; his rise, and the Yenan period, 267–275; and wartime ideological development, 275–282; in coalition government (1949), 327; his "shift to the cities," 335; and Confucianism, 350; and literature and art, 350; and Soviet aid, 351; on "permanent revolution," 357; on collectivization of agriculture, 358; and "the hundred flowers," 363; new belligerency in East-West relations, 367; strategy of dualism, 370; and the struggle within the Central Committee, 376; independent style of, 377–380; his approach to revolution, 380–383; in split with Soviet, 383–388; and the Cultural Revolution, 394–400; echoes of past in behavior of, 404–405
Mao-tzu ("hairy ones"), 142
Maoism, 278
"Maoist strategy," 267–269
Marco Polo, 80
Market community, 23–24
Marriage, law of *1950*, 340
Marshall, George C., 308–311
Marshall, Humphrey, 288
Marxism: on rural poverty, 27; a CCP monopoly, 261; Mao's nationalism related to, 378; Mao's understanding of, 384
Marxism-Leninism, 208, 344; Maoism added to, 278, 349, 386; Chinese history reappraised through, 351
"Mass line," concept of 333; versus party building, 381–382

Mass mobilization, and the Great Leap, 371
Mass organizations, under CCP, 332–335
Maternal relatives of ruler, 57, 93
May Fourth Movement (1919), 201–207, 248, 279, 378
May Thirtieth incident (1925), 212, 262
McCarthy, Joseph, 317, 318
Mecca, 128
Mechanized agriculture, 359
Medical missions, 146
Mediterranean, early American activity in, 284
Mencius, 58–59, 65
Mencius, 163; influence on Mao, 381
Merchant class: in traditional society, 36–42; growth of, in Ming and Ch'ing periods, 148; new, of modern times, 202–203, 206. *See also* Bourgeoisie
Mesopotamia, 42–43
Michael, Franz, 84, 435, 447
Middle Kingdom, 138, 348, 404
Militarism: in old society, 45–48; new, under KMT, 246–247; rise of PLA during Cultural Revolution, 393–394
Militarization: by gentry against White Lotus and Taipings, 158–159, 167; and warlords, 198–201; as dynamic element of modernization, 408
Military Affairs Commission, Nationalist, 246–247
Min (common people), 52
Min Pao, of T'ung Meng Hui, 191
Minerals, resources, 353
Mines, 176; in Manchukuo, 225. *See also* Kailan; Kaiping
Ming dynasty, 46, 81, 404, 415; Neo-Confucianism during, 64; rise of, 81, 94; decline of, 83–84; exploration during, 127–130; population, 149, 150
Minor parties, under KMT, 256–258; under CCP, 329
Minority peoples, *see* National minorities

Index

ing Nanking decade, 221–231; new militarism, 246–247; loss of moral prestige, 253–258; postwar politics, 256–258; alliance with CCP against Japan, 269; American support of, 302, 307, 366, 401, 402; and second Quemoy crisis, 368. *See also* Nanking government

Nationalist Revolution, 207–214

Nationalization, under CCP, 360, 406–412

Nature: harmony of man and, 11–15; relation of man to, in culture of East and West, 14; Confucian concept of, 54–55

Nazis, effect of on China policy, 289

Needham, Joseph, 66, 67, 429

Nemesis, steamer, 171

Neo-Confucianism, 61–64, 117

Neolithic culture, 9–10

Nepotism, 103

Nerchinsk, treaty of (1689), 133

Nestorian Christianity, 60

New Army, 193. *See also* Armies

New Citizen (Hsin Min Ts'ung Pao), edited by Liang Ch'i-ch'ao, 185

New Democracy, essay and doctrine of Mao Tse-tung (1940), 278–280; application of, 328; superseded by transition to socialism, 361

New Fourth Army, 270, 276, 281

New Life Movement, 243, 344

New Tide, liberal journal, 248

New Youth (Hsin Ch'ing Nien, La Jeunesse), 205, 248; Mao's article in, 377

New Zealand, 367

Nien rebels, 166–167

Night-soil industry, 6, 152

Nine Power Treaty of, *1922*, 299

Ningpo, treaty port, 145

Ninth Party Congress (1969), 399

Nirvana, Buddhist goal, 115, 116

Nivison, David, 349, 439

Nomad conquest, 73–76

"Nomadism," 73

Nonintervention, in American foreign policy, 299

Nonrecognition doctrine, 298

North Atlantic Treaty Organization (NATO), 421

North Korea, aggression against South Korea, 300, 351, 366, 421

North Vietnam, 369, 387, 417

North and South, contrast of, 1–8

Northern expeditions, 212, 215

Northern Sung dynasty, 77

Northern Wei dynasty, 74

Nuclear weapons, 386; in China's foreign policy, 417

Nurhachi (1559–1626), founder of Ch'ing dynasty, 83, 84

Odes, 58

Official class, *see* Bureaucracy

Oil resources, 353

Oksenberg, Michel, 392

"Old hundred names" *(lao-pai-hsing)*, colloquial name for populace, 52, 280

"Old Master" (Lao-tzu), 111

O-mi-t'o-fo (Amitabha), 115

"On the people's democratic dictatorship," 327–328

Open Door doctrine, 295–303, 419

Opium trade, 146; rise of, 141; end of Indian importation, 147; and the Taipings, 160, 166; suppression in late Ch'ing, 190

Opium War, 142

Ordo, barbarian military unit, 76; of Chingis Khan, 79

Ordos desert, 9

Organic Law, of Central People's Government, 328–329

"Oriental" society, and theory of Dr. K. A. Wittfogel, 42–48

Original sin, lack of in Confucianism, 63

Outer Mongolia, 362

Pai Ch'ung-hsi, Kwangsi general, 314

Pai-hsing ("hundred names"), 52

Pai-hua, spoken language, 205

Pakistan, 367

Pao-chia, mutual responsibility system in local government, 101–102, 152, 235, 406

Index

493

Index

Primogeniture, 22

Primordial ether (*ch'i*), in Neo-Confucianism, 62

Principles of form (*li*), in Neo-Confucianism, 62

Printing, 66

Private property: in traditional China, 42–43; in Communist China, 339

Production brigade, as basic agricultural unit, 273

Proletariat: potential for formation of, 202; in Comintern line, 262, 265; Chinese Communism independent of, 278; in "people's democratic dictatorship," 328

Protestant missionaries. *See* Christianity; Missionaries

Provinces, under empire, 98–99

Provincial assemblies, in late Ch'ing reforms, 189, 193

Public finance, of Nationalist government, 230–231

Public Health Administration, at Nanking, 241

Public works, gentry superintendence of, 29

Punishments, 106

Quebec, British-American conference at (1943), 306

Queen's College, Hong Kong, Sun Yat-sen at, 182

Quemoy, 367, 368

Quesnay, François, *The Despotism of China,* 136

Quotations from Chairman Mao Tsetung, 396

Racial stock, 10–11

Railroads: early building of, 176, 177, 222; loan agreements for, 193; mileage of (1942), 220; slow growth of, 223–224; role in warfare, 241; reopening by CCP, 337; building under CCP, 362

Rainfall, 3–5

Rebellion, *see* Revolutionary process

"Rectification," campaign to curb party cadres, 365, 371

Red versus expert, Mao slogan, 382; in army, 393

Red Army, 267–268, 270. *See also* Armies

Red Guards, 395

Red Spears, secret society, 233

Red Star over China, by Edgar Snow, 274

"Reform through labor," 341, 343

Reformers of *1898,* 179–181

Religion: Confucianism as, 59; in traditional society, 110–118. *See also* Christianity

Rents: collection of, 232; reduction of, by CCP, 272

Reorganization loan (1913), 198

Republic of China (1912), 192–194

"Resist America, Aid Korea" campaign, 341

"Resistance and Reconstruction," 255

Restoration, of Confucian government, 167–170, 243

Returned students: from Japan in 1900's, 188; CCP attitude toward those from Moscow, 277–278; predominantly from U.S. in 1930's, 289. *See also* Students

Revisionism: general problem of, 383; Soviet, 386; Mao's campaign against, 394

Revolution: industrial, in West, 123; Taipings as, 159; Sun Yat-sen and, 183; new nationalism as spur to, 189–192; Revolution of *1911,* 192–194, 198; Nationalist, 207–214; Lenin on, 209, 385; Sun Yat-sen's stages of, 216

Revolutionary colleges, 346

"Revolutionary committees," 398

Revolutionary process, 154–194; rebellion and restoration, 154–172; reform and revolution, 173–194

Ricci, Matteo, 131–132

Rice: economy based on, 13; double-cropping of, 151

Right conduct, 55

"Right of rebellion," 53

Index

Shantung: Germany ousted by Japan from, 196; in Versailles settlement, 206; rural reconstruction in, 238
Sheep economy of nomad, 73
Shen ("spirit"), 163
"Shift to the cities," 335
Shih, Vincent, on the Taiping religion, 163, 447
Shui-hu-chuan, novel, translated as *All Men Are Brothers*, 272, 437
Sian, 9; Chiang Kai-shek held at (1936), 50–51, 269
Siberia, 133
Silver purchase program, American, 228–229, 301–302
Sincerity (*ch'eng*), Confucian virtue, 63
Singapore, 305
Sinkiang, 362, 368; mining in, 353
Sinkiang Uighur Autonomous Region (1955), 368
Sino-American treaty (1943), 305
Sino-Burmese Friendship Association, 332
Sino-Foreign Empires, early, 76–78
Sino-Indian Friendship Association, 332
Sino-Soviet Friendship Association, 332
Sino-Soviet split, 383–388
Sino-Soviet Treaty: *1945*, 308; *1950*, 351
Six Ministries, or Boards, 97
Sixth Congress of CCP (1928), 264
Sixth Plenum of Central Committee (1958), 372
Skinner, G. William, 23, 441
Smith, Adam, 148
Smith, Arthur H., *Chinese Characteristics*, 294, 440
Snow, Edgar, 274, 455, 457, 459
Social mobility, myth and fact, 35
Social structure, traditional, 16–29; reformation under CCP, 340–344
Socialism: Marxian monopoly in China, 261; CCP struggle toward, 357–375
Society of Brothers and Elders (Ko Lao Hui), 233

Society for the Study of Self-strengthening, 180
Soils, 5–6
Son of Heaven, 55. *See also* Emperor
Soong: Charles Jones, 183; sisters, 183; T. V., 183, 227, 228, 230
South Korea, *see* Korea, Republic of
South Vietnam, 369, 421
Southeast Asia Treaty Organization (SEATO), 367
Southern Sung dynasty, 77, 78, 150
Southwest Associated University, at Kunming, 250
Sovereign rights, demand for recovery of, 190
Soviet aid, to Kuomintang, 208–211; to CCP, 311, 351–354
Soviet Union, *see* Russia
Soy beans, modern commercial crop, 225
Spain: colonial domains of, 131; trading settlements of, 319; U.S. treaty with (1898), 295
Spheres of interest, and Open Door, 298
Spinoza, Benedict de, 185
Spring and Autumn Annals, 58
"Squeeze," custom of, 104
Stakhanovite system, in Communist China, 342
Stalin, 121, 214, 263, 264, 279, 309; at Yalta, 308; death of, 353; Mao on, 381; and monolithic Communism, 383; party purges by, 395
State farms, 359
Steam tonnage, 222
Steel: low consumption per capita, 17; production, 225, 337
Steppe and sown, contrast of, 73
Stilwell, General Joseph W., 305, 307
Stimson, Henry L., 298; Stimson Doctrine, 290–291
Street committees, 333–334
Students: abroad for study, in 1900's, 188; movement of *1919*, 206–207; movement of *1925*, 212; in secondary schools (1942), 221; Kuomintang suppression of, 251–253; intellectual-emotional reconditioning of,

Index

T'ien-chu ("Lord of Heaven"), 163
Tientsin: treaties of, 143; Taipings near (1854), 162; industry in, 225; fall of (1949), 327
Ting-hsien, rural reconstruction center, 238
Ting Ling, 351
Tito, 278
Tobacco, introduction of, 151
Torture, 145
Tours, battle of (732), 126
Townsend, James, 333, 462
Toynbee, A. J., 91
Trade: routes, 8; of Sung, 60; in Central Asia, 78; under Mongols, 80; early European, 125; early Chinese maritime, 128–130; Canton, 131, 133, 140–142, 151; in tribute system, 137–142; under treaties, 142–149; under CCP, 353, 362
Trade unions, 207; exploited by CCP under Li Li-san, 265; All-China Federation of, 332
Trans-Siberian railroad, 362
Transcendentalists, New England school, 293
Translation, into Chinese: problems of, 115–116; of Western works, 174; of Scriptures, 205
Transport: a factor in modern warlordism, 199; a problem in modern development, 221; waterways, 222; railroads, 222–224; role in warfare, 241
Treaties: of Nanking (1842), 143; of Nerchinsk (1689), 133; of Tientsin (1858), 143. See also Sino-American; Sino-Soviet
Treaty system, 142–149; ports, 131, 143, 370; Chiang on, 137; and rights recovery movement, 216–218; on Taiwan, 319; abolition of, 217–218. See also Concessions; Tariffs
Triad Society, 160–161, 164–165, 182, 184
Tribute system, 137–142
Tripitaka (Buddhist canon), 115
Trotsky, Leon, 213–214, 263, 264, 267
Truman, Harry S., 352

Ts'ai Yuan-p'ei, 206
Tseng Kuo-fan, 169, 174, 176, 233, 243, 244
Tsinan, 201
Tsing Hua University, 249
Tsungli Yamen, 168, 172
Tsunyi conference, 269
Tung-lin ("Eastern forest") Academy, 118, 132
T'ung Meng Hui: formed, 191; succeeded by KMT, 259
Tungusic tribes, 79
Turkestan, 384; railroad to, 362
Turkey, opium from, 141
Turkish tribes, 78
Twentieth Bomber Command, 305
Twentieth Congress (1956) of Soviet party, 385
Twenty-one Demands, of Japan (1915), 196, 203
Tz'u-hsi, Empress Dowager, 96, 168, 181, 187

Uighur Turks, 78; script of, 79; in Sinkiang autonomous region, 368
Unequal treaties, 137, 143, 212; renounced by Russia, 209; abolished, 218, 244; American share in, 289. See also Treaty system
Unions, see Trade unions
United Front, of 1923–1927, Mao a worker in, 378; of 1937, Communist tactics of, 275–278
United Front Work Department, Yenan, 275
United Nations, 299–300; and Korean War, 366, 421; exclusion of People's Republic from, 417
United Nations Security Council, 321
United States: Chinese students in, 188, 249; misled by superficiality of China's modernization, 219–221; Christian colleges, 248; inherited China policy of, 283–303; role within Britain's informal empire, 287–289; ambivalence toward China, 289–295; and the Open Door policy, 295–300; nature of interest in China, 300–303; wartime China

498

Index

The American Foreign Policy Library